1990
underlined

#1

10/20

MMPI-2
Assessing Personality
and Psychopathology

MMPI-2
Assessing Personality and Psychopathology

John R. Graham
Professor of Psychology
Kent State University

New York   Oxford
OXFORD UNIVERSITY PRESS
1990

Oxford University Press

Oxford   New York   Toronto
Delhi   Bombay   Calcutta   Madras   Karachi
Petaling Jaya   Singapore   Hong Kong   Tokyo
Nairobi   Dar es Salaam   Cape Town
Melbourne   Auckland

and associated companies in
Berlin   Ibadan

Library of Congress Cataloging-in-Publication Data
Graham, John R. (John Robert), 1940–
MMPI-2: assessing personality and psychopathology /
John R. Graham.   p.   cm.
Includes bibliographical references.
1. Minnesota Multiphasic Personality Inventory.   I. Title.
RC473.M5G73   1990
155.2′83—dc20   89-29188
ISBN 0-19-506068-7

9 8 7 6 5 4 3

Printed in the United States of America
on acid-free paper

To Mary Ann

Foreword

In 1989—after nearly seven years of research and development—the MMPI-2 was published, replacing the original MMPI, the most widely used personality inventory. With imperfections removed, and its scope broadened, the MMPI-2 will likely continue to experience wide use and broadened applications in clinical practice and research.

Dr. Graham played a critical part in the development of the MMPI-2 throughout the restandardization project. As one of the four members of the MMPI Restandardization Committee (others included W. G. Dahlstrom, A. Tellegen, and myself) he contributed substantially to the revision. Without his motivation, effort, and clear vision about what the MMPI is to practitioners and what the MMPI-2 should be the project would never have succeeded. He was there during the initial conceptualization of the project, development of new items, collection and processing of normative data, collection of clinical data, and the final production of the MMPI-2 manual. Graham's commitment to making the MMPI-2 a practical, clinically usable instrument was evident throughout his participation in the restandardization project. His experience in using the MMPI in clinical and forensic settings helped the Restandardization Committee to keep sight of the practitioner's needs when alterations were to be made.

The publication of the MMPI-2 leaves a void with regard to an up-to-date introductory text. I was pleased when Jack Graham decided to write this book because, even though there is a technical manual for the MMPI-2 and a number of early research publications, no practical interpretative resources are available for the instrument. This book, like its predecessor *The MMPI: A Practical Guide* (first and second editions), will in all likelihood become the standard MMPI-2 text for years to come.

Graham is extremely well qualified to write the first interpretative clinical textbook on the MMPI-2. He has been a major contributor to the research on the MMPI and MMPI-2; has taught MMPI clinical interpretation to thousands of psychologists; has written major textbooks on MMPI interpretation; and has a detailed working knowledge of the MMPI-2 that can come only from experience through research, clinical practice, and extensive communication with test users. Graham's working knowledge of the MMPI and its replacement, the MMPI-2, is unsurpassed.

This timely book provides all the information needed to use the MMPI-2. It summarizes the similarities and differences between the MMPI and MMPI-2 and presents the revision and restandardization in an accurate, clear manner. The initial chapters detail how the MMPI-2 validity and clinical scales are contin-

uous with the original MMPI, and the author examines their construction, interrelationships, and empirical bases for description and prediction of behavior. The book includes a clear introduction to the development and structure of the new validity scales contained in the MMPI-2—the Fb, TRIN, and VRIN scales—and offers the most comprehensive interpretive guide available for these scales. This volume also introduces the new MMPI-2 Content Scales, which Graham played a major role in developing and validating. Moreover, an effective strategy is provided for interpreting MMPI-2 profiles.

This book continues in the tradition of the author's earlier MMPI texts in presenting test variables and interpretive strategies in a lucid, accurate, and authoritative manner. Graham's approach to teaching MMPI interpretation has always been straightforward—uncluttered by trivia but guided by a critical view of quality assessment measures—including a benign neglect of measures and indexes that do not work, such as the "subtle scales" which make promises they do not deliver. This text includes MMPI measures that have proved themselves in terms of validity and utility.

Apart from technical accuracy, comprehensiveness, and timeliness, Graham's book will be welcomed for its readability and didactic style. From an instructor's standpoint, it makes teaching an MMPI-2 course a joy, because the book contains all the necessities for understanding the MMPI-2. I'm of the view that teaching the basic MMPI course to graduate students should be fun (at least for the instructor), and let Graham's book do most of the preliminary work of introducing MMPI-2 constructs to students. At the beginning of the quarter I assign his book to be thoroughly read (and tested on) *before* I actually discuss the MMPI-2 in class. I am able to take this didactic approach because the book presents the basics of MMPI-2 interpretation in a highly digestible format. I used Graham's previous MMPI texts for my course at the University of Minnesota and recommend them to registrants in my workshops as the basic introduction to MMPI interpretation. The author's approach to MMPI provides the beginner with all of the necessary information in the context of an effective strategy for mastering profile interpretation. This new book follows in the tradition of Graham's previous texts and will introduce a new generation of MMPI-2 users to the concepts and interpretative strategies useful for understanding the workings of the MMPI-2.

Department of Psychology   James N. Butcher
University of Minnesota

Preface

In the five decades after work on the MMPI was initiated at the University of Minnesota by Starke Hathaway and J. Charnley McKinley, the instrument came to be widely used in the United States and around the world. It was administered routinely to clients in hospitals, clinics, and private practices and to nonclinical subjects in situations such as employment screening and marital counseling. The first and second editions of *The MMPI: A Practical Guide* (1977, 1987) provided students and practicing clinicians with information needed to learn about the MMPI and to interpret the instrument in clinical practice.

Recently the MMPI was updated and restandardized (Dahlstrom, Butcher, Graham, Tellegen, & Kaemmer, 1989). The revision involved a modernization of the content and language of test items, elimination of objectionable items, collection of nationally representative normative data, and development of some new scales. Although all of these changes have made the revised instrument, MMPI-2, a better tool for assessing personality and psychopathology, it has rendered inadequate existing reference works, such as *The MMPI: A Practical Guide*. The present book is appropriate for use as a textbook in personality assessment courses and as a reference guide for professionals who use the MMPI-2 in research and clinical work.

Chapter 1 describes the rationale underlying the MMPI and presents historical information about scale development and standardization of the original instrument. It discusses the revision of the MMPI and summarizes similarities and differences between the original MMPI and MMPI-2. Chapter 2 examines MMPI-2 test materials and procedures for administering and scoring the instrument and for coding the resulting profile of scores. Chapter 3 is devoted to the validity scales. The standard validity scales are considered singly and in combination, and several new validity scales are presented. Chapter 4 discusses each of the ten standard clinical scales and offers suggestions for interpreting scores at various T-score levels. The interpretation of two- and three-point code types and other profile configurations is covered in Chapter 5. Chapter 6 presents several different approaches to content interpretation. The concept of critical items is introduced. Content homogeneous subscales—including those developed by Harris and Lingoes—are considered, and a new set of content scales—developed especially for the revised item pool of MMPI-2—is presented. Chapter 7 covers some frequently used supplementary scales and introduces several new scales for MMPI-2. Chapter 8 examines psychometric characteristics of MMPI-2 (for example, reliability and validity) and discusses the instrument's use with special populations (adolescents, medical patients, ethnic groups, correctional subjects, nonclinical subjects). Chapter 9 presents the au-

thor's general strategy for interpreting MMPI-2, illustrated with several cases. Finally, Chapter 10 focuses on computerized administration, scoring, and interpretation of MMPI-2 and considers major professional and ethical issues associated with computerized use of the instrument. A sample computerized interpetation is presented and compared with a clinician-generated interpretation of the same data.

A guiding principle throughout the preparation of this book was that material should be presented in a way that will be most directly useful to students learning about the MMPI-2 and to practitioners using the instrument clinically. Thus, no attempt was made to include exhaustive technical information and research data about the MMPI or MMPI-2. However, enough information is included to permit the reader to evaluate the appropriateness of the MMPI-2 for various kinds of subjects and assessment tasks. Other sources, such as the test manuals (Hathaway & McKinley, 1983; Butcher, Dahlstrom, Graham, Tellegen, & Kaemmer, 1989) and the two-volume *MMPI Handbook* (Dahlstrom, Welsh, & Dahlstrom, 1972, 1975), are readily available for those who require more information about the original MMPI or MMPI-2.

Just as the MMPI came to be used widely in the United States and around the world, I am convinced that the MMPI-2 will be even more popular as a personality assessment instrument. If used appropriately, the MMPI-2 is a tool that can make assessment tasks more efficient and more fruitful. It is hoped that this book will help clinicians better understand the use of MMPI-2 in clinical assessment.

Kent, Ohio   J. R. G.
September 1989

Acknowledgments

Many persons have supported the completion of this book. I am indebted to the authors and publishers who granted permission to reproduce their works. Beverly Kaemmer, MMPI Manager at the University of Minnesota Press, facilitated access to information about the MMPI-2. The staff at Professional Assessment Services (National Computer Systems) was helpful in a variety of ways. The Department of Psychology at Kent State University provided clerical support. Auke Tellegen generated the data concerning percentile equivalents for uniform T-scores. Robert Archer and Theodore Henrichs reviewed the manuscript for the publisher and made many helpful comments. Jim Butcher was generally supportive and offered many helpful suggestions that were incorporated into the book. Mary Ann Stephens served as a sounding board for ideas and was a tremendous source of emotional support.

Contents

MMPI-2
Assessing Personality
and Psychopathology

1

Development of the MMPI and MMPI-2

DEVELOPMENT OF THE MMPI

Original Purpose

The MMPI was first published in 1943. Its authors, Starke Hathaway, Ph.D., and J. Charnley McKinley, M.D., were working in the University of Minnesota Hospitals and hoped that the MMPI would be useful for routine diagnostic assessments. During the 1930s and 1940s a primary function of psychologists and psychiatrists was to assign appropriate psychodiagnostic labels to individual cases. To assign such labels, an individual interview or mental status examination and individual psychological testing usually were utilized with each patient. It was hoped that a group-administered paper-and-pencil personality inventory would provide a more efficient way of arriving at appropriate psychodiagnostic labels.

Rationale

Hathaway and McKinley utilized the empirical keying approach in the construction of the various MMPI scales. This approach, which requires one to determine empirically items that differentiate between groups of subjects, is a common technique today but represented a significant innovation at the time of the MMPI's construction. Most prior personality inventories had been constructed according to a logical keying approach. With this approach, test items were selected or generated rationally according to face validity and responses keyed according to the subjective judgment of the test author concerning the kinds of responses likely to indicate the attributes being measured. Both clinical experience and research data seriously questioned the adequacy of this logical keying approach. Increasingly, it became apparent that subjects could falsify or distort their responses to items in order to present themselves in any way they chose. Further, empirical studies indicated that the subjectively keyed responses often were not consistent with differences actually observed between groups of subjects. In the newly introduced empirical keying procedure, responses to

individual test items were treated as unknowns, and empirical item analysis was utilized to identify test items that differentiated between criterion groups. This approach overcame many of the difficulties associated with the earlier, subjective approaches.

Clinical Scale Development

The first step in the construction of the basic MMPI scales was to collect a large pool of potential inventory items.[1] Hathaway and McKinley selected a wide variety of personality-type statements from such sources as psychological and psychiatric case histories and reports, textbooks, and earlier published scales of personal and social attitudes. From an initial pool of about 1000 statements the test authors selected a pool of 504 statements that they judged to be reasonably independent of one another.

The next step was to select appropriate criterion groups. One criterion group, referred to as the Minnesota normals, consisted primarily of relatives and visitors of patients in the University of Minnesota Hospitals. This group was augmented by several other groups of normal subjects, including a group of recent high school graduates attending precollege conferences at the University of Minnesota, a group of Work Progress Administration workers, and some medical patients at the University of Minnesota Hospitals. The second major group of subjects, referred to as clinical subjects, was made up of psychiatric patients at the University of Minnesota Hospitals. This second group included patients representing all the major psychiatric categories being utilized clinically at the time of the test construction. Clinical subjects were divided into subgroups of discrete diagnostic samples according to their clinically determined diagnostic labels. Whenever there was any doubt about a patient's clinical diagnosis or when more than one diagnosis was given, the patient was not included in this clinical reference group. The different subgroups of clinical subjects formed were hypochondriasis, depression, hysteria, psychopathic deviate, paranoia, psychasthenia, schizophrenia, and hypomania.

The next step in scale construction was to administer the original 504 test items to the Minnesota normals and to the patients in each of the clinical groups. In addition, an item analysis was conducted for each of the clinical groups to identify those items in the pool of 504 that differentiated significantly between the specific clinical group, other clinical groups, and a group of normal subjects. Individual MMPI items that were identified by this procedure were included in the resulting MMPI scale for that clinical group.

In an attempt to cross-validate each clinical scale (e.g., depression scale), the scale was administered to new groups of normal subjects, clinical subjects with

---

[1]Information concerning clinical and validity scale development is abstracted from a series of articles by Hathaway (1956, 1965), Hathaway and McKinley (1940, 1942), McKinley and Hathaway (1940, 1944), McKinley, Hathaway, and Meehl (1948), and Meehl and Hathaway (1946).

that particular clinical diagnosis, and clinical subjects with other diagnoses. If significant differences were found among scores for the normal group, the specific clinical group, and the group of other clinical subjects, the clinical scale was considered to have been adequately cross-validated and thus was ready for use in the differential diagnosis of new patients whose diagnostic features were unknown.

At a somewhat later time, two additional clinical scales were constructed. First, the Masculinity-Femininity (Mf) scale originally was intended to distinguish between homosexual males and heterosexual males. Because of difficulties in identifying adequate numbers of items that differentiated between these two groups, Hathaway and McKinley subsequently broadened their approach in the construction of the Mf scale. In addition to the all too few items that did discriminate between homosexual and heterosexual males, other items were identified that were differentially endorsed by normal male and female subjects. Also, a number of items from the Terman and Miles I scale (1936) were added to the original item pool and included in the Mf scale. Second, the Social Introversion (Si) scale was developed by Drake (1946) and has come to be included as one of the basic MMPI scales. Drake selected items for the Si scale by contrasting item response frequencies for a group of college women who participated in many extracurricular activities and a group who participated in few or no extracurricular activities. Subsequently, the scale's use has been extended to men as well as women.

Validity Scale Development

Hathaway and McKinley also developed four scales, hereafter referred to as the validity scales, whose purpose was to detect deviant test-taking attitudes. The Cannot Say scale or category is simply the total number of items in the MMPI either omitted or responded to as both true and false by the individual taking the test. Obviously, the omission of large numbers of items, which tends to lower the scores on the clinical scales, calls into question the interpretability of the whole resulting profile of scores.

The L scale, originally called the Lie scale of the MMPI, was designed to detect rather unsophisticated and naive attempts on the part of test subjects to present themselves in an overly favorable light. The L scale items were rationally derived and cover everyday situations in order to assess the strength of the person's unwillingness to admit even very minor weaknesses in character or personality. An example of an L scale item is "I do not read every editorial in the newspaper every day." Most people would be quite willing to admit that they do not read every editorial every day, but persons determined to present themselves in a very favorable light might not be willing to admit to such a perceived shortcoming.

The F scale of the MMPI was designed to detect individuals whose approach to the test-taking task is different from that intended by the test authors. F scale

items were selected by examining the endorsement frequency of the Minnesota normal group for each item and identifying those endorsed in a particular direction by fewer than 10 percent of the normals. Obviously, because few normal people endorse an item in that direction, a person who so endorses it is exhibiting a deviant response. A large number of such responses calls into question the extent to which a test subject complied with the test instructions when completing the MMPI.

The K scale of the MMPI was constructed by Meehl and Hathaway (1946) to identify clinical defensiveness. It was noted that some clearly abnormal subjects who took the MMPI obtained scores on the clinical scales that were not as elevated as was expected given their clinical status. Items in the K scale were selected empirically by comparing the responses of a group of patients who were known to be clinically deviant but who produced normal scores on the clinical scales of the MMPI with a group of people producing normal scores and for whom there was no indication of psychopathology. A high K score was intended to indicate defensiveness and call into question the person's responses to all the other items. The K scale also was later utilized to develop a correction factor for some of the clinical scales. Meehl and Hathaway reasoned that, if the effect of a defensive test-taking attitude, as reflected by a high K score, is to lower scores on the clinical scales, perhaps one might be able to determine the extent to which the scores on the clinical scales should be raised in order to reflect more accurately a person's behavior. By comparing the efficiency of each clinical scale with various portions of the K scale added as a correction factor, Meehl and Hathaway determined the appropriate weights of the K scale score for each clinical scale to correct for the defensiveness indicated by the K scale score. Some clinical scales were not K-corrected at all because the simple raw score on those clinical scales seemed to produce the most accurate prediction about a person's clinical condition. Other scales have proportions of K, ranging from .2 to 1.0, added in order to elevate the clinical scales appropriately.

Modified Approach to MMPI Utilization

After a decade of clinical use and additional validity studies it became apparent that the MMPI was not adequately successful for its original purpose, namely, the valid psychodiagnosis of a new patient. Although patients in any particular clinical category (e.g., depression) were likely to obtain high scores on the corresponding clinical scale, they also often obtained high scores on other clinical scales. Also, many normal subjects obtained high scores on one or more of the clinical scales. Clearly, the clinical scales are not pure measures of the symptom syndromes suggested by the scale names.

A number of different reasons have been suggested for the MMPI's failure to fulfill completely its original purpose. From further research it became apparent that many of the clinical scales of the MMPI are highly intercorrelated,

making it unlikely that only a single scale would be elevated for an individual. These intercorrelations are due, to a large extent, to item overlap between scales. Also, the unreliability of the specific psychiatric diagnoses of subjects used in the development of the MMPI scales contributes to their failure to differentiate among clinical groups.

Although the limited success of the MMPI scales in differentiating among clinical groups might have been bothersome in the 1940s, this limitation is not particularly critical today. Currently, practicing clinicians place less emphasis on diagnostic labels per se. Accumulating evidence suggests that psychiatric nosology is not as useful as medical diagnosis. A diagnosis of schizophrenia, for example, does not tell us much about the etiology of the disorder for that individual or the recommended therapeutic procedures.

For this reason, the MMPI came to be used in a way quite different from that originally intended. It was assumed that the clinical scales were measuring something other than error variance because reliable differences in scores were found among individuals known to differ in other important ways. In a modified approach, each MMPI scale was treated as an unknown; then, through clinical experience and empirical research, the correlates of each scale were identified. More than 10,000 studies have been published about the MMPI. When a person obtains a score on a particular scale, the clinician can refer to these studies in attributing to that person the characteristics and behaviors that through previous research and experience have been identified for other individuals with similar scores on that scale. To lessen the likelihood that excess meaning will be attributed because of the clinical scale names, the following scale numbers have been assigned to the original scales, replacing the clinical labels:

Present Scale Number	Original Scale Name
1	Hypochondriasis
2	Depression
3	Hysteria
4	Psychopathic Deviate
5	Masculinity-Femininity
6	Paranoia
7	Psychasthenia
8	Schizophrenia
9	Hypomania
0	Social Introversion

Thus, for example, when discussing a patient among themselves, MMPI-2 users refer to him or her as a "four-nine" or a "one-two-three," descriptive phrases in shorthand that communicate to the listener the particular behavior descriptions associated with the "4-9" or "1-2-3" syndrome.

In addition to identifying empirical correlates of high scores on each of the preceding numbered scales, it also is possible to identify empirical correlates for low scores and for various combinations of scores on the scales (e.g., highest scale in the profile, two highest scales in the profile). Some investigators have developed very complex rules for classifying individual profiles and have iden- tified behavioral-empirical correlates of profiles that meet the criteria (Gilberstadt & Duker, 1965; Marks, Seeman, & Haller, 1974). Thus, even though the MMPI was not particularly successful in terms of its original purpose (differential diagnosis of clinical groups believed in the 1930s to be discrete psychiatric types), it has proven possible subsequently to use the test to generate descriptions of and inferences about individuals (both normal subjects and patients) on the basis of their own profiles. It is this behavioral description approach to the utilization of the test in everyday practice that has led to the its great popularity among practicing clinicians.

DEVELOPMENT OF MMPI-2

Reasons for the Revision

In 1989 the MMPI was revised significantly, and the revised version of the test was called MMPI-2. Although the original MMPI came to be the most widely used personality test in the United States (Lubin, Larsen, & Matarazzo, 1984), and perhaps in the world, critics have expressed concern about some aspects of the instrument. Until the publication of MMPI-2 in 1989, the MMPI had not been revised since it was published in 1943.

There were serious concerns about the adequacy of the original standardiza- tion sample. That sample consisted of 724 persons who were visiting friends or relatives at the University of Minnesota Hospitals. The sample was one of convenience, and little effort was made to assure that it was representative of the U.S. population. Standardization subjects came primarily from the geo- graphical area around Minneapolis, Minnesota. All were white, and the typical subject was about 35 years of age, married, residing in a small town or rural area, working in a skilled or semiskilled trade (or married to a man of this occupational level), and having about 8 years of formal education (Dahlstrom, Welsh, & Dahlstrom, 1972). Hathaway and Briggs (1957) later refined this sample by eliminating persons with incomplete records or faulty background information. The refined sample was the one typically used for converting raw scores on supplementary MMPI scales to T-scores. In addition to concerns that the original standardization sample was not representative of the general popu- lation, there were concerns that the average American citizen had changed since the normative data were collected in the late 1930s.

There also were concerns about the item content of the original MMPI. Some

of the language and references in the items had become archaic or obsolete. For example, not many contemporary subjects could respond meaningfully to the item involving "drop the handkerchief" because the game had not been popular among children for many years. Likewise, references to sleeping powders and streetcars were largely inappropriate for contemporary subjects.

Some of the items of the original MMPI included sexist language that was not in accord with contemporary standards concerning the use of such language in psychological tests. Some items, such as those dealing with Christian religious beliefs, were judged inappropriate for many contemporary test subjects. Many test subjects found items dealing with sexual behavior and bowel and bladder functions to be irrelevant to personality assessment and therefore objectionable.

Because the original MMPI items were never subjected to careful editorial review, some of them included poor grammar and inappropriate punctuation. Some of the idioms were troublesome for test subjects with limited formal education.

Finally, there was concern that the original MMPI item pool was not broad enough to permit assessment of many characteristics judged important by many test users. For example, few items concerned suicide attempts, use of drugs other than alcohol, and treatment-related behaviors. Although many supplementary scales were developed using the original MMPI item pool, the success of these scales often was limited by the pool's inadequacy.

MMPI researchers and users had considered the need for revision and restandardization for quite some time. In 1970 the entire MMPI Symposium was devoted to the topic of revision (Butcher, 1972). The enormity of the task and the unavailability of funds delayed revision plans for quite some time. In 1982 the University of Minnesota Press appointed a Restandardization Committee, consisting of James N. Butcher, W. Grant Dalhstrom, and John R. Graham, to consider the need for and feasibility of a revision of the MMPI.[2] Based on the recommendations of the committee, a decision was made to revise the MMPI. Funds to support the revision were provided by the University of Minnesota Press. The test distributor, National Computer Systems, provided test materials, forms, and scanning and scoring of data.

Goals of the Restandardization Project

From the start of the Restandardization Project, it was determined that every effort would be made to maintain continuity between the original MMPI and its revision. This would assure that the considerable research base that had accumulated since the test's publication would still be relevant to the new version.

---

[2]Although not involved in the early stages of the restandardization project, Auke Tellegen later was appointed to the Restandardization Committee.

A primary goal of the project was to collect a contemporary normative sample that would be more representative of the general population than had been Hathaway's original sample. Additionally, efforts would be made to improve the MMPI item pool by rewriting some items, deleting others judged to be objectionable, and generating new items that would expand the content dimensions of the item pool.

Major revisions of the existing validity and clinical scales were not anticipated as part of the restandardization project, although it was hoped that the project would produce data that later could lead to improvements in the basic scales. Also, it was hoped that items that were added to the item pool would be useful in generating some new scales.

Preparing the Experimental Booklet

Preparing the experimental booklet (Form AX) involved several simultaneous processes. In order to maintain continuity between the original and revised forms of the MMPI, a decision was made to maintain all 550 unique items in Form AX. The second occurrences of 16 repeated items, originally included to facilitate early machine scoring, were deleted. They no longer served any useful purpose and also disturbed many test subjects, who assumed incorrectly that they were included to determine if the subject was responding consistently.

Eighty-two of the 550 items were rewritten for Form AX. Fifteen were reworded to eliminate reference to a specific gender. For example, "Any man who is willing to work hard has a good chance of succeeding" was changed to "Anyone who is willing to work hard has a good chance of succeeding." In other items, idiomatic or obsolete expressions were replaced with more contemporary wordings. For example, "irritable" was substituted for "cross," "bad behavior" for "cutting up," and "often" for "commonly." Some references that had become dated were replaced. For example, "sleeping powders" was changed to "sleeping pills," and "bath" was changed to "bath or shower." Some changes were directed at eliminating subcultural bias. For example, "I go to church almost every week" was changed to "I attend religious services almost every week."

Most of the item changes were slight, and all of them were made with the objective of preserving the original meaning of the items while using more acceptable, contemporary language. Data were collected and analyzed to assure that changes did not significantly effect endorsement patterns (Ben-Porath & Butcher, 1989).

A second major change in the item pool involved adding new items. The committee reviewed the content dimensions in the original MMPI item pool, and it sought recommendations from experts in personality measurement and clinical assessment concerning content dimensions that should be added to the pool. The 154 items generated by the committee were added to the item pool, bringing the Form AX booklet length to 704 items. The additional items covered

drug abuse, suicide potential, Type A behavior patterns, marital adjustment, work attitudes, and treatment amenability.

Normative Data Collection

To obtain a large normative group that was broadly representative of the United States population, certain procedures were developed (Butcher, Dalhstrom, Graham, Tellegen, & Kaemmer, 1989). 1980 Census data were used to guide subject solicitation. Seven testing sites (Minnesota, Ohio, North Carolina, Washington, Pennsylvania, Virginia, and California) were selected to assure geographic representativeness. Potential subjects in a particular region were selected primarily from community or telephone directories. They were then sent letters explaining the nature of the project and asking them to participate. After an initial trial period, it was decided that individual subjects would be paid $15.00, and couples who participated together $40.00 for their participation. Subjects were tested in groups in locations conveniently located in their communities. In order to assure representativeness of the sample, some subjects from special groups were added to the sample. These included military personnel and American Indians. In addition to completing Form AX of the MMPI, all subjects also completed a biographical information form and a life events form. Couples completed two additional forms describing the nature and length of their relationships and rating each other on 110 characteristics.

Using these procedures, approximately 2900 subjects were tested. After eliminating subjects because of test invalidity or incompleteness of other forms, a final sample of 2600 community subjects (1138 males and 1462 females) was constituted. The sample included 841 couples. To collect test-retest data, 111 female subjects and 82 male subjects were retested approximately a week after the initial testing.

Racial composition of the sample was as follows: white, 81%; black, 12%; Hispanic, 3%; American Indian, 3%; and Asian-American, 1%. Subjects ranged in age from 18 to 85 years (M = 41.04; SD = 15.29) and in formal education from 3 to 20 + years (M = 14.72; SD = 2.60). Most males (61.6%) and females (61.2%) in the sample were married. Approximately 32% of the males and 21% of the females had professional or managerial positions, and approximately 12% of the males and 5% of the females were laborers. The median family income was $30,000–35,000 for males and $25,000–30,000 for females. Approximately 3% of male subjects and 6% of female subjects in the normative sample indicated that they were involved in treatment for mental health problems at the time of their participation in the study.

Clearly, the normative sample for the revised MMPI is more representative of the general population than was Hathaway's original sample. Although higher educational levels seem to be overrepresented in the sample, it appears to be quite representative of persons who are likely to take the MMPI.

Adolescent Data Collection

Concurrently with the adult data collection, a large normative sample of adolescent subjects also was assembled. The adolescents were solicited from school rosters in most of the same cities where adult data were collected. A separate experimental booklet (Form TX) was utilized, and the adolescent subjects also completed biographical information forms and life events forms. Form TX also included the 550 unique items in the original MMPI (some of them in rewritten form) and some of the new items added to Form AX. In addition, new items were added to Form TX to cover content dimensions relevant to adolescents but not included in the original MMPI item pool. Although the Restandardization Committee decided that separate adolescent norms for the revised MMPI would be published, the adolescent norms were not included in the revised manual. Rather, the committee indicated that such norms would be published later. Other decisions about an adolescent version of the revised MMPI have not yet been made.

Additional Data Collection

In order to provide the data necessary for making decisions, such as which items from the Form AX booklet would be included in the final revised booklet, data were collected from a variety of additional subject groups. These included psychiatric patients, alcoholics, chronic pain patients, marital counseling clients, college students, and job applicants.

Development of the Final Booklet

The final version of the revised MMPI (MMPI-2) includes 567 items from the Form AX booklet. Several criteria were employed in deciding which items were to be included. First, all items entering into the standard validity and clinical scales were provisionally included, as were items needed to score supplementary scales judged to be important. Some items were maintained because they would be included in some new scales developed from the item pool. From this provisional item pool, some items were deleted because they were judged on the basis of previous research (Butcher & Tellegen, 1966) to be objectionable. These items dealt with religious attitudes and practices, sexual preferences, and bowel and bladder functions. Table 1.1 indicates for each validity and clinical scale the number of items deleted, changed, and remaining. Not very many items were changed in most scales, and even fewer items were deleted.

In summary, the MMPI-2 is similar in most ways to the original MMPI. The MMPI-2 booklet includes the items necessary for scoring the standard validity and clinical scales. Although not all of the supplementary scales that could be scored from the original MMPI can be scored from MMPI-2, many of them can.

Table 1.1. Item Changes and Deletions for Basic Validity and Clinical Scales

Scale	Number of Items			Types of Changes			
	Deleted	Remaining	Changed	A	B	C	D
L	0	15	2	1	1	0	0
F	4	60	12	1	5	6	0
K	0	30	1	0	1	0	0
Hs	1	32	5	0	1	3	1
D	3	57	2	1	1	0	0
Hy	0	60	9	0	4	2	3
Pd	0	50	4	0	2	1	1
Mf	4	56	6	1	2	1	2
Pa	0	40	2	1	0	0	1
Pt	0	48	2	0	0	1	1
Sc	0	78	13	0	1	7	5
Ma	0	46	7	4	2	1	0
Si	1	69	6	0	3	2	1
Not on Any Scale	—	—	16	3	7	3	3

Note: A = elimination of possibly sexist wording; B = modernization of idioms and usage; C = grammatical clarification; D = simplification.

Source: S. R. Hathaway & J. C. McKinley with J.N. Butcher, W. G. Dahlstrom, J. R. Graham, A. Tellegen, & B. Kaemmer. *Minnesota Multiphasic Personality Inventory-2: Manual for administration and scoring.* 1989. Minneapolis: University of Minnesota Press. Reproduced by permission.

Much of the research concerning interpretation of the original MMPI still applies directly to MMPI-2. Improvements in MMPI-2 include a more contemporary and representative standardization sample, updated and improved items, deletion of objectionable items, and some new scales. The following chapters will offer more discussion of similarities and differences between the original MMPI and MMPI-2.

2

Administration and Scoring

QUALIFICATIONS OF TEST USERS

The MMPI-2 is easily administered and scored by hand or by computerized procedures. Although these procedures can be completed by a clerk or secretary, the MMPI-2 is a sophisticated psychological test. Its use is restricted to qualified professionals who have adequate training in test theory, personality structure and dynamics, and psychopathology and psychodiagnosis. Additionally, users of MMPI-2 should have detailed knowledge of the inventory itself. Familiarity with all material included in the MMPI-2 manual is essential. Users also should be familiar with MMPI-2 interpretive procedures presented in books such as this one.

WHO CAN TAKE MMPI-2?

The MMPI-2 can be used with subjects who are 18 years old or older and who have at least an eighth grade reading level. The original MMPI should be used with subjects younger than 18 years of age, and separate, age-appropriate norms should be used with such subjects. More information about using the MMPI with adolescent subjects is presented in Chapter 8. As long as visual disabilities or other physical problems do not interfere, there is no upper age limit for those capable of taking the test.

The clinical condition of potential examinees is an important consideration in deciding who can take the MMPI-2. Completion of the test is a lengthy and tedious task for many subjects. Persons who are very anxious or agitated often find the task almost unbearable. It frequently is possible to break the testing session into several shorter periods for such individuals. Also persons who are confused may not be able to understand or to follow the standard instructions.

Such persons sometimes can complete the test if the items are presented using a standardized audio tape.

ADMINISTERING THE MMPI-2

The test can be administered to most persons either individually or in groups, using the forms of the test and answer sheets most convenient for the examiner. For those of average or above average intelligence, without complicating factors, the testing time typically is between 1 and 1½ hours. For less intelligent individuals, or those with other complicating factors, the testing time may exceed 2 hours. Although having the test subject take home the MMPI-2 to complete and return to the examiner sometimes seems more convenient, whenever possible it is desirable to have the test completed in the professional atmosphere of the clinician's office. This increases the likelihood that the test will be taken seriously and that the results will be valid and useful.

Before the MMPI-2 is administered, the examiner should establish rapport with test subjects. The best way to assure the subject's cooperation is to explain why the MMPI-2 is being administered, who will have access to the results, and why it is in the best interest of the test subject to cooperate with the testing.

The test should be administered in a quiet, comfortable place. The examiner or a proctor should be readily available to monitor the test-taking and to answer questions that may arise. Care should be taken to make sure that the test subject carefully reads the test instructions and understands them. Questions that arise during the course of testing should be handled promptly and confidentially. Most questions can be handled by referring the test subject to the standardized test instructions.

National Computer Systems (NCS) offers computer software that permits administration of the MMPI-2 using a personal computer. Test subjects follow directions on the computer monitor, where test items are displayed, and record their responses by using several identified keys on the computer keyboard. Moreland (1987) reviewed research studies concerning the equivalence of computerized and conventional test administration. Although the results of these studies are not all completely consistent, Moreland concluded that if the two types of administration are not completely equivalent, nonequivalence typically is small enough to be of no practical consequence. This conclusion is consistent with early studies indicating that the MMPI is a very robust instrument and that administration using booklet, card forms, or tape recordings of the original MMPI yielded comparable results (Cottle, 1950; MacDonald, 1952; Wiener, 1947). Thus, it probably can be assumed that computer administration will yield results comparable to use of the standard test booklet and answer sheets. An important consideration in deciding whether or not to use computer admin-

istration is the computer time required. A single administration of MMPI-2 can tie up a personal computer for several hours.

TESTING MATERIALS

Unlike the original MMPI, the MMPI-2 has only one booklet form. An optional hardcover version of the booklet is available for use when subjects may not have a table or desk surface on which to take the test. However, the order of items in both the softcover and hardcover versions is identical. Items are arranged so that those required for scoring the standard validity and clinical scales appear first. If only the standard scales are required, test subjects need only complete the first 370 items. However, if less than the entire test is completed, many of the supplementary scales available for MMPI-2 cannot be scored. Usually, if test subjects can complete 370 items, they can complete 567 items.

For subjects who may have difficulty completing the standard form of the test, several alternatives are available. A standardized tape-recorded version of the items is available from NCS. This version is useful for semiliterate persons and for persons with disabilities that make completion of the standard form difficult or impossible. A standardized Spanish version of the test is also available from NCS.

Almost since the MMPI was first published, there have been efforts to develop short forms of the test. However, except when administering the first 370 items in the booklet when only the standard validity and clinical scales are needed, the use of short forms of MMPI-2 is not acceptable. Research on the original MMPI clearly indicated that short forms are not adequate substitutes for the standard instrument (Butcher, Kendall, & Hoffman, 1980; Dahlstrom, 1980).

Several different answer sheets are available for MMPI-2. Which one to use depends on how the examiner plans to score the test. If the test is to be hand scored, one kind of answer sheet should be used. If it is to be computer scored, a different kind of answer sheet is indicated. Before administering the test, examiners should determine how scoring will be accomplished. Reference to the test manual or to a NCS test catalog will provide specific information about which answer sheets to use. It should be emphasized that none of the answer sheets designed for use with the original MMPI can be used with MMPI-2.

SCORING THE MMPI-2

Once the subject's responses to the MMPI-2 items have been recorded on an answer sheet, scoring can be accomplished by computer or by hand. As mentioned earlier, special answer sheets must be used for computer scoring. Computer scoring can be completed in several different ways. NCS sells computer

software that permits users to score the standard validity and clinical scales, as well as numerous supplementary scales, using their own personal computers. If the test has been computer administered, test responses are stored in the computer's memory and scoring programs applied directly to them. Another option, which is especially attractive for high-volume users, is to attach a scanner to the personal computer. Answer sheets are scanned quickly, and the responses are subjected to scoring programs. For those who do not require immediate availability of results, a final option for computer scoring is to forward subjects' responses to NCS in Minneapolis, where they are scored and returned to users by mail. From most locations in the United States the entire process can be accomplished in a week. For those who require faster turn-around time, a teleprocessing service is offered by NCS. A personal computer keyboard and modem are used to access the scoring services of NCS via telephone lines. The 567 items can be entered by a clerical person in approximately 10 minutes, and the resulting scores are returned immediately and printed out on the user's personal computer printer. All the computerized scoring options offered by NCS are paid for on a per use basis. Persons interested in available computer services should contact NCS for details.

Many persons, particularly those who are not high-volume users, may prefer to hand score the MMPI-2 using hand-scoring templates available from NCS. Scoring keys are available for the standard validity and clinical scales and for numerous supplementary scales. The scoring templates are quite easy to use. Each template is placed over an answer sheet designed especially for hand-scoring purposes. The number of blackened spaces is counted and represents the raw score for the scale in question. Care should be taken when scoring scale 5 (Masculinity-Femininity) to use the scoring key appropriate for the test subject's gender. For some scales only one scoring key is available, whereas for others two keys (front and back) are required. Obviously, when two keys are used, the raw score is the total number of blackened spaces on the front and back of the answer sheet. Raw scores for the standard validity and clinical scales are recorded in spaces provided on the answer sheet itself. For supplementary scales, raw scores are recorded in spaces provided on separate profile sheets. Although hand scoring the MMPI-2 is a simple clerical task, it should be completed with great care, as counting and recording errors are rather common.

CONSTRUCTING THE PROFILE

Profile sheets are available from NCS for the standard validity scales and for numerous supplementary scales. The standard profile sheet to be used routinely for MMPI-2 is one that applies a K-correction to some of the clinical scale raw scores. NCS offers separate profile sheets that permit construction of non–K-corrected profiles. Using the noncorrected scores is not recommended for most purposes. Almost all the information available concerning MMPI and

MMPI-2 interpretation is based on K-corrected scores, and it cannot be applied directly to noncorrected scores and profiles of scores. The test manual (Butcher, Dahlstrom, Graham, Tellegen, & Kaemmer, 1989) discusses circumstances when the noncorrected scores may be preferable. Generally speaking, K-corrected scores may lead to overestimates of deviance from nonclinical subjects, particularly those who are well educated. In such cases, the noncorrected scores may more accurately reflect the subjects' adjustment level compared with the normative sample. However, one should not use the noncorrected scores to generate statements concerning personality characteristics and symptoms of test subjects.

When the MMPI-2 is used with adolescent subjects, i.e., those younger than 18 years of age, the K-correction is not used. T-score transformations are based on noncorrected scores, and interpretive information is available concerning the meaning of noncorrected T-scores for adolescents. More information about using the MMPI-2 with adolescents can be found in Chapter 8 of this book.

A first step in constructing a profile of the standard validity and clinical scales is to transfer the raw scores from the answer sheet to appropriate blanks at the bottom of the profile sheet, making sure that the profile is the appropriate one for the person's gender. At this time it also is important to be certain that identifying data (name, age, date, education, etc.) are recorded on the profile sheet.

At this point a K-correction is added to the raw scores for the Hs, Pd, Pt, Sc, and Ma scales. The proportion of a person's K scale raw score that is to be added to each of these scales is indicated on the profile form. On these scales the total score (the original raw score plus the K-correction) is calculated and recorded in the appropriate blank on the profile sheet.

For each scale the examiner should refer to the number in the column above the scale label. The number in the column corresponding to the raw score (K-corrected if appropriate) on the scale is marked by the examiner either with a small x or a small dot. Raw scores on the Cannot Say (?) scale are recorded on the profile sheet but are not plotted as part of the profile. Care should be taken when plotting the scale 5 (Mf) scores. For men higher raw scores yield higher T-scores, whereas for women higher raw scores yield lower T-scores. After a dot or x has been entered in the column above each scale label, the MMPI-2 profile for the person examined is completed by connecting the plotted dots or x's with one another. Traditionally, the three validity scales are joined to one another but are not connected with the 10 clinical scale scores. Similar procedures are used to construct profiles for supplementary scales.

Because T-scores are printed on each side of the profile sheet, by plotting the scores in the manner described here, the raw scores for each scale can be converted visually to T-scores. A T-score has a mean of 50 and a standard deviation of 10. For scales L, F, K, 5, and 0 the T-scores used are linear, whereas for scales 1, 2, 3, 4, 6, 7, 8, and 9 special uniform T-scores are used. More information concerning characteristics of uniform T-scores and differences

between linear and uniform scores can be found in Chapter 8. The T-score conversions provided on the profile sheet are based on the responses of the contemporary standardization samples. Thus, a T-score of 50 for any particular scale indicates that a person's score is equal to the average or mean score for the standardization subjects of the test subject's same gender. Scores greater than 50 indicate scores higher than the average for the standardization sample, and scores below 50 indicate scores lower than the average for the standardization sample.

CODING THE PROFILE

Although it is possible to derive some useful information by interpreting an examinee's T-score on a single scale in isolation, much of the information relevant to interpretation of MMPI-2 protocols is *configural* in nature. Thus, in addition to interpreting individual scales, considering the pattern of the scales in relation to one another is necessary. To facilitate profile interpretation, coding is a procedure for recording concisely most of the essential information about a profile and for reducing the possible number of different profiles to a manageable size. Coding conveys information about the scores on scales relative to one another and also indicates an absolute range within which scores fall. It also permits easy grouping of similar profiles, using all or only part of the code.

Two major coding systems were utilized with the original MMPI: Hathaway's (1947) original system and a more complete system developed by Welsh (1948). Welsh's system is the only one used in recent years, and a slight modification of it is the one recommended in the test manual.

Welsh Code

Step 1

Utilize the number instead of the name for each scale.

Hs - 1	Pa - 6
D - 2	Pt - 7
Hy - 3	Sc - 8
Pd - 4	Ma - 9
Mf - 5	Si - 0

Step 2

Record the 10 numbers of the clinical scales in order of T-scores, from the highest on the left to the lowest on the right.

Step 3

To the right of and separated from the clinical scales, record the three validity scales (L,F,K) in order of T-scores with the highest on the left and the lowest on the right. Do not include the ? scale. The set of clinical scales and the set of validity scales are coded separately. No supplementary scales are included in the coding.

Step 4

When adjacent scales are within one T-score point, they are underlined. When adjacent scales have the same T-score, place in the ordinal sequence found on the profile sheet and underline.

Step 5

To indicate scale elevations, appropriate symbols are inserted after scale numbers as follows:

120 and above	!!
110–119	!
100–109	**
90–99	*
80–89	"
70–79	'
60–69	-
50–59	/
40–49	:
30–39	#
29 & less	to the right of #

If a 10-point T-score range does not contain any scale, the appropriate symbol for that elevation must be included. It is not necessary to include a symbol to the left of the scale with the highest score or to the right of the scale with the lowest score.

Step 6

Repeat steps 4 and 5 for the validity scales.

As a practice exercise, the reader might wish to cover the code at the bottom of Table 2.1 and code the T-scores into the Welsh code using the instructions given above.

Table 2.1. Example of Welsh Code

Scale Name	Scale No.	Raw Score	T-score
Cannot Say	— —	5	—
L	— —	6	61
F	— —	12	73
K	— —	11	41
Hypochondriasis	1	18	64
Depression	2	39	91
Hysteria	3	23	54
Psychopathic deviate	4	18	43
Masculinity-femininity	5	29	56
Paranoia	6	5	34
Psychasthenia	7	43	85
Schizophrenia	8	46	84
Hypomania	9	10	31
Social introversion	0	10	31

Welsh code: 2*<u>78</u>″ ′1–53/4:6#<u>90</u>   F′L–/K

3

The Validity Scales

For the MMPI-2 to yield maximally accurate and useful information, the test subject must approach the test-taking task in the manner indicated in the instructions. Subjects are instructed to read each item, consider its content, and give a direct and, as far as possible, honest response utilizing the true-false response format provided. When extreme deviations from these procedures occur, the resulting protocol should be considered invalid and should not interpreted further. Less extreme deviations should be taken into account when the resulting scores are interpreted.

Although Hathaway and McKinley hoped that the empirical keying procedure utilized in developing the MMPI would make such distortions less likely than in earlier face-valid inventories, they recognized the importance of assessing test-taking attitudes. Four validity indicators developed specifically to assess test-taking attitude with the original MMPI have been maintained with MMPI-2. In addition, three new validity indicators were developed specifically for MMPI-2.

In addition to providing important information about test-taking attitudes, the original validity scales of the MMPI also came to be used as sources of inferences about extratest behaviors. Both aspects of the four original validity indicators will be considered in this chapter. The items included in each of the original validity scales and the keyed response for each item are presented in Appendix A of this book.[1] T-score transformations for raw scores on the L, F, and K scales can be found in Appendix B. Appendix K reports information about items included in the three new validity scales and keyed responses for the items. T-score transformations for raw scores on the three new validity scales can be found in Appendix L.

CANNOT SAY (?) SCALE

The Cannot Say score simply is the number of omitted items (including items answered both true and false). People omit items on MMPI-2 for many reasons.

[1]Item numbers in Appendix A and elsewhere in this book are for the MMPI-2 booklet. Appendix J of the MMPI-2 manual (Butcher, Dahlstrom, Graham, Tellegen, & Kaemmer, 1989) includes a table for converting MMPI-2 item numbers to group form item numbers of the original MMPI.

Occasionally, items are omitted because of carelessness or confusion. Omitted items also can reflect an attempt to avoid admitting undesirable things about oneself without directly lying. People who cannot decide between the two response alternatives may leave many items unanswered. Others omit items because they lack the information or experience necessary for a meaningful response.

Regardless of the reasons for omitting items, a large number of such items can lead to lowered scores on other scales. Therefore, the validity of a protocol with many omitted items should be questioned. The MMPI-2 manual suggests that protocols with 30 or more omitted items should be considered invalid and not interpreted. This criterion seems to be far too liberal. This author's own prac-tice is to interpret with great caution protocols with more than 10 omitted items and not to interpret at all those with more than 30 omitted items. As indicated in Chapter 2, however, the best procedure is to ensure that few or no items are omitted. If encouraged before beginning MMPI-2 to answer all items, most people usually will omit only a very few. Also, if the examiner scans answer sheets at the time that the test is completed and encourages individuals to try to answer previously omitted items, most people will complete all or almost all of the items.

L SCALE

As indicated in Chapter 1, the L scale originally was constructed to detect a deliberate and rather unsophisticated attempt on the part of subjects to present themselves in a favorable light (Meehl & Hathaway, 1946). All 15 rationally derived items in the original L scale have been maintained in MMPI-2. The items deal with minor flaws and weaknesses to which most people are willing to admit. However, those who deliberately are trying to present themselves in a very favorable way are not willing to admit even such minor shortcomings. Such people produce high L scale scores.

Although most L scale items are not answered in the scored direction (false) by most people, many normal individuals endorse several of the items in the scored direction. The number of L items endorsed in the scored direction by subjects in the MMPI-2 normative samples was approximately three. Scores on the L scale are related to educational level, socioeconomic status, and psycho-logical sophistication. Better educated, brighter, more sophisticated people from higher social classes score lower on the L scale.

High Scores on L Scale

Because of the relationship between L scale scores and demographic variables, such variables must be taken into account when deciding if a score should be considered high. Whereas a raw score of 3 or 4 on the L scale would be about

average for a lower middle class laborer of average or below average intelligence, such a score would be considered moderately high for a college-educated person from an upper middle class background.

When the L scale score is higher than would be expected when demographic variables are taken into account, one should entertain the possibility that the person is not being frank in answering items on the inventory. As a result, the individual's scores on most or all of the clinical scales have been lowered artificially in the direction of appearing better adjusted psychologically.

In addition to suggesting a defensive test-taking attitude, high L scale scores tend to be associated with some other important characteristics and behaviors. High scorers on the L scale tend to be overly conventional and socially conforming. They are rigid and moralistic, and they overevaluate their own worth. They utilize repression and denial excessively, and they appear to have little or no insight into their own motivations. Also, they have little awareness of the consequences to other people of their behavior. In some rare cases, particularly when the F and K scales also are elevated, an extremely high L scale score may suggest a full-blown clinical confusion either organic or functional in nature.

Low Scores on L Scale

Low scores on the L scale usually indicate that the person responded frankly to the items and was self-confident enough to be able to admit to minor faults and shortcomings. Low scorers have been described as perceptive, socially responsive, self-reliant, and independent. They also appear to be strong, natural, and relaxed, and they function effectively in leadership roles. They are able to communicate their ideas effectively, although at times they may impress others as somewhat cynical and sarcastic.

Sometimes below average L scale scores suggest a deviant test-taking attitude in which subjects are being overly self-critical and may be exaggerating problems and negative characteristics. This interpretation is most appropriate when the K scale score also is quite low and the F scale score is very high. An all true response set also produces very low T-scores on the L scale.

Summary of L Scale Descriptors[2]

High L scale scores are indicative of persons who:

1. are trying to create a favorable impression of themselves by not being honest in responding to the items

[2]The reader should recognize that the descriptors listed in this and subsequent summaries are modal ones and that all descriptors will not apply necessarily to all individuals with a given score or configuration of scores. The descriptors should be viewed as hypotheses to be validated by reference to other test and nontest data.

2. may be defensive, denying, and repressing
3. may be confused
4. manifest little or no insight into their own motivations
5. show little awareness of consequences to other people of their behavior
6. overevalute their own worth
7. tend to be conventional and socially conforming
8. are unoriginal in thinking and inflexible in problem solving
9. are rigid and moralistic
10. have poor tolerance for stress and pressure

Low L scale scores are indicative of persons who:

1. probably responded frankly to the items
2. are confident enough about themselves to be able to admit to minor faults and shortcomings
3. in some cases may be exaggerating negative characteristics
4. are perceptive and socially reliant
5. are seen as strong, natural, and relaxed
6. are self-reliant and independent
7. function effectively in leadership roles
8. communicate ideas effectively
9. may be described by others as cynical and sarcastic

F SCALE

The F scale originally was developed to detect deviant or atypical ways of responding to test items (Meehl & Hathaway, 1946). The 64 items in the original F scale were ones answered in the scored direction by fewer than 10 percent of adult normal subjects. Several of the F scale items were deleted from MMPI-2 because of objectionable content, leaving the F scale with 60 items in the revised instrument.

A factor analysis of the original F scale (Comrey, 1958a) identified 19 content dimensions, assessing such diverse characteristics as paranoid thinking, antisocial attitudes or behavior, hostility, and poor physical health. A person can obtain a high F scale score by endorsing items in some, but not necessarily all, of these 19 content areas. In general, and because the scales of MMPI-2 are intercorrelated, high scores on the F scale usually are associated with high scores on the clinical scales, especially on scales 6 and 8. Scores on the F scale also have been found to correlate with age and with race, with adolescents and blacks scoring approximately 10 T-score points higher on the F scale than other groups.

As used by the practicing clinician, the F scale serves three important functions. First, it is an index of test-taking attitude and is useful in detecting

deviant response sets. Second, if one can rule out profile invalidity, the F scale is a good indicator of degree of psychopathology, with higher scores suggesting greater psychopathology. Finally, scores on the F scale can be used to generate inferences about other extratest characteristics and behaviors.

High Scores on F Scale

T-scores equal to or greater than 100 are indicative of persons who:

1. may have responded randomly to the MMPI-2 items
2. may have responded true to all the MMPI-2 items or false to all the MMPI-2 items
3. may have been faking bad responses when taking the MMPI-2
4. if hospitalized psychiatric patients, may manifest:
    a. delusions
    b. visual and/or auditory hallucinations
    c. reduced speech
    d. withdrawal
    e. poor judgment
    f. short attention span
    g. lack of knowledge of reasons for hospitalization
    h. psychotic diagnosis
    i. some extratest signs of organicity

T-scores in a range of 80 to 99 are indicative of persons who:

1. may be malingering
2. may be exaggerating symptoms and problems as a plea for help
3. may be quite resistant to the testing procedure
4. may be clearly psychotic by the usual criteria

T-scores in a range of 65 to 79 are indicative of persons who:

1. may have very deviant social, political, or religious convictions
2. may manifest clinically severe neurotic or psychotic disorders
3. if relatively free of psychopathology, are described as:
    a. moody
    b. restless
    c. dissatisfied
    d. changeable, unstable
    e. curious, complex
    f. opinionated
    g. opportunistic

T-scores in a range of 50 to 64 are indicative of persons who:

1. have endorsed items relevant to some particular problem area
2. typically function adequately in most aspects of their life situations

Low Scores on F Scale

T-scores that are below 50 are indicative of persons who:

1. answered items as most normal people do
2. are likely to be free of disabling psychopathology
3. are socially conforming
4. may have faked good in responding to the MMPI-2 items

K SCALE

When early experience with the MMPI indicated that the L scale was quite insensitive to several kinds of test distortion, the K scale was developed as a more subtle and more effective index of attempts by examinees to deny psycho-pathology and to present themselves in a favorable light or, conversely, to exaggerate psychopathology and to try to appear in a very unfavorable light (Meehl & Hathaway, 1946; McKinley, Hathaway, & Meehl, 1948). High scores on the K scale thus were thought to be associated with a defensive approach to the test, whereas low scores were thought to be indicative of an unusually frank and self-critical approach. In addition to identifying these deviations in test-taking attitudes, a statistical procedure also was developed for correcting scores on some of the clinical scales. (See discussion of the K-correction in Chapter 1.)

The original K scale included 30 items that were empirically identified by contrasting item responses of abnormal individuals who produced normal profiles with item responses of a group of normal subjects. The MMPI-2 version of the K scale includes all 30 of these original items.

Subsequent research and experience with the MMPI have indicated that the K scale is much more complex than was originally believed. Scores on the K scale are related to defensiveness, but they also are related to educational level and socioeconomic status, with better-educated and higher socioeconomic-level subjects scoring higher on the scale. It is not unusual for college-educated persons who are not being defensive to obtain T-scores on the K scale in a range of 55 to 60. Persons with even more formal education may obtain T-scores in a range of 60 to 70.

Moderate elevations on the K scale sometimes reflect ego strength and psychological resources. There is no definite way to determine when elevated

K scores indicate clinical defensiveness and when they indicate ego strength. However, if elevated K scores are found for persons who do not seem to be disturbed psychologically and who appear to be functioning reasonably well, the possibility that the K score is reflecting positive characteristics rather than defensiveness should be considered.

There has not been much research to support the routine use of the K-correction to the clinical scales. Although the K-correction may lead to better discriminative power for each clinical scale where it is applied, it does not necessarily improve the accuracy of the overall profile configuration. However, because virtually all information about profile interpretation is based on K-corrected scores, it is recommended that the K-correction be used routinely unless separate norms and interpretive data are available for uncorrected scores. Marks, Seeman, and Haller (1974) have used such an approach in utilizing uncorrected scores in their codebook for adolescents, but they are a notable exception within the ranks of test users. For persons who want to explore the possibility that uncorrected scores will be of greater utility in some particular setting, the test distributor provides profile sheets for plotting uncorrected scores. Occasionally, the MMPI research literature has reported data based on uncorrected scores. Clinicians should be sensitive to the nature of the data being presented in the literature so that they can apply the data clinically in an appropriate manner.

The 30 items in the K scale cover several different content areas in which a person can deny problems (e.g., hostility, suspiciousness, family dissension, lack of self-confidence, excessive worry). The K scale items tend to be much more subtle than items in the L scale; therefore, it is less likely that a defensive person will recognize the purpose of the items and will be able to avoid detection.

High Scores on the K Scale

When a K scale score is higher than is typically expected for a person's socioeconomic status, the possibility of either a deliberate attempt to deny problems and psychopathology and thereby to appear in a favorable light or of all false responding should be considered (see discussion of profile invalidity below for details about these two response sets). High K scale scorers may be trying to maintain an appearance of adequacy, control, and effectiveness. High scorers tend to be shy, inhibited, and hesitant about becoming emotionally involved with other people. In addition, they are intolerant and unaccepting of unconventional beliefs and behavior in other people. They lack self-insight and self-understanding. Delinquency is unlikely among people with high scores on the K scale. When high K scale scores are accompanied by marked elevations on the clinical scales, it is likely that the person is quite seriously disturbed psychologically but has little or no awareness of it. When moderately high scores are found for persons who do not seem to be disturbed psychologically and who

appear to be functioning reasonably well, they may be reflecting ego strength and other positive characteristics.

Average Scores on K Scale

When K scale scores fall within the range that is expected for a person's socioeconomic status, they suggest a healthy balance between positive self-evaluation and self-criticism. Such people tend to be well adjusted psychologically and to manifest few signs of emotional disturbance. They are independent, self-reliant, and capable of dealing with problems in their daily lives. They tend to have high intellectual abilities and wide interests and to be ingenious, enterprising, versatile, and resourceful. They are clear thinking and approach problems reasonably and systematically. In social situations, they mix well with other people, are enthusiastic and verbally fluent, and tend to take an ascendant role.

Low Scores on K Scale

When K scale scores are lower than expected for a person's socioeconomic status, the possibility of all true responding or a deliberate attempt to present themselves in an unfavorable light should be considered (see the following discussion of profile invalidity for details about these two response sets). Low scores also may indicate that subjects are exaggerating problems as a plea for help or that they are experiencing confusion that may be either organic or functional in nature. Low scorers tend to be very critical of themselves and of others and to be quite self-dissatisfied. They may be ineffective in dealing with problems in their daily lives, and they tend to have little insight into their own motives and behavior. They are socially conforming and tend to be overly compliant with authority. They are inhibited, retiring, and shallow and have a slow personal tempo. They tend to be rather awkward socially and to be blunt and harsh in social interactions. Their outlook toward life is characterized as cynical, skeptical, caustic, and disbelieving, and they tend to be quite suspicious about the motivations of other people.

Summary of Descriptors

High scores on the K scale are indicative of persons who:

1. may have responded false to most of the MMPI-2 items
2. may have tried to fake good in responding to the MMPI-2 items
3. may be trying to give an appearance of adequacy, control, and effectiveness

  4. are shy and inhibited
  5. are hesitant about becoming emotionally involved with people
  6. are intolerant and unaccepting of unconventional attitudes and beliefs in other people
  7. lack self-insight and self-understanding
  8. are not likely to display overt delinquent behavior
  9. if clinical scales also are elevated, may be seriously disturbed psychologically but have little awareness of it
  10. if not seriously disturbed psychologically, may have above-average ego strength and other positive characteristics

Average scores on the K scale are indicative of persons who:

  1. maintained a healthy balance between positive self-evaluation and self-criticism in responding to the MMPI-2 items
  2. are psychologically well adjusted
  3. show few overt signs of emotional disturbance
  4. are independent and self-reliant
  5. are capable of dealing with problems in daily life
  6. exhibit wide interests
  7. are ingenious, enterprising, versatile, and resourceful
  8. are clear thinking; approach problems in reasonable and systematic ways
  9. are good mixers socially
  10. are enthusiastic and verbally fluent
  11. take ascendant role in relationships

Low K scale scores are indicative of individuals who:

  1. may have responded true to most of the MMPI-2 items
  2. may have faked bad when responding to the MMPI-2 items
  3. may be exaggerating problems as plea for help
  4. may exhibit acute psychotic or organic confusion
  5. are critical of self and others and are self-dissatisfied
  6. are ineffective in dealing with problems of daily life
  7. show little insight into their own motives and behavior
  8. are socially conforming
  9. are overly compliant with authority
  10. have a slow personal tempo
  11. are inhibited, retiring, and shallow
  12. are socially awkward
  13. are blunt and harsh in social situations
  14. are cynical, skeptical, caustic, and disbelieving
  15. are suspicious about the motivations of other people

BACK-PAGE INFREQUENCY (Fb) SCALE

The Back-page Infrequency (Fb) scale originally was developed for the experimental booklet used in the normative data collection for MMPI-2 (Butcher, Dahlstrom, Graham, Tellegen, & Kaemmer, 1989). The procedures used to develop Fb were similar to those used in the development of the standard F scale. Since the items in the standard F scale appeared early in the experimental booklet, that scale did not offer evidence of the validity of responses to items appearing later in the 704-item booklet. The original Fb scale included 64 items that appeared later in the experimental booklet to which fewer than 10 percent of normal subjects responded in the scored direction. The version of the Fb scale included in MMPI-2 has 40 of the original 64 items.

In a protocol for which the standard F scale score is indicative of a valid approach to the instrument, an elevated Fb scale score could indicate that the subject stopped paying attention to the test items that occurred later in the booklet and shifted to an essentially random pattern of responding. In this situation, one could interpret the standard scales that are based on items that occur early in the booklet, but supplementary and content scales that are based on items that occur later in the booklet should not be interpreted. Of course, if the standard F scale is indicative of invalidity, the protocol should not be interpreted at all.

Because this is a newly developed scale, no research data are available concerning the optimal cutoff score for identifying invalid records. In a protocol resulting from random responding, we would expect about half (20) of the Fb items to be endorsed in the scored direction. Thus, a T-score greater than 120 would indicate that a protocol definitely should not be interpreted. However, T-scores greater than 80 on the Fb scale would suggest some sort of deviant responding on the items appearing later in the booklet and would indicate extreme caution in interpreting supplementary and content scales based on those items. Subjects who respond true to most of the MMPI-2 items or who fake bad in responding to the items also will produce very elevated scores on the Fb scale.

VARIABLE RESPONSE INCONSISTENCY (VRIN) SCALE

The Variable Response Inconsistency (VRIN) scale was developed for MMPI-2 as an additional validity indicator (Butcher, Dahlstrom, Graham, Tellegen, & Kaemmer, 1989). It provides an indication of subjects' tendencies to respond inconsistently to MMPI-2 items. The VRIN scale consists of 67 pairs of items with either similar or opposite content. Each time a subject answers items in a pair inconsistently, one raw score point is added to the score on the VRIN scale. For some item pairs two true responses result in a point being scored for the scale; for other item pairs two false responses result in a point being added;

and for still other item pairs a true response and a false response result in a point being added. This scale is very complicated to score, and it is recommended that it be scored by computer. Although hand scoring is possible, the procedure is complicated, suggesting that considerable care be taken in hand scoring it.

The MMPI-2 manual (Butcher, Dahlstrom, Graham, Tellegen, & Kaemmer, 1989) indicates that the VRIN scale is experimental at this time and interpretation of the scale requires caution until more empirical data are available. However, it is suggested that a raw score equal to or greater than 13 indicates inconsistent responding that probably invalidates the resulting protocol. A random response set will produce a very elevated T-score on VRIN (well above 100). In an all true or all false response set the VRIN T-score will be near 50. Subjects who deliberately are faking bad on the MMPI-2 will produce about average T-scores on VRIN.

In summary, VRIN was developed to identify subjects who respond to the MMPI-2 items inconsistently and whose resulting protocols therefore should not be interpreted. Such inconsistent responding typically results when subjects do not read the content of the items and respond instead in a random or near random way to the items.

VRIN will be most useful when it is used along with the F scale. A high F scale score and a high VRIN scale score would support the notion that the subject has responded randomly to the MMPI-2 items. However, a high F scale score and a low or moderate VRIN scale score would suggest a protocol that did not result from random responding or confusion. Instead, one would suspect that the protocol came either from a severely disturbed person who responded validly to the items or from a person who approached the items with an intention of appearing more disturbed than really is the case. Because an all true or all false response set would be likely to produce a high F scale score and an average VRIN scale score, those sets must also be considered.

TRUE RESPONSE INCONSISTENCY (TRIN) SCALE

The True Response Inconsistency (TRIN) scale was developed for MMPI-2 to identify subjects who respond inconsistently to items by giving true responses to items indiscriminately (acquiescence) or by giving false responses to items indiscriminately (nonacquiescence) (Butcher, Dahlstrom, Graham, Tellegen, & Kaemmer, 1989). In either case, the resulting profile may be invalid and uninterpretable.

The TRIN scale consists of 23 pairs of items that are opposite in content. Two true responses to some item pairs or two false responses to other item pairs would indicate inconsistent responding. The TRIN raw score is obtained by subtracting the number of pairs of items to which subjects responded inconsistently with two false responses from the number of pairs of items to which

subjects responded inconsistently with two true responses, and then adding a constant value of nine to the difference. TRIN scores can range from 0 to 23. Higher TRIN raw scores indicate a tendency to give true responses indiscriminately, and lower TRIN raw scores indicate a tendency to give false responses indiscriminately. When TRIN raw scores are converted to T-scores, both above average and below average raw scores are converted to higher T-scores, with the likelihood of a true or false response set indicated by letters T or F following the T-scores. As with the VRIN scale, the TRIN scale involves complex scoring that is best done by computer. If hand scoring is used, considerable care should be exercised.

TRIN also is considered to be experimental at this time, and interpretation should be done cautiously until additional empirical data are available (Butcher, Dahlstrom, Graham, Tellegen, & Kaemmer, 1989). However, the MMPI-2 manual suggests that as rough guidelines TRIN raw scores of 13 or more or of 5 or less may be suggestive of indiscriminate responding that might invalidate the protocol.

PROFILE INVALIDITY

Some MMPI-2 users consider any protocol invalid and uninterpretable that has more than 30 omitted items or a T-score greater than 70 on one or more of the standard validity scales. Although this is a very conservative practice that is not likely to result in labeling as valid profiles that are in fact invalid, it represents an oversimplified view of profile validity and causes many valid profiles to be discarded. For example, the MMPI-2 manual (Butcher, Dahlstrom, Graham, Tellegen, & Kaemmer, 1989) states that F scale scores in a T-score range of 71 to 90 can indicate psychosis. Gynther, Altman, and Warbin (1973) demonstrated that profiles with F scale T-scores equal to or greater than 100 can have reliable extratest personality and behavioral correlates (e.g., disorientation, hallucinations, delusions, short attention span). In addition, the experienced clinician is not very surprised to encounter a K scale T-score greater than 70 among well-educated persons. Thus, a more sophisticated approach to profile validity is indicated.

Some subjects approach the MMPI-2 with such deviant test-taking attitudes that the resulting protocols are not at all interpretable. For example, subjects who respond randomly to the MMPI-2 items or who approach the test with a deliberate and extreme attempt to feign psychopathology will produce a protocol that must not be interpreted. Other subjects do not follow the test instructions, but their deviant responding is not as extreme. For example, some clients who are seeking psychological or psychiatric treatment for the first time may tend to exaggerate symptoms and problems to some extent as a plea for help. These tendencies must be taken into account when the resulting protocol is interpreted, but they do not necessarily make the protocol uninterpetable.

Deviant Response Styles and Sets

To produce a valid MMPI-2 protocol a person must read and consider the content of each item and respond to it as true or false. Occasionally, individuals respond stylistically (e.g., false to each item) without reference to item content. Such behavior usually occurs among people who lack adequate reading skills, who are too confused to follow directions, or who have a very negativistic attitude toward the assessment procedure. Sometimes subjects are highly motivated to appear more or less well adjusted on the MMPI-2 than is actually the case for them, and they respond to item content in terms of the picture that they want to present of themselves rather than in terms of actual self-perceptions.

In ideal circumstances the test examiner should be aware of such response tendencies. Efforts should be made to assure that test subjects follow the standard instructions for completing the MMPI-2. If cooperation cannot be elicited, the test should not be administered. However, sometimes, particularly when large numbers of people are tested at once, some persons complete the MMPI-2 without following standard instructions. It is important for the MMPI-2 user to know how to detect the resulting invalid protocols. If profile invalidity is suspected, it may be helpful to consider what is known about the test subject's behavior from observation. Lack of congruence between the profile and observed behavior could be accounted for by the adoption of a response set or style.

If a particular MMPI-2 protocol is deemed invalid, the examiner may be able to discuss the situation with the test subject and readminister the test. Often a second testing yields a valid and interpretable protocol. If retesting is not possible or does not yield a valid protocol, no interpretation should be attempted. Further, it should be understood that the only thing an invalid protocol tells us about a test subject is that because responses to the test items were not valid, the resulting scores do not represent an accurate picture of what the person really is like. For example, it is tempting to conclude that the person who presents a fake good protocol, one in which even an average number of symptoms and problems are denied, is really a very maladjusted person who is trying to conceal that maladjustment. Such a conclusion is not justified. The person could just as well be a well-adjusted person who, because of circumstances, felt the need to present himself or herself as even better adjusted. For example, such motivation often is present when parents complete the MMPI-2 as part of a child custody evaluation.

Random Responding

One deviant response set involves a random or near random response to the test items. A person may respond in a clearly random manner or may use an idiosyncratic response pattern such as marking every block of eight items as true, true, false, false, true, true, false, false, or every block of six items as true, false, true, false, true, false, and repeating this pattern with each such subse-

quent block. Because the responses are made without regard to item content, the resulting protocol must be considered invalid. The profile configurations resulting from a completely random response set are shown in Figures 3.1A and 3.1B. In the random response profile, the F scale T-score is very elevated (usually greater than 100), the K scale is at or near a T-score of 50, and the L scale is moderately elevated (T = 60–70). The Fb scale also is quite elevated, usually at about the same T-score level as the F scale. The VRIN score is very elevated, again at about the same level as F and Fb. The TRIN score is somewhat elevated, but much less so than VRIN. The clinical scales are characterized by generally elevated scores, usually with the highest score on scale 8 and the second highest score on scale 6. Scales 5 and 0 are likely to be below 70. It should be understood that the random profiles in Figure 3.1A and 3.1B and the other invalid profiles presented in this section are modal profiles that would result if all items in the MMPI-2 were answered in an invalid manner. In practice, subjects may begin the MMPI-2 in a valid manner and then change to an invalid approach later in the test. Thus, many invalid profiles will approximate the modal ones presented here, but they will not match them exactly. A profile resulting from the random response set should under no circumstances be interpreted.

All True Responding

If a person answers all the items in the true direction, the resulting profiles look like the ones presented in Figures 3.2A and 3.2B. The salient features of the profile are an extremely elevated F scale score (usually well above a T-score of 100), L and K scale T-scores well below 50, and extreme elevation on the clinical scales on the right side of the profile, usually with the highest scores on scales 6 and 8. The Fb scale will also be quite elevated, usually at about the same level as the F scale. The TRIN scale will be quite elevated (T > 120), and the VRIN scale T-score will be near 50. A profile resulting from the all true responding should under no circumstances be interpreted.

All False Responding

The person who responds false to all the MMPI-2 items will produce profiles like those shown in Figures 3.3A and 3.3B. Note the simultaneous elevations on scales L, F, and K and the more elevated scores on the clinical scales on the left side of the profile. The T-scores on Fb and VRIN will be near 50 in the all false response set, and the TRIN T-score will be very high (above 110).

Negative Self Presentation

Faking Bad. Test subjects may be motivated to present an unrealistically negative impression when completing the MMPI-2. An extreme case of negative self presentation would be a person's deliberately responding to test items in a

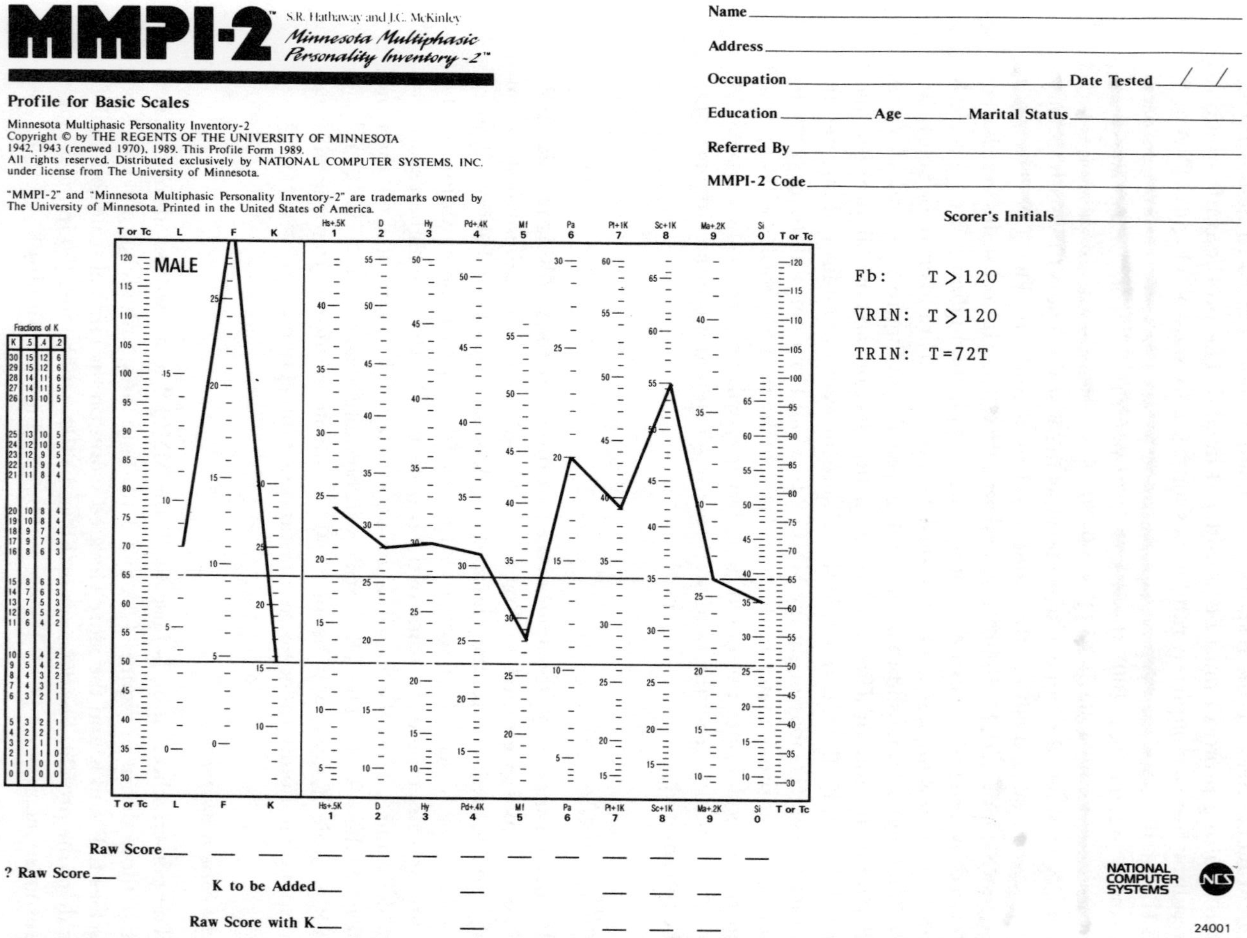
MMPI-2™ S.R. Hathaway and J.C. McKinley
Minnesota Multiphasic Personality Inventory-2™
Profile for Basic Scales
Minnesota Multiphasic Personality Inventory-2
Copyright © by THE REGENTS OF THE UNIVERSITY OF MINNESOTA
1942, 1943 (renewed 1970), 1989. This Profile Form 1989.
All rights reserved. Distributed exclusively by NATIONAL COMPUTER SYSTEMS, INC. under license from The University of Minnesota.
"MMPI-2" and "Minnesota Multiphasic Personality Inventory-2" are trademarks owned by The University of Minnesota. Printed in the United States of America.
Name
Address
Occupation
Date Tested
Education
Age
Marital Status
Referred By
MMPI-2 Code
Scorer's Initials
Fb: T > 120
VRIN: T > 120
TRIN: T=72T
MALE
Fractions of K
T or Tc
L
F
K
Hs+.5K 1
D 2
Hy 3
Pd+.4K 4
Mf 5
Pa 6
Pt+1K 7
Sc+1K 8
Ma+.2K 9
Si 0
Raw Score
? Raw Score
K to be Added
Raw Score with K
NATIONAL COMPUTER SYSTEMS
24001

Figure 3.1A. K-corrected profile for males indicative of random responding. (Copyright information appears on all MMPI-2 profiles and is therefore not repeated in figure captions.)

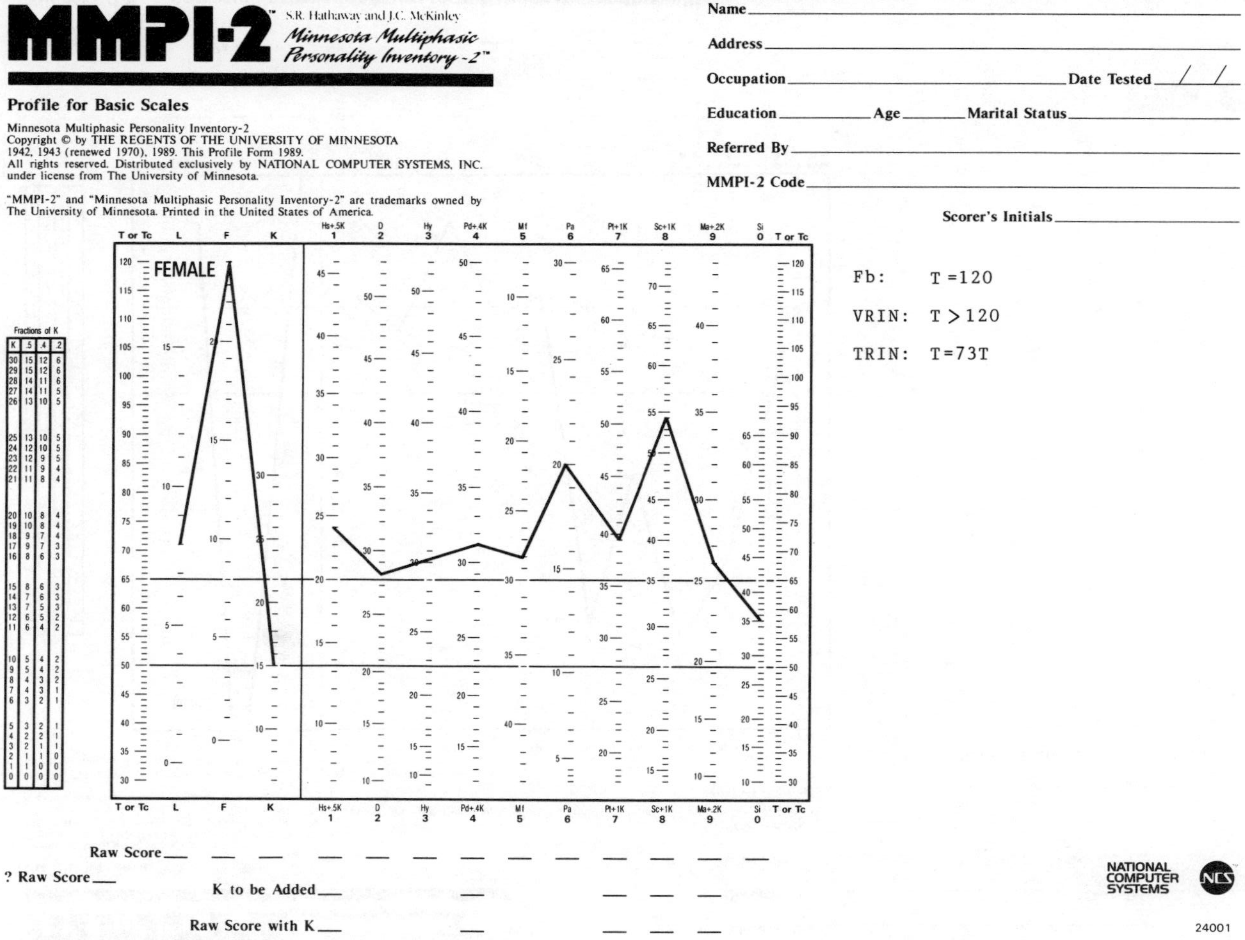

Figure 3.1B. K-corrected profile for females indicative of random responding.

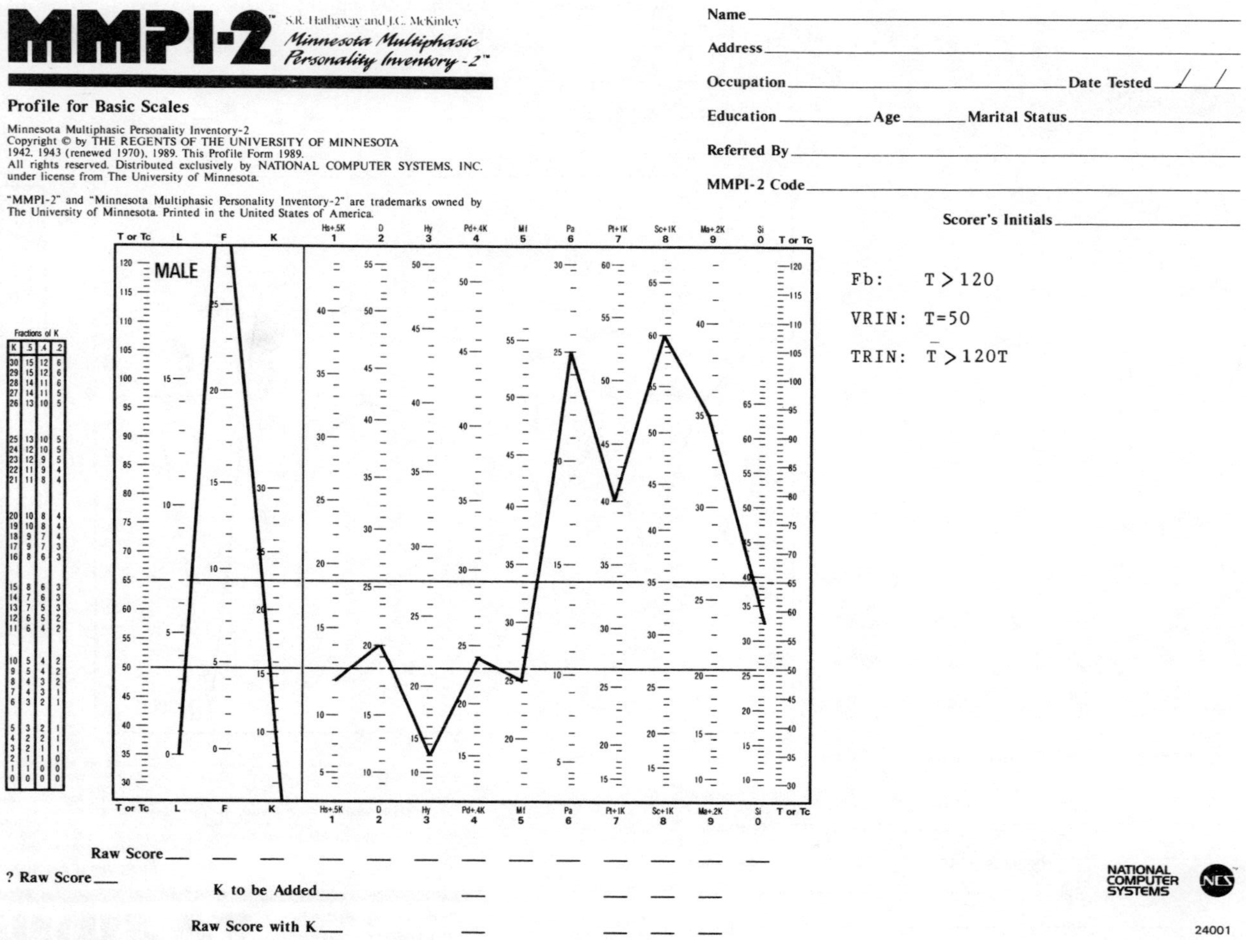

Figure 3.2A. K-corrected profile for males indicative of all true responding.

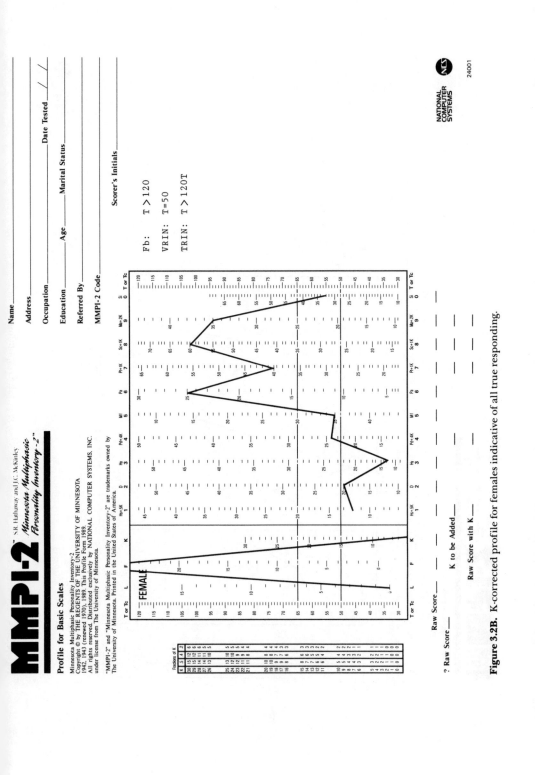

Figure 3.2B. K-corrected profile for females indicative of all true responding.

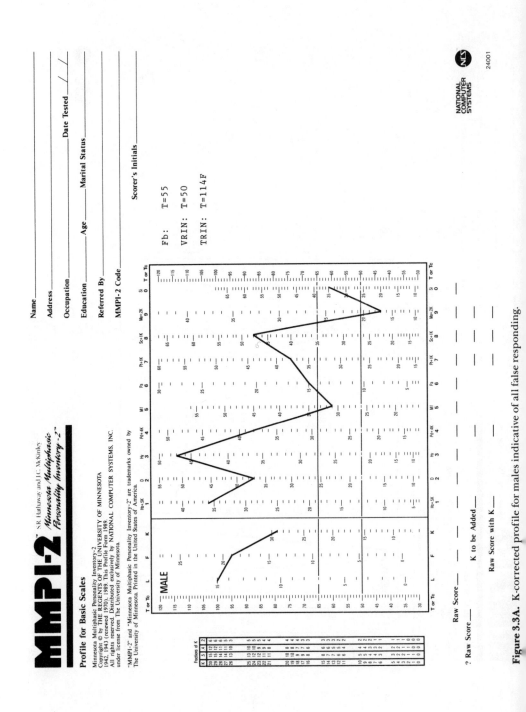

Figure 3.3A. K-corrected profile for males indicative of all false responding.

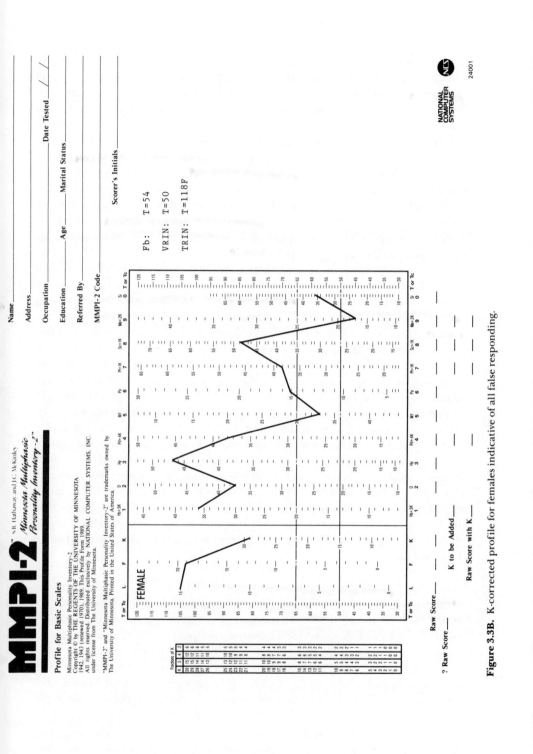

Figure 3.3B. K-corrected profile for females indicative of all false responding.

manner thought to communicate that he or she is very psychologically dis-turbed when in fact that is not the case. This response set often is referred to as "faking bad." Typical profiles for persons who are faking bad are presented in Figures 3.4A and 3.4B. These profiles are based on mean data for groups of male and female college students who took the MMPI-2 with instructions to present themselves as if they had serious psychological or emotional problems.[3] The fake bad profile is characterized by a very elevated F scale T-score (usually well above 100). Likewise, the Fb scale is elevated, usually at about the same level as the F scale. Since the subject who is faking bad is responding to the content of the items, both the TRIN scale and VRIN scale scores are not significantly elevated. Scores on the clinical scales are very elevated, with scales 6 and 8 typically being the most elevated. Scales 5 and 0 typically are the least elevated clinical scales in the fake bad profile.

Gough (1950) found that people who are trying to create the impression of severe psychopathology score considerably higher on the F scale than on the K scale. He suggested that the difference between the F scale *raw score* and the K scale *raw score* thus can serve as a useful index for detecting faking bad profiles. Gough (1950) and Meehl (1951) indicated that when such an index number is positive and is greater than 9, a profile should be considered as a fake bad profile. Carson (1969) suggested that a cutoff score of +11 yields more accurate identification of fake bad profiles. Although a single cutoff score cannot be established for all settings, whenever the F scale raw score is greater than the K scale raw score the possibility of faking bad should be considered, and as the difference becomes greater the likelihood of a fake bad profile becomes greater.

At first glance the fake bad profile looks similar to the profile one might expect to obtain from a person who is actually very psychologically disturbed. However, there are some important differences. First, the F scale score is usually higher for the fake bad profile. The usual range of F scale T-scores for a person who has been diagnosed as psychotic is 71 to 90, whereas in the fake bad profile the F scale T-score is well above 100. In addition, in a fake bad profile the clinical scales tend to be more extremely elevated than in a valid profile from a disturbed person.

Malingering. If a well-adjusted person responding to the MMPI-2 items with the intention of appearing to have psychological symptoms and problems does not do so in an extreme way (malingering), the resulting profile is harder to differentiate from a valid one for a disturbed person. In such a case the F scale is not as extremely elevated as in the fake bad profile, and the L and K scales usually are around 50. The most salient feature of the malingering profile is its *saw-toothed* appearance (see Figure 3.5). This appearance results because the person who is malingering tends to endorse a wide array of the obviously

[3]The data from this study by Graham and Watts have not yet been published. More information can be obtained by contacting John R. Graham, Department of Psychology, Kent State University, Kent, OH 44242.

pathological items on scales 2, 4, 6, and 8 but avoids endorsing the items that suggest very extreme psychopathology. Only very rarely does one encounter the saw-toothed pattern in the clinical scales in valid profiles.

Exaggeration. An even more difficult response set to identify is one in which a person who really has psychological symptoms and problems exaggerates them in responding to the MMPI-2 items. Because the resulting profile will depend, to a large extent, on the nature of the existing problems, no prototype can be presented for this response set. The major clue that such a response set may be present is that the level of elevations on the F scale and the clinical scales seems to be far greater than would be expected given the person's history and the observations made during interview and/or testing. Exaggeration does not completely invalidate a profile, but it is necessary to modify interpretive statements to take into account the probability of overreported symptoms and problems.

Positive Self Presentation

Faking Good. Sometimes persons completing the MMPI-2, including a surprising number of patients voluntarily seeking professional help, are motivated to deny problems and to appear better off psychologically than is in fact the case. In its most blatant form this tendency is referred to as "faking good." Typical profiles resulting from this test-taking attitude are presented in Figures 3.6A and 3.6B. These profiles are based on data from male and female college students who took the MMPI-2 with instructions to try to present a very positive impression as if they were being evaluated for a job that they really wanted.[4] The clearest indication of a fake good profile is a V-shaped or check mark–shaped validity scale configuration with elevations on scales L and K and an F scale T-score in a range of 40 to 50. Most of the clinical scales will be in a T-score range of 30 to 50, with scales 3, 5, and 9 often the highest of the clinical scales.

Because of the rather obvious nature of the L scale items, individuals who are bright, well educated, and psychologically sophisticated may detect the purpose of the items and will obtain lower scores on the L scale. However, because the K scale items are not as obvious as L scale items, even bright, well-educated, and psychologically sophisticated persons produce very elevated scores on the K scale if they adopt a fake good attitude toward the test. Before concluding that a high K scale score indicates a fake good strategy, however, the socioeconomic status of test subjects should be considered. Because higher socioeconomic status individuals tend to score higher on the K scale than do lower socioeconomic status individuals, for the former scores in a T-score range of 60 to 70 do not necessarily imply faking.

[4]The data from this study by Graham and Watts have not yet been published. More information can be obtained by contacting John R. Graham, Department of Psychology, Kent State University, Kent, OH 44242.

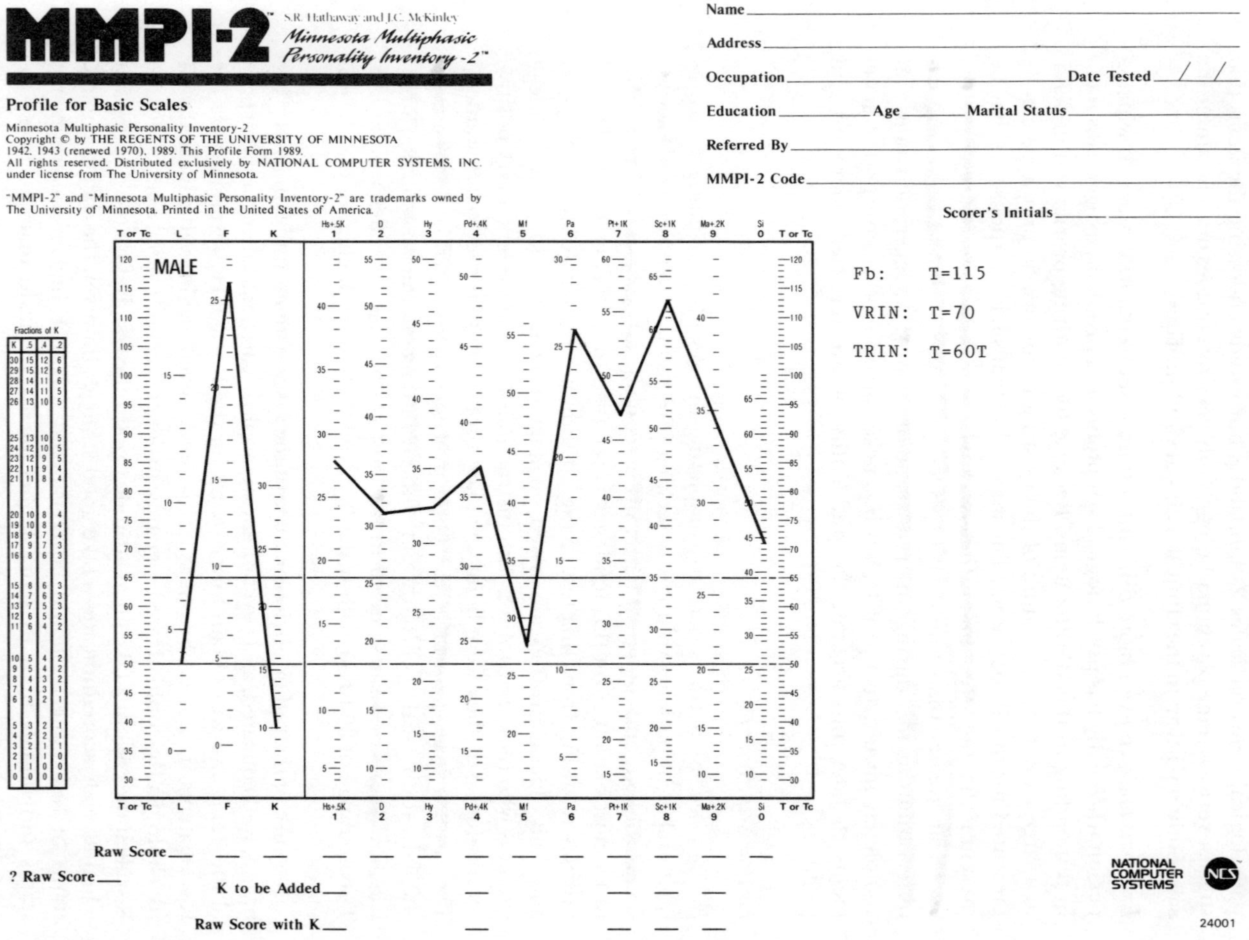

Figure 3.4A. K-corrected profile for males indicative of faking bad response set.

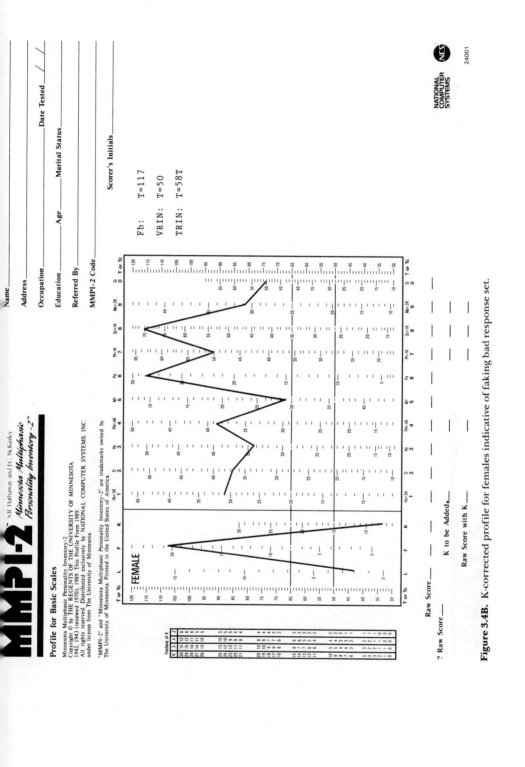

Figure 3.4B. K-corrected profile for females indicative of faking bad response set.

45

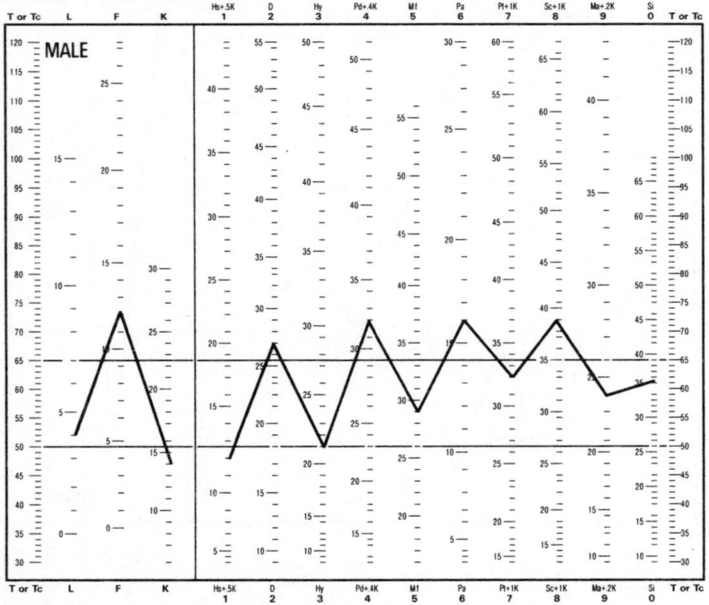

MMPI-2
S R Hathaway and J C McKinley

Minnesota Multiphasic
Personality Inventory -2

Name _____

Address _____

Occupation _____ Age _____ Marital Status _____

Education _____ Date Tested __ / __ / __

Referred By _____

MMPI-2 Code _____

Scorer's Initials _____

Profile for Basic Scales

Minnesota Multiphasic Personality Inventory-2
Copyright © by THE REGENTS OF THE UNIVERSITY OF MINNESOTA
1942, 1943 (renewed 1970), 1989. This Profile Form 1989.
All rights reserved. Distributed exclusively by NATIONAL COMPUTER SYSTEMS, INC.
under license from The University of Minnesota.

"MMPI-2" and "Minnesota Multiphasic Personality Inventory-2" are trademarks owned by
The University of Minnesota. Printed in the United States of America.

MALE

Raw Score _____

? Raw Score _____   K to be Added _____

Raw Score with K _____

NATIONAL COMPUTER SYSTEMS

24001

Figure 3.5. K-corrected saw-toothed profile indicative of malingering.

46

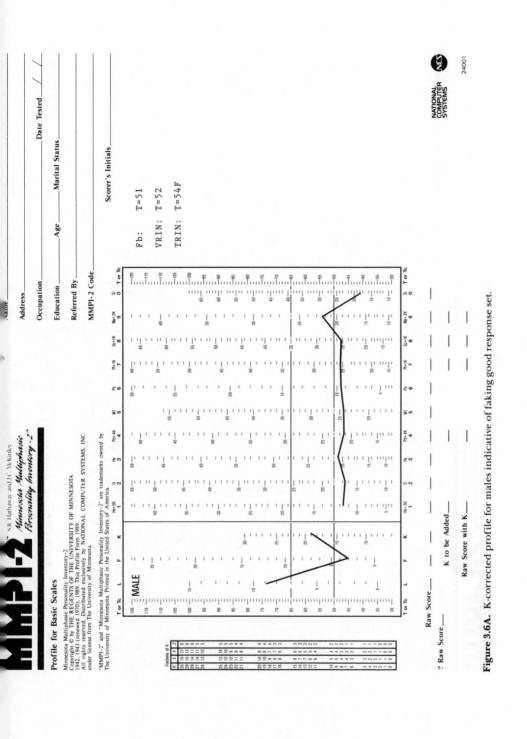

Figure 3.6A. K-corrected profile for males indicative of faking good response set.

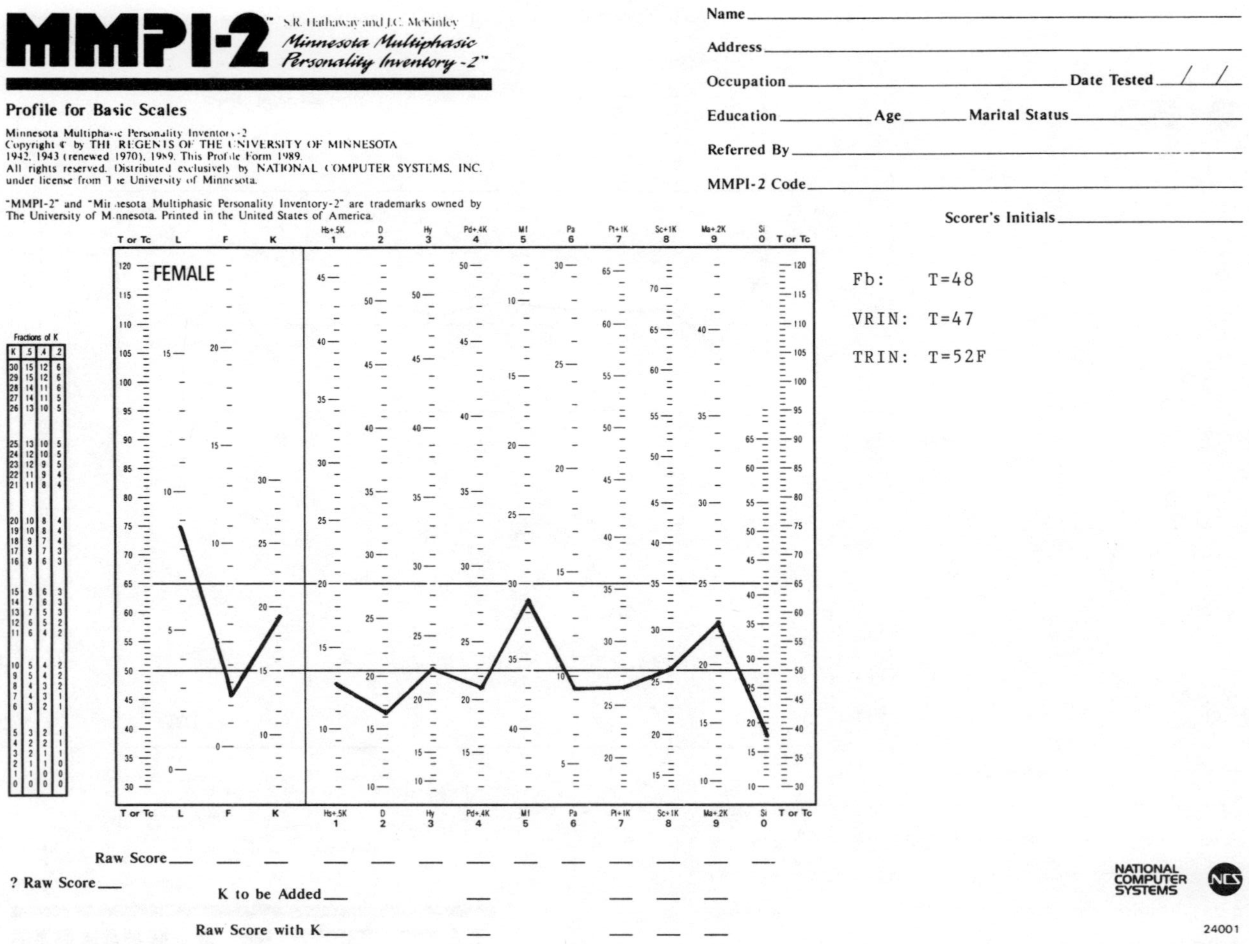
MMPI-2
S.R. Hathaway and J.C. McKinley
Minnesota Multiphasic Personality Inventory-2
Profile for Basic Scales
Minnesota Multiphasic Personality Inventory-2
Copyright © by THE REGENTS OF THE UNIVERSITY OF MINNESOTA 1942, 1943 (renewed 1970), 1989. This Profile Form 1989.
All rights reserved. Distributed exclusively by NATIONAL COMPUTER SYSTEMS, INC. under license from The University of Minnesota.
"MMPI-2" and "Minnesota Multiphasic Personality Inventory-2" are trademarks owned by The University of Minnesota. Printed in the United States of America.
Name
Address
Occupation
Date Tested
Education
Age
Marital Status
Referred By
MMPI-2 Code
Scorer's Initials
Fractions of K
FEMALE
T or Tc
L
F
K
Hs+.5K 1
D 2
Hy 3
Pd+.4K 4
Mf 5
Pa 6
Pt+1K 7
Sc+1K 8
Ma+.2K 9
Si 0
Fb: T=48
VRIN: T=47
TRIN: T=52F
Raw Score
? Raw Score
K to be Added
Raw Score with K
NATIONAL COMPUTER SYSTEMS
24001

Figure 2.6B K-corrected profile for females indicative of faking good response set.

Some clinicians tend to use the F minus K index to identify fake good profiles as well as fake bad profiles. If the F scale *raw score* minus the K scale *raw score* is negative (K greater than F) and large, it may be that a fake good attitude is present. However, this difference score cannot be used actuarially as an index of faking good. Whereas it is clear that a fake good profile has a higher K scale than F scale score, it is not as easy to determine a cutoff score as is the case with fake bad profiles. The F minus K index is especially inappropriate for higher socioeconomic status people, who tend to produce high K scale scores even if they are not faking good.

Defensive Profiles. Sometimes persons are motivated to present unrealistically favorable impressions but do not do so as blatantly as in the fake good response set. For example, persons taking the MMPI-2 as part of employment screening or child custody evaluations may want to emphasize positive characteristics and minimize negative ones. The resulting profile may underestimate problems and symptoms but is not necessarily uninterpretable.

In a defensive profile the L and K scores typically are more elevated that the F score. However, scores on these two scales will not be as extremely high as in the fake good response set. For some bright, well-educated persons, the L scale may not be significantly elevated in a defensive profile, but the K scale will be elevated. In a defensive profile, scores on the clinical scales will not be as low as in a fake good response set. A typical defensive profile is presented in Figure 3.7.

Butcher (1985a) suggested procedures for interpreting profiles for which the validity scale configuration is suggestive of defensiveness. If there are any clinical scales elevated above a T-score of 65, they should be interpreted using the standard correlates. It should be recognized that these scale elevations may reflect more significant problems because they were obtained when test subjects were trying to present the most favorable views of themselves. Since in a defensive profile the person is attempting to present an overly favorable view of his or her functioning, clinical scale T-scores in a 60 to 65 range should be considered significant. If all the clinical scale T-scores in a defensive profile are below 60, the profile is not providing much useful clinical information about the subject. One cannot tell whether such a profile is indicative of a well-adjusted person who is motivated to appear even more well adjusted or of a poorly adjusted person who is trying to appear to be well adjusted.

Other Indicators of Test Invalidity

Some authors (e.g., Greene, 1980) have suggested some additional ways of detecting invalid MMPI profiles. Gough (1954) developed the Dissimulation (Ds) scale to identify persons who are simulating or exaggerating psychopathology. Persons who were instructed to dissimulate scored higher on this scale. The test-retest (TR) index (Buechley & Ball, 1952) was the total number of the 16

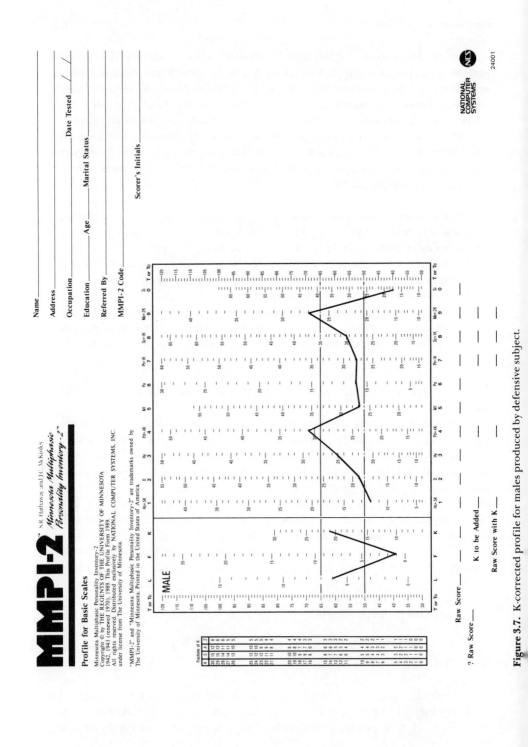

Figure 3.7. K-corrected profile for males produced by defensive subject.

repeated items in the MMPI that a subject answered inconsistently. The Care-lessness scale (Greene, 1978) consisted of 12 pairs of items that were judged to be psychologically opposite in content. This scale was thought to identify subjects who were careless in responding to the MMPI items. As will be dis-cussed in Chapter 7, Greene (1980) and others suggested that the relative endorsements of obvious versus subtle items may have merit in detecting fake good and fake bad response sets. This author's interpretation of existing data suggests that none of these additional scales or indexes was more effective than the standard validity and clinical scales in detecting invalid profiles. Except for the subtle-obvious subscales, these additional validity indicators are not in-cluded in MMPI-2.

4

The Clinical Scales

A primary goal of this chapter is to discuss the nature of each clinical scale in an attempt to help the MMPI-2 user understand the dimensions being assessed by the scale. In addition, descriptive material is presented for high scorers and low scorers on each scale. This material is based on an examination of previously reported data for the clinical scales of the original MMPI and consideration of new data concerning extratest correlates of the clinical scales of MMPI-2. Empirical validity studies for the original MMPI are summarized in Chapter 8. Likewise, that chapter describes several research studies conducted with MMPI-2 to determine extratest correlates of the clinical scales.

As indicated in Chapter 1, the clinical scales have been retained in MMPI-2 in basically the same form that they had in the original MMPI. A few items have been deleted from some of the scales because they had become dated or because they were judged to have objectionable content, usually having to do with religious beliefs or bowel or bladder function. Some of the items in the clinical scales were modified slightly to modernize them, to eliminate sexist references, or to improve readability. Table 1.1 summarizes these deletions and modifications. The items included in each clinical scale and the keyed response for each item are presented in Appendix A of this book.

The definition of a high score on the clinical scales has varied considerably in the literature and from one clinical scale to another. Some writers have considered a T-score above 70 as a high score. Others have defined high scores in terms of upper quartile in a distribution. Still others have presented descriptors for several T-score levels on each scale. Another approach has been to identify the highest scale in the profile (high point) irrespective of its T-score value. Low scores also have been defined in different ways in the literature, sometimes as T-scores below 40 and other times as scores in the lowest quartile of a distribution. Compared with high scores, limited information is available in the literature concerning the meaning of low scores. Although it often has been assumed that low scorers on a scale are characterized by the absence of characteristics that are present for high scorers, this is not always the case.

The approach used in this chapter will be to offer hypotheses about persons who score at various T-score levels on each of the clinical scales. At times it will be necessary to take some demographic characteristics into account in deter-

mining which hypotheses should be applied to a particular protocol. It should be understood that the T-score levels utilized have been established somewhat arbitrarily and that clinical judgment will be necessary in deciding which hypotheses should be applied to scores at or near the cutoff scores for the levels.

SCALE 1 (HYPOCHONDRIASIS)

Scale 1 originally was developed to identify patients who manifested a pattern of symptoms associated with the label of hypochondriasis. The syndrome was characterized in clinical terms by preoccupation with the body and concomitant fears of illness and disease. Although such fears usually are not delusional in nature, they tend to be quite persistent. An item deletion because of objectionable content reduced scale 1 from 33 items in the original MMPI to 32 items in MMPI-2.

Of all the clinical scales, scale 1 seems to be the most clearly homogeneous and unidimensional. All the items deal with somatic concerns or with general physical competence. Factor analysis (Comrey, 1957b) indicated that much of the variance in scale 1 is accounted for by a single factor: the denial of good health and the admission of a variety of somatic symptoms. Patients with bona fide physical problems typically show somewhat elevated T-scores on scale 1 (approximately 60). Elderly subjects tend to produce scale 1 scores that are slightly more elevated than those of the general adult standardization subjects.

High Scores on Scale 1

For persons with extremely high scores on scale 1 (T > 80), dramatic and sometimes bizarre somatic concerns should be suspected. If scale 3 also is elevated, the possibility of a conversion disorder should be considered. If scale 8 is very elevated along with scale 1, somatic delusions may be present.

Persons with more moderate elevations on scale 1 (T = 60–80) tend to have generally vague, nonspecific complaints. When specific symptoms are elicited, they tend to be epigastric in nature. Chronic weakness, lack of energy, and sleep disturbance also tend to be characteristic of high scorers. As stated above, medical patients with bona fide physical problems generally obtain T-scores of about 60 on this scale. When medical patients produce T-scores much above 60, one should suspect a strong psychological component to the illness. Moderately high scores on scale 1 tend to be associated with diagnoses such as somatoform disorders, somatoform pain disorders, anxiety disorders, and depressive disorders. Psychopathic acting out is rare among high scale 1 scorers.

High scale 1 scorers (T > 60) in both psychiatric and nonpsychiatric samples tend to be characterized by a distinctive set of personality attributes. They are likely to be selfish, self-centered, and narcissistic. Their outlook toward life

tends to be pessimistic, defeatist, and cynical. They are generally dissatisfied and unhappy and are likely to make those around them miserable. They complain a great deal and communicate in a whiny manner. They are demanding of others and are very critical of what others do, though they are likely to express hostility in rather indirect ways. Scores on scale 1 seem to correlate negatively with intellectual ability, and high scorers often are described as dull, unenthusiastic, unambitious, and lacking ease in oral expression. High scorers generally do not exhibit much manifest anxiety, and in general they do not show signs of major incapacity. Rather, they appear to be functioning at a reduced level of efficiency. Problems are much more likely to be longstanding in nature than situational or transient.

Extremely high and moderately high scorers typically see themselves as physically ill and are seeking medical explanations and treatment for their symptoms. They tend to lack insight and to resist psychological interpretations. These tendencies, coupled with their generally cynical outlook, suggest that they are not very good candidates for psychotherapy or counseling. They tend to be very critical of their therapists and to terminate therapy if they perceive the therapist as suggesting psychological reasons for their symptoms or as not giving them enough support and attention.

Low Scores on Scale 1

Because scale 1 is unidimensional in nature, low scorers tend to be very much the opposite of high scorers. In addition to being free of somatic preoccupation, they seem to be optimistic, alert, sensitive, insightful, and generally effective in their daily lives.

Summary of Descriptors for Scale 1

High scores on scale 1 indicate persons who:

1. have excessive bodily concern
2. may have conversion disorder or somatic delusions (if T > 80)
3. describe somatic complaints that generally are vague but if specific are likely to be epigastric in nature
4. complain of chronic weakness, lack of energy, and sleep disturbance
5. if medical patients, may have a strong psychological component to their illnesses
6. are likely to be diagnosed as having somatoform, somatoform pain, depressive, or anxiety disorders
7. are not likely to act out in psychopathic ways
8. seem selfish, self-centered, and narcissistic
9. have a pessimistic, defeatist, and cynical outlook toward life

10. are unhappy and dissatisfied
11. make others miserable
12. complain
13. communicate in whiny manner
14. are demanding and critical of others
15. express hostility indirectly
16. are described as dull, unenthusiastic, and unambitious
17. lack ease in oral expression
18. generally do not exhibit much manifest anxiety
19. seem to have functioned at a reduced level of efficiency for long periods of time
20. see themselves as medically ill and seek medical treatment
21. lack insight and resist psychological interpretations
22. are not very good candidates for psychotherapy or counseling
23. become critical of therapists
24. terminate therapy prematurely when therapists suggest psychological reasons for symptoms or are not perceived as giving enough attention and support

Low scores on scale 1 are indicative of persons who:

1. are free of somatic preoccupation
2. are alert, sensitive, and insightful
3. are generally effective in their daily lives

SCALE 2 (DEPRESSION)

Scale 2 was developed originally to assess symptomatic depression. The primary characteristics of symptomatic depression are poor morale, lack of hope in the future, and a general dissatisfaction with one's own life situation. Of the 60 items originally in scale 2, 57 have been retained in MMPI-2. Many of the items in the scale deal with various aspects of depression such as denial of happiness and personal worth, psychomotor retardation and withdrawal, and lack of interest in one's surroundings. Other items in the scale cover a variety of other symptoms and behaviors, including somatic complaints, worry or tension, denial of hostile impulses, and difficulty in controlling one's own thought processes. Scale 2 seems to be an excellent index of examinees' discomfort and dissatisfaction with their life situations. Whereas very elevated scores on this scale may suggest clinical depression, more moderate scores tend to indicate a general attitude or life-style characterized by poor morale and lack of involvement. Scale 2 scores seem to be related to age, with adolescent subjects scoring 5 to 10 T-score points lower than the adult standardization means and elderly subjects scoring 5 to 10 T-score points higher than the standardization sample

means. Some subjects who recently have been hospitalized or incarcerated tend to show moderate elevations on scale 2 that reflect dissatisfaction with current circumstances rather than clinical depression.

High Scores on Scale 2

High scorers on this scale (particularly if the T-scores exceed 70) often display depressive symptoms. They may report feeling depressed, blue, unhappy, or dysphoric. They tend to be quite pessimistic about the future in general and more specifically about the likelihood of overcoming their problems and making a better adjustment. Self-depreciation and guilt feelings are common. Behavioral manifestations may include lack of energy, refusal to speak, crying, and psychomotor retardation. Patients with such high scores often receive depressive diagnoses. Other symptoms found in high scorers include physical complaints, bad dreams, weakness, fatigue or loss of energy, agitation, and tension. They also are described as irritable, high-strung, and prone to worry and fretting.

High scorers also show a marked lack of self-confidence. They report feelings of uselessness and inability to function in a variety of situations. They give up easily when faced with stress. They see themselves as having failed to achieve adequately in school and at their jobs.

A life-style characterized by withdrawal and lack of intimate involvement with other people is common. High scorers tend to be described as introverted, shy, retiring, timid, seclusive, and secretive. Also, they tend to be aloof and to maintain psychological distance from other people. They often have a severely restricted range of interests and may withdraw from activities in which they previously participated. They are very cautious and conventional in their activities.

High scorers may have great difficulty in making even simple decisions, and they may be overwhelmed when faced with major life decisions such as vocation or marriage. They tend to be very overcontrolled and to deny their own impulses. They are likely to avoid unpleasantness and will make concessions in order to avoid confrontations.

Because high scale 2 scores suggest great personal distress, they may indicate a good prognosis for psychotherapy or counseling. There is some evidence, however, that high scorers may tend to terminate treatment prematurely when the immediate crisis passes.

Low Scores on Scale 2

Low scorers on scale 2 tend to be much more comfortable than high scorers. They indicate that they do not experience much tension, anxiety, guilt, and depression and that they feel relaxed and at ease. They tend to be self-confident

and generally are emotionally stable and capable of effective functioning in most situations. They are cheerful and optimistic and have little difficulty in verbal expression. They are alert, active, and energetic. They tend to seek out additional responsibilities and are seen as quite competitive by others.

Low scorers feel at ease in social situations and are rather quick to assume a leadership role. They appear to be clever, witty, and colorful, and they generally create very favorable first impressions.

Low scorers also tend to be somewhat impulsive and undercontrolled. Their lack of inhibitions leads them to be somewhat show-offish and exhibitionistic, and they may arouse hostility and resentment in other people. Also, they often find themselves in conflict with authority figures.

Summary of Descriptors for Scale 2

High scores on scale 2 are indicative of persons who:

1. display depressive symptoms (particularly if T-scores exceed 70)
2. feel blue, unhappy, and dysphoric
3. are quite pessimistic about the future
4. have self-deprecatory and guilt feelings
5. may cry, refuse to speak, and show psychomotor retardation
6. often are given depressive diagnoses
7. report bad dreams, physical complaints, weakness, fatigue, and loss of energy
8. are agitated and tense
9. are described as irritable, high-strung, and prone to worry and fretting
10. lack self-confidence
11. feel useless and unable to function
12. give up easily
13. feel like failures in school or at work
14. have life-styles characterized by withdrawal and lack of involvement with other people
15. are introverted, shy, retiring, timid, seclusive, and secretive
16. are aloof and maintain psychological distance from other people
17. have restricted range of interests
18. withdraw from activities in which they previously participated
19. are very cautious and conventional
20. have difficulty making decisions
21. feel overwhelmed when faced with major life decisions
22. are overcontrolled; deny own impulses
23. avoid unpleasantness; make concessions to avoid confrontations
24. because of personal distress, are likely to be good candidates for psychotherapy or counseling
25. may terminate therapy prematurely when immediate crisis passes

Low scores on scale 2 are indicative of persons who:

1. do not experience much tension, anxiety, guilt, or depression
2. feel relaxed and at ease
3. are self-confident
4. are emotionally stable and capable of effective functioning in most situations
5. feel cheerful and optimistic
6. have little difficulty in verbal expression
7. are alert, active, and energetic
8. are competitive and seek out additional responsibilities
9. are at ease in social situations
10. seek out leadership role
11. create favorable first impressions
12. are seen as clever, witty, and colorful
13. may be impulsive and undercontrolled
14. are show-offish and exhibitionistic
15. may arouse hostility and resentment in other people
16. often find themselves in conflict with authority figures

SCALE 3 (HYSTERIA)

This scale was developed to identify patients who were demonstrating hysterical reactions to stress situations. The hysterical syndrome is characterized by involuntary psychogenic loss or disorder of function.

All the 60 items in the original version of scale 3 have been retained in MMPI-2. Some of the items deal with a general denial of physical health and a variety of rather specific somatic complaints, including heart or chest pain, nausea and vomiting, fitful sleep, and headaches. Another group of items involves a rather general denial of psychological or emotional problems and of discomfort in social situations. Although these two clusters of items are reasonably independent in normal subjects, persons displaying hysterical defenses seem to score high on both clusters. In fact, it is not possible to obtain a T-score above 70 on scale 3 without endorsing both kinds of items.

Scale 3 scores are related to intellectual ability, educational background, and social class. Brighter, better-educated subjects of a higher social class tend to score higher on the scale. In addition, high scores are much more common among women than among men in both normal and psychiatric populations.

It is important to take into account the level of scores on scale 3. Whereas marked elevations (T > 80) suggest a pathological condition characterized by classical hysterical symptomatology, moderate levels are associated with a number of characteristics that are consistent with hysterical disorders but that do not include the classical hysterical symptoms. As with scale 1, patients with bona

fide medical problems lacking any evident psychological component tend to obtain T-scores of about 60 on this scale.

High Scores on Scale 3

Marked elevations on scale 3 (T > 80) may suggest persons who react to stress and avoid responsibility by developing physical symptoms. Their symptoms usually do not fit the pattern of any known organic disorder. They may include, in some combination, headaches, stomach discomfort, chest pains, weakness, and tachycardia. Nevertheless, symptoms may be absent most of the time but under stress may appear suddenly; they are likely to disappear just as suddenly when the stress subsides.

Except for the physical symptoms, high scorers tend to be relatively free of other symptoms. Although they sometimes describe themselves as prone to worry and to sleep disturbances, they are not likely to report severe anxiety, tension, or depression. Hallucinations, delusions, and suspiciousness also are rare. The most frequent diagnoses for high 3 scorers among psychiatric patients are conversion disorder and psychogenic pain disorder.

A salient feature of the day-to-day functioning of high scorers is a marked lack of insight concerning the possible underlying causes of their symptoms. In addition, they show little insight concerning their own motives and feelings.

High scorers often are described as extremely immature psychologically and at times even childish or infantile. They are quite self-centered, narcissistic, and egocentric, and they expect a great deal of attention and affection from others. They often use indirect and devious means to get the attention and affection that they crave. When others do not respond appropriately, they may become hostile and resentful, but these feelings are likely to be denied and not expressed openly or directly.

High scorers tend to be emotionally involved, friendly, talkative, enthusiastic, and alert. Although their needs for affection and attention drive them into social interactions, their interpersonal relationships tend to be rather superficial and immature. Their interest in people is based primarily on what they can get from them rather than on a sincere interest in others.

Occasionally high scorers will act out in a sexual or aggressive manner with little apparent attention to or understanding of what they are doing. When confronted with the realities of their behavior, they may act surprised and feel resentful and persecuted.

Because of their needs for acceptance and affection, high scorers may initially be quite enthusiastic about counseling and psychotherapy. However, they seem to view themselves as having medical problems and want to be treated medically. They are slow to gain insight into the underlying causes of their behavior and are quite resistant to psychological interpretations. If therapists insist on examining psychological causes of symptoms, premature termination of therapy is likely. High scorers may be willing to talk about problems in their

lives as long as they are not conceptualized as causing symptoms, and they often respond quite well to direct advice and suggestion.

When high scorers become involved in therapy, they often discuss worry about failure in school or work, marital unhappiness, lack of acceptance by their social groups, and problems with authority figures. Histories often include a rejecting father to whom females reacted with somatic complaints and males with rebellion and overt hostility.

Low Scores on Scale 3

Low scorers on scale 3 do not worry excessively about their health, and they do not present more than an average number of somatic symptoms. They tend to be rather constricted, conventional, and conforming in their everyday behaviors. They are described by others as unadventurous, as lacking industriousness, and as having a narrow range of interests.

Low scorers are cold and aloof and may display blunted affect. They are very limited in social interests and participation, and they tend to avoid leadership responsibilities. They are often seen as unfriendly and tough-minded, and they are hard to get to know. They may have difficulty trusting other people, and in general they seem to be rather suspicious. They are realistic, logical, and level-headed in their approach to problems and are not likely to make impulsive decisions. They seem to be content with what others would judge as a rather dull, uneventful life-style.

Summary of Descriptors for Scale 3

High scores on scale 3 are indicative of persons who:

1. react to stress and avoid responsibility through development of physical symptoms
2. may report headaches, stomach discomfort, chest pains, weakness, and tachycardia
3. have symptoms that may appear and disappear suddenly
4. do not report severe emotional turmoil
5. rarely report hallucinations, delusions, or suspiciousness
6. if psychiatric patients, receive diagnoses of conversion disorder or psychogenic pain disorder
7. lack insight concerning causes of symptoms
8. lack insight about their own motives and feelings
9. are psychologically immature, childish, and infantile
10. are self-centered, narcissistic, and egocentric
11. expect a great deal of attention and affection from others
12. use indirect and devious means to get attention and affection

13. do not express resentment and hostility openly
14. tend to be emotionally involved, friendly, talkative, and alert
15. have superficial and immature interpersonal relationships
16. are interested in what other people can do for them
17. occasionally act out in a sexual or aggressive manner with little apparent insight into their actions
18. initially are enthusiastic about treatment
19. view themselves as having medical problems and want medical treatment
20. are resistant to psychological interpretations
21. are likely to terminate treatment if therapists insist on examining psychological causes of symptoms
22. may be willing to talk about problems as long as they are not conceptualized as causing symptoms
23. often respond well to direct advice and suggestion
24. when involved in therapy, discuss worry about failure at work or school, marital unhappiness, lack of acceptance, problems with authority figures
25. have histories of rejecting fathers

Low scores on scale 3 are indicative of persons who:

1. do not worry excessively about their health
2. do not present somatic symptoms
3. are constricted, conventional, and conforming
4. are described as unadventurous, lacking industriousness, and having a narrow range of interests
5. are cold and aloof
6. may display blunted affect
7. have limited social interests and participation
8. avoid leadership responsibility
9. are seen as unfriendly, tough-minded, and hard to get to know
10. are suspicious and have difficulty trusting others
11. are realistic, logical, and level-headed in approach to problems
12. are not likely to make impulsive decisions
13. seem to be content with dull, uneventful life-style

SCALE 4 (PSYCHOPATHIC DEVIATE)

Scale 4 was developed to identify patients diagnosed as psychopathic personality, asocial or amoral type. Whereas subjects included in the original criterion group were characterized in their everyday behavior by such delinquent acts as lying, stealing, sexual promiscuity, excessive drinking, and the like, no major criminal types were included. All 50 of the items in the original scale have been maintained in MMPI-2. The items cover a wide array of topics, including

absence of satisfaction in life, family problems, delinquency, sexual problems, and difficulties with authorities. Interestingly, the keyed responses include both admissions of social maladjustment and assertions of social poise and confidence.

Scores on scale 4 tend to be related to age, with adolescents and college students often scoring in a T-score range of 55 to 60. It also has been reported that black subjects tend to score higher than white subjects on scale 4. This latter finding may reflect the tendency of blacks to view many social regulations as unfair and therefore as less important in influencing their behavior.

One way of conceptualizing what scale 4 assesses is to think of it as a measure of rebelliousness, with higher scores indicating rebellion and lower scores indicating an acceptance of authority and the status quo. The highest scorers on the scale rebel by acting out in antisocial and criminal ways; moderately high scorers may be rebellious but may express the rebellion in more socially acceptable ways; and low scorers are apt to be overly conventional and accepting of authority.

High Scores on Scale 4

Extremely high scores (T > 75) on scale 4 tend to be associated with difficulty in incorporating the values and standards of society. Such high scorers are likely to engage in a variety of asocial, antisocial, and even criminal behaviors. These behaviors may include lying, cheating, stealing, sexual acting out, and excessive use of alcohol and/or other drugs.

High scorers on scale 4 tend to be rebellious toward authority figures and often are in conflict with authorities of one kind or another. They often have stormy relationships with families, and family members tend to be blamed for their difficulties. Underachievement in school, poor work history, and marital problems are characteristic of high scorers.

High scorers are very impulsive persons who strive for immediate gratification of impulses. They often do not plan their behavior very well, and they may act without considering the consequences of their actions. They are very impatient and have a limited frustration tolerance. Their behavior may involve poor judgment and considerable risk taking. They tend not to profit from experiences and may find themselves in the same difficulties time and time again.

High scorers are described by others as immature and childish. They are narcissistic, self-centered, selfish, and egocentric. Their behavior often is ostentatious and exhibitionistic. They are insensitive to the needs and feelings of other people and are interested in others in terms of how they can be used. Although they tend to be seen as likable and generally create good first impressions, their relationships tend to be shallow and superficial. This may be due in part to rejection on the part of the people they mistreat, but it also seems to reflect their own inability to form warm attachments with others.

In addition, high scorers typically are extroverted and outgoing. They are talkative, active, adventurous, energetic, and spontaneous. They are judged by others to be intelligent and self-confident. Although they have a wide range of interests and may become involved in many activities, they lack definite goals and clear direction.

High scorers tend to be hostile and aggressive. They are resentful, rebellious, antagonistic, and refractory. Their attitude is characterized by sarcasm and cynicism. Both males and females with high scale 4 scores may act in aggressive ways, but females are likely to express aggression in more passive, indirect ways. Often there does not appear to be any guilt associated with aggressive behavior. Whereas high scorers may feign guilt and remorse when their behaviors get them into trouble, such responses typically are short-lived, disappearing when the immediate crisis passes.

Although high scorers typically are not seen as being overwhelmed by emotional turmoil, at times they may admit feeling sad, fearful, and worried about the future. They may experience absence of deep emotional response, which may produce feelings of emptiness and boredom. Among psychiatric patients high scorers tend to receive personality disorder diagnoses, with antisocial personality disorder or passive-aggressive personality disorder occurring most frequently.

Because of their verbal facility, outgoing manner, and apparent intellectual resources, high scorers often are perceived as good candidates for psychotherapy or counseling. Unfortunately, the prognosis for change is poor. Although they may agree to treatment to avoid something more unpleasant (e.g., jail or divorce), they generally are unable to accept blame for their own problems, and they terminate treatment as soon as possible. In therapy they tend to intellectualize excessively and to blame others for their difficulties.

Low Scores on Scale 4

Low scorers on scale 4 tend to be very conventional, conforming, and accepting of authority. They are rather passive, submissive, and unassertive. They are concerned about how others will react to them, and they tend to be sincere and trusting in their interpersonal relationships.

Low scorers are characterized by a low level of drive. Although they are concerned about status and security, they do not tend to be very competitive. They have a narrow range of interests, and although they are not creative or spontaneous in their approach to problems, they tend to be very persistent. Low scorers also are seen as moralistic and rigid in their views. Low scoring males do not have much sex drive, and some may actually be afraid of women.

Low scorers tend to be very critical of themselves, and unwarranted self-dissatisfaction is common. They are accepting of advice and suggestion. Although they may initially respond well to psychotherapy or counseling, they

tend to become very dependent on treatment and often seem to be afraid to accept responsibility for their own behavior.

Summary of Descriptors for Scale 4

High scores on scale 4 are indicative of persons who:

1. have difficulty incorporating values and standards of society
2. may engage in asocial and antisocial acts, including lying, cheating, stealing, sexual acting out, excessive use of alcohol and/or drugs (especially if T > 75)
3. are rebellious toward authority figures
4. have stormy relationships with families
5. blame family members for difficulties
6. have histories of underachievement
7. tend to experience marital problems
8. are impulsive and strive for immediate gratification of impulses
9. do not plan their behavior well
10. tend to act without considering the consequences of their actions
11. are impatient; have limited frustration tolerance
12. show poor judgment; take risks
13. tend not to profit from experiences
14. are seen by others as immature and childish
15. are narcissistic, self-centered, selfish, and egocentric
16. are ostentatious and exhibitionistic
17. are insensitive to the needs and feelings of others
18. are interested in others in terms of how they can be used
19. are likable; create good first impressions
20. have shallow and superficial relationships
21. seem unable to form warm attachments with others
22. are extroverted and outgoing
23. are talkative, active, adventurous, energetic, and spontaneous
24. are judged by others to be intelligent and self-confident
25. have wide range of interests but lack clear direction
26. tend to be hostile, aggressive, resentful, rebellious, antagonistic, and refractory
27. have sarcastic and cynical attitudes
28. may act in aggressive ways
29. if female, may express aggression in more passive, indirect ways
30. may feign guilt and remorse when in trouble
31. are not seen as overwhelmed by emotional turmoil
32. may admit feeling sad, fearful, and worried about the future
33. experience absence of deep emotional response
34. feel empty and bored

35. if psychiatric patients, are likely to receive antisocial or passive-aggressive personality disorder diagnoses
36. have poor prognosis for psychotherapy or counseling
37. may agree to treatment to avoid something more unpleasant
38. tend to terminate treatment prematurely
39. in treatment tend to intellectualize excessively and to blame others for difficulties

Low scores on scale 4 are indicative of persons who:

1. tend to be conventional, conforming, and accepting of authority
2. are passive, submissive, and unassertive
3. are concerned about how others will react to them
4. tend to be sincere and trusting in relationships
5. have a low level of drive
6. are concerned about status and security but tend not to be competitive
7. have a narrow range of interests
8. are not creative or spontaneous in their approach to problems
9. are persistent in problem solving
10. are moralistic and rigid in their views
11. if males, may not have much sex drive
12. are self-critical and dissatisfied with self
13. accept advice and suggestions
14. may become overly dependent on treatment
15. seem to be afraid to accept responsibility for their own behavior

SCALE 5 (MASCULINITY-FEMININITY)

Scale 5 originally was developed by Hathaway and McKinley to identify homosexual invert males. The test authors identified only a very small number of items that differentiated homosexual from heterosexual males. Thus, items also were added to the scale if they differentiated between normal men and women in the standardization samples. Some items from the Terman and Miles Attitude Interest Test also were added to the scale. Although Hathaway and McKinley considered this scale preliminary, it has come to be used in its original form as a standard clinical scale.

The test authors attempted unsuccessfully to develop a corresponding scale for identifying sexual inversion in females. As a result, the standard procedure is to use scale 5 for both male and female subjects. Fifty-two of the items are keyed in the same direction for both sexes, whereas four items, all dealing with frankly sexual material, are keyed in opposite directions for males and females. After obtaining raw scores, T-score conversions are reversed for the sexes so that a high raw score for males automatically is transformed by means of the profile

sheet itself to a high T-score, whereas a high raw score for females is trans-formed to a low T-score. The result is that a high T-score for both sexes is indicative of deviation from one's own sex.

In MMPI-2 56 of the 60 items in the original scale 5 have been maintained. Although a few of the items in scale 5 have frankly sexual content, most items are not sexual in nature and cover a diversity of topics, including work and recreational interests, worries and fears, excessive sensitivity, and family rela-tionships.

Scores on scale 5 are related to intelligence, education, and socioeconomic status. It is not uncommon for male college students and other college-educated males to obtain T-scores in the 60 to 65 range. These expected elevations are particularly important in determining whether scores should be considered to be extremely elevated. Although a T-score of 75 would be considered extreme for a male with limited formal education and from a lower social class, it would be only a moderate elevation for a better-educated male from a middle or upper middle class. Female college students and other college-educated females usu-ally score somewhat below 50 on scale 5. Women with graduate or professional level educations often score between 40 and 50 on scale 5.

Because of the reversal of scoring with scale 5, high T-scores have different meanings for males and females. Some writers have suggested that high scores for males are equivalent to low scores for females and that both indicate feminine interests and attitudes. A careful analysis of the data indicates that such an interpretation is a great oversimplification. Thus, high scores and low scores are discussed separately for males and females.

High Scores on Scale 5 (Males)

Scores that are markedly higher than expected based on subjects' intelligence, education, and social class should suggest the possibility of sexual concerns and problems. These concerns and problems may be associated with homoerotic trends or homosexual behavior, but they also can center around sexual prob-lems and behaviors of other kinds. High scorers may be experiencing conflicts in sexual identity and insecurity about masculine adequacy. Some high scorers on scale 5 display clearly effeminate behavior.

High scores for males on scale 5 are indicative of a lack of stereotyped masculine interests. High scorers tend to have aesthetic and artistic interests, and they are likely to participate in housekeeping and childrearing activities to a greater extent than do most men. The higher scores on scale 5 of more educated men may reflect a more androgynous orientation, one which effec-tively combines aspects of stereotypic masculinity and femininity.

High scoring males are seen by others as intelligent, capable persons who value cognitive pursuits. They are characterized as ambitious, competitive, and persevering. They are clever, clear-thinking, organized, and logical, and they

show good judgment and common sense. They are very curious and may be creative, imaginative, and individualistic in their approach to problems.

Sociability and sensitivity to others are also characteristics of high scoring males. They are empathic and tolerant, and they are capable of expressing warm feelings toward other people. High scoring males often are seen as passive and dependent in relationships. They seem to be peace loving persons who will make concessions to avoid unpleasant confrontations.

There are some data suggesting that high scores for males are indicative of good self-control. Acting out behavior is quite rare among high scorers. Even in subgroups with a high degree of delinquency, high scoring males on scale 5 are not likely to display delinquent behavior.

High Scores on Scale 5 (Females)

High scores on scale 5 are very uncommon among females subjects. When they are encountered, they generally indicate rejection of the traditional female role. Females having high scores are interested in sports, hobbies, and other activities that tend to be stereotypically more masculine than feminine. They are described as active, vigorous, and assertive. They also tend to be very competitive, aggressive, and dominating, and they are seen by others as rather coarse, rough, and tough.

High scoring females are very outgoing, uninhibited, and self-confident. They are easygoing, relaxed, and balanced. They are rather logical and calculated in their behavior and may be rather unemotional. They are seen as unfriendly by many people. Among hospitalized psychiatric patients, high scoring females tend to be diagnosed as psychotic. They may exhibit hallucinations, delusions, and suspiciousness, but acting out behavior is uncommon.

Low Scores on Scale 5 (Males)

Males who score low on scale 5 are presenting themselves as extremely masculine. They clearly have stereotypically masculine preferences in work, hobbies, and other activities. They overemphasize physical strength and prowess. They are described by others as aggressive, thrill-seeking, adventurous, and reckless. Coarse, crude, and vulgar talk and behavior are not uncommon. The exaggerated nature of their attitudes and behaviors suggests that they may be compensating for some basic doubts about their own masculinity.

Low scoring males are seen by others as having limited intellectual ability. They have a narrow range of interests and are rather inflexible and unoriginal in their approach to problems. They prefer action to thought and are practical and nontheoretical. They are not comfortable dealing with feelings.

Low Scores on Scale 5 (Females)

Comparatively little information is available concerning women who score low on scale 5. However, it seems clear that different interpretations should be made for low scores depending on educational level. Low scoring women with limited education (high school degree or less) are presenting themselves in terms of a stereotyped female role. Again, as with low scoring males, the exaggerated nature of their attitudes and behaviors suggests that they may be compensating for doubts about their own adequacy as women. They tend to be very passive, submissive, and yielding. They are likely to defer to men in decision making. They may be seen as self-pitying, complaining, and fault finding. Others may describe them as constricted, sensitive, modest, and idealistic.

A somewhat different interpretation should be made for low scoring women with college degrees or professional training. The general picture of these women is much more positive, and they seem to have a more balanced view of gender role behavior. Although they do not present themselves as stereotypically feminine, they have many interests, attitudes, and behaviors that are traditionally feminine. In addition, they see themselves as capable, competent, and conscientious. Others see more educated, low scoring women in very favorable ways. They are described as intelligent, capable, conscientious, and forceful. In addition, they are seen as considerate, easygoing, insightful, and unprejudiced.

Summary of Descriptors for Scale 5

High scale 5 scores for males are indicative of persons who:

1. may have sexual problems and concerns (especially if scores are markedly higher than expected for their intelligence, education, and social class)
2. may be experiencing conflicts in sexual identity and insecurity about masculine adequacy
3. may display clearly effeminate behaviors
4. lack stereotyped masculine interests
5. have aesthetic and artistic interests
6. are likely to participate in housekeeping and childrearing activities to a greater extent than most men
7. may have a more androgynous orientation (especially among more educated men)
8. are seen as intelligent, capable, valuing cognitive pursuits, ambitious, competitive, and persevering
9. are clever, clear-thinking, organized, and logical
10. show good judgment and common sense
11. are curious, creative, imaginative, and individualistic in their approach to problems

12. are sociable and sensitive to others
13. are empathic, tolerant, and capable of expressing warm feelings toward other people
14. often are seen as passive and dependent in relationships
15. seem to be peace loving persons who make concessions to avoid unpleasant confrontations
16. show good self-control
17. are not likely to act out in delinquent ways

High scale 5 scores for females indicate persons who:

1. are rejecting traditional female role
2. have interests that tend to be stereotypically more masculine than feminine
3. are active, vigorous, assertive, competitive, aggressive, and dominating
4. are seen by others as coarse, rough, and tough
5. are outgoing, uninhibited, and self-confident
6. are easygoing, relaxed, and balanced
7. are logical and calculated in their behavior
8. are unemotional
9. are seen as unfriendly by others
10. among hospitalized psychiatric patients, tend to be diagnosed as psychotic

Low scale 5 scores for males indicate persons who:

1. are presenting themselves as extremely masculine
2. have stereotypcially masculine interests
3. overemphasize strength and physical prowess
4. are described by others as aggressive, thrill-seeking, adventurous, and reckless
5. may show coarse, crude, vulgar talk and behavior
6. may be compensating for basic doubts about their own masculinity
7. are seen by others as having limited intellectual ability
8. have a narrow range of interests
9. are inflexible and unoriginal in their approach to problems
10. prefer action to thought
11. are practical and nontheoretical
12. are not comfortable dealing with feelings and emotions

Low scores for females with relatively less education indicate persons who:

1. are presenting themselves as stereotypically feminine
2. may be compensating for doubts about their own adequacy as women
3. tend to be passive, submissive, and yielding
4. are seen as self-pitying, complaining, and fault-finding
5. are described as constricted, sensitive, modest, and idealistic

Low scores for females with relatively more education indicate persons who:

1. have a balanced view of gender role behavior
2. see themselves as capable, competent, and conscientious
3. are described by others as intelligent, capable, conscientious, forceful, considerate, easygoing, insightful, and unprejudiced

SCALE 6 (PARANOIA)

Scale 6 originally was developed to identify patients who were judged to have paranoid symptoms such as ideas of reference, feelings of persecution, grandiose self-concepts, suspiciousness, excessive sensitivity, and rigid opinions and attitudes. Although the scale was considered preliminary because of problems in cross-validation, a major reason for its retention was that it produced relatively few false positives. Persons who score high on the scale usually have paranoid symptoms. However, some patients with clearly paranoid symptoms are able to achieve average scores on scale 6.

All 40 of the items in the original scale have been maintained in MMPI-2. Although some items deal with frankly psychotic behaviors (e.g., suspiciousness, ideas of reference, delusions of persecution, grandiosity), many items cover such diverse topics as sensitivity, cynicism, asocial behavior, excessive moral virtue, and complaints about other people. It is possible to obtain a T-score greater than 65 on this scale without endorsing any of the frankly psychotic items.

Although scores on scale 6 are reasonably independent of age, education, and intelligence, some data suggest that black subjects tend to score higher on the scale than white subjects. Rather than suggesting gross psychopathology, these higher scores probably reflect the views of many blacks that they are getting a raw deal in life and their generally suspicious attitudes concerning the motives of whites.

Interpretation of scale 6 is complicated because the scale clearly is not bipolar in nature. Very high scores (T > 70) generally are suggestive of frankly paranoid or psychotic behavior. More moderate scores (T = 60–70) are associated with a paranoid predisposition. Mild elevations (T = 50–60) indicate personality characteristics that could be described as paranoid in nature (e.g., suspicious, resentful, demanding). Moderately low scores (T = 35–45) tend to be associated with negative characteristics. Extremely low scores (T < 35), especially if the scale is the lowest one in the profile, suggest paranoid or psychotic behavior, but it may not be as obvious as with extreme elevations.

High Scores on Scale 6

Extreme Elevations

When scale 6 scores are above 70, and especially when it also is the highest scale in the profile, subjects may exhibit frankly psychotic behavior. Their thinking

may be disturbed, and they may have delusions of persecution or grandeur. Ideas of reference also are common. They may feel mistreated and picked on; they may be angry and resentful; and they may harbor grudges. Projection is a common defense mechanism. Diagnoses of schizophrenia or paranoid disorder are most frequent.

Moderate Elevations

When scale 6 scores are within a T-score range of 60 to 70, frankly psychotic symptoms are not as common. However, persons with scores in this range are characterized by a variety of traits and behaviors that suggest a paranoid predisposition. They tend to be excessively sensitive and overly responsive to the opinions of others. They feel that they are getting a raw deal out of life and tend to rationalize and to blame others for their own difficulties. Also, they are seen as suspicious and guarded and commonly exhibit hostility, resentment, and an argumentative manner. They tend to be very moralistic and rigid in their opinions and attitudes, overemphasizing rationality greatly. Women who score in this range may describe sadness, withdrawal, and anxiety, and they are seen by others as emotionally labile and moody. The prognosis for psychotherapy is poor because these subjects do not like to talk about emotional problems and are likely to rationalize most of the time. They have great difficulty in establishing rapport with therapists. In therapy, they are likely to reveal hostility and resentment toward family members.

Mild Elevations

Scores in a T-score range of 50 to 60 are not likely to have psychotic symptoms. However, they may have a paranoid orientation toward life. They see the environment as demanding and not particularly supportive. They tend to be very sensitive to what other people think of them, and they are suspicious of the motives of others. Anger and resentment are common.

Low Scores on Scale 6

Moderately Low Scores

It is not clear from the existing literature how scores in a T-score range of 35 to 45 should be interpreted. Some studies of normal subjects have indicated that scores at this level are associated with positive characteristics. Such scorers tend to be socially interested and to face life situations adequately. They are seen as balanced, orderly, and reasonable. They tend to be cautious, conventional, and self-controlled in their approach to problems. Scores in this same range, if obtained from subjects in clinical settings, may have more negative implications. Persons with such scores are seen as stubborn, evasive, and guarded. They are likely to be self-centered, overly sensitive, and dissatisfied. They tend to have narrow interests and to approach problems in inflexible ways. Among

hospitalized psychiatric patients, psychotic symptoms or diagnoses are not uncommon.

Extremely Low Scores

T-scores below 35 on scale 6 should alert the clinician to the possibility of a frankly paranoid disorder, particularly if scale 6 is the lowest clinical scale and if the validity scales suggest a defensive test-taking attitude. Whereas subjects with scores in this range may have delusions, suspiciousness, and ideas of reference, these may be less obvious to others than is true for extremely high scorers. They tend to be evasive, defensive, and guarded. Rather than being openly hostile, aggressive, and abrasive, they seem more shy, secretive, and withdrawn.

Summary of Descriptors for Scale 6

Extreme elevations (T > 70) on scale 6 indicate persons who:

1. may exhibit frankly psychotic behavior
2. have disturbed thinking, delusions of persecution or grandeur, and ideas of reference
3. feel mistreated and picked on
4. feel angry and resentful
5. harbor grudges
6. utilize projection as a defense mechanism
7. often receive diagnoses of schizophrenia or paranoid disorder

Moderate elevations (T = 60–70) on scale 6 are indicative of persons who:

1. have a paranoid predisposition
2. tend to be excessively sensitive and overly responsive to opinions of others
3. feel they are getting a raw deal out of life
4. tend to rationalize and blame others for difficulties
5. are suspicious and guarded
6. have hostility, resentment, and an argumentative manner
7. are moralistic and rigid in opinions and attitudes
8. overemphasize rationality
9. if female, may describe sadness, withdrawal, and anxiety
10. if female, are seen by others as emotionally labile and moody
11. have a poor prognosis for therapy
12. do not like to talk about emotional problems
13. rationalize excessively in therapy
14. have difficulty establishing rapport with therapists
15. in therapy reveal hostility and resentment toward family members

Mild elevations (T = 50–60) on scale 6 are indicative of persons who:

1. have a paranoid orientation toward life
2. see the environment as demanding and not supportive
3. are very sensitive to what other people think of them
4. are suspicious of the motives of others
5. commonly feel angry and resentful

Moderately low scores (T = 35–45) on scale 6 for normal persons are indicative of persons who:

1. are socially interested
2. face life situations adequately
3. are seen as balanced, orderly, and reasonable
4. tend to be cautious, conventional, and self-controlled

Moderately low scores (T = 35–45) on scale 6 for clinical subjects are indicative of persons who:

1. are seen as stubborn, evasive, and guarded
2. are likely to be self-centered, overly sensitive, and dissatisfied
3. have narrow interests
4. approach problems in inflexible ways
5. if hospitalized psychiatric patients, commonly have psychotic symptoms and receive psychotic diagnoses

Extremely low scores (T < 35) on scale 6 are indicative of persons who:

1. may have a frankly paranoid disorder
2. may have delusions, suspiciousness, and ideas of reference
3. have paranoid symptoms that are not as obvious as those of high scorers of this scale
4. tend to be evasive, defensive, and guarded
5. may be shy, secretive, and withdrawn

SCALE 7 (PSYCHASTHENIA)

Scale 7 originally was developed to measure the general symptomatic pattern labeled psychasthenia. Although this diagnostic label is not used commonly today, it was popular when the scale was developed. Among currently popular diagnostic categories, the obsessive-compulsive disorder probably is closest to the original psychasthenia label. The thinking of persons diagnosed as psychasthenic was characterized by excessive doubts, compulsions, obsessions, and

unreasonable fears. This symptom pattern was much more common among outpatients than among hospitalized patients, so the number of cases available for scale construction was small. All 48 items in the original scale have been maintained in MMPI-2. They cover a variety of symptoms and behaviors but deal primarily with uncontrollable or obsessive thoughts, feelings of fear and/or anxiety, and doubts about one's own ability. Unhappiness, physical complaints, and difficulties in concentration also are represented in the scale.

High Scores on Scale 7

Scale 7 is a good index of psychological turmoil and discomfort, with higher scorers experiencing greater turmoil. High scorers tend to be very anxious, tense, and agitated. They worry a great deal, even over very small problems, and they are fearful and apprehensive. High-strung and jumpy, they report difficulties in concentrating and often receive anxiety disorder diagnoses.

High scorers tend to be very introspective, and they sometimes report fears that they are losing their minds. Obsessive thinking, compulsive and ritualistic behavior, and ruminations, often centered around feelings of insecurity and inferiority, are common among very high scorers. Such individuals lack self-confidence and are self-critical, self-conscious, self-degrading, and plagued by self-doubts. They tend to be very rigid and moralistic and to have high standards of behavior and performance for themselves and others. They are likely to be quite perfectionistic and conscientious; they may feel guilty about not living up to their own standards and depressed about falling short of goals.

In general, high scorers are neat, orderly, organized, and meticulous. They are persistent and reliable, but they lack ingenuity and originality in their approach to problems. They are seen by others as dull and formal. They have great difficulties in decision making, and they may vacillate over very small, routine decisions. In addition, they are likely to distort the importance of problems and to be quite overreactive to stressful situations.

High scorers tend to be shy and do not interact well socially. They are described as hard to get to know, and they worry a great deal about popularity and social acceptance. Some people see them as sentimental, peaceable, soft-hearted, trustful, sensitive, and kind, others as dependent, unassertive, and immature.

Some high scorers express physical complaints that may center around the heart, the gastrointestinal system, or the genitourinary system. Complaints of fatigue, exhaustion, insomnia, and bad dreams are common.

Although high scorers may be motivated for therapy because they feel so uncomfortable and miserable, they are not very responsive to brief psychotherapy or counseling. Despite some insight into their problems, they tend to rationalize and to intellectualize a great deal. They often are resistant to interpretations and may express much hostility toward the therapist. However, they tend to remain in therapy longer than most patients, and they may show

very slow but steady progress. Problems presented in therapy may include difficulties with authority figures, poor work or study habits, or concern about homosexual impulses.

Low Scores on Scale 7

Low scorers on scale 7 are free of disabling fears and anxieties and are very self-confident. They are perceived as warm, cheerful, and friendly. They have a wide range of interests and are responsible, efficient, realistic, and adaptable. Success, status, and recognition are important to them.

Summary of Descriptors for Scale 7

High scores on scale 7 are indicative of persons who:

1. experience psychological turmoil and discomfort
2. feel anxious, tense, and agitated
3. are worried, fearful, apprehensive, high-strung, and jumpy
4. report difficulties in concentrating
5. often receive anxiety disorder diagnoses
6. are introspective
7. may report fears that they are losing their minds
8. experience obsessive thinking, compulsive and ritualistic behavior, and ruminations
9. feel insecure and inferior
10. lack self-confidence
11. are self-critical, self-conscious, and self-degrading
12. are plagued by self-doubts
13. tend to be very rigid and moralistic
14. have high standards of performance for self and others
15. are perfectionistic and conscientious
16. feel depressed and guilty about falling short of goals
17. are neat, organized, and meticulous
18. are persistent and reliable
19. lack ingenuity in their approach to problems
20. are seen by others as dull and formal
21. have difficulties making decisions
22. distort the importance of problems; overreact to stressful situations
23. tend to be shy; do not interact well socially
24. are described as hard to get to know
25. worry about popularity and social acceptance
26. are seen by others as sentimental, peaceable, soft-hearted, trustful, sensitive, and kind

27. are described as dependent, unassertive, and immature
28. may have physical complaints centering on:
    a. the heart
    b. the genitourinary system
    c. the gastrointestinal system
    d. fatigue, exhaustion, insomnia, and bad dreams
29. may be motivated for therapy because of turmoil
30. are not responsive to brief therapy or counseling
31. show some insight into problems
32. rationalize and intellectualize excessively
33. are resistant to interpretations
34. may express hostility toward therapist
35. remain in therapy longer than most patients
36. make slow but steady progress in therapy
37. discuss in therapy problems including difficulty with authority figures, poor work or study habits, and concerns about homosexual impulses

Low scores on scale 7 are indicative of persons who:

1. are free of disabling fears and anxieties
2. are self-confident
3. are perceived as warm, cheerful, and friendly
4. have a wide range of interests
5. are responsible, efficient, realistic, and adaptable
6. value success, status, and recognition

SCALE 8 (SCHIZOPHRENIA)

Scale 8 was developed to identify patients diagnosed as schizophrenic. This category included a heterogeneous group of disorders characterized by disturbances of thinking, mood, and behavior. Misinterpretations of reality, delusions, and hallucinations may be present. Ambivalent or constricted emotional responsiveness is common. Behavior may be withdrawn, aggressive, or bizarre.

All 78 of the items in the original scale have been maintained in MMPI-2. Some of the items deal with such frankly psychotic symptoms as bizarre mentation, peculiarities of perception, delusions of persecution, and hallucinations. Other topics covered include social alienation, poor family relationships, sexual concerns, difficulties in impulse control and concentration, and fears, worries, and dissatisfactions.

Scores on scale 8 are related to age and to race. Adolescents and college students often obtain T-scores in a range of 50 to 60, perhaps reflecting the turmoil associated with that period in life. Black subjects, particularly males, tend to score higher than white subjects. The elevated scores for blacks do not

necessarily suggest greater overt psychopathology but may simply indicate the alienation and social estrangement experienced by many blacks. Some elevations of scale 8 can be accounted for by subjects who are reporting a large number of unusual experiences, feelings, and perceptions related to the use of prescription and nonprescription drugs, especially amphetamines. Also, some medical conditions, such as epilepsy, have been associated with scale 8 elevations (e.g., Dikmen, Hermann, Wilensky, & Rainwater, 1983; Dodrill, 1986).

High Scores on Scale 8

Although one should be cautious about concluding that a subject is schizophrenic on the basis of only the score on scale 8, T-scores in a range of 75 to 90 suggest the possibility of a psychotic disorder. Confusion, disorganization, and disorientation may be present. Unusual thoughts or attitudes, perhaps even delusional in nature, hallucinations, and extremely poor judgment may be evident. Extreme scores (T > 90) usually are not produced by psychotic subjects. They are more likely to indicate an individual who is in acute psychological turmoil or a less disturbed person who is endorsing many deviant items as a cry for help. However, some recently hospitalized psychiatric patients often obtain high ranging scores on scale 8 that accurately reflect their severe psychopathology.

High scores on scale 8 may suggest a schizoid life-style. High scorers tend to feel as if they are not a part of their social environments. They feel isolated, alienated, misunderstood, and unaccepted by their peers. They are withdrawn, seclusive, secretive, and inaccessible and may avoid dealing with people and with new situations. They are described by others as shy, aloof, and uninvolved.

High scorers experience a great deal of apprehension and generalized anxiety. They may feel very resentful, hostile, and aggressive, but they are unable to express such feelings. A typical response to stress is withdrawal into daydreams and fantasies, and some subjects may have a difficult time separating reality and fantasy.

High scorers may be plagued by self-doubts. They feel inferior, incompetent, and dissatisfied. Sexual preoccupation and sex role confusion are common. Their behavior often is characterized by others as nonconforming, unusual, unconventional, and eccentric. Physical complaints may be present, and they usually are vague and longstanding in nature.

High scorers may at times be very stubborn, moody, and opinionated. At other times they are seen as generous, peaceable, and sentimental. Other adjectives used to describe high scorers include immature, impulsive, adventurous, sharp-witted, conscientious, and high-strung. Although they may have a wide range of interests and may be creative and imaginative in approaching problems, their goals generally are abstract and vague, and they seem to lack basic information that is required for problem solving.

The prognosis for psychotherapy is not good because of the longstanding

nature of high scorers' problems and their reluctance to relate in a meaningful way to the therapist. However, high scorers tend to stay in therapy longer than most patients, and eventually they may come to trust the therapist. Medical consultation to evaluate the appropriateness of chemotherapy may be indicated.

Low Scores on Scale 8

Low scorers on scale 8 tend to be friendly, cheerful, good-natured, sensitive, and trustful. They are seen as well-balanced and adaptable, and they are responsible and dependable. However, low scorers tend to be somewhat restrained in their relationships, and they avoid deep, emotional involvement with other people. In interpersonal relationships they are submissive and compliant, and they are overly accepting of authority. Low scorers tend to be cautious, conventional, conservative, and unimaginative in their approach to problems, and they tend to be very practical and concrete in their thinking. They are concerned about success, status, and power, but they are so overcontrolled that they are reluctant to place themselves in clearly competitive situations.

Summary of Descriptors for Scale 8

High scores on scale 8 are indicative of persons who:

1. may have a psychotic disorder (especially if T = 75–90)
2. may be confused, disorganized, and disoriented
3. may report unusual thoughts or attitudes, or hallucinations
4. may show extremely poor judgment
5. may be in acute psychological turmoil
6. may be exaggerating deviance as a cry for help
7. tend to have a schizoid life-style
8. do not feel a part of their environments
9. feel isolated, alienated, misunderstood, and unaccepted
10. are withdrawn, seclusive, secretive, and inaccessible
11. avoid dealing with people and new situations
12. are described as shy, aloof, and uninvolved
13. experience apprehension and generalized anxiety
14. may feel resentful, hostile, and aggressive
15. are unable to express negative feelings
16. typically respond to stress by withdrawing into daydreams and fantasies
17. may have difficulty separating reality and fantasy
18. are plagued by self-doubts
19. feel inferior, incompetent, and dissatisfied

20. may experience sexual preoccupation and/or sex role confusion
21. are nonconforming, unusual, unconventional, and eccentric
22. have vague and longstanding physical complaints
23. may at times be stubborn, moody, and opinionated
24. may at times be seen as generous, peaceable, and sentimental
25. are described as immature, impulsive, adventurous, sharp-witted, conscientious, and high-strung
26. may have a wide range of interests
27. may be creative and imaginative in approaching problems
28. have abstract and vague goals
29. seem to lack basic information required for problem solving
30. have poor prognosis for psychotherapy because of the longstanding nature of their problems and the reluctance to relate in meaningful way to therapist
31. tend to stay in therapy longer than most patients
32. may eventually come to trust therapist
33. may require medical referral to evaluate appropriateness of chemotherapy

Low scores on scale 8 are indicative of persons who:

1. tend to be friendly, cheerful, good-natured, sensitive, and trustful
2. are seen as well-balanced, and adaptable
3. are responsible and dependable
4. tend to be restrained in relationships
5. avoid deep, emotional involvement with other people
6. are submissive, compliant, and overly accepting of authority
7. tend to be cautious, conventional, conservative, and unimaginative in approach to problems
8. are practical and concrete in thinking
9. are concerned about success, status, and power
10. are reluctant to place themselves in clearly competitive situations

SCALE 9 (HYPOMANIA)

Scale 9 originally was developed to identify psychiatric patients manifesting hypomanic symptoms. Hypomania is characterized by elevated mood, accelerated speech and motor activity, irritability, flight of ideas, and brief periods of depression.

All 46 items in the original scale have been maintained in MMPI-2. Some of them deal specifically with features of hypomanic disturbance (e.g., activity level, excitability, irritability, grandiosity). Others cover topics such as family relationships, moral values and attitudes, and physical or bodily concerns. No

single dimension accounts for much of the variance in scores, and most of the sources of variance represented in the scale are not duplicated in other clinical scales.

Scores on scale 9 clearly are related to age and to race. Younger subjects (e.g., adolescents and college students) typically obtain scores in a T-score range of 55 to 60, and for elderly subjects scale 9 scores below a T-score of 50 are common. Black subjects typically score higher than white subjects on the scale; scores in a T-score range of 55 to 65 are common for black subjects.

Scale 9 can be viewed as a measure or psychological and physical energy, with high scorers having excessive energy and low scorers lacking even an average amount of energy. When scores are high, one expects characteristics suggested by other aspects of the profile to be acted out, whereas low scores suggest that they will not be acted out. For example, high scores on scale 4 suggest asocial or antisocial tendencies. If scale 9 is elevated along with scale 4, these tendencies are likely to be expressed overtly in behavior. However, a person with scale 4 elevated and scale 9 in an average or low range is not likely to express overtly his or her asocial or antisocial attitudes.

High Scores on Scale 9

Extreme elevations (T > 80) on scale 9 may suggest a manic episode. Patients with such scores are likely to show excessive, purposeless activity and accelerated speech; they may have hallucinations and/or delusions of grandeur; and they are very emotionally labile. Some confusion may be present, and flight of ideas is not uncommon.

Subjects with more moderate elevations are not likely to exhibit frankly psychotic symptoms, but there is a definite tendency toward overactivity and unrealistic self-appraisal. High scorers are energetic and talkative, and they prefer action to thought. They have a wide range of interests and are likely to have many projects going at once. However, they do not utilize energy very wisely and often do not see projects through to completion. They may be creative, enterprising, and ingenious, but they have little interest in routine or in details. High scorers tend to become bored and restless very easily, and their frustration tolerance is quite low. They have great difficulty in inhibiting expression of impulses, and periodic episodes of irritability, hostility, and aggressive outbursts are not uncommon. An unrealistic and unqualified optimism is also characteristic of high scorers. They seem to think that nothing is impossible, and they have grandiose aspirations. Also, they have an exaggerated appraisal of their own self-worth and self-importance and are not able to see their own limitations.

High scorers are very outgoing, sociable, and gregarious. They like to be around other people and generally create good first impressions. They impress others as being friendly, pleasant, enthusiastic, poised, and self-confident. Their relationships with other people are usually quite superficial, and as others get

to know them better they become aware of their manipulations, deceptions, and unreliability.

Despite the outward picture of confidence and poise, high scorers are likely to harbor feelings of dissatisfaction concerning what they are getting out of life. They may feel upset, tense, nervous, anxious, and agitated, and they describe themselves as prone to worry. Periodic episodes of depression may occur.

In psychotherapy, high scorers may reveal negative feelings toward domineering parents, report difficulties in school or at work, and admit to a variety of delinquent behaviors. Female subjects may be rebelling against the stereotyped female role, and some male subjects may be concerned about homosexual impulses. The prognosis for psychotherapy is poor. High scorers are resistant to interpretations, irregular in their attendance, and likely to terminate therapy prematurely. They engage in a great deal of intellectualization and may repeat problems in a stereotyped manner. They do not become dependent on the therapist, who may be a target for hostility and aggression.

Low Scores on Scale 9

Low scorers on scale 9, particularly if the scale is the lowest one in the profile, are characterized by low energy and activity levels. They appear to be lethargic, listless, apathetic, and phlegmatic, and they are difficult to motivate. Chronic fatigue and physical exhaustion are common. Depression, accompanied by tension and anxiety, may be present.

Low scorers are reliable, responsible, and dependable. They approach problems in a conventional, practical, and reasonable way, and they are conscientious and persevering. They may lack self-confidence, and they are seen by others as sincere, quiet, modest, and humble. They also tend to be somewhat withdrawn and seclusive, and they see themselves as not being very popular. They tend to be overcontrolled and are not likely to express their feelings directly or openly.

Low scoring males have home and family interests and seem willing to settle down. For hospitalized psychiatric patients, low scores have favorable prognostic implications.

Summary of Descriptors for Scale 9

High scores on scale 9 are indicative of persons who:

1. if T > 80, may exhibit behavioral manifestations of a manic episode, including:
   a. excessive, purposeless activity
   b. accelerated speech
   c. hallucinations

    d. delusions of grandeur

    e. emotional lability

    f. confusion

    g. flight of ideas

2. are overactive
3. have unrealistic self-appraisal
4. are energetic and talkative
5. prefer action to thought
6. have a wide range of interests
7. may have many projects going at once
8. do not utilize energy wisely
9. often do not see projects through to completion
10. may be creative, enterprising, and ingenious
11. have little interest in routine and detail
12. tend to become bored and restless very easily
13. have low frustration tolerance
14. have difficulty in inhibiting expression of impulses
15. have periodic episodes of irritability, hostility, and aggressive outbursts
16. are characterized by unrealistic, unqualified optimism
17. have grandiose aspirations
18. have an exaggerated appraisal of self-worth
19. are unable to see their own limitations
20. are outgoing, sociable, and gregarious
21. like to be around other people
22. create good first impressions
23. impress others as friendly, pleasant, enthusiastic, poised, and self-confident
24. have quite superficial relationships with other people
25. eventually are seen by others as manipulative, deceptive, and unreliable
26. beneath an outward picture of confidence and poise, harbor feelings of dissatisfaction
27. may feel upset, tense, nervous, anxious, and agitated
28. may describe themselves as prone to worry
29. may experience periodic episodes of depression
30. in psychotherapy may reveal negative feelings toward domineering parents, difficulties in school or at work, and a variety of delinquent behaviors
31. if females, may be rebelling against stereotyped female role
32. if males, may be concerned about homosexual impulses
33. have a poor prognosis for psychotherapy
34. are resistant to interpretations
35. are irregular in therapy attendance
36. are likely to terminate therapy prematurely
37. engage in a great deal of intellectualization
38. repeat problems in a stereotyped manner
39. do not become dependent on therapists
40. may make therapists targets of hostility and aggression

Low scores on scale 9 indicate persons who:
1. are characterized by low energy and activity levels
2. appear to be lethargic, listless, apathetic, and phlegmatic
3. are difficult to motivate
4. may report chronic fatigue and physical exhaustion
5. may report depression, accompanied by tension and anxiety
6. are reliable, responsible, and dependable
7. approach problems in conventional, practical, reasonable ways
8. are conscientious and persevering
9. may lack self-confidence
10. are seen by others as sincere, quiet, modest, and humble
11. tend to be somewhat withdrawn and seclusive
12. see themselves as not being very popular
13. tend to be overcontrolled; are not likely to express feelings directly or openly
14. if males, have home and family interests and seem willing to settle down
15. if hospitalized psychiatric patients, have a more favorable prognosis than most hospitalized patients

SCALE 0 (SOCIAL INTROVERSION)

Although scale 0 was developed later than the other clinical scales, it has come to be treated as a standard clinical scale. The scale was designed to assess a subject's tendency to withdraw from social contacts and responsibilities. Items were selected by contrasting high and low scorers on the Social Introversion-Extroversion scale of the Minnesota T-S-E Inventory. Only female subjects were used to develop the scale, but its use has been extended to male subjects as well.

All but one of the 70 items in the original scale have been maintained in MMPI-2. The items are of two general types. One group of items deals with social participation, whereas the other group deals with general neurotic maladjustment and self-depreciation. High scores can be obtained by endorsing either kind of item, or both. Scores on scale 0 are quite stable over extended periods of time.

High Scores on Scale 0

The most salient characteristic of high scorers on scale 0 is social introversion. High scorers are very insecure and uncomfortable in social situations. They tend to be shy, reserved, timid, and retiring. They feel more comfortable when alone or with a few close friends, and they do not participate in many social activities. They may be especially uncomfortable around members of the opposite sex.

High scorers lack self-confidence, and they tend to be self-effacing. They are hard to get to know and are described by others as cold and distant. They are sensitive to what others think of them and are likely to be troubled by their lack of involvement with other people. They are quite overcontrolled and are not likely to display their feelings directly. They are submissive and compliant in interpersonal relationships, and they are overly accepting of authority.

High scorers also are described as serious and as having a slow personal tempo. Although they are reliable and dependable, their approach to problems tends to be cautious, conventional, and unoriginal, and they give up easily. They are somewhat rigid and inflexible in their attitudes and opinions. They also have great difficulty in making even minor decisions. They seem to enjoy their work and get pleasure from productive personal achievement.

High scorers tend to worry, to be irritable, and to feel anxious. They are described by others as moody. Guilt feelings and episodes of depression may occur. High scorers seem to lack energy and do not have many interests.

Low Scores on Scale 0

Low scorers on scale 0 tend to be sociable and extroverted. They are outgoing, gregarious, friendly, and talkative. They have a strong need to be around other people, and they mix well. They are seen as intelligent, verbally fluent, and expressive. They are active, energetic, and vigorous. They are interested in power, status, and recognition, and they tend to seek out competitive situations.

Low scorers have problems with impulse control, and they may act without considering the consequences of their actions. They are somewhat immature and self-indulgent. Relationships with other people may be superficial and insincere. A tendency to manipulate other people and to be opportunistic may be evident. Their exhibitionistic and ostentatious styles may arouse resentment and hostility in others.

Summary of Descriptors for Scale 0

High scores on scale 0 indicate persons who:

1. are socially introverted
2. are very insecure and uncomfortable in social situations
3. tend to be shy, reserved, timid, and retiring
4. feel more comfortable alone or with a few close friends
5. do not participate in many social activities
6. may be especially uncomfortable around members of the opposite sex
7. lack self-confidence; tend to be self-effacing
8. are hard to get to know
9. are described by others as cold and distant

10. are sensitive to what others think of them
11. are likely to be troubled by their lack of involvement with other people
12. are quite overcontrolled; are not likely to display feelings openly
13. are submissive and compliant in interpersonal relationships
14. are overly accepting of authority
15. are described as serious and as having a slow personal tempo
16. are reliable and dependable
17. tend to have a cautious, conventional, and unoriginal approach to problems
18. tend to give up easily
19. are somewhat rigid and inflexible in their attitudes and opinions
20. have great difficulty in making even minor decisions
21. seem to enjoy their work and get pleasure from productive personal achievement
22. tend to worry, to be irritable, and to feel anxious
23. are described by others as moody
24. may experience episodes of depression
25. seem to lack energy
26. do not have many interests

Low scores on scale 0 are indicative of persons who:

1. are sociable and extroverted
2. are outgoing, gregarious, friendly, and talkative
3. have a strong need to be around other people
4. mix well
5. are seen as intelligent, expressive, and verbally fluent
6. are active, energetic, and vigorous
7. are interested in power, status, and recognition
8. seek out competitive situations
9. have problems with impulse control; may act without considering the consequences of their actions
10. are somewhat immature and self-indulgent
11. may have superficial and insincere relationships with other people
12. may be manipulative and opportunistic
13. may arouse resentment and hostility in others

5

Profile Configurations

From the MMPI's inception, Hathaway and McKinley made clear that the configural interpretation of an examinee's scores was diagnostically richer and thus more useful than an interpretation that examined single scales without regard for relationships among the scales. Meehl (1951), Meehl and Dahlstrom (1960), Taulbee and Sisson (1957), and others also stressed configural approaches to MMPI interpretation. Thus, some of the earlier MMPI validity studies (e.g., Black, 1953; Guthrie, 1952; Meehl, 1951) grouped profiles according to the two highest clinical scales in the profile and tried to identify reliable extratest behaviors that were uniquely related to each profile type. Other investigators (e.g., Gilberstadt & Duker, 1965; Marks & Seeman, 1963) developed complex rules for classifying profiles into homogeneous groups and tried to identify extratest correlates for each group. For example, the following criteria must be met in order for a profile to be classified as a 4-9 type in the Gilberstadt and Duker system: (1) Pd and Ma greater than T-score 70; (2) no other scales greater than T-score 70; (3) L less than T-score 60; (4) Ma 15 or more T-score points greater than Sc; and (5) Pd 7 or more T-score points greater than Mf. Although clinicians initially were quite enthusiastic about this complex approach to profile classification, they became disenchanted as accumulating research and clinical evidence indicated that only a small proportion of the MMPI protocols encountered in a typical psychiatric setting could be classified using the complex types defined by the existing classification systems (Fowler & Coyle, 1968; Huff, 1965; Meikle & Gerritse, 1970).

More recently, interest in complex rules for classifying profiles has diminished, replaced by a resurgent interest in the simpler (two-scale, three-scale) approach to the classification of profiles. Gynther and his colleagues (Gynther, Altman, & Sletten, 1973) and Lewandowski and Graham (1972) demonstrated that reliable extratest correlates can be identified for profiles that are classified according to their two highest clinical scales. An obvious advantage of the simpler approaches is that a large proportion of the profiles encountered in most settings can be classified into codes that have been studied empirically. Marks, Seeman, and Haller (1974), in their revision and extension of the earlier work by Marks and Seeman (1963), acknowledged that no appreciable loss in

accuracy of extratest descriptions resulted when they used two-point codes instead of their more complex codes for classifying MMPI profiles.

This chapter presents interpretive data for some configurations of MMPI-2 scales. Because no data have been reported concerning correlates of code types for MMPI-2, the descriptions reported here are based on studies of code types with the original MMPI. This approach seems justified because there are data indicating considerable continuity between the original MMPI and MMPI-2. Additionally, external correlates for the individual clinical scales of MMPI-2 are markedly similar to those previously identified for the clinical scales of the original MMPI. Of course, it will be important for researchers to verify that the same descriptors are appropriate for MMPI and MMPI-2 code types.

DEFINING CODE TYPES

Described very simply, code types are ways of classifying MMPI profiles that take into account more than a single clinical scale at a time. The simplest code types are high-points and low-points. A high-point code (e.g., high-point 2) simply tells us that the scale, in this example scale 2, is higher than any other clinical scale in the profile. The high-point code does not tell us anything about the absolute level of the highest scale. A low-point code (e.g, low-point 7) simply tells us that the scale, in this example scale 7, is lower than any other clinical scale in the profile. Again, the low point code does not tell us anything about the absolute level of the lowest scale.

There can only be one high-point code or low-point code for any particular profile. In an earlier chapter, we defined high and low scores in terms of absolute T-score levels and not in relation to other scales in the profile. In this conceptualization, a subject could have several high or low scores. A careful examination of the MMPI literature suggests that basically the same general picture of high scoring or low scoring individuals emerges regardless of whether we are dealing with high or low scores or with high-point or low-point code types. Thus, no additional interpretive information will be presented in this chapter for high-point codes or low-point codes.

Two-point code types tell us which two clinical scales are the highest ones in the profile. Thus, a 2-7 two-point code tells us that scale 2 is the highest clinical scale in the profile and scale 7 is the second highest clinical scale in the profile. For most two-point codes the scales are interchangeable. For example, we often talk about code types such as 27/72, and we make basically the same interpretations for the 2-7 code as we do for the 7-2 code. Whenever the order of the scales in the two-point code makes a difference in interpretation, specific mention is made in the descriptive data for those particular codes in this chapter. As with high-point codes, two-point codes tell us nothing about the absolute level of scores for the two scales in the code type.

Three-point code types tell us which three clinical scales are the highest ones in the profile. For example, a 2-7-8 code type is one in which scale 2 is the highest in the profile, scale 7 is the second highest, and scale 8 is the third highest. For most three-point codes the order of scales is interchangeable. Whenever the order is important in terms of the interpretations of code types, specific mention is made when the descriptive data for those codes are presented in this chapter.

Sometimes it is very easy to determine the code type for a particular profile. If two or three scales are much more elevated that the rest of the scales in the profile, the appropriate code type classification may be obvious. However, sometimes it is difficult to determine a code type because several or more clinical scales are of about equal elevation. In such cases, each possible code type should be considered and interpretive statements about each generated. For example, consider a profile in which scale 2 has a T-score of 75, scale 7 has a T-score of 66, scale 8 has a T-score of 65, and no other clinical scales have T-scores above 60. The appropriate three-point code for this profile would be 2-7-8. However, one would want to consider both 2-7 and 2-8 two-point codes. When dealing with a profile in which many clinical scales are elevated at about the same level, it probably does not make much sense to generate all the possible two- or three-point codes. Rather, one would infer that the person producing such a profile is presenting many different symptoms and problems whose nature could be elucidated by consideration of the correlates of scores on each of the scales.

For both two- and three-point codes the descriptors presented are more likely to fit a particular subject when the scales in the code are more elevated (particularly if T-scores are greater than 65) and are significantly higher than the rest of the clinical scales in the profile. The descriptors for the various code types include symptoms and personality or life-style characteristics. When the scales in the code are significantly elevated, (especially when they are above T = 65) both kinds of descriptors are likely to fit the examinee. However, when the scales in the code are less elevated, it may be appropriate to delete the descriptors dealing with more extreme symptoms and to maintain those dealing with personality and life-style characteristics.

As more aspects of the MMPI-2 profile are taken into consideration in classifying profiles into code types, the profiles that fit into each type are more homogeneous. Likewise, the persons producing those profiles are more likely to be like each other. Thus, we expect that the descriptors for more complex code types are more likely to apply to a particular examinee with one of those code types than will be the case for descriptors derived from less complex code types.

TWO-POINT CODE TYPES

If two-point codes are used interchangeably, there are 40 possible two-point combinations of the 10 clinical scales. The two-point codes included in this

chapter are those that occur reasonably frequently in a variety of settings and for which an adequate amount of interpretive information is available in the literature.[1] The reader will note that few codes including scales 5 and 0 are presented. The reason is that in many research studies with two-point codes, scales 5 and 0 have been excluded because they were added after the original publication of the MMPI and thus were not available for some subjects in some of the early studies. The descriptions that follow represent modal patterns and obviously do not describe unfailingly each and every person with the code types. For profiles that do not fit any of the two-point codes presented here, the clinician will have to rely on interpretation of high and low scores on individual clinical scales (see Chapter 4).

12/21

The most prominent features of the 12/21 code are somatic discomfort and pain. Individuals with this code present themselves as physically ill, although there may be no clinical evidence of an organic basis for their symptoms. They are very concerned about health and bodily functions and are likely to overreact to minor physical dysfunction. They may present multiple somatic complaints, or the symptoms may be restricted to one particular system. Although headaches and cardiac complaints may occur, the digestive system is more likely to be involved. Ulcers, particularly of the upper gastrointestinal tract, are common, and anorexia, nausea, and vomiting may be present. Individuals with the 12/21 code also may complain of dizziness, insomnia, weakness, fatigue, and tiredness. They tend to react to stress, including responsibility, with physical symptoms, and they resist attempts to explain their symptoms in terms of emotional or psychological factors.

12/21 individuals are generally anxious, tense, and nervous. Also, they are high-strung and prone to worry about many things, and they tend to be restless and irritable. Although pronounced clinical depression is not common for persons with the 12/21 code, they may report feelings of unhappiness or dysphoria, brooding, and loss of initiative.

Persons with the 12/21 code report feeling very self-conscious. They are introverted and shy in social situations, particularly with members of the opposite sex, and they tend to be somewhat withdrawn and seclusive. They harbor many doubts about their own abilities, and they vacillate about even minor, everyday matters. They are hypersensitive concerning what other people think about them, and they may be somewhat suspicious and untrusting in interpersonal relations. They also tend to be passive-dependent in their rela-

[1]Sources consulted in preparing Chapter 5: Anderson & Bauer (1985); Carson (1969); Dahlstrom, Welsh, & Dahlstrom (1972); Davis & Sines (1971); Drake & Oetting (1959); Duckworth & Anderson (1986); Gilberstadt & Duker (1965); Good & Brantner (1961); Gynther, Altman, & Sletten (1973); Hovey & Lewis (1967); Lachar (1974b); Lewandowski & Graham (1972); Marks, Seeman, & Haller (1974); Nelson & Marks (1985); Persons & Marks (1971); Schubert (1973).

tionships, and they may harbor hostility toward people who are perceived as not offering enough attention and support.

Excessive use of alcohol may be a problem for 12/21 individuals, especially among psychiatric patients. Their histories may include blackouts, job loss, arrests, and family problems associated with alcohol abuse. Persons with the 12/21 code most often are given diagnoses of anxiety disorders, depressive disorders, or somatoform disorders, although a small proportion of individuals with this code may be diagnosed as schizophrenic. In this latter group, scale 8 usually also is elevated along with scales 1 and 2.

Individuals with the 12/21 code are not seen as good risks for traditional psychotherapy. They can tolerate high levels of discomfort before becoming motivated to change. They utilize repression and somatization excessively, and they lack insight and self-understanding. In addition, their passive-dependent life-styles make it difficult for them to accept responsibility for their own behavior. Although long-term change after psychotherapy is not very likely, short-lived symptomatic changes often occur.

13/31

The 13/31 code is more common among women and older persons than among men and younger persons. Psychiatric patients with the 13/31 code usually receive somatoform disorder diagnoses. Classical conversion symptoms may be present, particularly if scale 2 is considerably lower than scales 1 and 3 (i.e., the so-called conversion V pattern). Whereas some tension may be reported by 13/31 persons, severe anxiety and depression usually are absent, as are clearly psychotic symptoms. Rather than being grossly incapacitated in functioning, the 13/31 individual is likely to continue functioning but at a reduced level of efficiency.

The somatic complaints presented by 13/31 persons include headaches, chest pain, back pain, and numbness or tremors of the extremities. Eating problems, including anorexia, nausea, vomiting, and obesity, are common. Other physical complaints include weakness, fatigue, dizziness, and sleep disturbance. The physical symptoms increase in times of stress, and there is clear secondary gain associated with the symptoms.

Individuals with the 13/31 code present themselves as normal, responsible, and without fault. They make excessive use of denial, projection, and rationalization, and they blame others for their difficulties. They prefer medical explanations for their symptoms, and they lack insight into psychological factors underlying their symptoms. They manifest an overly optimistic and Pollyannaish view of their situations and of the world in general, and they do not show appropriate concern about their symptoms and problems.

13/31 persons tend to be rather immature, egocentric, and selfish. They are insecure and have a strong need for attention, affection, and sympathy. They are very dependent, but they are uncomfortable with the dependency and experi-

ence conflict because of it. Although they are outgoing and socially extroverted, their social relationships tend to be shallow and superficial, and they lack genuine emotional involvement with other people. They tend to exploit social relationships in an attempt to fulfill their own needs. They lack skills in dealing with the opposite sex, and they may be deficient in heterosexual drive.

13/31 individuals harbor resentment and hostility toward other people, particularly those who are perceived as not fulfilling their needs for attention. Most of the time they are overcontrolled and likely to express their negative feelings indirectly and passively, but they occasionally lose their tempers and express themselves in angry, but not violent, ways. Behaving in a socially acceptable manner is important to 13/31 persons. They need to convince other people that they are logical and reasonable, and they are conventional and conforming in their attitudes and values.

Because of their unwillingness to acknowledge psychological factors underlying their symptoms, 13/31 persons are difficult to motivate in traditional psychotherapy. They are reluctant to discuss psychological factors that might be related to somatic symptoms, and if therapists insist on doing so, they are likely to terminate therapy prematurely. Sometimes it is possible to get them to discuss problems, as long as no direct link to somatic symptoms is suggested. In therapy they expect therapists to provide definite solutions to their problems, and they may terminate therapy when therapists fail to do so. 13/31 persons tend to be suggestible, and they often will try activities suggested by therapists.

14/41

The 14/41 code is not encountered frequently in clinical practice and is much more common among males than among females. Persons with the 14/41 code frequently report severe somatic symptoms, particularly nonspecific headaches. They also may appear to be indecisive and anxious. Although they are socially extroverted, they lack skills with members of the opposite sex. They may feel rebellious toward home and parents, but direct expression of these feelings is not likely. Excessive use of alcohol may be a problem, and 14/41 persons may have a history of alcoholic benders, job loss, and family problems associated with their drinking behavior. In school or on the job, the 14/41 persons lack drive and do not have well-defined goals. They are dissatisfied and pessimistic in their outlook toward life, and they are demanding, grouchy, and referred to as bitchy in interpersonal relationships. Because they are likely to deny psychological problems, they tend to be resistant to traditional psychotherapy.

18/81

Persons with the 18/81 code harbor many feelings of hostility and aggression, and they are not able to express these feelings in a modulated, adaptive manner.

Either they inhibit expression almost completely, which results in feelings of being "bottled up," or they are overly belligerent and abrasive.

18/81 persons feel socially inadequate, especially around members of the opposite sex. They lack trust in other people, keep them at a distance, and feel generally isolated and alienated. A nomadic life-style and a poor work history are common.

Psychiatric patients with the 18/81 code most often are diagnosed on strictly clinical criteria as schizophrenic, although diagnoses of anxiety disorders and schizoid personality disorder are sometimes given. 18/81 persons tend to be unhappy and depressed, and they may display flat affect. They present somatic concerns (including headaches and insomnia), which at times are so intense that they border on being delusional. 18/18 persons also may be confused in their thinking, and they are very distractible.

19/91

Persons with the 19/91 code are likely to be experiencing a great deal of distress and turmoil. They tend to be very anxious, tense, and restless. Somatic complaints, including gastrointestinal problems, headaches, and exhaustion, are common, and these people are reluctant to accept psychological explanations of their symptoms. Although on the surface 19/91 individuals appear to be verbal, socially extroverted, aggressive, and belligerent, they are basically passive-dependent persons who are trying to deny this aspect of their personalities.

19/91 persons have a great deal of ambition. They expect a high level of achievement from themselves, but they lack clear and definite goals. They are frustrated by their inability to achieve at a high level. The 19/91 code is sometimes found for brain-damaged individuals who are having difficulties coping with their limitations.

23/32

Although persons with the 23/32 code typically do not experience disabling anxiety, they report feeling nervous, agitated, tense, and worried. They also report feeling sad, unhappy and depressed. Fatigue, exhaustion, and weakness are common. They lack interest and involvement in their life situations, and they have difficulty getting started on a project. Decreased physical activity is likely, and somatic complaints, usually gastrointestinal in nature, may occur.

23/32 individuals are rather passive, docile, and dependent. They are plagued by self-doubts, and they harbor feelings of inadequacy, insecurity, and helplessness. They tend to elicit nurturant and helpful attitudes from other people. Persons with the 23/32 code are very interested in achievement, status, and power. They may appear to be competitive, industrious, and driven, but they do not really place themselves in directly competitive situations where they might

experience failure. They seek increased responsibility, but they dread the stress and pressure associated with it. They often feel that they do not get adequate recognition for their accomplishments, and they are easily hurt by even mild criticism.

23/32 persons are extremely overcontrolled. They have difficulty expressing their feelings, and they may feel bottled up much of the time. They tend to deny unacceptable impulses, and when denial fails they feel anxious and guilty. Persons with the 23/32 code feel socially inadequate, and they tend to avoid social involvement. They are especially uncomfortable with members of the opposite sex, and sexual maladjustment, including frigidity and impotence, is common.

The 23/32 code is much more common for women than for men. Rather than indicating incapacitating symptoms, it suggests a lowered level of efficiency for prolonged periods. Problems are longstanding, and the 23/32 person has learned to tolerate a great deal of unhappiness. Among psychiatric patients, the diagnosis most frequently assigned to persons with the 23/32 code is depressive disorder. Antisocial personality disorder diagnoses are very rare among persons with this code type.

Response to traditional psychotherapy is likely to be poor for the 23/32 persons. They are not introspective; they lack insight into their own behavior; they resist psychological formulations of their problems; and they tolerate a great deal of unhappiness before becoming motivated to change.

24/42

When persons with the 24/42 code come to the attention of professionals, it usually is after they have been in trouble with their families or with the law. They are impulsive and unable to delay gratification of their impulses. They have little respect for social standards and often find themselves in direct conflict with societal values. Their acting out behavior is likely to involve excessive use of alcohol, and their histories often include alcoholic benders, arrests, job loss, and family discord associated with drinking.

24/42 persons feel frustrated by their own lack of accomplishment and are resentful of demands placed on them by other people. They may react to stress by drinking excessively or by using addictive drugs. After periods of acting out, they express a great deal of remorse and guilt about their misdeeds. They may report feeling depressed, anxious, and worthless, but these feelings do not seem to be sincere. Despite their resolutions to change, they are likely to act out again in the future. It has been noted in the literature that when scales 2 and 4 are grossly elevated, suicidal ideation and attempts are quite possible. Often the suicide attempts are directed at making other people feel guilty.

When they are not in trouble, 24/42 persons may seem to be energetic, sociable, and outgoing. They create favorable first impressions, but their tendencies to manipulate others produce feelings of resentment in long-term rela

tionships. Beneath the outer facade of competent, comfortable persons, 24/42 individuals tend to be introverted, self-conscious, and passive-dependent. They harbor feelings of inadequacy and self-dissatisfaction, and they are uncomfortable in social interactions, particularly ones involving the opposite sex. At times they appear to be rigid and overly intellectualized.

Although persons with the 24/42 code may express the need for help and the desire to change, the prognosis for traditional psychotherapy is not good. They are likely to terminate therapy prematurely when the situational stress subsides or when they have extracted themselves from their current difficulties. Even when they stay in therapy, not much improvement is likely.

27/72

27/72 individuals tend to be anxious, nervous, tense, high-strung, and jumpy. They worry excessively, and they are vulnerable to real and imagined threat. They tend to anticipate problems before they occur and to overreact to minor stress. Somatic symptoms are common among 27/72 persons. They usually involve rather vague complaints of fatigue, tiredness, and exhaustion, but insomnia, anorexia, and cardiac pain may be reported. Depression also is an important feature of the 27/72 code. Although 27/72 persons may not report feeling especially sad or unhappy, they show symptoms of clinical depression, including weight loss, slow personal tempo, and retarded thought processes. They are extremely pessimistic about the world in general and more specifically about the likelihood of overcoming their problems, and they brood about their problems much of the time.

Individuals with the 27/72 code have a strong need for achievement and for recognition for their accomplishments. They have high expectations for themselves, and they feel guilty when they fall short of their goals. They tend to be rather indecisive, and they harbor feelings of inadequacy, insecurity, and inferiority. They are intropunitive, blaming themselves for all problems in their life situations. 27/72 individuals are rigid in their thinking and problem solving, and they are meticulous and perfectionistic in their daily activities. They also may be excessively religious and extremely moralistic.

Persons with the 27/72 code tend to be rather docile and passive-dependent in their relationships with other people. In fact, they often find it difficult to be even appropriately assertive. They have the capacity for forming deep, emotional ties, and in times of stress they become overly clinging and dependent. They are not aggressive or belligerent, and they tend to elicit nurturance and helping behavior from other people. Because of the intense discomfort they experience, they are motivated for psychotherapy. They tend to remain in psychotherapy longer than many patients, and slow but steady progress can be expected.

Psychiatric patients with the 27/72 code are likely to receive a diagnosis of anxiety disorder, depressive disorder, or obsessive-compulsive disorder. Anti-

social personality disorder diagnoses are very rare among persons with this code type.

28/82

Persons with the 28/82 code report feeling anxious, agitated, tense, and jumpy. Sleep disturbance, inability to concentrate, confused thinking, and forgetfulness also are characteristic of 28/82 people. Such persons are inefficient in carrying out their responsibilities, and they tend to be unoriginal in their thinking and problem solving. They are likely to present themselves as physically ill, with somatic complaints that include dizziness, blackout spells, nausea, and vomiting. They resist psychological interpretations of their problems, and they are resistant to change. They underestimate the seriousness of their problems, and they tend to be unrealistic about their own capabilities.

28/82 individuals are basically dependent and ineffective, and they have problems in being assertive. They are irritable and resentful much of the time; they fear loss of control and do not express themselves directly. They attempt to deny undesirable impulses, and cognitive dissociative periods during which negative emotions are expressed may occur. Such periods are followed by guilt and depression. 28/82 persons are rather sensitive to the reactions of others, and they are quite suspicious of the motivations of others. They may have a history of being hurt emotionally, and they fear being hurt more. They avoid close interpersonal relationships, and they keep people at a distance emotionally. This lack of meaningful involvement with other people increases their feelings of despair and worthlessness.

If both scales 2 and 8 are very elevated, the 28/82 code suggests serious psychopathology. The most common diagnoses given to psychiatric patients with this code are bipolar disorder and schizoaffective disorder. 28/82 individuals have chronic, incapacitating symptomatology. They are guilt-ridden and appear to be clinically depressed. Withdrawal, soft and reduced speech, retarded stream of thought, and tearfulness also are common. Psychiatric patients with the 28/82 code may be preoccupied with suicidal thoughts, and they are likely to have a specific plan for doing away with themselves.

29/92

29/92 persons tend to be self-centered and narcissistic, and they ruminate excessively about self-worth. Although they may express concern about achieving at a high level, it often appears that they set themselves up for failure. In younger persons, the 29/92 code may suggest an identity crisis characterized by lack of personal and vocational direction.

29/92 persons report feeling tense and anxious, and somatic complaints, often centering in the upper gastrointestinal tract, are common. Although they

may not appear to be clinically depressed at the time that they are examined, their histories typically suggest periods of serious depression. Excessive use of alcohol may be employed as an escape from stress and pressure.

The 29/92 code is found primarily among individuals who are denying under-lying feelings of inadequacy and worthlessness and defending against depres-sion through excessive activity. Alternating periods of increased activity and fatigue may occur. Whereas the most common diagnosis for psychiatric patients with the 29/92 code is bipolar disorder, it sometimes is found for patients with brain damage who have lost emotional control or who are trying to cope with deficits through excessive activity.

34/43

The most salient characteristic of 34/43 persons is chronic, intense anger. They harbor hostile and aggressive impulses, but they are unable to express their negative feelings appropriately. If scale 3 is higher than scale 4, passive, indirect expression of anger is likely. Persons with scale 4 higher than scale 3 appear to be overcontrolled most of the time, but brief episodes of aggressive acting out may occur. Prisoners with the 4-3 code have histories of assaultive, violent crimes. In some rare instances, individuals with the 34/43 code successfully dissociate themselves from their aggressive acting out behavior. 34/43 individ-uals lack insight into the origins and consequences of their behavior. They tend to be extrapunitive and to blame other people for their difficulties. Other people may define the 34/43 person's behavior as problematic, but he or she is not likely to view it that way.

Persons with the 34/43 code are reasonably free of disabling anxiety and depression, but complaints of headaches, upper gastrointestinal discomfort, and other somatic distress may occur. Although these persons may feel upset at times, the upset does not seem to be related directly to external stress.

Most of the 34/43 person's difficulties stem from deep, chronic feelings of hostility toward family members. They demand attention and approval from others. They are very sensitive to rejection, and they become hostile when criticized. Although they appear outwardly to be socially conforming, inwardly they are quite rebellious. They may be sexually maladjusted, and marital in-stability and sexual promiscuity are common. Suicidal thoughts and attempts are characteristic of 34/43 individuals; these are most likely to follow episodes of excessive drinking and acting out behavior. Personality disorder diagnoses are most commonly associated with the 34/43 code, with passive-aggressive personality being most common.

36/63

Individuals with the 36/63 code may report moderate tension and anxiety and may have physical complaints, including headaches and gastrointestinal discom-

fort, but their problems do not seem to be acute or incapacitating. Most of their difficulties stem from deep, chronic feelings of hostility toward family members. They do not express these feelings directly, and much of the time they may not even recognize them. When they do become aware of their anger, they try to justify it in terms of the behavior of others. In general, 36/63 individuals are defiant, uncooperative, and hard to get along with. They may express mild suspiciousness and resentment about others, and they are very self-centered and narcissistic. They deny serious psychological problems and express a very naive, Pollyannaish attitude toward the world.

38/83

Persons with the 38/83 code appear to be in a great deal of psychological turmoil. They report feeling anxious, tense, and nervous. Also, they are fearful and worried, and phobias may be present. Depression and feelings of hopelessness are common among 38/83 individuals, and they have difficulties in making even minor decisions. A wide variety of physical complaints (gastrointestinal and musculoskeletal discomfort, dizziness, blurred vision, chest pain, genital pain, headaches, insomnia) may be presented. 38/83 persons tend to be quite vague and evasive when talking about their complaints and difficulties.

38/83 persons are rather immature and dependent, and they have strong needs for attention and affection. They display intropunitive reactions to frustration. They are not involved actively in their life situations, and they are apathetic and pessimistic. They approach problems in an unoriginal, stereotyped manner.

The 38/83 code suggests the presence of disturbed thinking. Individuals with this code complain of not being able to think clearly, of problems in concentration, and of lapses of memory. They express unusual, unconventional ideas, and their ideational associations may be rather loose. Obsessive ruminations, blatant delusions and/or hallucinations, and irrelevant, incoherent speech may be present. The most common diagnosis for psychiatric patients with the 38/83 code is schizophrenia, but they are sometimes diagnosed as somatoform disorders. Although response to insight-oriented psychotherapy is not likely to be good for 38/83 persons, they often benefit from a supportive psychotherapeutic relationship.

45/54

Persons with the 45/54 code tend to be rather immature and narcissistic. They are emotionally passive, and they harbor very strong unrecognized dependency needs. They have difficulty in incorporating societal values into their own personalities. They are nonconforming, and they seem to be defying convention through their dress, speech, and behavior. In the 45/54 configuration, scale 5 indicates that these individuals have adequate control and are not likely to act

out in obviously delinquent ways. However, a low frustration tolerance, coupled with intense feelings of anger and resentment, can lead to brief periods of aggressive acting out. Temporary remorse and guilt may follow the acting out behavior, but 45/54 persons are not likely to be able to inhibit similar episodes in the future. The modal diagnosis for psychiatric patients with the 45/54 code is passive-aggressive personality disorder.

45/54 persons are likely to be experiencing difficulty with sex role identity. They are rebelling against stereotyped sex roles, and overt homosexuality is a definite possibility, particularly if scales 4 and 5 are markedly elevated. Males with the 45/54 code fear being dominated by females, and they are extremely sensitive to demands of females.

46/64

Persons with the 46/64 code are immature, narcissistic, and self-indulgent. They are passive-dependent individuals who make excessive demands on others for attention and sympathy, but they are resentful of even the most mild demands made on them by others. Females with the 46/64 code seem overly identified with the traditional female role and are very dependent on males. Both 46/64 males and females do not get along well with others in social situations, and they are especially uncomfortable around members of the opposite sex. They are suspicious of the motivations of others and avoid deep emotional involvement. They generally have poor work histories, and marital problems are quite common. Repressed hostility and anger are characteristic of 46/64 persons. They appear to be irritable, sullen, argumentative, and generally obnoxious. They seem to be especially resentful of authority and may derogate authority figures.

Individuals with the 46/64 code tend to deny serious psychological problems. They rationalize and transfer blame to others, and they accept little or no responsibility for their own behavior. They are somewhat unrealistic and grandiose in their self-appraisals. Because they deny serious emotional problems, they generally are not receptive to traditional counseling or psychotherapy.

Among psychiatric patients, diagnoses associated with the 46/64 code are about equally divided between passive-aggressive personality disorder and schizophrenia (paranoid type). In general, as the elevation of scales 4 and 6 increases and as scale 6 becomes higher than scale 4, a prepsychotic or psychotic disorder becomes more likely. 46/64 individuals present vague emotional and physical complaints. They report feeling nervous and depressed, and they are indecisive and insecure. Physical symptoms may include asthma, hay fever, hypertension, headaches, blackout spells, and cardiac complaints.

47/74

Persons with the 47/74 code may alternate between periods of gross insensitivity to the consequences of their actions and excessive concern about the effects of

their behavior. Episodes of acting out, which may include excessive drinking and sexual promiscuity, may be followed by temporary expressions of guilt and self-condemnation. However, the remorse does not inhibit further episodes of acting out. 47/74 individuals may present vague somatic complaints, including headaches and stomach pain. They also may report feeling tense, fatigued, and exhausted. They are rather dependent, insecure individuals who require almost constant reassurance of their self-worth. In psychotherapy they tend to respond symptomatically to support and reassurance, but long-term changes in personality are unlikely.

48/84

48/84 individuals do not seem to fit into their environments. They are seen by others as odd, peculiar, and queer. They are nonconforming and resentful of authority, and they often espouse radical religious or political views. Their behavior is erratic and unpredictable, and they have marked problems with impulse control. They tend to be angry, irritable, and resentful, and they act out in asocial or antisocial ways. Crimes committed by 48/84 persons tend to be vicious and assaultive and often appear to be senseless, poorly planned, and poorly executed. Prostitution, promiscuity, and sexual deviation are fairly common among 48/84 individuals. This is the most common code among male rapists. Excessive drinking and drug abuse (particularly involving hallucinogens) may also occur. Histories of 48/84 individuals usually indicate underachievement, uneven performance, and marginal adjustment.

Persons with the 48/84 code harbor deep feelings of insecurity, and they have exaggerated needs for attention and affection. They have poor self-concepts, and it seems as if they set themselves up for rejection and failure. They may have periods during which they become obsessed with suicidal ideation. 48/84 persons are quite distrustful of other people, and they avoid close relationships. When they are involved interpersonally, they have impaired empathy and try to manipulate others into satisfying their needs. They lack basic social skills and tend to be socially withdrawn and isolated. The world is seen as a threatening and rejecting place, and their response is to withdraw or to strike out in anger as a defense against being hurt. They accept little responsibility for their own behavior, and they rationalize excessively, blaming their difficulties on other people. 48/84 persons tend to harbor serious concerns about their masculinity or femininity. They may be obsessed with sexual thoughts, but they are afraid that they cannot perform adequately in sexual situations. They may indulge in antisocial sexual acts in an attempt to demonstrate sexual adequacy.

Psychiatric patients with the 48/84 code tend to be diagnosed as schizophrenia (paranoid type) or antisocial, schizoid, or paranoid personality disorder. If both scales 4 and 8 are very elevated, and particularly if scale 8 is much higher than scale 4, the likelihood of psychosis and bizarre symptomatology, including unusual thinking and paranoid suspiciousness, increases.

49/94

The most salient characteristic of 49/94 individuals is a marked disregard for social standards and values. They frequently get in trouble with the authorities because of antisocial behavior. They have poorly developed consciences, easy morals, and fluctuating ethical values. Alcoholism, fighting, marital problems, sexual acting out, and a wide array of delinquent acts are among the difficulties in which they may be involved. This is a common code among persons who abuse alcohol and other substances.

49/94 individuals are narcissistic, selfish, and self-indulgent. They are quite impulsive and are unable to delay gratification of their impulses. They show poor judgment, often acting without considering the consequences of their acts, and they fail to learn from experience. They are not willing to accept responsibility for their own behavior, rationalizing shortcomings and failures and blaming difficulties on other people. They have a low tolerance for frustration, and they often appear to be moody, irritable, and caustic. They harbor intense feelings of anger and hostility, and these feelings get expressed in occasional emotional outbursts.

49/94 persons tend to be ambitious and energetic, and they are restless and overactive. They are likely to seek out emotional stimulation and excitement. In social situations they tend to be uninhibited, extroverted, and talkative, and they create a good first impression. However, because of their self-centeredness and distrust of people, their relationships are likely to be superficial and not particularly rewarding. They seem to be incapable of deep emotional ties, and they keep others at an emotional distance. Beneath the facade of self-confidence and security, the 49/94 individuals are immature, insecure, and dependent persons who are trying to deny these feelings. A diagnosis of antisocial personality disorder is usually associated with the 49/94 code, although patients occasionally are diagnosed as having a bipolar disorder.

68/86

Persons with the 68/86 code harbor intense feelings of inferiority and insecurity. They lack self-confidence and self-esteem, and they feel guilty about perceived failures. Withdrawal from everyday activities and emotional apathy are common, and suicidal ideation may be present. 68/86 persons are not emotionally involved with other people. They are suspicious and distrustful of others, and they avoid deep emotional ties. They are seriously deficient in social skills, and they are most comfortable when alone. They are quite resentful of demands placed on them, and other people see them as moody, irritable, unfriendly, and negativistic. In general, their life-styles can be characterized as schizoid.

Although some persons with the 68/86 code are diagnosed as paranoid or schizoid personality disorders, among psychiatric patients this configuration usually is associated with a diagnosis of schizophrenia (paranoid type), par-

ticularly if scales 6 and 8 are considerably higher than scale 7. 68/86 individuals are likely to manifest clearly psychotic behavior. Thinking is described as autistic, fragmented, tangential, and circumstantial, and thought content is likely to be bizarre. Difficulties in concentrating and attending, deficits in memory, and poor judgment are common. Delusions of persecution and/or grandeur and hallucinations may be present, and feelings of unreality may be reported. Persons with the 68/86 code often are preoccupied with abstract or theoretical matters to the exclusion of specific, concrete aspects of their life situations. Affect may be blunted, and speech may be rapid and at times incoherent. Effective defenses seem to be lacking, and these persons respond to stress and pressure by withdrawing into fantasy and daydreaming. Often it is difficult for the 68/86 persons to differentiate between fantasy and reality. Medical consultation to determine appropriateness of psychotropic medication should be considered.

69/96

69/96 individuals are rather dependent and have strong needs for affection. They are vulnerable to real or imagined threat, and they feel anxious and tense much of the time. In addition, they may appear to be tearful and trembling. A marked overreaction to minor stress also is characteristic of persons with the 69/96 code. A typical response to severe stress is withdrawal into fantasy. 69/96 individuals are unable to express emotions in an adaptive, modulated way, and they may alternate between overcontrol and direct, undercontrolled emotional outbursts.

Psychiatric patients with the 69/96 code almost always receive a diagnosis of schizophrenia, paranoid type, and they are likely to show signs of a thought disorder. They complain of difficulties in thinking and concentrating, and their stream of thought is retarded. They are ruminative, overideational, and obsessional. They may have delusions and hallucinations, and their speech seems to be irrelevant and incoherent. They appear to be disoriented and perplexed, and they may show poor judgment.

78/87

78/87 individuals typically are in a great deal of turmoil. They are not hesitant to admit to psychological problems, and they seem to lack adequate defenses to keep themselves reasonably comfortable. They report feeling depressed, worried, tense, and nervous. When first seen professionally, they may appear to be confused and in a state of panic. They show poor judgment and do not seem to profit from experience. They are introspective and are characterized as ruminative and overideational.

Persons with the 78/87 code harbor chronic feelings of insecurity, inadequacy, and inferiority, and they tend to be quite indecisive. They lack even an average number of socialization experiences, and they are not socially poised or confident. As a result, they withdraw from social interactions. They are passive-dependent individuals who are unable to take a dominant role in interpersonal relationships. Mature heterosexual relationships are especially difficult for 78/87 persons. They feel quite inadequate in the traditional sex role, and sexual performance may be poor. In an apparent attempt to compensate for these deficits, they engage in rich sexual fantasies.

Diagnoses of schizophrenia, depressive disorders, obsessive-compulsive disorders, and personality disorders are all represented among individuals with the 78/87 code. Schizoid is the most common personality disorder diagnosis assigned to persons with this code. The relative elevations of scales 7 and 8 are important in differentiating psychotic from nonpsychotic disorders. As scale 8 becomes greater than scale 7, the likelihood of a psychotic disorder increases. Even when a psychotic label is applied, blatant psychotic symptoms may not be present.

89/98

Persons with the 89/98 code tend to be rather self-centered and infantile in their expectations of other people. They demand a great deal of attention and may become resentful and hostile when their demands are not met. Because they fear emotional involvement, they avoid close relationships and tend to be socially withdrawn and isolated. They seem especially uncomfortable in heterosexual relationships, and poor sexual adjustment is common.

89/98 persons also are characterized as hyperactive and emotionally labile. They appear to be agitated and excited, and they may talk excessively in a loud voice. They are unrealistic in self-appraisal, and they impress others as grandiose, boastful, and fickle. They are vague, evasive, and denying when they talk about their difficulties, and they may state that they do not need professional help.

Although 89/98 persons have a high need to achieve and may feel pressured to do so, their actual performance tends to be mediocre. Their feelings of inferiority and inadequacy and their low self-esteem limit the extent to which they involve themselves in competitive or achievement-oriented situations.

The 89/98 code is suggestive of serious psychological disturbance, particularly if scales 8 and 9 are grossly elevated. The modal diagnosis for 89/98 persons is schizophrenia. Severe disturbance in thinking is likely. 89/98 individuals are confused, perplexed, and disoriented, and they report feelings of unreality. They have difficulty concentrating and thinking, and they are unable to focus on issues. Thinking also may appear to be odd, unusual, autistic, and circumstantial. Speech may be bizarre and may involve clang associations, neologisms,

and echolalia. Delusions and hallucinations may be present. The 89/98 code frequently is found among adolescents who are using drugs.

THREE-POINT CODE TYPES

As stated earlier in this chapter, three-point code types tell us which three clinical scales are the highest ones in the profile. Far less research has been conducted concerning three-point codes than concerning two-point codes or single-scale scores. The three-point codes included in this section are those that occur reasonably frequently in a variety of clinical settings and for which some research data are available. Because profiles classified according to three-point codes result in rather homogeneous groupings, the descriptors presented for any particular code are likely to fit many individuals with that code rather well. However, it must again be emphasized that the descriptions provided represent modal patterns. Not every descriptor will apply to every person with a particular three-point code.

123/213/231

Persons with this code usually are diagnosed as somatoform disorder, anxiety disorder, or depressive disorder. Somatic complaints, particularly those associated with the gastrointestinal system, are common, and often there appears to be clear secondary gain associated with the symptoms. Sleep disturbance, perplexity, despondency, and feelings of hopelessness occur. Persons with this code are in conflict about dependency and self-assertion, and they often keep other people at an emotional distance. They tend to have a low energy level, and they are lacking in sex drive. Such persons often show good work and marital adjustment, but they rarely take risks in their lives.

132/312

This configuration, in which scales 1 and 3 often are significantly higher than scale 2, has been referred to as the "conversion valley." Persons with this code type may show classic conversion symptoms, and diagnoses of conversion disorder or somatoform pain disorder are common. Stress is often converted into physical symptoms. Persons with this code use denial and repression excessively, they lack insight into the causes of their symptoms, and they resist psychological explanations of their problems. Although these individuals tend to be rather sociable, they tend to be passive-dependent in relationships. It is important for them to be liked and approved of by others, and their behavior typically is conforming and conventional.

138

Persons with this code usually are diagnosed as schizophrenic disorder (paranoid type) or paranoid personality disorder. They are likely to have rather bizarre somatic symptoms that may be delusional in nature. Depressive episodes and suicidal preoccupation, as well as sexual and religious preoccupation, may occur. Clear evidence of thought disorder may be observed. These individuals are agitated, excitable, loud, and short-tempered. They often have histories of excessive use of alcohol and feel restless and bored much of the time. They are ambivalent about forming close relationships, and they often feel suspicious and jealous.

139

Persons with this code type often are diagnosed as somatoform disorder or organic brain syndrome. If they have the latter diagnosis, they may show spells of irritation, assaultiveness, and temper outbursts.

247/274/472

The modal diagnosis for persons with this code is passive-aggressive personality disorder, and symptoms of depression and anxiety may be present. This is a very common code type among patients who abuse alcohol and/or other substances. Family and marital problems are common among these individuals, who may feel fearful, worried, and high-strung. They overreact to stress and undercontrol impulses. They tend to be angry, hostile, and immature, with strong unfilled needs for attention and support. They are in conflict about dependency and sexuality. They tend to be phobic, ruminative, and overideational and experience guilt associated with anger. Although they often have strong achievement needs, they are afraid to compete for fear of failing. They have difficulty enduring anxiety during treatment, and they may respond best to directive, goal-oriented treatment.

278/728

Persons with this code often present a mixed picture diagnostically. They are experiencing a great deal of emotional turmoil, and they tend to have a rather schizoid life-style. Brief, acute psychotic episodes may occur. They tend to feel tense, nervous, and fearful, and they have problems in concentrating and attending. They feel depressed, despondent, and hopeless, and they often ruminate about suicide. Affect appears to be blunted or otherwise inappropriate. These persons lack basic social skills and are shy, withdrawn, introverted, and

socially isolated. They feel inadequate and inferior. They tend to set high standards for themselves and to feel guilty when the standards are not met. They tend to show interest in obscure, esoteric subjects.

687/867

This code type, in which scales 6 and 8 typically are much more elevated than scale 7, has been referred to as the "psychotic valley." It suggests very serious psychopathology, and the most common diagnosis for persons with the code type is schizophrenic disorder (paranoid type). Hallucinations, delusions, and extreme suspiciousness are common. Affect tends to be blunted. Persons with this code tend to be shy, introverted, and socially withdrawn, but they may become quite aggressive when drinking. They tend to have problems with memory and concentration. Although persons with this code type may not be experiencing disabling emotional turmoil, they often are unable to handle the responsibilities of everyday life and require inpatient treatment. Psychotropic medications often are prescribed.

OTHER CONFIGURAL ASPECTS

Regardless of their absolute elevations and whether or not they are the highest scales in the profile, the relative elevations of scales 1, 2, and 3 provide important interpretive information. When scales 1 and 3 are 10 or more T-score points higher than scale 2, individuals probably are using denial and repression excessively. They tend to have little or no insight into their own needs, conflicts, or symptoms. They are reasonably free of depression, anxiety, and other emotional turmoil, but somatic symptoms are likely. These persons want medical explanations for their problems, resisting psychological explanations. When scale 2 is equal to or higher than scales 1 and 3, the individuals are not likely to be so well defended, and they may report a wide variety of symptoms and complaints.

The relationship between scales 3 and 4 gives important information about impulse control. Even when these two scales are not the most elevated ones in the profile, their relative positions are meaningful. When scale 4 is 10 or more T-score points higher than scale 3, we expect problems with impulse control. Such persons tend to act without adequately considering the consequences of their actions. When scale 3 is 10 or more T-score points higher than scale 4, we expect persons to have adequate control and not to act impulsively. When scores on scales 3 and 4 are about equally elevated, and especially when they are both above T-scores of 65, persons may be overly controlled and not even appropriately assertive most of the time, but periods of impulsive acting out may occur.

Scale 5's position in the profile of male subjects also tells us something about control. Regardless of the scores on other scales in the profile, elevation of scale

5 suggests an element of control. High scale 5 men are not likely to act out impulsively. Hathaway and Monachesi (1963) found that even in environments where the base rate for delinquency was very high, adolescent boys who scored high on scale 5 did not become involved in delinquent acts.

A profile configuration in which scales 4 and 6 are at above average levels suggests rather intense anger that is expressed in rather passive-aggressive ways. This configuration occurs for both men and women, but it is more common for women and often is accompanied by scale 5 scores that are lower than would be expected for their educational levels. Women with this configuration often have mislabeled their feelings and present themselves as depressed rather than angry. They may feel trapped in a role (e.g., housewife, mother) that is not very satisfying to them.

The relationship between scales 7 and 8 gives important information about chronicity of problems and about the likelihood of thought disorder. When scale 7 is 10 or more T-score points greater than scale 8, problems tend to be acute rather than chronic and thought disorder is not likely. As scale 8 becomes greater than scale 7, problems tend to be more chronic, and the likelihood of thought disorder increases. When both scales 7 and 8 are elevated, persons may be rather confused, but a well-developed delusional system is not to be expected.

6

Content Interpretation

In the construction of the original MMPI scales, Hathaway and McKinley utilized empirical keying procedures. Items were included in a scale if they empirically differentiated between external criterion groups. No emphasis was placed on the content of the items identified in this manner, and only for scale 7 were attempts made to ensure that the resulting scales were homogeneous or internally consistent. In fact, early in the history of the MMPI some clinicians seemed to believe that examination of the content of items endorsed by test subjects would spoil the empirical approach to assessment.

More recently, clinicians and researchers have become increasingly aware that consideration of item content adds significantly to MMPI interpretation. The purpose of this chapter is to discuss some approaches to the interpretation of the content dimensions in the MMPI-2. It should be emphasized that these approaches are viewed as supplementary to the interpretation of the standard MMPI-2 scales and should not be used instead of the standard scales.

THE HARRIS-LINGOES SUBSCALES

Subscale Development

As mentioned above, the standard MMPI clinical scales were constructed by empirical keying procedures. Because little attention was given by Hathaway and McKinley to scale homogeneity, most of the standard clinical scales are quite heterogeneous in terms of item content. The same total raw score on a clinical scale can be achieved by individuals endorsing combinations of quite different kinds of items. A number of investigators have suggested that the systematic analysis of these subgroups of items within the standard clinical scales can add significantly to the interpretation of protocols (e.g., Comrey, 1957abc, 1958bcde; Comrey & Marggraff, 1958; Graham, Schroeder, & Lilly, 1971; Harris & Lingoes, 1955, 1968; Pepper & Strong, 1958). The subscales developed by Harris and Lingoes represent the most comprehensive effort of this kind. Their scales have come to be widely used clinically and are routinely scored and reported by some of the automated scoring and interpretation services.

Harris and Lingoes (1955, 1968) reported the construction of subscales for six of the 10 standard clinical scales (scales 2, 3, 4, 6, 8, and 9). They did not develop subscales for scales 1 or 7 because they considered them homogeneous in content. Whereas a factor analytic study by Comrey (1957b) suggested that Harris and Lingoes were correct about the unidimensionality of scale 1, factor analyses of scale 7 items have not been as conclusive. Comrey (1958d) factor-analyzed scale 7 item responses and identified several factors, but Strenger (1989) was not able to develop reliable and valid subscales for scale 7, largely because of the homogeneity of the scale. Harris and Lingoes did not develop subscales for scale 5 and 0, because those scales were not considered standard clinical scales. Subsequent efforts to develop subscales for scale 5 and 0 will be discussed later in this chapter.

Each of the Harris-Lingoes subscales was constructed logically by examining the content of items within a standard clinical scale and grouping together items that seemed similar in content or were judged to reflect a single attitude or trait. A label was assigned to each subscale on the basis of the investigators' clinical judgments of the content of items in the subscale. Although it was assumed that the resulting subscales would be more homogeneous than their parent scales, no statistical estimates of homogeneity were provided by Harris and Lingoes. Altogether 31 subscales were developed, but three subscales that are obtained by summing scores on other subscales generally are not used in clinical interpretation.

Because the MMPI-2 includes most of the items in the standard clinical scales, the Harris-Lingoes subscales can be scored. Several changes were made in the subscales from the original MMPI to the MMPI-2. First, several items that are scored on some of the subscales were deleted, so those scales have fewer items in the MMPI-2 than in the original MMPI. Although only a few items were deleted, some of the subscales were already so short that deletions are of serious concern. Second, Harris and Lingoes included in some of the subscales items that were not on the parent scales, apparently because they were using preliminary versions of some of the clinical scales. In the MMPI-2 the items found in the subscales but not in the parent scales have been deleted from the subscales. Finally, the Harris-Lingoes subscales have been renumbered to eliminate the lettered subscripts for some of the subscales.

Table 6.1 presents the names of the 28 Harris-Lingoes subscales and the number of items in each scale. Appendix D presents the MMPI-2 booklet numbers of items for each scale and the scored response for each item. NCS offers scoring templates and profile sheets for the Harris-Lingoes subscales. Appendix E presents linear T-score transformations for raw scores on each of the subscales.

Harris and Lingoes did not avoid placing an item in more than one subscale. Thus, item overlap among the subscales is considerable and may account for the high correlations between subscales. Table 6.2 summarizes these intercorrelations for the MMPI-2 standardization samples.

Table 6.1. Internal consistency (Alpha) and test-retest coefficients, Harris-Lingoes subscales

	Subscale	Internal Consistency[a]		Test-retest Reliability[b]	
		Males (N = 1138)	Females (N = 1462)	Males (N = 82)	Females (N = 111)
D1	Subjective Depression	.71	.74	.85	.84
D2	Psychomotor Retardation	.24	.28	.74	.76
D3	Physical Malfunctioning	.23	.29	.64	.74
D4	Mental Dullness	.60	.63	.76	.81
D5	Brooding	.63	.65	.81	.77
Hy1	Denial of Social Anxiety	.73	.74	.86	.85
Hy2	Need for Affection	.64	.62	.76	.80
Hy3	Lassitude-Malaise	.67	.73	.86	.88
Hy4	Somatic Complaints	.59	.68	.81	.77
Hy5	Inhibition of Aggression	.17	.11	.61	.68
Pd1	Familial Discord	.51	.57	.81	.73
Pd2	Authority Problems	.31	.23	.68	.62
Pd3	Social Imperturbability	.57	.55	.85	.77
Pd4	Social Alienation	.48	.52	.81	.75
Pd5	Self Alienation	.62	.67	.78	.78
Pa1	Persecutory Ideas	.59	.64	.78	.69
Pa2	Poignancy	.39	.43	.66	.69
Pa3	Naiveté	.56	.57	.58	.73
Sc1	Social Alienation	.66	.69	.78	.75
Sc2	Emotional Alienation	.29	.34	.69	.74
Sc3	Lack of Ego Mastery, Cognitive	.66	.68	.68	.64
Sc4	Lack of Ego Mastery, Conative	.58	.62	.76	.81
Sc5	Lack of Ego Mastery, Defective Inhibition	.50	.56	.72	.70
Sc6	Bizarre Sensory Experiences	.64	.66	.78	.67
Ma1	Amorality	.29	.32	.72	.78
Ma2	Psychomotor Acceleration	.53	.50	.81	.68
Ma3	Imperturbability	.43	.46	.65	.70
Ma4	Ego Inflation	.32	.48	.74	.58

[a]Cronbach's coefficient Alpha

[b]Average retest interval was nine days

Source: Unpublished data from MMPI Restandardization Project. John R. Graham, Department of Psychology, Kent State University, Kent, OH 44242.

Table 6.2. Intercorrelations for Harris-Lingoes subscales for 1138 males and 1462 females in the standardization sample

	D	D1	D2	D3	D4	D5
D	—	88	56	58	77	67
D1	85	—	43	45	85	83
D2	61	44	—	08	40	20
D3	52	41	87	—	41	34
D4	70	82	36	34	—	70
D5	57	79	20	25	65	—

	Hy	Hy1	Hy2	Hy3	Hy4	Hy5
Hy	—	35	40	52	52	31
Hy1	39	—	32	−25	−22	15
Hy2	54	32	—	−30	−32	28
Hy3	43	−27	−28	—	54	−17
Hy4	45	−20	−25	53	—	−15
Hy5	47	16	36	−09	−09	—

	Pd	Pd1	Pd2	Pd3	Pd4	Pd5
Pd	—	68	46	13	68	73
Pd1	63	—	17	−15	46	49
Pd2	52	19	—	32	15	15
Pd3	13	−12	25	—	−10	−22
Pd4	66	39	21	−07	—	71
Pd5	67	41	21	−26	69	—

	Pa	Pa1	Pa2	Pa3
Pa	—	50	62	38
Pa1	48	—	36	−39
Pa2	57	32	—	−19
Pa3	44	−37	−18	—

	Sc	Sc1	Sc2	Sc3	Sc4	Sc5	Sc6
Sc	—	83	56	76	74	73	75
Sc1	81	—	42	51	53	54	46
Sc2	53	39	—	36	70	27	31
Sc3	74	47	34	—	69	50	58
Sc4	72	49	68	69	—	40	43
Sc5	71	50	24	46	38	—	60
Sc6	68	38	26	49	32	55	—

	Ma	Ma1	Ma2	Ma3	Ma4
Ma	—	51	74	26	66
Ma1	57	—	24	03	21
Ma2	73	33	—	−05	41
Ma3	29	00	−13	—	−14
Ma4	64	21	41	−06	—

Note: Correlations for females are above diagonal; correlations for males are below diagonal.

Source: Unpublished data from MMPI Restandardization Project. John R. Graham, Department of Psychology, Kent State University, Kent, OH 44242.

Subscale Norms

Harris and Lingoes (1955) did not present any normative data when their subscales were first described, but a later paper (Harris & Lingoes, 1968) reported means and standard deviations for psychiatric patients at the Langley Porter Clinic. Gocka and Holloway (1963) presented means and standard deviations for 68 male veteran psychiatric patients. Appendix E presents T-score transformations for Harris-Lingoes subscale raw scores based on data from the contemporary standardization samples. These are the T-scores used to construct the profile sheets available from NCS for the Harris-Lingoes subscales.

Subscale Reliability

Table 6.1 reports internal consistency (Alpha) coefficients for men and women in the standardization sample. Although several of the subscales have rather low Alpha coefficients, most have a high degree of internal consistency. The table also reports test-retest coefficients for subsamples of the standardization subjects who took the MMPI-2 twice. The test-retest data suggest that the temporal stability of the subscales is less than that of the parent scales, but stability is adequate for most scales. As one would expect, the shorter subscales have the lower test-retest coefficients.

Subscale Validity

Although the Harris-Lingoes subscales have been in existence for more than 30 years and are used fairly widely among clinicians (largely because they are scored routinely by some automated scoring and interpretation services), only limited empirical research concerning the subscales has been published. The factor analytic work of Comrey (1957abc, 1958bcde; Comrey & Marggraff, 1958) indirectly offers some support for the construct validity of the Harris-Lingoes subscales. For each clinical scale of the MMPI (excluding scales 5 and 0), Comrey reported factor analyses of the intercorrelations of items. Although there are some significant differences between the logically derived Harris-Lingoes subscales and the corresponding factor analytically derived Comrey factors, in general the Comrey studies revealed factors within each clinical scale that are similar to the Harris-Lingoes subscales and supported Harris's notion that the clinical scales are not homogeneous and unidimensional.

Lingoes (1960) factor-analyzed scores on the Harris-Lingoes subscales and on the Wiener Subtle-Obvious subscales of the MMPI (Wiener, 1948) in an attempt to determine the statistical factor structure of the MMPI. He concluded that the dimensionality of the MMPI was more complex than that of the six standard scales from which the various subscales were derived but simpler than that of the 36 subscales (Harris-Lingoes, Wiener) included in his own factor analysis. Harris and Lingoes (1955) reasoned intuitively that the subscales should be

more homogeneous than the parent scales from which they were drawn, but they did not offer any evidence in this regard. Calvin (1974) statistically examined the homogeneity of the five Harris-Lingoes subscales for scale 2 (Depression). Separately factor-analyzing inter-item correlations for each of the five subscales, he concluded that four of the subscales appeared to be unidimensional, whereas one subscale (Psychomotor Retardation) was two-dimensional (loss of interest in life activities and inhibition of hostility). Examination of the internal consistency coefficients in Table 6.1 indicates that there is considerable variability among the Harris-Lingoes subscales. Some of them, such as D1 (Subjective Depression) and Hy1 (Denial of Social Anxiety), have good internal consistency, whereas others, such as D2 (Psychomotor Retardation) and Hy5 (Inhibition of Aggression), have very poor internal consistency.

Harris and Christiansen (1946) studied pretherapy MMPI differences between neurotic patients who were judged to have been successful in psychotherapy and similar patients who were judged to have been unsuccessful. They found that the successful patients scored lower on scales 4, 6, 8, and 9 of the MMPI, suggesting that they had more ego strength. Significant differences between successful and unsuccessful patients also were identified for eight Harris-Lingoes subscales. Successful patients scored lower on the Familial Discord, Authority Problems, and Social Alienation subscales of scale 4, on the Persecutory Ideas subscale of scale 6, and on the Defective Inhibition and Bizarre Sensory Experiences subscales of scale 8. Harris and Christiansen did not consider whether greater accuracy of prediction of psychotherapy outcome was possible with the subscales than with only the standard clinical scales. They felt, however, that the subscale information could lead to a better understanding of how successful therapy patients view themselves and the environments in which they live.

Gocka and Holloway (1963) correlated the scores of psychiatric patients on the Harris-Lingoes subscales with their scores on other MMPI scales assessing social desirability, introversion-extroversion, and dissimulation; with a number of demographic variables (intelligence, occupational level, marital status); with legal competency status at the time of hospital admission; and with number of days of hospitalization. Most Harris-Lingoes subscales were related to the social desirability scale, and some subscales were related to the introversion-extroversion and dissimulation scales. Few significant correlations were found between Harris-Lingoes subscale scores and demographic variables. Two subscale scores correlated significantly with competency status, and no subscale correlated significantly with length of hospitalization.

Panton (1959) compared the Harris-Lingoes subscale scores of black and white prison inmates. He found that whites scored higher on Authority Problems, suggesting that whites had more authority problems and aggressive tendencies than blacks. Blacks scored higher on Persecutory Ideas, Social Alienation, and Ego Inflation, suggesting more psychotic trends for blacks than for whites. Panton also compared the Harris-Lingoes subscale scores of prison inmates with the psychiatric norms presented by Harris and Lingoes (1968). He found that

inmates' scores were higher than those of the psychiatric patients on the Social Alienation, Self Alienation, and Amorality subscales. Inmates' scores were lower than those of psychiatric patients on the Subjective Depression, Psychomotor Retardation, Mental Dullness, Need for Affection, Lassitude-Malaise, Inhibition of Aggression, Lack of Cognitive Ego Mastery, Lack of Conative Ego Mastery, and Psychomotor Acceleration subscales.

Calvin (1975) attempted to identify empirical behavioral correlates for the Harris-Lingoes subscales for a sample of hospitalized psychiatric patients. He compared high scorers on each Harris-Lingoes subscale with other scorers on that subscale on a number of extratest variables, including psychiatric diagnosis, reasons for hospitalization, nurses' ratings, and psychiatrists' ratings. Although 10 of the 28 subscales were determined to have reliable behavioral correlates, Calvin concluded that in most cases the subscales are not likely to add significantly to protocol analysis based on the standard clinical scales for psychiatric patients. The results of Calvin's study are included in the interpretive descriptions presented in the following section.

Interpretation of Harris-Lingoes Subscales

Scores on the Harris-Lingoes subscales provide information concerning the kinds of items that subjects endorsed in the scored direction to obtain a particular score on a clinical scale. Although such information is generally useful, there are two circumstances in which it seems especially helpful. First, it can help to explain why a subject receives an elevated score on a clinical scale when that elevation was not expected from history and other information available to the clinician. For example, a patient whose primary symptom is depression could produce a profile with elevations on scales 2, 7, and 8. The scale 2 and 7 elevations are consistent with history and clinical observation. However, the scale 8 elevation is somewhat troublesome. Why does this patient, for whom there is no history or clinical indication of schizophrenia or thought disorder, score relatively high on scale 8? Reference to the Harris-Lingoes subscale scores might reveal that most of the scale 8 elevation results from items in the Sc4 (Lack of Conative Ego Mastery) subscale. This subscale assesses feelings of depression and despair and of life's being a strain much of the time. These characteristics are very consistent with those based on the rest of the profile and with the patient's history.

Second, the Harris-Lingoes subscales can be very useful in interpreting clinical scale scores that are marginally elevated (T = 60–65). Often it does not seem that many of the interpretations suggested for a high score on a scale are appropriate for the less-elevated scores. For example, there would be some reluctance to attribute the antisocial characteristics often suggested for high scores on scale 4 to a subject receiving a T-score of 67 on that scale. The Harris-Lingoes subscales could be very helpful in this instance. A high score on Pd1 (Familial Discord), for example, could explain the moderately elevated score on

scale 4 without requiring inferences about more deviant asocial or antisocial behaviors.

As with the other supplementary scores discussed in this book, it is not possible to establish absolutely firm cutoff scores to define high and low scorers on the subscales. As clinicians gain experience with the subscales, they will come to establish cutoff scores for the settings in which the MMPI-2 is used. The individual who is just beginning to use the subscales for MMPI-2 interpretation should find it useful to consider T-scores greater than 65 as high scores and T-scores less than 40 as low scores.

The descriptions that follow for high and low scorers on each of the subscales are based on the descriptions provided by Harris and Lingoes (1955, 1968), the validity studies reviewed in the previous section, the author's own clinical experience, and examination of the content of the items in each subscale. These descriptions should be used to generate hypotheses about subjects that can be validated from other data sources. They are modal and as such will not apply completely to every examinee who achieves high or low scores on the subscales. It should be emphasized again that the Harris-Lingoes subscales should be used to supplement the standard validity and clinical scales and should not replace them.

Subjective Depression (D1)

High scores on the D1 subscale indicate persons who:

1. feel unhappy, blue, or depressed much of the time
2. lack the energy to cope with the problems of their everyday lives
3. are not interested in what goes on around them
4. feel nervous or tense much of the time
5. have difficulties concentrating and attending
6. have a poor appetite and trouble sleeping
7. brood and cry frequently
8. lack self-confidence
9. feel inferior and useless
10. are easily hurt by criticism
11. feel uneasy, shy, and embarrassed in social situations
12. tend to avoid interactions with other people, except for relatives and close friends
13. if hospitalized psychiatric patients, are likely to receive a diagnosis of depressive disorder

Low scores on the D1 subscale indicate persons who:

1. feel happy and satisfied
2. are interested in and stimulated by their environments
3. deny tension, difficulties in concentration and attention, poor appetite, sleep disturbances, and frequent brooding or crying

4. are self-confident
5. are socially extroverted
6. like to be around other people
7. are at ease in social situations

Psychomotor Retardation (D2)

High scores on the D2 subscale indicate persons who:

1. are characterized as immobilized and withdrawn
2. lack the energy to cope with everyday activities
3. avoid other people
4. deny hostile or aggressive impulses or actions

Low scores on the D2 subscale indicate persons who:

1. describe themselves as active and involved
2. have no difficulty getting started on things
3. view everyday life as interesting and rewarding
4. admit having hostile and aggressive impulses at times

Physical Malfunctioning (D3)

High scores on the D3 subscale indicate persons who:

1. are preoccupied with their own physical functioning
2. deny good health
3. report a wide variety of specific somatic symptoms that may include weakness, hay fever or asthma, poor appetite, nausea or vomiting, and convulsions

Low scores on the D3 subscale indicate persons who:

1. present themselves as being in good physical health
2. do not report the wide variety of specific somatic symptoms characteristic of high scorers on this subscale

Mental Dullness (D4)

High scores on the D4 subscale indicate persons who:

1. lack the energy to cope with the problems of everyday life
2. feel tense
3. complain of difficulties in concentrating
4. complain of poor memory or judgment
5. lack self-confidence
6. feel inferior to others

7. get little enjoyment out of life
8. appear to have concluded that life is no longer worthwhile

Low scores on the D4 subscale indicate persons who:

1. view life as interesting and worthwhile
2. feel capable of coping with everyday problems
3. deny tension
4. deny difficulties in concentration
5. claim that memory and judgment are satisfactory
6. are self-confident
7. compare themselves favorably with other people

Brooding (D5)

High scores on the D5 subscale indicate persons who:

1. brood, ruminate, and cry much of the time
2. lack the energy to cope with problems
3. seem to have concluded that life is no longer worthwhile
4. feel inferior, unhappy, and useless
5. are easily hurt by criticism
6. feel that they are losing control of their thought processes

Low scores on the D5 subscale indicate persons who:

1. feel happy most of the time
2. feel that life is worthwhile
3. deny lack of energy, brooding, and frequent crying
4. are self-confident
5. are not excessively sensitive to criticism

Denial of Social Anxiety (Hy1)

High scores on the Hy1 subscale indicate persons who:

1. are socially extroverted
2. feel quite comfortable in interacting with other people
3. find it easy to talk with other people
4. are not easily influenced by social standards and customs

Low scores on the Hy1 subscale indicate persons who:

1. are socially introverted
2. are shy and bashful in social situations
3. find it difficult to talk with other people
4. are greatly influenced by social standards and customs

Need for Affection (Hy2)

High scores on the Hy2 subscale indicate persons who:

1. have strong needs for attention and affection from others and fear that those needs will not be met if they are more honest about their feelings and attitudes
2. express naively optimistic and trusting attitudes toward other people
3. claim to see others as honest, sensitive, and reasonable
4. deny having negative feelings about other people
5. try to avoid unpleasant confrontations whenever possible

Low scores on the Hy2 subscale indicate persons who:

1. have very negative, critical, and suspicious attitudes toward other people
2. see others as dishonest, selfish, and unreasonable
3. admit to negative feelings toward other people who are perceived as treating them badly

Lassitude-Malaise (Hy3)

High scores on the Hy3 subscale indicate persons who:

1. feel uncomfortable and not in good health
2. feel weak, fatigued, or tired
3. do not present specific somatic complaints
4. report difficulties in concentrating, poor appetite, and sleep disturbance
5. feel unhappy and blue
6. describe their home environments as unpleasant and uninteresting

Low scores on the Hy3 subscale indicate persons who:

1. report being comfortable and in good health
2. do not have difficulties in concentrating, poor appetite, or disturbed sleep
3. feel happy and satisfied with their life situations

Somatic Complaints (Hy4)

High scores on the Hy4 subscale indicate persons who:

1. present multiple somatic complaints
2. complain of pain in heart and/or chest
3. complain of fainting spells, dizziness, or balance problems
4. complain of nausea and vomiting, poor vision, shakiness, or feeling too hot or too cold
5. utilize repression and conversion of affect
6. express little or no hostility toward other people

Low scores on the Hy4 subscale indicate persons who:

1. do not report the multiple somatic symptoms characteristic of high scorers on the scale
2. admit to hostility and other negative feelings

Inhibition of Aggression (Hy5)

High scores on the Hy5 subscale indicate persons who:

1. deny hostile and aggressive impulses
2. say they are not interested in reading about crime and violence
3. are sensitive about how others respond to them
4. say they are decisive

Low scores on the Hy5 subscale indicate persons who:

1. admit to hostile and aggressive impulses
2. express interest in reading about crime and violence
3. see themselves as indecisive
4. say they are not very concerned about how other people view them

Familial Discord (Pd1)

High scores on the Pd1 subscale indicate persons who:

1. describe their home and family situations as quite unpleasant
2. have felt like leaving their home situations
3. describe their homes as lacking in love, understanding, and support
4. describe their families as critical, quarrelsome, and refusing to permit adequate freedom and independence

Low scores on the Pd1 subscale indicate persons who:

1. describe their home and family situations in very positive terms
2. see their families as offering love, understanding, and support
3. describe their families as not being overly controlling or domineering

Authority Problems (Pd2)

High scores on the Pd2 subscale indicate persons who:

1. resent societal and parental standards and customs
2. admit to having been in trouble in school or with the law
3. have definite opinions about what is right and wrong
4. stand up for what they believe
5. are not greatly influenced by the values and standards of others

Low scores on the Pd2 subscale indicate persons who:

1. tend to be very socially conforming and accepting of authority
2. do not express personal opinions or beliefs openly
3. are easily influenced by other people
4. deny having been in trouble in school or with the law

Social Imperturbability (Pd3)

High scores on the Pd3 subscale indicate persons who:

1. present themselves as comfortable and confident in social situations
2. like to interact with other people
3. experience no difficulty in talking with other people
4. tend to be somewhat exhibitionistic and show-offish
5. have strong opinions about many things and are not reluctant to defend them vigorously

Low scores on the Pd3 subscale indicate persons who:

1. experience a great deal of discomfort and anxiety in social situations
2. do not like to meet new people
3. find it difficult to talk in interpersonal situations
4. are socially conforming
5. do not express personal opinions and attitudes openly

Social Alienation (Pd4)

High scores on the Pd4 subscale indicate persons who:

1. feel alienated, isolated, and estranged
2. believe that other people do not understand them
3. feel lonely, unhappy, and unloved
4. feel that they get a raw deal from life
5. blame other people for their problems and shortcomings
6. are concerned about how other people react to them
7. are self-centered and insensitive to the needs and feelings of others
8. act in inconsiderate ways toward other people
9. verbalize regret and remorse for their actions

Low scores on the Pd4 subscale indicate persons who:

1. feel that they belong in their social environments
2. see other people as loving, understanding, and supportive
3. find interpersonal relationships gratifying
4. are not overly influenced by the values and attitudes of others
5. are willing to settle down; find security in routine

Self Alienation (Pd5)

High scores on the Pd5 subscale indicate persons who:

1. describe themselves as uncomfortable and unhappy
2. have problems concentrating
3. do not find daily life interesting or rewarding
4. verbalize regret, guilt, and remorse for past deeds but are vague about the nature of this misbehavior
5. find it hard to settle down
7. may use alcohol excessively

Low scores on the Pd5 subscale indicate persons who:

1. present themselves as comfortable and happy
2. find daily life stimulating and rewarding
3. are willing to settle down
4. deny excessive use of alcohol
5. do not express regret, remorse, or guilt about past misdeeds

Persecutory Ideas (Pa1)

High scores on the Pa1 subscale indicate persons who:

1. view the world as a threatening place
2. feel that they are getting a raw deal from life
3. feel misunderstood
4. feel that others have unfairly blamed or punished them
5. are suspicious and untrusting of other people
6. blame others for their own problems and shortcomings
7. in extreme cases may have delusions of persecution

Low scores on the Pa1 subscale indicate persons who:

1. feel that they are understood and fairly treated
2. are able to trust other people
3. do not project blame for problems and shortcomings
4. deny the persecutory ideas expressed by high scorers on this subscale

Poignancy (Pa2)

High scores on the Pa2 subscale indicate persons who:

1. see themselves as more high-strung and more sensitive than other people
2. say that they feel more intensely than others

3. feel lonely and misunderstood
4. look for risky or exciting activities to make them feel better

Low scores on the Pa2 subscale indicate persons who:

1. feel understood and accepted
2. do not present themselves as more sensitive than others
3. avoids risky or dangerous activities

Naiveté (Pa3)

High scores on the Pa3 subscale indicate persons who:

1. express extremely naive and optimistic attitudes about other people
2. see others as honest, unselfish, generous, and altruistic
3. present themselves as trusting
4. say they have high moral standards
5. deny hostility and negative impulses

Low scores on the Pa3 subscale indicate persons who:

1. have rather negative and suspicious attitudes toward other people
2. see others as dishonest, selfish, and untrustworthy
3. admit to some hostility and resentment toward people who make demands on or take advantage of them

Social Alienation (Sc1)

High scores on the Sc1 subscale indicate persons who:

1. feel that they are getting a raw deal from life
2. feel that other people do not understand them
3. feel that other people have it in for them
4. feel that other people are trying to harm them
5. describe family situations as lacking in love and support
6. feel that families treat them more as children than adults
7. feel lonely and empty
8. admit that they have never had love relationships with anyone
9. report hostility and hatred toward family members
10. avoid social situations and interpersonal relationships whenever possible

Low scores on the Sc1 subscale indicate persons who:

1. feel understood and loved
2. report having rewarding emotional involvements with other people

3. describe their family situations in positive terms
4. deny feelings of hatred and resentment toward family members

Emotional Alienation (Sc2)

High scores on the Sc2 subscale indicate persons who:

1. report feelings of depression and despair; wish they were dead
2. are apathetic and frightened
3. may exhibit sadistic and/or masochistic needs

Low scores on the Sc2 subscale indicate persons who:

1. deny feelings of depression and despair
2. are not apathetic and frightened
3. feel that life is worth living
4. deny sadistic or masochistic needs

Lack of Ego Mastery, Cognitive (Sc3)

High scores on the Sc3 subscale indicate persons who:

1. feel that they might be losing their minds
2. report strange thought processes and feelings of unreality
3. report difficulties in concentration and memory

Low scores on the Sc3 subscale indicate persons who:

1. deny concern about loss of control of thought processes
2. do not admit to strange or unusual thought processes
3. do not admit to feelings of unreality
4. do not admit difficulties in concentration and memory

Lack of Ego Mastery, Conative (Sc4)

High scores on the Sc4 subscale indicate persons who:

1. feel that life is a strain; admit feelings of depression and despair
2. have difficulty in coping with everyday problems; worry excessively
3. respond to stress by withdrawing into fantasy and daydreaming
4. do not find their daily activities interesting and rewarding
5. have given up hope of things getting better
6. may wish that they were dead

Low scores on the Sc4 subscale indicate persons who:

1. feel that life is interesting and very much worthwhile
2. have the energy to cope with everyday problems
3. deny feelings of depression, excessive worry, suicidal ideation

Lack of Ego Mastery, Defective Inhibition (Sc5)

High scores on the Sc5 subscale indicate persons who:

1. feel that they are not in control of their emotions and impulses and are frightened by this perceived loss of control
2. tend to be restless, hyperactive, and irritable
3. may have periods of laughing and crying that they cannot control
4. may report episodes during which they did not know what they were doing and later could not remember what they had done

Low scores on the Sc5 subscale indicate persons who:

1. deny concern about loss of control of impulses and emotions
2. do not admit to restlessness, hyperactivity, or irritability
3. do not admit to periods of activity that they could not control or could not later remember

Bizarre Sensory Experiences (Sc6)

High scores on the Sc6 subscale indicate persons who:

1. experience feelings that their bodies are changing in strange and unusual ways
2. report skin sensitivity, feeling hot or cold, voice changes, muscle twitching, clumsiness, problems in balance, ringing or buzzing in the ears, paralysis, weakness
3. admit to hallucinations, unusual thought content, ideas of external influence

Low scores on the Sc6 subscale indicate persons who:

1. deny bodily changes, feelings of depersonalization, and other strange experiences that are characteristic of high scorers on this subscale

Amorality (Ma1)

High scores on the Ma1 subscale indicate persons who:

1. perceive other people as selfish, dishonest, and opportunistic, and because of these perceptions feel justified in behaving in similar ways
2. seem to derive vicarious satisfaction from the manipulative exploits of others

Low scores on the Ma1 subscale indicate persons who:

1. deny that other people are selfish, dishonest, or opportunistic and find such behaviors unacceptable in themselves

2. deny receiving vicarious gratification from the manipulative exploits of others

Psychomotor Acceleration (Ma2)

High scores on the Ma2 subscale indicate persons who:

1. experience acceleration of speech, thought processes, and motor activity
2. feel tense and restless
3. feel excited or elated without cause
4. become bored easily and seek out risk, excitement, or danger as a way of overcoming the boredom
5. admit to impulses to do something harmful or shocking

Low scores on the Ma2 subscale indicate persons who:

1. are calm and placid
2. deny hyperactivity, restlessness, or tension
3. are satisfied with a life situation that many other people might judge to be dull or boring
4. avoid situations or activities involving risk or danger

Imperturbability (Ma3)

High scores on the Ma3 subscale indicate persons who:

1. deny social anxiety
2. feel comfortable around other people
3. have no problem in talking with others
4. profess little concern about or sensitivity to the opinions, values, and attitudes of other people
5. feel impatient and irritable toward others

Low scores on the Ma3 subscale indicate persons who:

1. feel quite uncomfortable around other people
2. have problems talking with others
3. are easily influenced by the opinions, values, and attitudes of those around them
4. deny resentment, impatience, and irritability toward others

Ego Inflation (Ma4)

High scores on the Ma4 subscale indicate persons who:

1. have unrealistic evaluations of their own abilities and self-worth
2. are resentful when others make demands on them, particularly if the persons making the demands are perceived as less capable

Low scores on the Ma4 subscale indicate persons who:

1. have realistic notions about their own self-worth or may even be extremely self-critical
2. deny resentment toward others who make demands on them

SERKOWNEK SUBSCALES FOR SCALES 5 AND 0

As stated previously, Harris and Lingoes (1955, 1968) did not develop subscales for scales 5 and 0. Their omission of these scales was consistent with other early research efforts that did not consider scales 5 and 0 as standard clinical scales.

An early effort by Pepper and Strong (1958), who used clinical judgment in forming subgroups of items for scale 5, received little attention among MMPI users. Graham, Schroeder, and Lilly (1971) factor-analyzed the scale 5 and 0 item responses of psychiatric inpatients, psychiatric outpatients, and normal subjects. For each of the two scales, seven factors emerged, one of which represented demographic variables included in the analyses.

Serkownek (1975) utilized the data from the Graham et al. (1971) factor analyses to develop subscales for scales 5 and 0. Items that loaded higher than .30 on a factor were selected for the scale to assess that factor dimension. Labels were assigned to the subscales on the basis of an examination of the content of the items included in the scale. Prior to the publication of the MMPI-2 the Serknownek subscales gained popularity among MMPI users. However, several concerns about these subscales led to a decision not to include them in the MMPI-2.

One major concern about Serkownek's scale 5 subscales was that the factor analysis on which they were based may have had methodological problems. Graham et al. (1971) combined male and female data in their analysis, and this could have created artificial masculine interest and feminine interest factors. Another concern was that some of the items in the Serkownek subscales were scored in the opposite direction from the parent scales. Finally, for females the raw scores on the scale 5 subscales were transformed to T-scores in the opposite direction from the parent scale. High raw scores on scale 5 subscales yielded high T-scores, whereas for scale 5 itself, higher raw scores yield lower T-scores.

SUBSCALES FOR MMPI-2 SCALE 0

Development of the Scale 0 Subscales

Ben-Porath, Hostetler, Butcher, and Graham (1989) developed scale 0 subscales for the MMPI-2 to replace the Serkownek subscales for that scale. Factor analyses of scale 0 item responses of normal college men and women were utilized to

construct provisional subscales. Internal consistency procedures were then utilized to refine the subscales. The three subscales resulting from these procedures are mutually exclusive, internally consistent, moderately independent, and representative of the major content dimensions of scale 0. Item numbers and scored directions for each of the subscales are reported in Appendix F. Linear T-score values for raw scores on the subscales can be found in Appendix G.

Reliability and Validity of Scale 0 Subscales

Internal consistency coefficients (Alphas) were computed for the subscales for college and normative samples (Ben-Porath et al., 1989). These coefficients are reported in Table 6.3. The internal consistency of the subscales compares quite favorably with that of other MMPI-2 scales and subscales.

Test-retest reliability coefficients were computed for the subscales using a subsample of 82 men and 111 women from the MMPI-2 normative samples who took the test twice with approximately a one week interval between testings (Ben-Porath et al., 1989). The test-retest coefficients are reported in Table 6.3. The temporal stability of the subscales seems to be greater than for most other MMPI-2 scales and subscales.

Ben-Porath et al. (1989) reported some preliminary validity data for the subscales. Scores on the subscales were correlated with behavioral ratings for a sample of 822 couples from the normative samples who participated in the study together and independently rated each other. The patterns of correlations were judged to offer support for the convergent and divergent validity of the subscales.

Table 6.3. Internal consistency and test-retest reliability coefficients for scale 0 subscales

| | | Alpha Coefficients | | | Test-Retest Coefficients | |
| | College | | Normative | | Normative | |
Subscale	Male (N = 525)	Female (N = 797)	Male (N = 1138)	Female (N = 1462)	Male (N = 82)	Female (N = 111)
Si1 Shyness/ Self-Consiousness	.82	.82	.81	.84	.91	.90
Si2 Social Avoidance	.77	.75	.77	.75	.88	.87
Si3 Self/Other Alienation	.77	.77	.75	.78	.77	.88

Source: Y. S. Ben-Porath, K. Hostetler, J. N. Butcher, & J. R. Graham. New subscales for the MMPI-2 Social Introversion (Si) scale. *Psychological Assessment: A Journal of Consulting and Clinical Psychology*, 1989, *1*, 169–174. Copyright © 1989 by the American Psychological Association. Adapted by permission of the publisher.

Interpretation of Scale 0 Subscales

Because the subscales have only recently been developed, only limited data are available concerning their interpretation. Examination of the content of items in the subscales and of the correlations between scores on the subscales and external behavioral ratings can be used to generate some tentative hypotheses concerning persons who score high or low on the subscales. Ben-Porath et al. (1989) recommended that T-scores of 65 or greater be considered high scores on the subscales. Although the subscale developers did not recommend any cutoff for low scores, it seems reasonable to use the same cutoff ($T < 40$) that has been recommended for other MMPI-2 scales and subscales.

Shyness/Self-Consciousness (Si1)

High scores on the Si1 subscale indicate persons who:

1. feel shy around others
2. feel easily embarrassed
3. feel ill at ease in new situations
4. are not talkative or friendly
5. lack self-confidence and give up easily

Low scores on the Si1 subscale indicate persons who:

1. are extroverted
2. initiate social contact with other people
3. are talkative and friendly
4. are self-confident and do not give up easily

Social Avoidance (Si2)

High scores on the Si2 subscale indicate persons who:

1. do not enjoy being involved with groups or crowds of people
2. actively avoid getting involved with other people

Low scores on the Si2 subscale indicate persons who:

1. enjoy being involved with groups or crowds of people
2. initiate social contact with other people

Self/Other Alienation (Si3)

High scores on the Si3 subscale indicate persons who:

1. have low self-esteem

2. lack interest in activities
3. feel unable to effect changes in their life situations

Low scores on the Si3 subscale indicate persons who:

1. have high self-esteem
2. appear to be interested in activities
3. feel able to effect changes in their life situations

WIGGINS CONTENT SCALES

Whereas Harris and Lingoes had formed content scales within individual clinical scales, Wiggins (1969) used the entire MMPI item pool to form content
scales. Starting with 26 content categories suggested by Hathaway and McKinley
(1940), Wiggins used a combination of rational and statistical procedures to
develop his scales. The resulting 13 scales were psychometrically sound and
seemed to represent well the content dimensions of the original MMPI. Unfortunately, when the MMPI was revised in 1989, Wiggins's scales were no longer
adequate. Some of his scales could no longer be scored from the MMPI-2 items
because of item deletions. In addition, the Wiggins scales did not represent
adequately the new content dimensions introduced into the MMPI-2 by the
addition of new items.

NEW CONTENT SCALES FOR MMPI-2

New content scales for MMPI-2 were developed by Butcher, Graham, Williams,
and Ben-Porath (1990) to assess the content dimensions of the revised instrument. These scales were developed using a combination of rational and statistical procedures.

Development of the Content Scales

The first step in the development of the content scales was to define clinically
relevant content areas represented by the items in Form AX of the MMPI.
Twenty-two categories were rationally identified and definitions written for
each. Three clinical psychologists served as judges and assigned items to the
content categories. They were free to add categories, if that seemed indicated,
and to assign items to more than one category. Items assigned to a category by
two or three of the judges were placed into provisional scales. Three raters then
met and reviewed all item placements. Any disagreements were discussed until

there was full agreement concerning placement. For one of the original categories, sufficient items could not be identified, so it was dropped from further consideration.

In the next step of scale development, item responses for two samples of psychiatric patients and two samples of college students were used to identify items in the provisional scales that did not correlate highly with total scores for the scales and that detracted from their internal consistency. Such items were dropped from the scales. At this stage, four additional scales were dropped from further consideration because of unacceptably low internal consistencies. Also, the data indicated that another content category, Cynicism, which had been previously identified by item factor analysis, was not represented in the content scales. Thus, a 20-item cynicism scale was added.

Another way of assuring appropriate item placement was to examine correlations between each item in the inventory and total scores on the new content scales. Items that correlated higher with a score from a scale other than the one on which it was placed were deleted or moved to the other scale.

A final step involved examination of the content of items in each content scale to determine rationally whether the items fit conceptually with the definition of the content domain. Some items that were statistically related to the total score for a scale but whose content did not seem appropriate for that scale were eliminated. This final step was judged to be important because items in the MMPI clinical scales whose content is not obviously related to the contructs being assessed do not contribute significantly to the validity of those scales. (See Chapter 7 for a discussion of Subtle-Obvious items.)

The multistage procedures used to develop the scales yielded a set of 15 scales that were judged to be internally consistent, relatively independent, and representative of clinically relevant content dimensions in the item pool. Although item overlap between scales was kept minimal, some overlap was permitted when the constructs assessed by the scales were conceptually related. Table 6.4 presents a listing of the 15 content scales. Item numbers and scored directions for each of the content scales are reported in Appendix H.

Norms for the Content Scales

Data from the male and female normative samples (Butcher, Dahlstrom, Graham, Tellegen, & Kaemmer, 1989) were used to generate T-score conversions for content scale raw scores. The same uniform T-scores used for the validity and clinical scales of MMPI-2 are used with the content scales. Raw scores for the content scales were regressed on percentile-corresponding T-scores from the uniform distribution derived for the clinical scales. This procedure permits scores for the content scales to be expressed on the same metric as the clinical scales, thus assuring comparability within the set of content scales and between content scales and clinical scales. Uniform T-score transformations for the content scales are reported separately for males and females in Appendix I.

Table 6.4. Reliability of MMPI-2 content scales

Scale		No. Items	Internal[a] Consistency		Test-retest[b] Reliability	
			Males (N = 1138)	Females (N = 1462)	Males (N = 82)	Females (N = 111)
ANX	Anxiety	23	.82	.83	.90	.87
FRS	Fears	23	.72	.75	.81	.86
OBS	Obsessiveness	16	.74	.77	.83	.85
DEP	Depression	33	.85	.86	.87	.88
HEA	Health Concerns	36	.76	.80	.81	.85
BIZ	Bizarre Mentation	24	.73	.74	.78	.81
ANG	Anger	16	.76	.73	.85	.82
CYN	Cynicism	23	.86	.85	.80	.89
ASP	Antisocial Practices	22	.78	.75	.81	.87
TPA	Type A	19	.72	.68	.82	.79
LSE	Low Self Esteem	24	.79	.83	.84	.86
SOD	Social Discomfort	24	.83	.84	.91	.90
FAM	Family Problems	25	.73	.77	.84	.83
WRK	Work Interference	33	.82	.84	.90	.91
TRT	Negative Treatment Indicators	26	.78	.80	.79	.88

[a]Cronbach's coefficient alpha.

[b]Average retest interval was nine days.

Source: J. N. Butcher, J. R. Graham, C. L. Williams, & Y. S. Ben-Porath. *Development and use of the MMPI-2 content scales*. The University of Minnesota Press, Minneapolis. Copyright © 1990 by the University of Minnesota. Reproduced by permission.

Reliability of the Content Scales

Table 6.4 reports test-retest reliability coefficients for the content scales for 82 males and 111 females in the standardization sample. The average retest interval was approximately nine days. These coefficients indicate that the content scales are quite stable over this short time interval. In fact, the content scales appear to be more reliable than the basic clinical scales.

Table 6.4 also reports internal consistency (Alpha) coefficients for the content scales based on responses of the male and female standardization samples. The internal consistency of the content scales is quite high. In general, the content scales are more internally consistent than the clinical scales and similar in internal consistency to the Wiggins scales that they were developed to replace.

Validity of the Content Scales

Butcher et al. (1990) reported several kinds of preliminary validity data for the content scales. Correlations between the content scales and other MMPI-2 scales are reported in Table 6.5. These correlational data contribute significantly to

our understanding of the construct validity of the content scales. Some of the content scales correlate very highly with standard scales, suggesting that they can be interpreted in similar ways. For example, the HEA (Health Concerns) scale and the Hs (Hypochondriasis) scale correlate .89 for men and .91 for women, suggesting that both are measures of health concern. Likewise, the SOD (Social Discomfort) scale and the Si (Social Introversion) scale correlate .85 for men and .84 for women. However, other content scales are not so highly correlated with standard scales with similar labels, suggesting that these scales are assessing some unique characteristics as well as some common ones. For example, the correlation between DEP (Depression) and D (Depression) was .52 for men and .63 for women, suggesting that these two measures of depression are not interchangeable.

Butcher et al. (1990) also presented some data concerning behavioral correlates for the content scales. More than 800 couples participated in the MMPI-2 standardization project. In addition to responding to the MMPI items, these couples, most of whom were married to each other, independently rated each other on 110 items concerning personality and behavior. Butcher et al. correlated ratings on these items and on factor scales derived from the items with scores on the content scales. The resulting correlations were used to generate behavioral descriptors for high and low scorers on each of the content scales.

Butcher et al. (1990) reported data concerning scores of chronic pain patients, psychiatric patients, and normal subjects on the HEA (Health Concerns) scale. As expected, chronic pain patients scored significantly higher than the other groups on the HEA scale. A T-score cutoff of 65 of the HEA scale correctly classified most of the chronic pain patients and incorrectly classified very few of the other subjects.

Butcher, Graham, Williams, and Ben-Porath (1990) also presented some preliminary data concerning the WRK (Negative Work Attitudes) scale scores for several groups of men who could be assumed to differ on this scale. The scores of pilot applicants, military personnel, alcoholics in treatment, and psychiatric inpatients were compared. The pilot applicants, who would be expected to have the most positive work attitudes, scored lowest on the WRK scale, whereas the alcoholics and psychiatric patients obtained the highest scores.

Clearly, more empirical data are needed before the validity of the content scales can be judged adequately. However, the preliminary data presented by the scale developers is impressive and encouraging.

Interpretation of Content Scales

Although the validity data for the content scales are limited at this time, the data presented by Butcher et al. (1990) and examination of the content of items in each content scale can be used to offer some tentative interpretive inferences about persons who score relatively high or low on each scale. As with the Harris-Lingoes subscales discussed earlier, until additional data are available, users of the content scales should consider T-scores greater than 65 as high scores and

Table 6.5. Correlations of content scales with MMPI-2 validity and clinical scales for males and females in MMPI-2 normative samples

	?	L	F	K	Hs	D	Hy	Pd	Mf	Pa	Pt	Sc	Ma	Si
						Males (N = 1138)								
ANX	−04	−27	47	−61	50	45	04	50	20	33	80	69	31	43
FRS	00	−07	24	−29	34	22	02	16	01	09	37	35	06	28
OBS	−02	−30	40	−63	40	26	−16	29	12	18	77	64	31	44
DEP	01	−17	57	−56	48	52	02	58	16	38	80	75	27	48
HEA	02	−06	47	−29	89	45	39	35	10	25	50	55	18	29
BIZ	03	−14	51	−44	38	03	−09	36	08	33	51	62	48	11
ANG	−03	−38	34	−66	33	01	−21	36	−02	15	55	53	42	19
CYN	−01	−17	39	−71	33	07	−43	26	−17	−16	51	53	42	32
ASA	−03	−34	42	−60	26	01	−36	37	−15	−12	45	50	51	18
TPA	−06	−37	29	−68	29	05	−30	22	−05	04	53	48	38	25
LSE	−01	−19	48	−52	42	42	−11	27	07	18	72	61	11	59
SOD	−01	−07	31	−31	24	39	−19	04	11	09	40	36	−20	85
FAM	02	−27	53	−55	32	21	−11	57	18	21	59	66	43	31
WRK	00	−26	53	−63	49	44	−09	41	14	21	81	73	23	59
TRT	00	−19	54	−57	46	40	−12	40	02	19	72	68	20	56
						Females (N = 1462)								
ANX	−05	−24	47	−67	58	60	17	51	10	39	83	71	34	48
FRS	−05	02	16	−41	34	20	−01	13	00	06	39	33	11	32
OBS	−04	−26	39	−69	45	40	−06	36	08	25	79	65	36	47
DEP	00	−19	58	−63	54	63	12	61	01	44	83	77	31	55
HEA	01	−07	42	−43	91	45	48	33	00	25	55	59	29	31
BIZ	00	−07	49	−46	36	11	−03	39	−14	31	51	65	50	15
ANG	−04	−34	38	−69	39	20	−06	44	00	25	62	60	44	27
CYN	−05	−08	41	−70	41	17	−24	32	−24	−06	51	54	46	35
ASA	−05	−30	41	−57	30	09	−25	37	−28	−09	44	51	51	23
TPA	−03	−29	31	−65	32	15	−16	23	−05	13	53	49	36	28
LSE	−04	−16	44	−60	44	53	−04	31	01	23	74	61	14	65
SOD	−03	−04	28	−38	24	43	−17	06	07	19	43	35	−17	84
FAM	−01	−21	56	−57	40	32	04	61	04	33	60	72	45	33
WRK	−04	−23	50	−69	52	58	02	44	04	29	82	72	27	63
TRT	−01	−15	50	−63	45	50	−05	42	−04	26	72	69	24	61

Source: J. N. Butcher, J. R. Graham, C. L. Williams, & Y. S. Ben-Porath. *Development and use of the MMPI-2 content scales*. The University of Minnesota, Minneapolis. Copyright © 1990 by the University of Minnesota. Reproduced by permission.

T-scores lower than 40 as low scores. As additional validity data accumulate, it may be possible to state more precise cutoff scores when using some of the content scales for specific purposes.

Anxiety (ANX)

High scores on the ANX scale indicate persons who:

1. feel anxious, nervous, worried, and apprehensive
2. have problems with concentration
3. complain of sleep disturbance
4. are uncomfortable making decisions

5. may report feeling sad, blue, or depressed
6. feel that life is a strain and are pessimistic about things getting better
7. lack self-confidence
8. feel overwhelmed by the responsibilities of daily life
9. if female, may appear to be irritable and hostile

Low scores on the ANX scale indicate persons who:

1. are not likely to report symptoms of anxiety or depression
2. are self-confident and decisive and feel able to meet the demands of daily life

Fears (FRS)

High scores on the FRS scale indicate persons who:

1. feel fearful and uneasy much of the time
2. report multiple specific fears or phobias

Low scores on the FRS scale indicate persons who:

1. are not generally fearful and uneasy
2. do not report multiple specific fears or phobias

Obsessiveness (OBS)

High scores on the OBS scale indicate persons who:

1. have great difficulty making decisions
2. are rigid and dislike change
3. engage in compulsive behaviors such as counting or hoarding
4. fret, worry, and ruminate about trivial things
5. may feel dysphoric and despondent; lack interest in things
6. lack self-confidence

Low scores on the OBS scale indicate persons who:

1. do not have difficulty making decisions
2. do not fret, worry, and ruminate excessively
3. can handle change in routine
4. are self-confident and interested in things

Depression (DEP)

High scores on the DEP scale indicate persons who:

1. feel depressed, sad, blue, or despondent
2. feel fatigued and lack interest in things

   3. are pessimistic and feel hopeless
   4. may recently have been preoccupied with thoughts of death and suicide
   5. cry easily
   6. are indecisive and lack self-confidence
   7. feel guilty
   8. have health concerns
   9. feel lonely and empty much of the time
10. if female, may be resentful and demanding

Low scores on the DEP scale indicate persons who:

1. are not likely to report symptoms of depression
2. have energy and are interested in things
3. are decisive and self-confident

Health Concerns (HEA)

High scores on the HEA scale indicate persons who:

1. deny good physical health
2. are preoccupied with bodily functioning
3. feel worn out and lack energy
4. report a variety of specific somatic symptoms, including some that could be suggestive of neurological disorder

Low scores on the HEA scale indicate persons who:

1. claim to be in good physical health
2. are not preoccupied with bodily functioning
3. do not report multiple specific somatic symptoms

Bizarre Mentation (BIZ)

High scores on the BIZ scale indicate persons who:

1. may have psychotic thought processes
2. may report auditory, visual, or olfactory hallucinations
3. report feelings of unreality
4. feel that other people say bad things about them
5. may believe that other people are trying to harm them
6. may believe that other people can read their minds or control their thinking or behavior

Low scores on the BIZ scale indicate persons who:

1. are not likely to have psychotic thought processes
2. probably are not reporting hallucinations, delusions, or feelings of unreality

Anger (ANG)

High scores on the ANG scale indicate persons who:

1. feel angry and hostile much of the time
2. are seen by others as irritable, grouchy, impatient, and stubborn
3. may feel like swearing or smashing things
4. have temper tantrums
5. may lose control and be physically abusive
6. if female, may express anger and hostility in passive, indirect ways

Low scores on the ANG scale indicate persons who:

1. deny feeling generally angry or hostile
2. claim not to lose control and act abusively

Cynicism (CYN)

High scores on the CYN scale indicate persons who:

1. see other people as dishonest, selfish, and uncaring
2. question the motives of others
3. are guarded and untrusting in relationships
4. may be hostile and overbearing
5. may be demanding themselves but resent even mild demands placed on them by others
6. are not friendly or helpful

Low scores on the CYN scale indicate persons who:

1. express generally positive perceptions of other people
2. are trusting in relationships
3. are not seen as hostile and overbearing
4. are friendly and helpful

Antisocial Practices (ASP)

High scores on the ASP scale indicate persons who:

1. are likely to have been in trouble in school or with the law
2. believe that there is nothing wrong with getting around laws as long as they aren't broken
3. may enjoy hearing about the antics of criminals
4. have generally cynical attitudes about other people, seeing them as selfish and dishonest
5. resent authority
6. if males, may express anger and hostility by cursing, swearing, or having temper tantrums

7. if males, may use nonprescription drugs
8. if females, may express anger and hostility less directly than males
9. if females, may be seen by others as dishonest and not helpful or considerate of others

Low scores on the ASP scale indicate persons who:

1. do not report having been in trouble in school or with the law
2. are not particularly resentful of authority
3. are not seen by others as cynical or hostile

Type A (TPA)

High scores on the TPA scale indicate persons who:

1. are hard-driving, fast-moving, and work-oriented
2. feel that there is never enough time to get things done
3. do not like to wait or be interrupted
4. frequently are hostile, irritable, and easily annoyed
5. tend to be overbearing and critical in relationships
6. tend to hold grudges and want to get even
7. if females, may be seen as tense, restless, nervous, and suspicious

Low scores on the TPA scale indicate persons who:

1. are not particularly competitive, driven, or fast-moving
2. do not feel great time pressure in getting things done
3. are not seen by others as critical and overbearing
4. are not perceived as hostile, irritable, or easily annoyed

Low Self Esteem (LSE)

High scores on the LSE scale indicate persons who:

1. have very poor self-concepts
2. anticipate failure and give up easily
3. are overly sensitive to criticism and rejection
4. find it difficult to accept compliments
5. are passive in relationships
6. have difficulty making decisions
7. may have many worries and fears

Low scores on the LSE scale indicate persons who:

1. are self-confident and expect to succeed
2. are decisive

3. are not particularly passive
4. are not especially sensitive to criticism or rejection
5. do not report many worries and fears

Social Discomfort (SOD)

High scores on the SOD scale indicate persons who:

1. are shy and socially introverted
2. would rather be alone than around other people
3. dislike parties and other group activities
4. do not initiate conversations

Low scores on the SOD scale indicate persons who:

1. are socially extroverted and sociable
2. like parties and other group activities
3. find it easy to initiate conversations

Family Problems (FAM)

High scores on the FAM scale indicate persons who:

1. describe considerable discord in their current families and/or families of origin
2. describe their families as lacking in love, understanding, and support
3. resent the demands and advice of their families
4. feel angry and hostile toward their families
5. see marital relationships as involving unhappiness and lack of affection

Low scores on the FAM scale indicate persons who:

1. describe their families in generally positive terms
2. see their families as loving, understanding, and supportive
3. deny feelings of anger and resentment toward their families
4. do not see marital relationships as involving unhappiness and lack of affection

Work Interference (WRK)

High scores on the WRK scale indicate persons who:

1. report a wide variety of attitudes and behaviors likely to contribute to poor work performance
2. may be questioning their own career choices
3. say that their families have not approved of their career choices

4. are not ambitious and are lacking in energy
5. express negative attitudes toward co-workers
6. have poor self-concepts
7. are obsessive and have problems concentrating
8. have difficulty making decisions and may show poor judgment
9. feel tense, worried, and fearful

Low scores on the WRK scale indicate persons who:

1. do not report attitudes and behaviors that are likely to contribute to poor work performance
2. seem to be ambitious and energetic
3. express positive attitudes toward co-workers
4. seem comfortable with their career choices
5. are self-confident
6. are not tense, worried, fearful, or obsessive
7. can concentrate and make decisions without great difficulty

Negative Treatment Indicators (TRT)

High scores on the TRT scale indicate persons who:

1. have negative attitudes toward doctors and mental health treatment
2. feel that no one can understand them
3. believe that they have problems that they cannot share with anyone
4. give up easily when problems are encountered
5. feel unable to make significant changes in their lives
6. are poor problem solvers
7. often show poor judgment

Low scores on the TRT scale indicate persons who:

1. have generally positive attitudes toward doctors and mental health treatment
2. believe that others can understand and help them
3. can share problems with others
4. do not give up easily when problems are encountered
5. feel capable of making significant changes in their lives
6. show good judgment and are good problem solvers

CRITICAL ITEMS

Critical items are items in the inventory whose content is judged to indicate serious psychopathology. Grayson (1951) identified the first set of MMPI critical

items, basing them on subjective clinical judgment. The 38 items dealt primarily with severe psychotic symptoms and overlapped considerably with scales F and 8. Grayson believed that responses in the scored direction to any of these items suggested potentially serious emotional problems that should be studied further. Caldwell (1969) intuitively generated a more comprehensive set of critical items that he intended for use with computerized scoring and interpretive services. Investigating the validity of the Grayson and Caldwell critical items as indicators of crises, Koss, Butcher, and Hoffman (1976) concluded that both sets of items performed poorly as indices of serious malfunctioning.

Koss-Butcher Critical Items

Koss, Butcher, and Hoffman (1976) asked clinicians to nominate MMPI items that seemed to be related to six crisis areas (acute anxiety state, depressed suicidal ideation, threatened assault, situational stress due to alcoholism, mental confusion, and persecutory ideas). The nominated items were then compared with criterion measures of the crises, resulting in a list of 73 valid critical items. Following the revision of the MMPI in 1989 the Koss-Butcher critical item set was revised to reflect changes in the item pool (Butcher, Dahlstrom, Graham, Tellegen, & Kaemmer, 1989). The revised Koss-Butcher critical items are reprinted in Appendix J.

Lachar-Wrobel Critical Items

Lachar and Wrobel (1979) used a similar approach in identifying 111 critical items related to 14 problem areas frequently encountered in inpatient and outpatient samples. All but four of the original Lachar-Wrobel critical items are included in the MMPI-2. These items are listed in Appendix J. It should be noted that the Lachar-Wrobel critical items have not been revised to include new items that were added to the original MMPI item pool.

Recommendations Concerning Use of Critical Items

Koss (1979, 1980) has summarized the usefulness of critical items, reviewing research suggesting that the Koss-Butcher and Lachar-Wrobel critical items are more valid than the Grayson or Caldwell critical items. However, she also pointed out some cautions in using critical items. All the critical item sets overlap considerably with scales F and 8, and most critical items are keyed in the true direction. Thus, critical item endorsements can be misleading for persons displaying an acquiescence response set or exaggerating their symptoms and problems.

MMPI-2 users who interpret critical item endorsements should seriously consider Koss's (1980) cautions and recommendations, noting especially her conclusion that critical items should not be used as a quick assessment of level of maladjustment. Data indicate that the critical items perform poorly in separating normal and psychiatric subjects. Also, critical item lists are not as reliable as scales because of the vulnerability of single item responses to error. A test subject can misinterpret and/or mismark a single item, leading the test interpreter to an erroneous conclusion, whereas that same mistake in the context of a longer scale would not have much impact on the individual's total score on that scale.

The potential value of using critical items is the same as with the other content approaches discussed in this chapter. Examination of the content of subjects' responses can clarify the kinds of things that they are telling us about themselves. However, critical item responses should not be overinterpreted. In a valid MMPI-2 protocol, endorsement of critical items should lead the clinician to inquire further in the areas assessed by the items.

7

Supplementary Scales

In addition to its use in the construction of the standard validity and clinical scales, the MMPI item pool was used to develop numerous other scales by variously recombining the 566 items using item analytic, factor analytic, and intuitive procedures. Dahlstrom, Welsh, and Dahlstrom (1972, 1975) presented more than 450 supplementary scales. The scales had quite diverse labels, ranging from more traditional ones, such as Dominance and Suspiciousness, to more unusual ones, such as Success in Baseball and Yeshiva College Subcultural Scale. They varied considerably in terms of what they were supposed to measure, how they were constructed, their reliabilities, the extent to which they were cross-validated, the availability of normative data, and how much additional validity data was generated. They also varied in terms of how frequently they were utilized in clinical and research settings. Some scales were used only by their constructors, whereas others were employed extensively in research studies and used routinely in clinical interpretation of the MMPI.

Not all supplementary scales could be maintained in the MMPI-2 (Butcher, Dahlstrom, Graham, Tellegen, & Kaemmer, 1989) because that would have increased the length of the test booklet beyond a point judged acceptable for routine clinical use. For the most part, the extent to which existing research data supported a scale's reliability and validity determined which scales were maintained. However, some scales were maintained on the basis of less scientific criteria. For example, the Harris-Lingoes subscales were maintained because they were judged a very helpful supplementary source of information in interpreting the clinical scales. The Wiener Subtle-Obvious subscales were maintained because some persons believe that they are useful in detecting some response sets that invalidate profiles.

In addition to maintaining some of the existing supplementary scales, Butcher, Dahlstrom, Graham, Tellegen, & Kaemmer (1989) developed some new scales for MMPI-2. The new validity scales were described in Chapter 3 and new content scales in Chapter 6. Several other new scales that also were developed are described in this chapter.

The same format will be used for discussing each supplementary scale. Scale development information will be presented, and, to the extent that they are available, reliability and validity data will be reported. Interpretive information for high and low scores on each scale also will be summarized. As with the clinical and validity sales, no absolute cutoffs for high and low scores can be

determined. In general, T-scores greater than 65 should be considered high scores, and T-scores below 40 should be considered low scores. Whenever information about specific cutoff scores for a scale is available, such information will be presented. The higher the scores, the more likely it is that the interpretive information for high scores will apply. Similarly, the lower the scores, the more likely it is that interpretive information for low scores will apply. Although an attempt was made to rely on research studies for interpretive information, in some cases examining item content and clinical impressions was necessary in generating descriptors. For supplementary scales developed from the original MMPI and maintained in the MMPI-2, research data from the original MMPI were utilized to generate interpretive statements. Because these scales are essentially the same in the two versions of the test, this approach seems to be appropriate. It should be emphasized that the supplementary scales are not intended to replace the standard validity and clinical scales but to be used in addition to them.

The composition and scoring of each supplementary scale are presented in Appendix K. It should be noted that the supplementary scales can be scored only if the entire 567-item MMPI-2 is administered. The test publisher provides scoring keys for the supplementary scales discussed in this chapter. Appendix L presents T-score conversions for the supplementary scales, and the test publisher provides profile sheets for plotting scores on the supplementary scales. The norm groups used to transform raw scores to T-scores are the same ones used for the standard validity and clinical scales. Linear T-score transformations are used for all supplementary scales discussed in this chapter.

ANXIETY (A) AND REPRESSION (R) SCALES

Scale Development

Whenever the basic validity and clinical scales of the MMPI or MMPI-2 have been factor-analyzed to reduce them to their most common denominators, two basic dimensions have emerged consistently (e.g., Butcher, Dahlstrom, Graham, Tellegen, & Kaemmer, 1989; Block, 1965; Eichman, 1961, 1962; Welsh, 1956). Welsh (1956) developed the Anxiety (A) and Repression (R) scales to assess these two basic dimensions.

By factor-analyzing MMPI scores for male Veterans Administration patients, Welsh identified a factor that he originally labeled "general maladjustment." A scale was developed to assess this factor by identifying the items most highly associated with it. The original scale was administered to new groups of psychiatric patients and refined by utilizing internal consistency procedures. The original A scale included 39 items, all of which have been maintained in the MMPI-2 version of the scale. Welsh suggested from an examination of the items that the content of the A scale items falls into four categories: thinking and thought processes; negative emotional tone and dysphoria; lack of energy and

pessimism; and malignant mentation. The items are keyed in such a way that high scores on the A scale are associated with increased psychopathology.

The R scale was constructed by Welsh (1956) to measure the second major dimension emerging from factor analyses of the basic validity and clinical scales of the MMPI. A procedure similar to that used in developing the A scale also was employed with the R scale. It resulted in a final scale containing 40 items, 37 of which have been maintained in the MMPI-2 version of the scale. Welsh suggested the following clusters based on the content of the R scale items: health and physical symptoms; emotionality, violence, and activity; reactions to other people in social situations; social dominance, feelings of personal adequacy, and personal appearance; and personal and vocational interests.

Reliability and Validity

Welsh (1965) reported reliability data for the A and R scales based on research by E. Kooser and P. Stevens. For 108 college undergraduates, the split-half reliability coefficients for A and R were .88 and .48, respectively. Gocka (1965) reported Kuder-Richardson 21 (internal consistency) values of .94 and .72 for the A and R scales, respectively, for 220 male Veterans Administration psychiatric patients. For the MMPI-2 normative samples, internal consistency coefficients for the A scale were .89 for men and .90 for women. Corresponding internal consistency coefficients for the R scale were .67 and .57 (Butcher, Dahlstrom, Graham, Tellegen, & Kaemmer, 1989).

When 60 college sophomores were given the A and R scales on two occasions, separated by four months, test-retest reliability coefficients for A and R were .70 and .74, respectively (Welsh, 1956). Test-retest coefficients for the A scale for college students, with a six-week interval, were .90 for men and .87 for women. Corresponding values for the R scale were .85 and .84, respectively (Moreland, 1985b). For the MMPI-2 normative samples, test-retest reliabilities (with an average interval of one week) for the A scale were .91 for men and .91 for women. For the R scale test-retest reliabilities were .79 for men and .77 for women (Butcher, Dahlstrom, Graham, Tellegen, & Kaemmer, 1989). The stability of scores on the A and R scales over these relatively short periods of time is quite high.

It has been suggested by some writers that the major sources of variance in MMPI responses were associated with response sets. A response set exists when test items are answered from a particular perspective that presents the examinee as he or she would like to appear to be. Edwards (1964) argued that the first factor of the MMPI, the one assessed by the A scale, simply assesses the examinees' willingness while describing themselves on the test to admit to or endorse socially undesirable items. Messick and Jackson (1961) suggested that R scores simply indicate the extent to which examinees are willing to admit (acquiesce) on the test to all kinds of emotional difficulties. This interpretation appeared to be supported by the fact that all the items in the R scale are keyed in the false

direction. Block (1965) refuted the response set or bias arguments by demonstrating that the same two major factor dimensions emerged even when the MMPI scales were altered to control for social desirability and acquiescence effects with the use of techniques developed by Edwards (1964) and others. Block also was able to identify through his research reliable extratest correlates for the two factor dimensions.

Welsh (1956) reported some unpublished data supplied by Gough for a group of normal subjects. Gough found that A scale scores correlated negatively with the K and L scales and with scale 1 of the MMPI and correlated positively with the F scale and with scales 9 and 0. Gough also reported that high A scorers showed slowness of personal tempo, pessimism, vacillation, hesitancy, and inhibitedness. Sherriffs and Boomer (1954) found that high A scorers showed more self-doubts in examination situations. Welsh (1956) reported a study by Welsh and M. Roseman indicating that patients who showed the most positive change during insulin shock therapy also showed marked decreases in A scale scores after such therapy. There also is evidence that A scores tend to decrease during psychiatric hospitalization (Lewinsohn, 1965). Duckworth and Duckworth (1975) suggested that a high A scale score indicates that a person is experiencing enough discomfort to likely be motivated to change in psychotherapy. Block and Bailey (1955) reported reliable extratest correlates for high and low scores on the A scale. These correlates are presented below in the discussion of the interpretation of high and low A scores.

Welsh (1956) also reported that in the study by Welsh and Roseman the patients who were judged as most improved during their course of insulin shock therapy showed some decreases in R scores in addition to the decrease in A scores. Lewinsohn (1965) found that only small changes appeared in R scores during psychiatric hospitalization. Welsh (1956) reported data provided by Gough indicating that in a sample of normal subjects, R scale scores were positively correlated with the L and K scales and with scales 1 and 2 of the MMPI and negatively correlated with scale 9. Duckworth and Duckworth (1975) described high R scorers as denying, rationalizing, and lacking self-insight. Block and Bailey (1955) identified extratest correlates of high and low R scores. These correlates are included below in connection with the interpretation of high and low scores on the R scale.

Interpretation of High A Scores

High scores on the A scale indicate persons who:

1. are anxious and uncomfortable
2. have a slow personal tempo
3. are pessimistic
4. are apathetic, unemotional, and unexcitable
5. are shy and retiring

6. lack confidence in their own abilities
7. are hesitant and vacillating
8. are inhibited and overcontrolled
9. are influenced by diffuse personal feelings
10. are defensive
11. rationalize; blame others for difficulties
12. lack poise in social situations
13. are conforming and overly accepting of authority
14. are submissive, compliant, and suggestible
15. are cautious
16. are fussy
17. if males, have behavior that tends to be effeminate
18. are seen as cool, distant, and uninvolved
19. become confused, disorganized, and maladaptive under stress
20. are uncomfortable enough to be motivated to change in psychotherapy

In summary, high scoring A persons from a normal population are rather miserable and unhappy people. High scoring A persons in a psychiatric setting fit such summarizing rubrics as neurotic, maladjusted, submissive, and over-controlled. Because of their discomfort, high A scorers usually are highly motivated for counseling or psychotherapy.

Interpretation of Low A Scores

Low scores on the A scale indicate persons who:

1. do not feel anxious or uncomfortable
2. are active and vigorous
3. are expressive, colorful, and verbally fluent
4. are frank and outspoken
5. are outgoing, sociable, friendly, and informal
6. assume ascendant roles in relation to others
7. are persuasive
8. are ostentatious and exhibitionistic
9. are efficient, capable, and clear thinking
10. are versatile and resourceful
11. are self-confident
12. are competitive; value success and achievement
13. are interested in power, status, and recognition
14. manipulate other people
15. are unable to delay gratification of impulses
16. prefer action to thought; act without considering the consequences of actions

In summary, low scorers on the A scale are characterized as extroverted, competent, confident, and somewhat impulsive. Although such individuals are not likely to be experiencing serious psychological turmoil, they may or may not have adjustment problems.

Interpretation of High R Scores

High scores on the R scale indicate persons who:

1. are submissive
2. are unexcitable
3. are conventional and formal
4. are clear thinking
5. are slow and painstaking

In summary, high R scorers are internalizing individuals who have adopted careful and cautious life-styles.

Interpretation of Low R Scores

Low scores on the R scale indicate persons who:

1. are outgoing, outspoken, and talkative
2. are excitable and emotional
3. are enthusiastic
4. are spunky and daring
5. are informal
6. are robust and jolly
7. are courageous
8. are generous
9. are dominant
10. are impulsive
11. are aggressive and bossy
12. are sarcastic and argumentative
13. are self-seeking, self-indulgent
14. are shrewd, wary, guileful, and deceitful

In summary, low R scorers tend to be rather outgoing, emotional, and spontaneous in their life-styles, and they take ascendant roles in interpersonal relationships.

Conjoint Interpretation of A and R Scales

Welsh (1956, 1965) suggested that a more complete understanding of an examinee is possible if the A and R scores are considered conjointly. Welsh (1956) reported some preliminary work carried out by Welsh and John Pearson in which protocols of Veterans Administration psychiatric inpatients were cate-

gorized as high A–low R, high A–high A, low A–low R, and low A–high R. Different psychiatric diagnostic labels were associated with cases in the four quadrants (e.g., depressive diagnoses most often occurring in the high A–high R quadrant and personality disorder diagnoses most often occurring in the low A–low R quadrant). Gynther and Brillant (1968) reported that Welsh's results were not replicated when they utilized the quadrant approach with their own sample of psychiatric outpatients.

Subsequently, Welsh (1965) suggested dividing each scale (A and R) into high, medium, and low levels to form nine categories or novants. Using male Veterans Administration patients, Welsh identified protocols that fit each of his novants. He then determined the typical profiles for the novants and inferred personality descriptions from the profile configurations. Welsh noted that the descriptions are biased toward patient groups rather than normal individuals and that the descriptions are intended to lead to hypotheses for further investigation; they should not be taken literally and should not be used for "cookbook" interpretation of profiles. Duckworth and Duckworth (1975) reported that they did not find Welsh's descriptions of the novants to be very accurate for college counselees, except for the high A–high R interpretation.

EGO STRENGTH (Es) SCALE

Scale Development

The Ego Strength (Es) scale was developed by Barron (1953) specifically to predict the response of neurotic patients to individual psychotherapy. The original Es scale had 68 items, of which 52 were included in the MMPI-2 version. To identify items for the scale, item responses of 17 patients who were judged independently as clearly improved after six months of psychotherapy were compared with item responses of 16 patients who were judged as unimproved after six months of psychotherapy. Items are scored in the direction most often chosen by the improved patients. The Es scale items deal with physical functioning, seclusiveness, moral posture, personal adequacy, ability to cope, phobias, and anxieties.

Reliability and Validity

Barron (1953) reported that the odd-even reliability of the Es scale for a sample of 126 patients was .76. Gocka (1965) reported a Kuder-Richardson 21 (internal consistency) value of .78 for the Es scale for 220 male Veterans Administration psychiatric patients. For males and females in the MMPI-2 normative samples, internal consistency values for the Es scale were .60 and .65, respectively.

Barron (1953) reported a test-retest reliability coefficient of .72 for a group of 30 patients using a test-retest interval of three months. Moreland (1985b)

reported test-retest coefficients for male and female college students (with a six-week interval) of .80 and .82, respectively. Test-retest coefficients for sub-samples of male and female subjects in the MMPI-2 normative samples were .78 and .83, respectively (Butcher, Dahlstrom, Graham, Tellegen, & Kaemmer, 1989).

The Es scale was cross-validated by Barron (1953) using three different samples of neurotic patients for whom ratings of improvement during brief, psychoanalytically oriented psychotherapy were available. Because pretherapy Es scores were positively related to rated improvement for all three samples, Barron concluded that the Es scale is useful in predicting responsiveness to psychotherapy. Unfortunately, subsequent attempts by others to cross-validate the Es scale as a predictor of response to psychotherapy or other treatment approaches have yielded inconsistent findings. Some data indicate that psychiatric patients who change most during treatment have higher pretreatment Es scores than patients who show less change (e.g., Wirt, 1955, 1956), whereas other data suggest that change in treatment is unrelated to pretreatment Es scores (e.g., Ends & Page, 1957; Fowler, Teel, & Coyle, 1967; Getter & Sundland, 1962; Sullivan, Miller, & Smelser, 1958). Distler, May, and Tuma (1964) found that pretreatment Es scores were positively related to hospitalization outcome for male psychiatric patients and negatively related to hospitalization outcome for female psychiatric patients. Simmett (1962) reported that Veterans Administration psychiatric patients with higher pretreatment Es scores showed more personality growth during treatment, which included psychotherapy, than did patients with lower scores, but pretreatment Es scores were unrelated to rated symptomatic change for these same patients. It should be noted that many of the failures to replicate Barron's finding utilized change after hospitalization and therefore did not represent a true replication of his study.

Dahlstrom, Welsh, and Dahlstrom (1975) tried to explain the inconsistent findings concerning the relationship between Es scores and treatment outcome. They suggested that when high Es scores occur for persons who obviously are having difficulties but who are denying them, the high Es scores may not be predictive of a favorable treatment outcome. However, high Es scores for persons who are admitting to emotional problems may suggest a favorable response to treatment. Clayton and Graham (1979) were not able to validate the Dahlstrom et al. hypothesis with a sample of hospitalized psychiatric patients. It is clear from the existing literature that the relationship between Es scores and treatment outcome is not a simple one and that factors such as kind of patients, type of treatment, and nature of the outcome measure must be taken into account. In general, however, high Es scores are predictive of positive personality change for neurotic patients who receive traditional, individual psychotherapy.

One must be very cautious in interpreting Es scores in profiles suggesting defensiveness. In such profiles Es scores tend to be artificially high and thus not predictive of positive response to therapy. Likewise, caution should be exercised in interpreting Es scores in profiles suggesting exaggeration of symp-

toms. In such exaggerated profiles, Es scores tend to be artificially low and thus not predictive of a negative response to therapy.

Research data also suggest that the Es scale can be viewed as an indication of overall psychological adjustment. Higher scores on the Es scale are associated with more favorable adjustment levels as assessed by other MMPI-2 indexes and extratest criteria. Es scores tend to be lower for psychiatric patients than for nonpatients and for people receiving psychiatric or psychological treatment than for persons not receiving such treatment (Gottesman, 1959; Himelstein, 1964; Kleinmuntz, 1960; Quay, 1955; Spiegel, 1969; Taft, 1957). However, it has been reported that the Es scale fails to differentiate between delinquent and nondelinquent adolescents (Gottesman, 1959). Whereas Es scores tend to be higher for neurotic patients than for psychotic patients, the scale fails to discriminate among more specific diagnostic categories (Hawkinson, 1961; Rosen, 1963; Tamkin, 1957; Tamkin & Klett, 1957).

Some data indicate that Es scores tend to increase as a result of psychotherapy or other treatment procedures. Lewinsohn (1965) reported that psychiatric patients showed an increase in level of Es scores from hospital admission to discharge. However, Barron and Leary (1955) found that Es scores did not change more for patients who received individual or group psychotherapy than for patients who remained on a waiting list for a similar period of time. It also was reported that psychotherapy patients who were self-referred scored higher on the Es scale than those who were referred by someone else (Himelstein, 1964), suggesting that high Es scorers are more aware of internal conflicts than are low Es scorers.

Scores on the Es scale are related positively to intelligence (Tamkin & Klett, 1957; Wirt, 1955) and to formal education (Tamkin & Klett, 1957). The relationship between Es scores and age is less clear. Tamkin and Klett (1957) found no relationship between Es scores and age, but Getter and Sundland (1962) reported that older persons tended to score lower on the Es scale. Consistent sex differences in Es scores have been reported, with males obtaining higher scores than females (Distler, May, & Tuma, 1964; Getter & Sundland, 1962; Taft, 1957). This sex difference originally was interpreted as reflecting the greater willingness of females to admit to problems and complaints (Getter & Sundland, 1962). However, a more reasonable explanation is that males score higher than females because the scale contains a number of items dealing with masculine role identification (Holmes, 1967).

Interpretation of High Es Scores

From the preceding discussion, it may be concluded that high scorers on the Es scale generally tend to show more positive personality change during treatment than do low scorers. However, the relationship between Es scores and treatment prognosis is not a simple one, and patient and treatment variables must be

taken into account. Also, high Es scorers tend to be better adjusted psychologically and thus more able to cope with problems and stresses in their life situations. Among psychiatric patients, high Es scores are likely to be associated with neurotic diagnoses and low Es scores with psychotic diagnoses. In addition, high scores on the Es scale indicate individuals who:

1. lack chronic psychopathology
2. are stable, reliable, and responsible
3. are tolerant; lack prejudice
4. are alert and adventuresome
5. are determined and persistent
6. are self-confident, outspoken, and sociable
7. are intelligent, resourceful, and independent
8. have a secure sense of reality
9. deal effectively with others
10. create favorable first impressions
11. gain acceptance of others
12. are opportunistic and manipulative
13. have strongly developed interests
14. if male, have an appropriately masculine style of behavior
15. are hostile and rebellious toward authority
16. are competitive
17. may be sarcastic and cynical
18. seek help because of situational problems
19. can tolerate confrontations in psychotherapy

In summary, people with high Es scores appear to be fairly well put together emotionally. In nonpsychiatric settings, they are not likely to have serious emotional problems. If they do have emotional problems, these problems are likely to be situational rather than chronic. Further, high scorers have psychological resources to draw upon in helping them to solve the problems, and the prognosis for positive change in counseling or psychotherapy is good.

Interpretation of Low Es Scores

In general, low Es scorers tend to be less well adjusted psychologically than high Es scorers, and they are not well equipped to deal with problems and stresses. In general, low scorers are likely to show less positive personality change during treatment. Among psychiatric patients, low Es scorers are more likely to be diagnosed as psychotic than as neurotic or personality disorder. In addition, Barron (1953, 1956), Dahlstrom and Welsh (1960), Dahlstrom, Welsh, and Dahlstrom (1975), Duckworth and Duckworth (1975), and Good and Brantner (1961) suggested that low scores on the Es scale indicate individuals who:

1. have poor self-concepts; feel worthless; brood
2. feel helpless
3. are confused
4. have chronic physical complaints
5. have chronic fatigue
6. have fears and phobias
7. are withdrawn and seclusive
8. are inhibited and unadaptive
9. show stereotyped and unoriginal approach to problems
10. are mannerly and mild
11. are rigid and moralistic
12. if males, have an effeminate style of behavior
13. exaggerate problems as a "cry for help"
14. have poor work histories
15. have problems that are characterological rather than situational in nature
16. express good intentions to change in psychotherapy but do not act on them

In summary, individuals with low Es scores do not seem to be very well put together psychologically. They are likely to be seriously maladjusted. Their problems are likely to be longstanding in nature, their personal resources for coping with problems extremely limited, and the prognosis for positive change in psychotherapy poor.

MACANDREW ALCOHOLISM-REVISED SCALE (MAC-R)

Scale Development

The MacAndrew Alcoholism (MAC) scale (MacAndrew, 1965) was developed to differentiate alcoholic from nonalcoholic psychiatric patients. The scale was constructed by contrasting the MMPI responses of 200 male alcoholics seeking treatment at an outpatient clinic with responses of 200 male nonalcoholic psychiatric patients from the same facility. These analyses identified 51 items that differentiated the two groups. Because MacAndrew was interested in developing a subtle scale, two of the 51 items that deal directly with excessive drinking behavior were eliminated from the scale. The items are scored so that higher scores are more indicative of alcohol abuse.

Four of the original MAC items were among those eliminated from the MMPI-2 because of objectionable content. Because the MAC scale typically is interpreted in terms of raw scores, a decision was made to maintain a 49-item scale in the MMPI-2. Thus, the four objectionable items were replaced with four new items selected because they differentiated alcoholic from nonalcoholic males. Schwartz and Graham (1979) reported that the major content dimen-

sions of the MAC scale are cognitive impairment, school maladjustment, interpersonal competence, risk taking, extroversion and exhibitionism, and moral indignation.

Reliability and Validity

No internal consistency data were reported for the original MAC scale, but the MAC-R scale does not seem to have particularly good internal consistency. Internal consistency coefficients (Coefficient Alpha) for the MMPI-2 normative samples were .56 for males and .45 for females (Butcher, Dahlstrom, Graham, Tellegen, & Kaemmer, 1989). A factor analysis reported by Schwartz and Graham (1979) indicated that the original MAC scale was not unidimensional.

Moreland (1985b) reported test-retest reliability coefficients (six-week interval) for the MAC scale with samples of normal college men and women. The coefficients were .82 and .75, respectively. For subsamples of male and female subjects in the MMPI-2 normative samples, test-retest reliability coefficients (one-week interval) for the MAC-R scale were .62 and .78, respectively. These relatively modest test-retest reliability coefficients for normal samples could be explained, at least in part, by the limited variability of scores in these groups.

Several studies reported that MAC scores did not change significantly during treatment programs ranging in length from 60 to 90 days or during a one-year follow-up period after treatment (Chang, Caldwell, & Moss, 1973; Huber & Danahy, 1975; Rohan, 1972; Rohan, Tatro, & Rotman, 1969). Hoffman, Loper, & Kammeier (1974) compared the MMPIs of male alcoholics at the time of treatment to MMPIs taken 13 years earlier when they had entered college and found no differences in MAC scores over this extended period of time.

MacAndrew (1965) reported cross-validation data for his scale. A cutoff score of 24 correctly classified approximately 82 percent of the alcoholic and nonalcoholic subjects. Subsequent research has indicated that groups of alcoholic and nonalcoholic subjects in a variety of settings tend to obtain significantly different mean scores on the MAC (Apfeldorf & Huntley, 1975; Rhodes, 1969; Rich & Davis, 1969; Rohan, 1972; Rosenberg, 1972; Schwartz & Graham, 1979; Uecker, 1970; Williams, McCourt, & Schneider, 1971). There also are data suggesting that drug addicts score higher than other psychiatric patients but not differently from alcoholics on the MAC scale (Fowler, 1975; Kranitz, 1972). Graham (1978) reported that pathological gamblers scored similarly to alcoholics and heroin addicts on the MAC.

In a longitudinal study, Hoffman, Loper, & Kammeier (1974) located MMPIs of alcoholic males in treatment; these MMPIs had been completed approximately 13 years previously when they entered college. When the MAC scores of these men were compared with those of their classmates who did not become alcoholics, significant differences were found. Data also suggest that persons who drink excessively but who are not alcoholics score higher on the MAC scale than persons who do not drink excessively (Apfeldorf & Huntley, 1975;

Williams, McCourt, & Schneider, 1971). The MAC scale also seems to be effective in identifying adolescents who have significant problems with alcohol and/or drug abuse (Wisniewski, Glenwick, & Graham, 1985; Wolfson & Erbaugh, 1984).

Several studies have suggested caution in using the MAC scale with black subjects (Graham & Mayo, 1985; Walters, Greene, & Jeffrey, 1984; Walters, Greene, Jeffrey, Kruzich, & Haskin, 1983). Although black alcoholics tend to obtain scores in the addictive range, classification rates in these studies have not been very good because nonalcoholic black subjects also tended to score rather high on the MAC scale. Further, in all these MAC studies of black alcoholics, the samples have involved military personnel or veterans. The extent to which these findings can be generalized to other kinds of subjects remains to be determined. Likewise, additional research is needed to determine the MAC-R scale's effectiveness with other minority subjects.

In a recent review article, Gottesman and Prescott (1989) questioned the routine use of the MAC in clinical and employment settings. They indicated that evidence that the MAC can identify substance abusers is not as compelling as many users assume. Further, accuracy of classification using the MAC is considerably lower when the scale is used in settings where the base rate for substance abuse is markedly different from that of the study in which the scale was developed. Gottesman and Prescott's observations are appropriate, but their conclusion that the MAC should not be used outside of research settings seems extreme. Instead, this author recommends that no decisions be made on the basis of MAC (or MAC-R) scores alone. High scores on the scale should alert clinicians to obtain corroborating information concerning the possibility of substance abuse.

Interpretation of MAC-R

Except for the four objectionable items that were replaced in MAC-R, the revised scale is essentially the same as the original scale so its interpretation can be similar to that of the original MAC scale. High scores on the MAC-R scale suggest the possibility of alcohol or other substance abuse, though obviously it would not be responsible clinical practice to reach conclusions about substance abuse without obtaining corroborating information from other sources. In general, MAC-R raw scores of 28 and above strongly suggest substance abuse. Scores between 24 and 27 are somewhat suggestive of such abuse, but there will be many false positives (i.e., persons identified as abusers because of their scores who really are not abusers) at this level. Scores below 24 strongly contraindicate a substance abuse problem. Incorrect classification of nonabusers as abusers is especially likely to occur for individuals who have the extroverted, activity-oriented style commonly found among high MAC-R scorers who do not abuse substances. Blacks who abuse substances are likely to obtain elevated MAC-R scores, but the tendency for black nonabusers to have elevated scores on

the scale will lead to more false positives than with white subjects. It should be noted that persons who previously abused substances but no longer do so tend to obtain high MAC-R scores.

In addition to the possibility of substance abuse, high MAC-R scores indicate individuals who:

1. are socially extroverted
2. are exhibitionistic
3. may experience blackouts
4. have difficulties in concentrating
5. may have histories of behavior problems in school
6. are self-confident and assertive
7. enjoy competition and risk taking

In addition to suggesting less likelihood of substance abuse than high scores, low MAC-R scores indicate individuals who:

1. are shy and socially introverted
2. are conventional and conforming
3. are lacking in self-confidence

OVERCONTROLLED-HOSTILITY (O-H) SCALE

Scale Development

Megargee, Cook, and Mendelsohn (1967) suggested that there are two major types of persons who commit acts of extreme physical aggression. Habitually aggressive (undercontrolled) persons have not developed appropriate controls against the expression of aggression, so that when they are provoked they respond with aggression of an intensity proportional to the degree of provocation. Chronically overcontrolled persons have very rigid inhibitions against the expression of any form of aggression. Most of the time the overcontrolled individuals do not respond even with aggression appropriate to provocation, but occasionally, when the provocation is great enough, they may act out in an extremely aggressive manner. Megargee and his associates believed that the most aggressive acts typically are committed by overcontrolled rather than undercontrolled persons.

The original O-H scale was constructed by identifying items that were answered differently by extremely assaultive prisoners, moderately assaultive prisoners, prisoners convicted of nonviolent crimes, and men who had not been convicted of any crime. Items were scored so that higher scores on O-H indicated more assaultive (overcontrolled) persons. The original O-H scale contained 31 items, of which 28 were retained by the MMPI-2.

Reliability and Validity

Megargee, Cook, & Mendelsohn (1967) reported a coefficient of internal consistency (Kuder-Richardson 21) of .56 for the O-H scale for a combined group of criminals and college students. Internal consistency coefficients (Coefficient Alpha) for the MMPI-2 normative male and female samples were .34 and .24, respectively. Clearly, the O-H scale is not very internally consistent. Moreland (1985b) reported test-retest coefficients for male and female college students of .72 and .56, respectively. Test-retest coefficients of males and females from the MMPI-2 normative samples were .68 and .69, respectively.

Although some studies (e.g., Megargee, Cook, & Mendelsohn, 1967; Deiker, 1974; Fredericksen, 1976) found that more violent criminals scored higher on the O-H scale, other studies (e.g., Fisher, 1970) failed to find O-H differences between assaultive and nonassaultive prisoners. Lane (1976) suggested that some of the negative findings could be due to a confounding of race and the assaultiveness criterion and to the manner in which the O-H scale was administered. Although no data were presented to support the contention, Lane stated that the O-H scale must be administered in the context of the entire MMPI. Data also suggest that when the O-H scale is used to identify assaultive prisoners, cutoff scores should be established individually for each setting in which the scale is used. Little evidence suggests that high O-H sores in groups other than prisoners are associated with violent acts.

Interpretation of High O-H Scores

In correctional settings, high O-H scores tend to be associated with aggressive and violent acts. However, the validity of the O-H scale is such that individual predictions of violence from O-H scores are not likely to be very accurate. In addition, cutoff scores for predicting violence should be established separately in each setting where the scale is used. The O-H scale has some potential use in other settings because it tells clinicians something about how subjects typically respond to provocation. Higher O-H scorers tend not to respond to provocation even appropriately most of the time, but occasional exaggerated aggressive responses may occur. High O-H scores also indicate persons who:

1. are impunitive
2. report fewer angry feelings
3. express less verbal hostility in reaction to frustration
4. are more socialized and responsible
5. have strong needs to excel
6. are dependent on others
7. are trustful
8. describe nurturant and supportive family backgrounds

Interpretation of Low O-H Scores

Relatively little data exist concerning the interpretation of low scores on O-H. We do not expect the low scorers to display the overcontrolled-hostility syndrome described for high scorers. Low scorers may be either chronically aggressive persons or persons who are quite appropriate in the expression of their aggression.

DOMINANCE (DO) SCALE

Scale Development

The Dominance (Do) scale was developed by Gough, McClosky, and Meehl (1951) as part of a larger project concerned with political participation. Because the 60-item scale included 28 MMPI items, it was possible to score an abbreviated version of the scale from standard administration of the MMPI. The MMPI-2 version of the Do scale retained 25 of the original 28 items. To develop the Do scale, high school and college students were given a definition of dominance (strong in face-to-face personal situations; able to influence others; not readily intimidated or defeated; safe, secure, and confident in face-to-face situations) and were asked to nominate peers who were most and least dominant. High- and low-dominance criterion groups were defined on the basis of these peer nominations, and both groups were given a 150-item questionnaire, which included some MMPI items. Item analyses of the responses identified items that differentiated between high- and low-dominance criterion groups. The items are keyed so that a high score on the Do scale suggests high dominance. The Do scale items deal with a number of different content areas, including concentration, obsessive-compulsive behaviors, self-confidence, discomfort in social situations, concern about physical appearance, perseverance, and political opinions.

Reliability and Validity

Gough et al. (1951) reported an internal consistency coefficient (Kuder-Richardson 21) of .79 for the 60-item Do scale, and Gocka (1965) reported a Kuder-Richardson value of .60 for the 28-item Do scale for 220 male Veterans Administration psychiatric patients. Internal consistency coefficients (Coefficient Alpha) for males and females in the MMPI-2 normative samples were .74 and .79, respectively.

A test-retest coefficient of .86 for Marine Corps officers was reported by Knapp (1960). Moreland (1985b) reported test-retest coefficients (six-week interval) for male and female college students of .85 and .83, respectively. Test-retest coefficients (one-week interval) for subsamples of males and females in

the MMPI-2 normative samples were .84 and .86, respectively. Knapp (1960) reported correlations of .75 and .79 between Do scores based on the 28 MMPI items and Do scores based on the total 60-item scale for samples of enlisted men and officers.

Gough et al. (1951) found that a raw score cutoff of 36 on the 60-item scale identified 94 percent of their high- and low-dominance high school subjects, whereas a raw score cutoff of 39 on the 60-item scale identified 92 percent of high- and low-dominance college students. Correlations between Do scores based on the 28 MMPI items and peer ratings and self-ratings of dominance were .52 and .65, respectively, for college students and .60 and .41, respectively, for high school students.

Knapp (1960) found that Marine Corps officer pilots scored significantly higher on the 28-item Do scale than did enlisted men. The mean scores for the officers and enlisted men were quite similar to mean scores reported for high- and low-dominance high school and college students. Knapp interpreted his data as supporting the use of the Do scale as a screening device in selecting officers. However, Olmstead and Monachesi (1956) reported that the MMPI Do scale was not able to differentiate between firemen and fire captains. Eschenback and Dupree (1959) found that Do scores did not change as a result of situational stress (a realistic survival test). It would be interesting to know whether Do scores change as individuals change their dominance roles (e.g., when an enlisted person becomes an officer). Unfortunately, no data of this kind are available at this time.

Interpretation of High Do Scores

High scorers on the Do scale see themselves and are seen by others as stronger in face-to-face personal situations, not readily intimidated, and feeling safe, secure, and self-confident. Although there is some limited evidence to suggest that high scores on the Do scale are more common among persons holding positions of greater responsibility and leadership, no data are available concerning the adequacy of performance in such positions as a function of Do scores. Also, high Do scores indicate individuals who:

1. appear poised and self-assured
2. are self-confident
3. appear free to behave in straightforward manner
4. are optimistic
5. are resourceful and efficient
6. are realistic and task-oriented
7. feel adequate to handle problems
8. are persevering
9. have dutiful sense of morality
10. have strong need to face reality

In summary, high Do scorers are people who are confident of their abilities to cope with problems and stresses in their life situations.

Interpretation of Low Do Scale Scores

Low scorers on the Do scale see themselves and are seen by others as submissive, weaker in face-to-face contacts, unassertive, unable to stand up for their own rights and opinions, and easily influenced by other people. Low Do scorers are less likely than high Do scorers to be in positions of responsibility and leadership. Based on an examination of the content of the Do scale items, it appears that low Do scores indicate individuals who:

1. lack self-confidence
2. are pessimistic
3. are inefficient and stereotyped in approach to problems
4. feel inadequate to handle problems
5. give up easily
6. do not feel a sense of duty to others
7. do not face up to the realities of their life situations

In summary, low Do scorers tend to have difficulty in asserting themselves. In addition, they are not very effective in handling problems and stresses in their life situations.

SOCIAL RESPONSIBILITY (RE) SCALE

Scale Development

The Social Responsibility (Re) scale was developed by Gough, McClosky, and Meehl (1952) as part of a larger project concerning political participation. The original scale contained 56 items, with 32 items coming from the MMPI item pool. A score based on the 32 MMPI items could be obtained, and normative data were available for the 32 item Re scale. In MMPI-2, 30 of the original 32 MMPI items were retained.

The samples used in constructing the Re scale were 50 college fraternity men, 50 college sorority women, 123 social science students from a high school, and 221 ninth-grade students. In each sample, the most and least responsible individuals were identified. Responsibility was defined as willingness to accept the consequences of one's own behavior, dependability, trustworthiness, integrity, and sense of obligation to the group. For the high school and college samples, peer nominations were used to identify subjects high and low in responsibility. Teachers provided ratings of responsibility for the ninth-grade sample. The responses of the most responsible and least responsible subjects in each sample to the items in the MMPI item pool and to a questionnaire

containing rationally generated items were then examined. The items that best discriminated between the most and least responsible subjects in all samples became the Re scale. In the MMPI-2, these items deal with concern for social and moral issues, disapproval of privilege and favor, emphasis on duties and self-discipline, conventionality versus rebelliousness, trust and confidence in the world in general, and poise, assurance, and personal security (Gough et al., 1952).

Reliability and Validity

Gough et al. (1952) reported an uncorrected split-half reliability coefficient of .73 for the 56-item scale for a sample of ninth-grade students. Gocka (1965) reported a Kuder-Richardson 21 (internal consistency) value of .63 for the 32-item Re scale for 220 male Veterans Administration psychiatric patients. Internal consistency values (Coefficient Alpha) for males and females in the MMPI-2 normative samples were .67 and .61, respectively (Butcher, Dahlstrom, Graham, Tellegen, & Kaemmer, 1989).

Moreland (1985b) reported test-retest coefficients (six-week interval) for male and female college students of .85 and .76, respectively. Test-retest coefficients (with one-week interval) for subsamples of males and females in the MMPI-2 normative samples were .85 and .74, respectively (Butcher, Dahlstrom, Graham, Tellegen, & Kaemmer, 1989). Gough and his colleagues reported correlations of .84 and .88 between Re scores based on all 56 items and scores based on the 32 MMPI items in the Re scale for their college and high school samples.

Correlations between MMPI Re scale scores and criterion ratings of responsibility in the derivation samples were .47 for college students and .53 for high school students. For college students the correlation between MMPI Re scores and self-ratings of responsibility was .20, and the correlation between these two variables for high school students was .23. Optimal cutting scores for the MMPI Re scale yielded correct classification of 78 percent and 87 percent, respectively, of the most and least responsible individuals in the various derivation samples. Gough et al. (1952) reported some limited cross-validational data for the total (56-item) Re scale. They obtained a correlation of .22 between scores and ratings of responsibility for a sample of medical students. A correlation of .33 between Re scores and ratings of positive character integration was reported for a sample of fourth-year graduate students.

In two studies, it was shown that persons with higher Re scores tended to have positions of leadership and responsibility. Knapp (1960) found that Marine Corps officers scored significantly higher on the MMPI Re scale than did enlisted men. Olmstead and Monachesi (1956) reported that fire captains scored higher on the MMPI Re scale than firemen, but the difference was not statistically significant.

Duckworth and Duckworth (1975) suggested that the Re scale measures acceptance (high score) or rejection (low score) of a previously held value system, usually that of one's parents. High Re scorers over age 25 tend to accept their

present value system and intend to continue using it, whereas low scorers may be questioning their current value system or rejecting their most recently held value system. For younger persons, high Re scores indicate acceptance of parental value systems, whereas low Re scores indicate questioning or rejection of parental value systems. Duckworth and Duckworth (1975) also suggested that high Re scorers, regardless of age, are more rigid in acceptance of values and are less willing to explore other values. They also indicated that older persons tend to score higher than younger persons on the Re scale and that college students who are questioning parental values often receive quite low Re scores.

Interpretation of High Re Scores

High Re scorers tend to see themselves and are seen by others as willing to accept the consequences of their own behavior, as dependable and trustworthy, and as having integrity and a sense of responsibility to the group. They also are more likely than low Re scorers to be in positions of leadership and responsibility. High Re scorers are rigid in their acceptance of values and are unwilling to explore other values. Younger persons with high Re scores tend to accept the values of their parents. Also, high Re scores indicate individuals who:

1. have deep concern over ethical and moral problems
2. have a strong sense of justice
3. set high standards for themselves
4. reject privilege and favor
5. place excessive emphasis on carrying their own share of burdens and duties
6. are self-confident
7. have trust and confidence in the world in general

In summary, high Re scorers have incorporated societal and cultural values and are committed to behaving in a manner consistent with those values. In addition, they place high value on honesty and justice.

Interpretation of Low Re Scores

Low Re scorers do not see themselves and are not seen by others as willing to accept responsibility for their own behavior. They are lacking or deficient in dependability, trustworthiness, integrity, and a sense of responsibility to the group. They are less likely than high Re scorers to be in positions of leadership and responsibility. Low Re scorers also are less rigid than high Re scorers in their acceptance of values and are more willing to explore other values. Younger persons with low Re scores tend to deny the value system of their parents and to substitute another value system for the parental one. Older persons with low Re scores question or deny their most recently held value system and may have adopted new religious or political outlooks.

COLLEGE MALADJUSTMENT (MT) SCALE

Scale Development

The College Maladjustment (Mt) scale was constructed to discriminate between emotionally adjusted and maladjusted college students (Kleinmuntz, 1960). Mt items were selected from the MMPI item pool by comparing responses of 40 adjusted male and female students and 40 maladjusted male and female students. The adjusted students had contacted a university clinic to arrange for a routine mental health screening examination as part of teacher certification procedures, and none of them admitted to a history of psychiatric treatment. The maladjusted students had contacted the same clinic for help with emotional problems and had remained in psychotherapy for three or more sessions. Item analytic procedures yielded 43 items that discriminated between the adjusted and maladjusted students. The MMPI-2 Mt scale retains 41 of the original 43 items, with items scored such that higher scores on the scale are more indicative of maladjustment. Kleinmuntz (1961) found that scores on the 43-item scale administered separately corresponded quite well to Mt scores derived from a standard MMPI administration.

Reliability and Validity

Internal consistency coefficients (Coefficient Alpha) for males and females in the MMPI-2 normative samples were .84 and .86, respectively (Butcher, Dahlstrom, Graham, Tellegen, & Kaemmer, 1989). When Kleinmuntz (1961) administered the Mt scale to college students twice within an interval of three days, a test-retest reliability coefficient of .88 was obtained. Moreland (1985b) reported test-retest coefficients (six-week interval) for male and female college students of .89 and .86, respectively. Test-retest coefficients (one-week interval) for subsamples of males and females in the MMPI-2 normative samples were .91 and .90, respectively (Butcher, Dahlstrom, Graham, Tellegen, & Kaemmer, 1989).

Kleinmuntz (1961) reported that college students who took the Mt scale when they entered college and later sought "emotional" counseling scored higher on the scale than did a similar group of students who sought out "vocational-academic" counseling. Using a Mt scale cutoff of 15, Parker (1961) was able to classify correctly 74 percent of maladjusted students who completed the Mt scale at the time that they sought counseling, but only 46 percent when the Mt scale was completed as part of a battery administered at the time of college admission. Parker's data and Kleinmuntz's own data led Kleinmuntz (1961) to conclude that the Mt scale is more accurate when used for identifying existing emotional problems than for predicting future emotional problems. Higher Mt scores for maladjusted than for adjusted students were reported subsequently in several different settings (Kleinmuntz, 1963). Wilderman (1984) found that within a college counseling sample higher Mt scores were associated with more

elevated MMPI profiles and with more severe psychopathology as indicated by therapist ratings than were relatively lower Mt scores.

Female students tend to score higher than male students on the Mt scale. Mt scores of adjusted and maladjusted college students vary considerably from one college setting to another and among divisions within each college. This variation indicates that separate norms and cutoff scores should be established for each specific setting where the Mt scale is used.

Interpretation of High Mt Scores

Because of variations in Mt scores among college settings, it is not possible to identify an absolute cutoff score above which students should be considered maladjusted. However, among college students within a given setting, higher Mt scores are more suggestive of maladjustment. Because the Mt scale has not been studied systematically in settings other than colleges and universities, its use is not recommended with subjects who are not college students. In addition to suggesting general maladjustment, high Mt scores for college students indicate individuals who:

1. are ineffectual
2. are pessimistic
3. procrastinate
4. are anxious and worried
5. somatize
6. feel that life is a strain much of the time

Interpretation of Low Mt Scores

Within a given college setting, students with lower Mt scores generally are better adjusted emotionally than students with higher scores on the scale. In addition, low Mt scores for college students indicate individuals who:

1. are optimistic
2. are conscientious
3. are relatively free of emotional discomfort

MASCULINE GENDER ROLE (GM) AND FEMININE GENDER ROLE (GF) SCALES

Scale Development

Peterson (1989) developed the Masculine Gender Role (GM) and Feminine Gender Role (GF) scales for the MMPI-2 as separate measures of the masculine

and feminine components in the bipolar Masculinity-Femininity (Mf) scale of the MMPI. Items in the GM scale were those endorsed in the scored direction by a majority of men in the MMPI-2 normative sample and endorsed in that same direction by at least 10 percent fewer women in the MMPI-2 normative sample. Correspondingly, items for GF were those endorsed in the scored direction by a majority of women in the MMPI-2 normative sample and endorsed in that same direction by at least 10 percent fewer men in the MMPI-2 normative sample. Only nine of 47 items in GM and 16 of the 46 items in GF also appear on the Mf scale.

Examination of the content of items in the GM scale suggests that they deal primarily with the denial of fears, anxieties, and somatic symptoms. Some GM items have to do with interest in stereotypically masculine activities, such as reading adventure stories, and denial of interests in stereotypically feminine occupations such as nursing and library work. Other groups of GM items have to do with denial of excessive emotionality and presentation of one's self as independent, decisive, and self-confident. The largest group of items in the GF scale has to do with the denial of asocial or antisocial acts, such as getting in trouble with the law or at school and excessive use of alcohol or other drugs. Many GF items also have to do with liking stereotypically feminine activities, such as cooking and growing house plants, and disliking stereotypically masculine activities, such as reading mechanics magazines and auto racing. Some GF items involve admission of excessive sensitivity. There also are several items expressing early identification with a female figure and satisfaction with being female or wishing that one were not male.

Reliability and Validity

Internal consistency estimates (Coefficient Alpha) for the GM scale for males and females in the MMPI-2 normative samples were .67 and .75, respectively (Butcher, Dahlstrom, Graham, Tellegen, & Kaemmer, 1989). Test-retest reliability coefficients (one-week interval) for the GM scale for subsamples of males and females in the MMPI-2 normative samples were .73 and .89, respectively (Butcher et al., 1989).

The internal consistency coefficient (Alpha) for the GF scale was .57 for both males and females in the MMPI-2 normative samples (Butcher et al., 1989). Test-retest reliability coefficients (one-week interval) for the GF scale were .86 and .78, respectively, for subsamples of males and females in the MMPI-2 normative samples (Butcher et al., 1989).

Peterson (1989) reported some preliminary data concerning behavioral correlates of GM and GF scales. He found that for males the GM scale is related to high self-confidence, persistence, and wide interests, as well as a lack of fears or feelings of self-reference. For females the GM scale also is related to high self-confidence, as well as honesty, a willingness to try new things, and a lack of worries or feelings of self-reference. For males the GF scale is related to re-

ligiosity, avoidance of swearing or cursing, and frankness in pointing out to others their personal faults. For males the GF scale also is related to bossiness, poor control over one's temper, and susceptibility to the abuse of alcohol and nonprescription drugs. For females, the GF scale also is related to religiosity and use of nonprescription drugs.

Interpretation of GM and GF Scores

Because these scales have been developed recently and very limited validity data are available concerning them, it is difficult to generate descriptors that can be applied with confidence to high and low scorers on the scales. The preliminary data by Peterson (1989) and the content of items in the scales suggest that both males and females who obtain high scores on GM are characterized in positive ways. They tend to be self-confident and free from fears and worries. For both males and females, higher scores on GF are related to religiosity and to abuse of alcohol and nonprescription drugs. In addition, males scoring higher on GF are seen as bossy and as having poor control over their tempers.

Peterson (1989) suggested that the conjoint interpretation of the GM and GF scales can yield a gender role typology similar to that used with other instruments. A high score on GM and a low score on GF indicate stereotypic masculinity; a high score on GF and a low score on GM indicate stereotypic femininity; high scores on both GM and GF indicate androgyny; and low scores on both GM and GF indicate an undifferentiated orientation.

Peterson (1989) further reported that high raw scores on the Mf scale indicate stereotypically feminine subjects, and low raw scores on the Mf scale indicate stereotypically masculine subjects. However, persons falling in the middle range on the Mf scale can be either androgynous or undifferentiated. He hypothesized that the conjoint interpretation of GM and GF can be helpful in making such distinctions concerning the patterning of gender roles in persons in this middle range on the Mf scale. It should be emphasized that the GM and GF scales have not been sufficiently validated to permit their routine clinical use. They should be considered experimental scales to be used for research purposes.

POST-TRAUMATIC STRESS DISORDER (PK) SCALE

Scale Development

The Post-traumatic Stress Disorder (PK) scale was developed by Keane, Malloy, and Fairbank (1984) by contrasting the MMPI item responses of 60 male Vietnam combat veterans who had diagnoses of post-traumatic stress disorder (PTSD) based on structured interviews and a psychophysiological assessment procedure and 60 male veterans who had diagnoses other than PTSD. They

identified 49 items that these two groups answered significantly differently. A raw score cutoff of 30 correctly classified 82 percent of the subjects used in developing the scale and also 82 percent of cross-validation groups of PTSD and non-PTSD veterans. The MMPI-2 version of the PK scale includes 46 of the original items.

The content of the PK scale items suggests great emotional turmoil. Some items deal with anxiety, worry, and sleep disturbance. Others suggest guilt and depression. In some items subjects are reporting the presence of unwanted and disturbing thoughts, and in others they are describing lack of emotional control. Feeling misunderstood and mistreated is also present in some item content.

Reliability and Validity

Internal consistency coefficients for the PK scale for males and females in the MMPI-2 normative samples were .85 and .87, respectively. Test-retest reliability coefficients for subsamples of males and females in the MMPI-2 normative samples were .86 and .89, respectively.

Subsequent to the development of the PK scale by Keane et al. (1984), several investigations of its utility in diagnosing PTSD patients have been published. Gayton, Burchstead, and Matthews (1986) found that a cutoff score of 30 on the PK scale correctly classified 57 percent of PTSD Vietnam veterans and 55 percent of non-PTSD veterans. Cannon, Bell, Andrews, and Finkelstein (1987) found that the PK scale correctly classified 76 percent of PTSD Vietnam veterans and 64 percent of non-PTSD veterans. Classification rates of 57 percent for PTSD Vietnam veterans and 84 percent for non-PTSD veterans were reported by Vanderploeg, Sison, and Hickling (1987). Query, Megran, and McDonald (1986) used the PK scale with World War II veterans who had been POWs and later had been diagnosed as having PTSD or not having PTSD. They found that the former POWs who had subsequent diagnoses of PTSD scored significantly higher on the PK scale than former POWs without diagnoses of PTSD. Hyer, Fallon, Harrison, and Boudewyns (1987) indicated that caution should be used with the PK scale because it contains no subtle items and therefore may be susceptible to faking by veterans who are motivated to appear to have PTSD in order to gain monetary compensation.

In summary, there appears to be considerable evidence that scores on the PK scale are related to PTSD diagnoses among veterans. Studies, such as that by Keane et al. (1984), that have used well-defined criteria to establish the diagnosis of PTSD report higher classification rates than other studies that used less reliable diagnostic procedures. Using the PK scale to classify veterans as PTSD or non-PTSD will produce more false positive than false negative errors. It is not clear to what extent scores on the PK scale are susceptible to faking by persons who are motivated to appear to have PTSD but who really do not. It has been suggested that high F scale scores ($T > 88$) indicate attempts to fabricate symptoms of PTSD. No data have been published concerning the utility of the

PK scale with noncombat-related cases of PTSD. As with other MMPI-2 scales, it is not responsible clinical practice to use a single scale to assign diagnostic labels.

Interpretation of High PK Scores

In addition to being associated with diagnoses of post-traumatic stress disorder, high scores on the PK scale indicate individuals who:

1. report intense emotional distress
2. report symptoms of anxiety and sleep disturbance
3. feel guilty and depressed
4. may be having unwanted and disturbing thoughts
5. fear loss of emotional and cognitive control
6. feel misunderstood and mistreated

Interpretation of Low PK Scores

In addition to being less likely to be associated with diagnoses of post-traumatic stress disorder, low scores on the PK scale indicate persons who:

1. do not report emotional distress such as anxiety, depression, and sleep disturbance
2. do not report unwanted and disturbing thoughts
3. do not fear loss of emotional and cognitive control
4. do not feel misunderstood and mistreated

POST-TRAUMATIC STRESS DISORDER (PS) SCALE

The 60 items listed for the Post-traumatic Stress Disorder (PS) scale in the MMPI-2 manual do not really represent a formal scale. Rather, they are items that Schlenger and his associates (Schlenger & Kulka, 1987; Schlenger, Kulka, Fairbank, Hough, Jordan, Marmar, & Weiss, 1989) at the Research Triangle Institute in North Carolina found to differentiate among Vietnam veterans who had been diagnosed as PTSD, Vietnam veterans with psychiatric diagnoses other than PTSD, and nonpatient Vietnam veterans. Forty-five of the items are also included in the PK scale described earlier. The additional 15 items are ones from the experimental form of the MMPI (AX) that were endorsed differentially by the three groups of veterans.

No research has yet been published concerning this group of items. Internal consistency coefficients for males and females in the MMPI-2 standardization

samples were .89 and .91, respectively. In a personal communication with this author, Schlenger reported a corrected split-half reliability coefficient of .94 for a scale based on the 45 PS items that also are in the PK scale. Test-retest reliability coefficients for the PS scale for subsamples of males and females in the MMPI-2 normative samples were .92 and .88, respectively. Schlenger also reported that the 45-item scale correctly classified 81.6 percent of Vietnam veterans who had been diagnosed as PTSD based on structured interviews and other information and 87.7 percent of Vietnam veterans who did not have PTSD diagnoses.

In summary, the 60 items listed in the MMPI-2 manual for the PS scale do not really comprise a scale. Rather, they are items from the PK scale and other items from the MMPI-2 that were endorsed differentially by veterans with and without developed from these items remains to be demonstrated. Schlenger and his associates plan to continue their research efforts with the items.

SUBTLE-OBVIOUS SUBSCALES

Wiener (1948) differentiated between MMPI items that were easy to detect as indicating emotional disturbance and items that were relatively difficult to detect as indicating emotional disturbance. The former were labeled as obvious items and the latter as subtle items. They rationally developed obvious and subtle subscales for scales 2, 3, 4, 6, and 9 of the original MMPI. Wiener hypothesized that test subjects who were trying to fake bad on the MMPI would endorse many of the obvious and few of the subtle items in the clinical scales. Correspondingly, test subjects who were trying to fake good on the MMPI would endorse many of the subtle items and few of the obvious items in the clinical scales.

Although the Subtle-Obvious subscales are discussed in the MMPI-2 manual and the test publisher provides scoring keys and T-score transformation tables for the subscales, they will not be considered in detail in this chapter because of this author's belief that they are of little or no value in clinical practice. It seems likely that the subtle items are ones that were identified in the original item analyses due to chance. Had Hathaway and McKinley cross-validated their item analyses, these items probably would not have been included in the clinical scales.

Considerable research evidence indicates that nontest behaviors are most accurately predicted by the obvious rather than by the subtle items (Duff, 1965; Gynther, Burkhart, & Hovanitz, 1979; Burkhart, Gynther, & Fromuth, 1980; Snyter & Graham, 1984; Butcher, 1989). In fact, including subtle items in the clinical scales may actually detract from the prediction of criterion variables.

The data concerning the utility of the Subtle-Obvious subscales in detecting deviant test-taking attitudes is somewhat more complex. Subjects who were known to be exaggerating psychopathology when responding to MMPI items

tended to endorse many more obvious than subtle items. However, because all the clinical scales except scale 9 have many more obvious than subtle items, persons who actually have considerable psychopathology also endorse more obvious than subtle items (Schretlen, 1988). Thus, the differential endorsement of the subtle and obvious items is not particularly useful in differentiating between exaggerated profiles and valid profiles indicating severe psycho-pathology. Several studies have suggested that the standard validity scales are as accurate as or more accurate than the Subtle-Obvious subscales in discriminating between exaggerated and valid profiles indicating severe psychopathology (Anthony, 1971; Schretlen, 1988).

When subjects have been instructed to fake good on the MMPI, they have endorsed fewer obvious items than under standard instructions. Interestingly, with the fake good instructions subjects tended to endorse more of the subtle items than with standard instructions. This may be because the subtle items are seen by test subjects as representing socially desirable attitudes or actions (Burkhart, Christian, & Gynther, 1978). Studies that have examined the utility of the Subtle-Obvious subscales in identifying fake good response sets have not found them to be particularly accurate (Dubinsky, Gamble, & Rogers, 1985; Schretlen, 1988).

Several conclusions can be reached concerning the Subtle-Obvious subscales. First, the subtle items probably were included in the clinical scales because the item analyses were not cross-validated. Second, it is the obvious and not the subtle items that are most related to nontest behaviors. Third, although subjects who approach the MMPI-2 with motivation to minimize or to exaggerate psy-chopathology may endorse the subtle and obvious items differentially, the Subtle-Obvious subscales do not permit very accurate differentiation of faked and valid profiles. Fourth, the standard validity scales of MMPI-2 work as well as or better than the Subtle-Obvious subscales in identifying these deviant response sets. Because of complex relationships between subtle-obvious item endorsements, invalid response sets, and subject characteristics, this author does not use the Subtle-Obvious subscales in his own clinical work and does not recommend that others use them. Instead, it is recommended that scores and patterns of scores on the standard validity scales (see Chapter 3) be used in making decisions about test invalidity.

8

Psychometric Considerations and Use with Special Groups

Although the major purpose of this book is to help students and clinicians learn to use and interpret the MMPI-2 clinically, it also is very important for test users to understand the strengths and weaknesses of the instrument so that they can evaluate the appropriateness of its use in various settings and for various purposes. This chapter is intended as a brief summary of information concerning the psychometric properties of the MMPI-2 and its use with subjects different from those for whom the MMPI was designed and on whom it was standardized. Because of the considerable continuity between the original MMPI and MMPI-2, some information about both versions will be included. Coverage will not be exhaustive, and readers who require more information about topics covered here should consult other references such as the test manual (Butcher, Dahlstrom, Graham, Tellegen, & Kaemmer, 1989) and *An MMPI Handbook*, Volumes I and II (Dahlstrom, Welsh, & Dahlstrom, 1972, 1975).

PSYCHOMETRIC CONSIDERATIONS

The MMPI was the most widely used psychological test in the United States (Lubin, Larsen, & Matarazzo, 1984; Keller & Piotrowski, 1989; Piotrowski & Lubin, in press), and it seems likely that the MMPI-2 will be even more widely used. Far more research papers have been published about the MMPI than about any other personality inventory (Graham & Lilly, 1984). Reviewers of the MMPI have generally endorsed its utility. Alker (1978) concluded that the MMPI can provide reliable indications of psychological treatments that will or will not work for specific patients. King (1978) concluded his review of the MMPI by stating: "The MMPI remains matchless as the objective instrument for the assessment of psychopathology . . . and still holds the place as the sine qua non in the psychologist's armamentarium of psychometric aids" (p. 938). Although the MMPI-2 has not yet undergone critical review, the continuity between it and the original MMPI is such that the new version is also likely to be received positively.

Standardization

Unlike many projective techniques, the MMPI was well standardized in terms of materials, administration, and scoring. Essentially the same items, scales, and profile sheets were used from its inception in the 1930s until the publication of the MMPI-2 in 1989. Although there were some variations in the interpretation of scores, most users based interpretations on the sizable research literature that has accumulated. This standardization of materials and procedures ensured that data collected in diverse settings were comparable and led to the accumulation of a significant data base for interpreting results.

Although the MMPI-2 was somewhat modified, considerable effort was made to maintain continuity between the original test and the revised version. Although some items were updated, some deleted, and some new ones added, the basic item pool is quite similar to that of the original MMPI. The new instrument maintains the true-false response format of the original test. The basic validity and clinical scales remain essentially unchanged. Scores are arrayed on a profile sheet that bears remarkable resemblance to the original one. Although uniform T-scores are used for eight of the clinical scales, the resulting scores are essentially equivalent to the original ones. Later in this chapter data will be reviewed suggesting that the large body of research literature that has accumulated for the MMPI can be applied directly to MMPI-2. Clearly, enough continuity exists between the MMPI and MMPI-2 to assure that much of what we have learned about the original instrument is relevant to the revised version.

Scale Construction

As was discussed briefly in Chapter 1, the clinical scales of the MMPI were constructed according to empirical keying procedures. Items were selected for inclusion in a scale if subjects diagnosed as having a particular clinical syndrome (e.g., hypochondriasis, depression) responded to the items significantly differently from other patients and from normal subjects. The reader interested in details concerning original scale construction should consult a series of articles by Hathaway and his associates in *Basic Readings on the MMPI* (Dahlstrom & Dahlstrom, 1980). In order to maintain continuity between the original and revised instruments, MMPI-2 maintains the basic clinical scales with only minor deletions and changes (see Table 1.1 in Chapter 1). Scale 5 had the most items deleted (four), and these dealt primarily with objectionable sexual content. Correlations between scores on the original clinical scales and the clinical scales of MMPI-2 are all above .98, suggesting that the two sets of scales essentially are equivalent.

Although the empirical keying approach was an improvement over the face-valid approach used in earlier personality inventories, the scale construction procedures were rather unsophisticated by current psychometric standards. The clinical samples were often very small. For example, only 20 criterion

subjects were used to select items for scale 7. Although the test authors stressed that they tried to identify criterion groups composed of patients with only one kind of psychopathology, no data were presented concerning the reliability of the criterion placements. For most scales, cross-validation procedures were employed. The statistical analyses were not very sophisticated, and often only descriptive statistics were presented.

Because no attempt was made to ensure that items would appear on only one scale, there is considerable overlap between some of the scales. For example, 13 of the 39 items in the MMPI-2 scale 6 also appear in scale 8. This item overlap contributes to high intercorrelations among the scales and limits the extent to which scores on a single scale contribute uniquely to the prediction of appropriate criterion measures. The intercorrelations of the basic MMPI-2 scales for the normative samples are presented in Appendix M.

The empirical keying approach used with the MMPI precluded attention to item content and scale homogeneity. Hathaway and McKinley (1940) noted that the MMPI item content was heterogeneous, but they did not give attention to the homogeneity of the individual scales. As a result, the internal consistency of the scales is not very high. More information about the internal consistency of MMPI-2 scales will be presented later in this chapter.

Norms

Test norms provide a summary of results obtained when the test is given to a representative sample of individuals. The sample is referred to as the normative sample or standardization sample. A person's score on a test typically has meaning only when it is compared with a standardization sample.

The normal subjects used in constructing the original scales of the MMPI included 724 persons who were visiting friends or relatives at the University of Minnesota Hospitals. Only persons who reported that they were under the care of a physician were excluded from the sample. Other normal subjects used in various phases of scale development were 265 high school graduates who came to the University of Minnesota Testing Bureau for precollege guidance, 265 skilled workers involved with local Works Progress Administration projects, and 243 medical patients who did not report psychiatric problems.

Only the 724 hospital visitors were included in the sample that was used to determine T-score values for the original MMPI. All the subjects in the standardization sample were white, and the typical person was about 35 years of age, married, residing in a small town or rural area, working in a skilled or semi-skilled trade (or married to a man of this occupational level), and having about eight years of formal education (Dahlstrom, Welsh, & Dahlstrom, 1972). Hathaway and Briggs (1957) later refined this sample by eliminating persons with incomplete records or faulty background information. The refined sample was the one typically used for converting raw scores on supplementary MMPI scales to T-scores.

Although some data collected on nonclinical subjects in a variety of research projects suggested that the original MMPI norms were still appropriate, concern was expressed that the MMPI norms had become outdated. Colligan, Osborne, and Offord (1980) collected contemporary data from normal subjects in the same geographical area where the original MMPI norms were collected. These investigators found that on some MMPI scales contemporary subjects endorsed more items in the scored direction than did Hathaway's normal subjects. The Colligan et al. data were of limited utility because their subjects were limited geographically and demographically. In addition, their data were presented as normalized T-scores. Although Colligan et al. argued that normalized scores were more appropriate, Hsu (1984) offered some convincing arguments to the contrary, and Graham and Lilly (1986) demonstrated that the use of normalized T-scores led to underdiagnosis of psychopathology of psychiatric patients.

The normative samples for MMPI-2 are larger and more representative than those for the original MMPI (Butcher, Dahlstrom, Graham, Tellegen, & Kaemmer, 1989). The 1138 males and 1462 females in the MMPI-2 normative samples were selected from diverse geographical areas of the United States, and their demographic characteristics closely parallel 1980 census data. They were community residents who were solicited randomly for participation in the restandardization study. Approximately 3 percent of the males and 6 percent of the females indicated that they were in treatment for mental health problems at the time of their participation in the study. The samples include representatives of minority groups (i.e., blacks, Hispanics, Asian-Americans, American Indians). Although the educational level of subjects in the MMPI-2 normative samples (mean = 14.72 years) is somewhat higher than that of the general population, it probably is representative of persons to whom the MMPI-2 is likely to be administered. Normative subjects ranged in age from 18 to 85 years. In a separate project, MMPI-2 normative data were collected from large, diverse samples of adolescent subjects. Separate norms for adolescents will be published at a later date.

Analyses of MMPI-2 scores were conducted for various subgroupings of normative subjects. These analyses indicated that separate norms were not needed for subjects of differing ages, geographic areas, or ethnicity. There were important differences between the males and females, so separate norms were developed for these two groups.

In summary, whereas the normative samples for the original MMPI were small and not very representative of the general population of the United States, the normative samples for the MMPI-2 are large and quite representative of the population on major demographic variables. This represents a very significant improvement in the instrument.

T-Score Transformations

As indicated in Chapter 2, raw scores on the various MMPI-2 scales are converted to T-scores to facilitate interpretation. With the original MMPI, raw

scores were converted to linear T-scores having a mean of 50 and a standard deviation of 10. Because the distribution of raw scores for the MMPI and MMPI-2 scales are not normally distributed, linear T-scores, which maintain the same distributions as the raw scores on which they are based, do not have exactly the same meaning for every scale. For example, a T-score of 70 on one clinical scale of the original MMPI did not have the same percentile equivalent as a T-score of 70 on another MMPI clinical scale. Although the percentile equivalents were not greatly different from one scale to another, the differences led to some problems in interpretation.

For the eight basic clinical scales (excluding scales 5 and 0), the MMPI-2 utilizes a different kind of T-score transformation from that used with the original MMPI. This transformation, called a uniform T-score, assures that a T-score of a given level (e.g., 70) has the same percentile equivalent for all scales (Butcher, Dahlstrom, Graham, Tellegen, & Kaemmer, 1989). A composite (or average) distribution of the raw scores of the normative samples on the eight basic clinical scales was derived. The distribution of each of the eight clinical scales was adjusted so that it would match the composite distribution. This procedure resulted in uniform T-scores that are percentile equivalent and whose distributions are closely matched in terms of skewness and kurtosis. The change in the distribution of any particular scale is not great, so the profile retains most of its familiar characteristics. Percentile equivalents for various uniform T-scores are reported in Appendix N.

Uniform T-scores were not derived for scales 5 and 0 or for the validity scales because the distributions of scores of these scales differ considerably from those of the eight clinical scales. For these scales, linear T-score transformations, comparable to those used with the original MMPI, were derived. The norms for most MMPI-2 supplementary scales are expressed as linear T-scores. The exceptions are the new content scales for which uniform T-scores were derived using the same composite distributions used for the eight clinical scales. This permits direct comparison between the basic clinical scales and the content scales.

Temporal Stability

That scores on tests of ability, interest, and aptitude should have high temporal stability is quite accepted by most psychologists. What temporal stability should be expected from personality tests is not as clear. Although personality test scores should not be influenced by sources of error variance, such as room temperature, lack of sleep, and the like, it must be recognized that many personality attributes change over relatively short periods of time. Dahlstrom (1972) pointed out that many of the inferences made from personality test data involve current emotional status, whereas others deal with personality structure. Scales assessing personality structure should have high temporal stability, but those designed to measure current emotional status should be sensitive to rather short-term fluctuations.

From the MMPI's inception there has been an awareness of the importance of

scale stability. Dahlstrom, Welsh, and Dahlstrom (1972), Graham (1977a), and Schwartz (1977) summarized temporal stability data for the individual validity and clinical scales of the MMPI. Table 8.1 reports ranges and typical values of test-retest correlations of the original MMPI scales for various samples and varying test-retest intervals. For normal subjects the test-retest coefficients for relatively short intervals were relatively high and comparable to coefficients for other personality tests. For longer intervals the coefficients were considerably lower. The data for psychiatric patients were very similar to those for normals. For criminal samples the short-term coefficients were a bit lower than for the normal and psychiatric samples. Schwartz (1977) concluded that the temporal stability of the original MMPI scales was not related systematically to the gender of subjects or the MMPI form used. Further, no MMPI scale appeared to be consistently more stable than other scales. In summary, short-term temporal stability of the original MMPI scales compared favorably with that of scores from other personality inventories.

The MMPI-2 manual (Butcher, Dahlstrom, Graham, Tellegen, & Kaemmer, 1989) reports test-retest reliability coefficients for the basic MMPI-2 validity and clinical scales for 82 males and 111 females in the normative samples. The retest interval for these subjects was approximately one week. Table 8.2 summarizes these coefficients. The short-term temporal stability of the MMPI-2 scales for normal subjects appears to be at least as high as or higher than that of the original MMPI scales. The reliability coefficients for the MMPI-2 scales compare quite favorably with those of other personality scales.

Because MMPI interpretive strategies have emphasized the configural aspects of profiles, it is important to consider the stability of such configurations. Many clinicians assume that because the individual clinical scales have reasonably good temporal stability, the configurations based on those scales also have good temporal stability. Only limited data are available concerning the stability of scale configurations for the original MMPI, and no data have yet been published concerning the stability of configurations for the MMPI-2. However, because of the considerable continuity between the original and revised instru-

Table 8.1. Summary of test-retest reliability coefficients for original MMPI scales

Samples	Test-Retest Interval					
	One Day or Less		One to Two Weeks		One Year or More	
	Actual Range	Typical Range	Actual Range	Typical Range	Actual Range	Typical Range
Normal	.49–.96	.80–.85	.29–.92	.70–.80	.13–.73	.35–.45
Psychiatric	.61–.94	.80–.85	.43–.86	.80–.85	.22–.72	.50–.60
Criminal	.40–.86	.70–.80	.21–.84	.60–.70	—	—

Source: G. F. Schwartz, *An investigation of the stability of single scale and two-point MMPI code types for psychiatric patients*. Unpublished doctoral dissertation, Kent State University, Kent, OH, 1977. Reproduced by permission.

Table 8.2. Test-retest coefficients for MMPI-2 scales for male and female subjects in the normative samples (one-week interval)

Scales	Males (N = 82)	Females (N = 111)
L	.77	.81
F	.78	.69
K	.84	.81
Hs	.85	.85
D	.75	.77
Hy	.72	.76
Pd	.81	.79
Mf	.82	.73
Pa	.67	.58
Pt	.89	.88
Sc	.87	.80
Ma	.83	.68
Si	.92	.91

Source: Minnesota Multiphasic Personality Inventory-2 (MMPI-2): Manual for administration and scoring. (1989) S. R. Hathaway & J. C. McKinley with J. N. Butcher, W. G. Dahlstrom, J. R. Graham, A. Tellegen, & B. Kaemmer. Minneapolis: The University of Minnesota Press. Reproduced by permission.

ments, one can assume that the stability of the MMPI-2 configurations will be very similar to that on the original MMPI.

Table 8.3 summarizes the results of studies that have reported stability of high-point, two-point, and three-point code types for the original MMPI. Although the kinds of subjects and test-retest intervals have differed across studies, the results have been rather consistent. About one half of subjects have had the same high-point code on two administrations; about one fourth to one third have had the same two-point code; and about one fourth have had the same three-point code.

Graham, Smith, and Schwartz (1986) concluded that no particular high-point code or two-point code was significantly more stable than other codes. Graham et al. (1986) also reported that configurations tended to be more stable when the scales in the code types were more elevated initially and when there was a greater difference between these scales and other scales in the profile. When code types of subjects changed from test to retest administrations, the second code type often was in the same diagnostic grouping (neurotic, psychotic, characterological) as the first. From one half to two thirds of subjects had code types in the same diagnostic grouping on test and retest. When the code types were from different diagnostic groupings on test and retest, the most frequent change was from psychotic on the initial test to characterological on the retest. The implication of these data is that many of the inferences made would be the same even though the patients did not have exactly the same two-point code on the two occasions.

Table 8.3. Percentages of high-point, two-point, and three-point MMPI codes remaining the same on retest[a]

Source	Sample	N	Sex	Test-Retest Interval	High-Point	Two-Point	Three-Point
Graham (1977a)	College student	43	M	1 week	51	35	23
Graham (1977a)	College student	36	F	1 week	50	31	28
Faschingbauer (1974)	College student/ Psychiatric	61	M/F	1 day	63	41	23
Lichtenstein & Bryan (1966)	Volunteer/ Psychiatric	82	M/F	1–2 days	50	—	—
Kincannon (1968)	Psychiatric	60	M/F	1–2 days	61	—	—
Pauker (1966)	Psychiatric	107	F	13–176 days	44	25	—
Sivanich (1961)[b]	Psychiatric	202	F	2–2230 days	48	20	—
Uecker (1969)	Organic	30	M	1 week	—	23	—
Lauber & Dahlstrom (1953)	Delinquent	19	F	?	90	95	—

[a]For two-point and three-point codes, scales are used interchangeably.

[b]Used only four two-point codes (4-6, 4-2, 6-8, 2-7).

Source: J. R. Graham, R. L. Smith, & G. F. Schwartz (1986). Stability of MMPI configurations for psychiatric inpatients. *Journal of Consulting and Clinical Psychology, 54,* 375–380. Copyright © 1986 by the American Psychological Association. Reproduced by permission of the publisher.

What about subjects whose code types changed from one major diagnostic grouping on the initial test to another major grouping on the retest? Were these changes due to the unreliability of the MMPI, or did they reflect significant changes in the status of the patients? Graham et al. (1986) addressed this issue to a limited extent. They studied psychiatric inpatients who produced psychotic two-point codes on the initial testing and nonpsychotic codes on retesting and then compared these patients with those who had psychotic codes for both administrations or for neither administration. External psychiatric ratings of psychotic behaviors were available for all patients, and those who changed from psychotic to nonpsychotic showed concomitant changes in psychiatric ratings. Patients who had nonpsychotic codes on both administrations were given relatively low psychosis ratings on both occasions. Complicating the results of the study was the finding that patients who had psychotic codes on both test and retest were given lower psychosis ratings at retest than at the time of the initial test. It is important to note, however, that the psychiatrists who did the rating also were case managers for the patients they rated. Consequently, they may have been reluctant to indicate that patients that they were treating, and perhaps were about ready to discharge from the hospital, had not shown decreases in psychotic behaviors.

Several summary statements can be made about the temporal stability of MMPI-2 scores. Individual MMPI-2 scales seem to be as reliable temporally as the scales of the original MMPI and as other personality measures. Code types are likely to be more stable when their scales are more elevated and when they

are significantly more elevated than other scales in the profile. Although configurations probably are not as stable as they are assumed to be by test users, many subjects are likely to produce the same code types on different admin- istrations of the test. Furthermore, when the code types change from one administration to another, they are likely to remain in the same diagnostic grouping. When the code types change dramatically, concomitant behavioral changes are likely.

Internal Consistency

Because of the empirical keying procedures used in constructing the basic validity and clinical scales, little or no attention was given by the test authors to internal consistency of scales. Dahlstrom, Welsh, and Dahlstrom (1975) sum- marized internal consistency data for a variety of samples. Estimates of internal consistency varied considerably (from $-.05$ to $+.96$), with typical values ranging from .60 to .90. Scales 3, 5, and 9 appeared to be the least consistent, whereas scales 1, 7, and 8 appeared to be the most internally consistent. The MMPI-2 manual (Butcher, Dahlstrom, Graham, Tellegen, & Kaemmer, 1989) reports internal consistency values for the standard validity and clinical scales of MMPI-2. These values are summarized in Table 8.4. The coefficients are similar to the typical values previously reported for the original MMPI scales. Scales

Table 8.4. Internal consistency estimates (Alpha) for MMPI-2 validity and clinical scales for the normative samples

Scales	Males (N = 1138)	Females (N = 1462)
L	.62	.57
F	.64	.63
K	.74	.72
Hs	.77	.81
D	.59	.64
Hy	.58	.56
Pd	.60	.62
Mf	.58	.37
Pa	.34	.39
Pt	.85	.87
Sc	.85	.86
Ma	.58	.61
Si	.82	.84

Source: Minnesota Multiphasic Personality Inventory-2 (MMPI-2): Manual for administration and scoring. (1989) S. R. Hathaway & J. C. McKinley with J. N. Butcher, W. G. Dahlstrom, J. R. Graham, A. Tellegen, & B. Kaemmer. Minneapolis: The University of Minnesota Press. Re- produced by permission.

1, 7, 8, and 0 appear to be the most internally consistent, whereas scales 5, 6, and 9 appear to be the least internally consistent.

Factor analyses of items within each standard scale of the MMPI have indicated that most of the scales are not unidimensional (Comrey, 1957abc, 1958abcde; Comrey & Marggraff, 1958; Graham, Schroeder, & Lilly, 1971; Ben-Porath, Hostetler, Butcher, and Graham, 1989). The one exception seems to be scale 1, where most of the variance is associated with a single dimension: concern about health and bodily functioning. Because little attention was given to internal consistency when the original MMPI scales were constructed, it is not surprising that the scales are not as internally consistent as some other personality scales developed according to internal consistency procedures.

Factor Structure

Two consistent dimensions have emerged whenever scores on the basic MMPI validity and clinical scales have been factor-analyzed (Block, 1965; Eichman, 1961, 1962; Welsh, 1956). Scales 7 and 8 had high positive loadings on Factor I, and the K scale had a high negative loading on that factor. Welsh and Eichman both labeled this factor "Anxiety," whereas Block scored it in the opposite direction and called it "Ego Resiliency." Welsh developed the Anxiety (A) scale to assess this dimension. This scale seems to assess a general maladjustment dimension.

Scales 1, 2, and 3 had high positive loadings on Factor II and scale 9 a moderately high negative loadings. Welsh and Eichman labeled this dimension "Repression," and Block called it "Ego Control." The Repression (R) scale, developed by Welsh to assess this dimension, seems to assess denial, rationalization, lack of insight, and overcontrol of needs and impulses.

The MMPI-2 manual (Butcher, Dahlstrom, Graham, Tellegen, & Kaemmer, 1989) reports results of factor analyses of the MMPI-2 scales for subjects in the normative samples. The results are quite consistent with previous studies reported in the literature for the original MMPI. One major factor seems related to general maladjustment and psychotic mentation, whereas another major factor seems more related to neurotic characteristics. Smaller factors seem to be related to gender role identification and personality disorder. Butcher, Dahlstrom, Graham, Tellegen, and Kaemmer (1989) noted that the factor structure was somewhat different for males and females, suggesting that some MMPI-2 patterns may have somewhat different interpretive meanings for each gender.

Some investigators factor- or cluster-analyzed responses to the entire original MMPI item pool (Barker, Fowler, & Peterson, 1971; Chu, 1966; Johnson, Null, Butcher, & Johnson, 1984; Lushene, 1967; Stein, 1968; Tryon, 1966; Tryon & Bailey, 1965). Most of these early studies were limited by small sample sizes or analyses based on subsets of the total MMPI item pool. Only the study of Johnson et al. (1984) utilized a very large sample (more than 11,000 subjects) and analyzed the entire item pool in a single computational pass.

Using replication procedures, Johnson et al. (1984) identified the following 21 factors in the MMPI item pool: Neuroticism (General Anxiety and Worry); Psychoticism (Peculiar Thinking); Cynicism (Normal Paranoia); Denial of Somatic Problems; Social Extroversion; Stereotypic Femininity; Aggressive Hostility; Psychotic Paranoia; Depression; Delinquency; Inner Directedness; Assertiveness; Stereotypic Masculinity; Neurasthenic Somatization; Phobias; Family Attachment; Well-being (Health); Intellectual Interests; Rebellious Fundamentalism; Sexual Adjustment; and Dreaming. The authors noted the similarity of these factors to the content dimensions represented in the Wiggins content scales and in the original content categories presented by Hathaway and McKinley. They also commented that the item pool seemed to be measuring more aspects of personality than merely emotional stability. No data have yet been published concerning the factor structure of MMPI-2 item responses. However, because of the considerable overlap between items in the original MMPI and MMPI-2, one would expect to find some of the same factors represented in MMPI-2 item response data. However, because of item deletions and additions, some factors present in the original MMPI item data might not emerge from analysis of MMPI-2 item data, and some factors not present in the original MMPI item data probably would be identified with MMPI-2 item data.

Studies of the factor structure of item responses to the original MMPI offered some interesting insights into the psychometric properties of the MMPI and suggested the basis for new and potentially useful scales. Barker et al. (1971) and Tryon, Stein, and Chu (Stein, 1968) developed scales to assess their factor dimensions and demonstrated them to be as reliable as the standard MMPI scales and as good as or better than the standard scales in discriminating among diagnostic groups. However, the limited amount of data concerning the utility of scales based on factor analyses precluded recommending their routine clinical use. Whether or not reliable and valid scales can be developed through factor analyses of items responses to the MMPI-2 remains to be determined.

Response Sets and Styles

Over the years some critics, such as Messick and Jackson (1961) and Edwards (1957, 1964) argued that the MMPI scales were of limited utility because most of the variance in their scores could be attributed to response sets or styles. Messick and Jackson argued that subjects who obtained high scores on the MMPI scales did so only because of an acquiescence response style (i.e., a tendency to agree passively with inventory statements). In support of their argument, Messick and Jackson pointed out an imbalance in the proportion of items keyed true or false on the standard MMPI scales. Further, it was shown that scores on Welsh's Anxiety scale (a measure of one major source of variance in MMPI responses) correlated positively with an acquiescence measure.

Edwards maintained that scores on the standard scales of the MMPI were grossly confounded with a social desirability response set. Subjects who obtained higher scores on the clinical scales were hypothesized to be those willing

to admit to socially undesirable behaviors, whether or not these behaviors really were characteristic of them. Major support for this position came from data indicating that scores on the standard MMPI scales and on Welsh's Anxiety scale had high negative correlations with a social desirability scale.

Although a number of persons argued against the acquiescence and social desirability interpretations of the MMPI scales, Block (1965) most thoroughly reviewed the arguments supporting them and pointed out some statistical and methodological problems. He also presented some new evidence clearly rebutting them. Block modified the standard MMPI scales, balancing the number of true and false items within each scale. Contrary to the prediction of Messick and Jackson, with these modified scales the factor structure of the MMPI was essentially the same as with the standard scales. Block also developed a measure of Welsh's Anxiety factor that was free of social desirability influences. Correlations between this modified Anxiety scale and standard MMPI scales were essentially the same as for Welsh's original scale. Finally, Block demonstrated that MMPI scales had reliable corrrelates with important nontest behaviors even when the effects of social desirability and acquiescence were removed.

In summary, the criticism directed at the MMPI by critics such as Messick, Jackson, and Edwards was severe. However, the MMPI withstood their challenges. Because of the continuity between the original MMPI and the MMPI-2, the data presented by Block concerning response sets probably can be generalized to the MMPI-2 as well.

Validity

In Volume II of *An MMPI Handbook*, Dahlstrom, Welsh, and Dahlstrom (1975) cited over 6000 studies involving the MMPI. Because of the continuity between the MMPI and the MMPI-2, the research base that supported the validity of the original MMPI also supports the validity of MMPI-2. Here we review briefly the validity data for the original MMPI, report data concerning the congruence between the MMPI and the MMPI-2, and present some initial external validity data for the MMPI-2.

In trying to reach some conclusions about the MMPI, it seems helpful to group research studies into three general categories. First, studies have compared the MMPI profiles of relevant criterion groups. Most of these studies have identified significant differences on one or more of the MMPI scales among groups formed on the basis of diagnosis, severity of disturbance, treatment regimes, and numerous other criteria. Lanyon (1968) published average or typical profiles for many of these criterion groups. Efforts to develop classification rules to discriminate among groups of subjects also investigated the validity of the MMPI (Goldberg, 1965; Henrichs, 1964; Meehl & Dahlstrom, 1960; D. R. Peterson, 1954; Taulbee & Sisson, 1957). Most of these classification studies have indicated that rules could be developed to discriminate among groups of interest.

A second category of studies included efforts to identify reliable behavioral correlates of MMPI scales and configurations. Nontest correlates of high or low scores on individual clinical scales have been identified for adolescents (Hathaway & Monachesi, 1963; Archer, Gordon, Giannetti, & Singles, 1988), normal college students (Black, 1953; Graham & McCord, 1985), student nurses (Hovey, 1953), normal Air Force officers (Block & Bailey, 1955; Gough, McKee, & Yandell, 1955), medical patients (Guthrie, 1949), and psychiatric patients (Boerger, Graham, & Lilly, 1974; Hedlund, 1977). Correlates for configurations of two or more MMPI scales were reported for normal adults (Hathaway & Meehl, 1952), normal college students (Black, 1953), medical patients (Guthrie, 1949), and psychiatric patients (Boerger, Graham, & Lilly, 1974; Gilberstadt & Duker, 1965; Gynther, Altman, & Sletten, 1973; Lewandowski & Graham, 1972; Marks, Seeman, & Haller, 1974; Meehl, 1951). The results of these numerous empirical studies with adults are synthesized in Chapters 4 and 5 and have been summarized previously by Dahlstrom, Welsh, and Dahlstrom (1972), Greene (1980), and Graham (1987). Archer (1987) has summarized the data for adolescent subjects. Clinicians drew heavily on the results of these studies in making inferences about MMPI scores and configurations. These data suggested that there are reliable nontest correlates for MMPI scores and configurations, but they also indicated that exactly the same correlates may not always be found for subjects of differing demographic backgrounds.

A third category of studies considered the MMPI scores and the person interpreting them as an integral unit and examined the accuracy of inferences based on the MMPI. In an early study of this type, Little and Shneidman (1959) asked expert test interpreters to provide diagnoses, ratings, and descriptions of subjects based on data from the MMPI, Rorschach, Thematic Apperception Test (TAT), and Make a Picture Story Test (MAPS). The accuracy of these judgments was determined by comparing them with judgments based on extensive case history data. The average correlations between judges' descriptions of subjects based on the MMPI, Rorschach, TAT, and MAPS were .28, .16, .17, and .11, respectively. Kostlan (1954) reported data suggesting that the MMPI leads to the most accurate inferences when used in conjunction with social case history data. Sines (1959) reported a mean correlation of .38 between judgments based on the MMPI and interview data and criterion ratings provided by patients' therapists. In a study limited to MMPI data, Graham (1967) reported correlations between MMPI-based descriptions and criterion descriptions of .31, .37, and .29 for judges of high, medium, and low experience, respectively.

Reviewing clinical judgment research, of which the above cited studies are a part, Goldberg (1968) concluded that, in general, clinical judgments tend to be rather unreliable, only minimally related to the confidence and the amount of experience of test judges, relatively unaffected by the amount of information available to judges, and rather low in validity on an absolute basis. In a more recent review of the clinical judgment literature, Garb (1984) was more optimistic, concluding that adding MMPI data to demographic information led to significant increases in validity of inferences. Graham and Lilly (1984) pointed

out that, compared with Rorschach and other projective techniques, personality descriptions based on the MMPI have been relatively more accurate. Also, descriptions based on MMPI data have been more accurate than descriptions based on judges' stereotypes of typical patients. When MMPI data have been used in conjunction with social history and/or interview data, the resulting descriptions have been more valid than when the MMPI data have been used alone.

To the extent that it can be demonstrated that scores and configurations of scores based on the original MMPI and on MMPI-2 are congruent, the considerable validity data that have accumulated for the original MMPI can be generalized to the MMPI-2. Graham (1988) reported data suggesting that scores on the standard validity and clinical scales of MMPI-2 and of the original MMPI are equivalent. The two sets of scores were correlated for normal and psychiatric subjects, and all correlations were greater than .98.

Graham (1968) also reported that for all scales except L the MMPI-2 normative subjects endorsed more items in the deviant direction than did the original MMPI normative subjects. On the L scale, the MMPI-2 normative subjects endorsed slightly fewer items in the scored direction. Thus, for most scales a given raw score will be equivalent to a somewhat lower T-score when the MMPI-2 norms are used than when the original MMPI norms are used. For the L scale a somewhat higher T-score will result when the MMPI-2 norms are used. For reasons that are not completely explainable, an F scale raw score also will result from using the MMPI-2 norms than from using the original MMPI norms. This seems to happen because Hathaway did not use a simple linear transformation for the F scale. Rather, he made some adjustments to take into account demographic characteristics of subjects.

Graham (1988) also reported data concerning the congruence of code types using MMPI-2 normative data and data from the original MMPI normative subjects. Raw scores for 232 male and 191 female psychiatric patients were converted to T-scores using both the original MMPI norms and MMPI-2 norms. The resulting T-scores were used to determine high-point and two-point code types for the subjects. Table 8.5 summarizes data concerning the agreement of code types when the different norms were used. Clearly, most subjects produced the same high-point and two-point codes using the two sets of norms. These data support the comparability of code types for the MMPI-2 and the original MMPI.

Because the basic validity and clinical scales of the original MMPI have been maintained relatively unchanged in the MMPI-2 and because data suggest that scores and code types for the MMPI-2 and the original MMPI are congruent, one can infer that the two instruments are basically comparable. Existing empirical data concerning the validity of the original MMPI therefore can be assumed to be relevant to the MMPI-2 as well.

It also is important to establish the validity of a revised instrument by comparing scores on that instrument with relevant external criterion measures. Graham (1988) reported some preliminary data concerning the external correlates of MMPI-2 scores. Utilizing data from 822 normal couples who partici-

Table 8.5. Congruence of high-point and two-point code types for male and female psychiatric patients

Code Type	Cutoff Score	Percentage Agreement MMPI-2 and MMPI	
		Male (N = 232)	Female (N = 191)
High-Point	None	79	77
	70	80	78
	80	81	81
	90	78	90
	100	84	93
Two-Point	None	70	65
	70	66	60
	80	64	62
	90	65	74
	100	71	94

Source: Graham, J. R. (1988, August). Establishing validity of the revised form of the MMPI. Symposium presentation at the 96th Annual Convention of the American Psychological Association, Atlanta, GA.

pated in the restandardization research together, scores on the basic clinical scales of the MMPI-2 (abstracted from Form AX) were correlated with be-havioral ratings of subjects provided by their partners. Table 8.6 lists the behavioral ratings that were most highly correlated with the clinical scales. The pattern of correlations suggests both convergent and discriminant validity for the clinical scales of the MMPI-2. Most of the correlates are quite consistent with those previously reported for the original MMPI. However, it should be noted that there were some important differences in correlates between males and females. For example, on scale 4, higher scoring males were more likely to get in trouble with the law and use nonprescription drugs than were lower scoring males. This relationship did not hold true for females. Also, higher scoring females on scale 6 were more likely than lower scoring females to be moody and lacking in emotional control. This relationship did not hold true for males. These gender differences suggest that additional research is needed to clarify the extent to which different interpretations should be considered for males and females.

Graham (1988) also reported behavioral correlate data for psychiatric pa-tients. Scores on the MMPI-2 clinical scales (abstracted from Form AX) were correlated with ratings of symptoms completed by psychiatrists and psycholo-gists who had observed and interviewed the patients. Table 8.7 lists the symp-toms most highly correlated with the clinical scales of the MMPI-2. As with the data for the normal subjects, the data from this study suggest that there are reliable extratest correlates for MMPI-2 scores and that these extratest corre-lates are quite similar to those previously reported for the original MMPI. Again, as with normal subjects, different correlates were found for males and females for some of the scales. For example, male patients scoring higher on

Table 8.6. External correlates for MMPI-2 clinical scales for 822 men and 822 women in the MMPI-2 normative samples

| Scale | Rating Scale Item | Correlation Coefficients | |
		Male	Female
1—Hs	Worries about health	27	23
	Lacks energy	22	18
	Headaches, stomach trouble	22	27
	Trouble sleeping	20	21
2—D	Lacks energy	29	24
	Lacks interest	23	23
	Self-confident	−22	−24
	Worries, frets	22	23
	Sad, blue	21	23
3—Hy	Trouble sleeping	18	20
	Worries about health	17	15
4—Pd	Angry, yells	09	25
	Cooperative	−11	−24
	Irritable, grouchy	10	23
	Trouble with law	21	13
	Uses nonprescription drugs	16	13
5—Mf	NONE		
6—Pa	Sad, blue	11	21
	Moody	12	19
	Bad dreams	08	19
	Cries easily	11	19
	Lacks emotional control	03	15
7—Pt	Bad dreams	14	23
	Many fears	21	21
	Self-confident	−18	−21
	Indecisive	17	18
8—Sc	Many fears	19	18
	Bad dreams	17	16
9—Ma	Uses nonprescription drugs	22	14
	Wears unusual clothing	10	22
	Bossy	18	06
	Talks too much	15	21
0—Si	Shy	28	28
	Self confident	−28	−28
	Avoids people	24	28
	Lacks interest	23	20

Note: Because of the large sample sizes correlations greater than .06 are statistically significant. Only items with correlations of .15 or greater for at least one gender are reported.

Source: J. R. Graham (1988, August). Establishing validity of the revised form of the MMPI. Symposium presentation at the 96th Annual Convention of the American Psychological Association, Atlanta, GA.

Table 8.7. Symptom descriptors for MMPI-2 clinical scales for 232 male and 191 female psychiatric patients

		Correlation Coefficients	
Scale	Symptom Descriptor	Male	Female
1—Hs	Somatic concern	18	14
	Hallucinatory behavior	14	17
	Grandiosity	−13	−16
	Unusual thought content	13	02
2—D	Depressive mood	30	26
	Grandiosity	−25	−36
	Guilt feelings	24	25
	Hallucinatory behavior	23	27
3—Hy	Grandiosity	−19	−25
	Somatic concern	18	15
	Depressive mood	17	12
4—Pd	Guilt feelings	17	02
	Grandiosity	−16	−21
	Emotional withdrawal	03	20
	Depressive mood	11	21
5—Mf	Motor retardation	−01	19
6—Pa	Suspiciousness	02	20
	Emotional withdrawal	−02	19
	Unusual thought content	18	05
	Motor retardation	−15	−03
	Anxiety	−10	19
7—Pt	Hallucinatory behavior	22	09
	Grandiosity	−22	−27
	Guilt feelings	21	15
	Unusual thought content	21	00
	Depressive mood	18	20
8—Sc	Suspiciousness	04	25
	Unusual thought content	22	02
9—Ma	Depressive mood	−17	−05
	Hostility	09	16
	Conceptual disorganization	15	18
0—Si	Grandiosity	−23	−25
	Hallucinatory behavior	23	17
	Depressive mood	22	15
	Unusual thought content	20	14
	Guilt feeling	15	21

Note: With these sample sizes correlations greater than .11 are statistically significant. Only descriptors with correlations equal to or greater than .15 for at least one gender are listed.

Source: J. R. Graham (1988, August). Establishing validity of the revised form of the MMPI. Symposium presented at the 96th Annual Convention of the American Psychological Association, Atlanta, GA.

scale 7 were more likely to manifest hallucinatory behavior and unusual thought content than males scoring lower on this scale, but the relationship was not found for female patients.

In summary, although research with the MMPI-2 is very limited at this time, there are some data suggesting that the instrument has validity. First, because of the congruence between scores and configurations of scores for the MMPI-2 and the original MMPI, the existing body of research literature concerning the MMPI can be applied rather directly to the MMPI-2. Second, preliminary research has indicated that there are reliable extratest correlates for MMPI-2 clinical scales and that these correlates are quite consistent with previously reported correlates for the original MMPI. Of course, it is likely that publication of the MMPI-2 will stimulate a great deal of additional research that will clarify more completely the validity of the MMPI-2 for various kinds of subjects and for various clinical purposes.

USE WITH SPECIAL GROUPS

The original MMPI was developed for use with adult psychiatric patients. Its norms were based on white adult normals in the cities and towns surrounding the University of Minnesota. Considerable caution was indicated in using the instrument with subjects whose demographic characteristics were different from those of the standardization sample or in other than traditional psychiatric settings. Although the norms for the MMPI-2 are more representative of the population of the United States than were those for the original MMPI, very little is known about the use of the MMPI-2 with special groups. This section reviews some information about the use of the original MMPI with some special groups. Because of the continuity between the MMPI-2 and the original MMPI, much of this information probably will be applicable to the MMPI-2. The limited data that exist concerning the use of the MMPI-2 with special populations also is reviewed.

Adolescents

The version of the MMPI-2 published in 1989 is intended for subjects 18 years of age or older. Contemporary normative data for adolescent subjects also have been collected. Although the test publisher has indicated that adolescent norms will be published, they are not included in the MMPI-2 manual, and it is not clear whether a separate booklet for adolescents will be made available. In addition, though the experimental version of the MMPI that was administered to the adolescent normative subjects included a number of new items designed especially for adolescents, it is still too soon to know whether these new items will be useful in developing new scales for adolescent subjects. Until new data

for adolescents are provided, the original MMPI should be used with subjects who are younger than 18 years of age. Later in this section we discuss appropriate norms for adolescent subjects and strategies for interpreting profiles of adolescent subjects.

Although the MMPI was developed for use with adults, it was administered to large groups of adolescents in Minnesota as early as 1947 (Hathaway & Monachesi, 1963). These early data and those of subsequent researchers (e.g., Ball, 1962; Baughman & Dahlstrom, 1968; Marks, Seeman, & Haller, 1974) indicated that on some MMPI scales normal adolescents obtained higher scores than the adult standardization sample. More specifically, mean profiles for groups of normal adolescents typically have had T-scores of approximately 60 on the F scale and on scales 4, 8, and 9. In several samples the mean profiles also show moderate elevation on scale 7.

The meaning of these elevated scores is not clear. They could suggest the turmoil and instability that some believe even normal adolescents experience. They could indicate more frequent psychopathology in adolescents, although this may be unlikely, given that studies have found only a slightly higher prevalence rate of psychiatric disorders in adolescence compared with middle childhood (e.g., Rutter, Graham, Chadwick, & Yule, 1976). They could result from experiences, unique to adolescent subjects, that are not particularly disturbing nor pathological but part of normal adolescent development. They could be due, at least in part, to differences in sampling and administration procedures in the adult and adolescent studies. However, it is clear that these differences between normal adult and normal adolescent scores create some problems when we try to interpret the profiles of adolescent subjects.

Ehrenworth and Archer (1985) reported that adolescent psychiatric patients produced different code types depending on whether adult or adolescent norms were used. Only 25 percent of the adolescent patients had the same two-point code for both adult and adolescent norms. When adult norms were used with adolescent patients, psychotic code types were much more likely to emerge than when adolescent norms were used (Chase, Chaffin, & Morrison, 1975; Ehrenworth, 1984).

Given that for adolescents different norms lead to differences in scores and code types, which norms lead to the most accurate judgments and inferences about adolescents? Archer (1987) and C. L. Williams (1986) concluded that adolescent norms are more appropriate than adult norms for adolescent subjects. For example, Ehrenworth (1984) found that adolescent norms led to a lower false positive rate for psychotic diagnoses for adolescent patients. Moore and Handal (1980) found that clinical scale elevations obtained when the MMPIs of normal adolescents scored on adult norms were not accompanied by indications of pathology on the Affect Checklist. Whereas Newmark, Gentry, and Whitt (1983) indicated that MMPIs scored on adult norms were not very effective in identifying schizophrenia in adolescents, Archer and Gordon (1988) found scores based on adolescent norms useful in identifying schizophrenia in adolescent inpatients. Archer, Ball, and Hunter (1985) found that adolescent

MMPIs scored on adolescent norms were useful in identifying borderline personality disorders in an inpatient psychiatric setting.

Another important issue in the use of the MMPI with adolescents centers on the source of descriptors to be used in generating inferences about profiles, whether they result from adolescent or adult norms. Should one use adult descriptors, such as those reported in other chapters of this book, or descriptors developed specifically for adolescents? Marks, Seeman, and Haller (1974) determined empirical correlates of two-point codes for adolescent psychiatric patients. These correlates were based on a sample of adolescents who were literate, white, 12 to 18 years of age, living with natural or adoptive parents, and lacking organic brain syndrome but who did have emotional problems and were in treatment for them. Although Marks and his colleagues are to be commended for conducting one of the few adequate research studies to date concerning the empirical correlates of adolescent code types, little subsequent research has replicated their findings. More recently, Williams and Butcher (in press, ab) reported empirical correlates for clinical scales and code types for adolescent subjects in a variety of treatment settings. These investigators concluded that the correlates reported previously for adult subjects also applied to their adolescent subjects.

Several studies have addressed the issue of whether adolescent profiles should be interpreted using descriptors based on adults or those based on adolescents. Lachar, Klinge, and Grisell (1976) found that computer interpretations generated from adolescent norms and adult-based descriptors were more accurate than those generated from adult norms and adult-based descriptors. However, these investigators did not examine the accuracy of descriptors generated from adolescent norms and adolescent-based descriptors. Ehrenworth and Archer (1985) examined the accuracy of interpretations of adolescent MMPIs under three conditions: adult norms and adult-based descriptors; adolescents norms and adolescent-based descriptors; and adolescent norms and adult-based descriptors. Accuracy of interpretations was rated by therapists of the adolescent inpatients. Although accuracy for all conditions was less than the investigators had expected, the interpretations generated from adolescent norms and adolescent-based descriptors were the least accurate. Wimbish (1984) reached a different conclusion about this matter. Her data indicated that the most accurate inferences about adolescent subjects came from the use of adolescent norms and adolescent-based descriptors.

Archer (1987) suggested that a "common-sense compromise" appears most appropriate in interpreting the profiles of adolescent subjects. He recommended using adolescent norms to convert raw scores to T-scores and subsequently interpreting the resulting profiles by combining information from both adolescent samples (e.g., Marks, Seeman, & Haller, 1974) and adult samples (e.g., Graham, 1977b; Lachar, 1974b). Although this compromise has much to recommend it, the clinician still is in a difficult position when the adolescent and adult descriptors lead to significantly different impressions of adolescent subjects. In these circumstances, other data sources (interview, history, observa-

tions, etc.) must be utilized in determining which kinds of descriptors are likely to be most accurate for a given subject.

Clearly, several kinds of additional research are needed. First, more up-to-date and representative normative data are needed for adolescent subjects. The adolescent norms presented in Dahlstrom, Welsh, and Dahlstrom (1972), utilized by Marks et al. (1974), and reprinted in Appendix C of this book are limited. Some of the data were collected by Hathaway in Minnesota as early as 1947. All of Hathaway's subjects were in the ninth grade, which makes the older and younger ones atypical. The Hathaway data were supplemented by data collected by Briggs in 1964 and 1965 in Alabama, California, Kansas, Missouri, North Carolina, and Ohio. There are serious reservations about how representative the samples are. We know that they included almost exclusively white subjects. Clearly, there is a pressing need for new normative data based on census representative samples of adolescents. As stated earlier in this section, a large sample of contemporary adolescent subjects has been assembled, and normative data based on the sample will be published in the near future.

Another pressing need is for more empirical research to establish empirical correlates of scores and configurations for adolescent subjects. The investigators working on the adolescent norms also have collected data in several clinical settings. These data should provide the basis for establishing empirical correlates for adolescent scores and configurations of scores. The availability of representative, contemporary adolescent norms and additional data concerning empirical correlates should help to resolve some of the uncertainty that exists concerning the interpretation of adolescent MMPIs.

Some practical suggestions can be made concerning the use of the MMPI with adolescents. A sixth- or seventh-grade reading level is needed, and Williams (1986) suggested screening for reading problems prior to administering the MMPI. In addition to reading level, an adolescent's developmental level also must be considered. The adolescent must be willing to stick to the task of answering the items, and he or she must have a wide enough range of experience to make the content of the items psychologically and semantically meaningful. In choosing to administer the MMPI to an adolescent, the examiner must decide if the task is appropriate to his or her cognitive, social, and emotional stage of development.

Once the MMPI is administered to adolescents and the raw scores are determined, two profiles should be plotted, one for adult norms and one for adolescent norms. The adult profile can be plotted on a standard MMPI answer sheet. To plot an adolescent profile the examiner must consult adolescent norm tables, such as those found in Appendix C of this book. The tables are entered using raw scores that are *not K-corrected*. T-scores are then plotted on a standard profile sheet.

For some adolescent subjects the profiles based on the two kinds of normative data will be quite similar and will yield the same code type. For others the two profile types will differ significantly. Typically, the adult norms will yield scores for adolescents that make them appear to be more psychopathological than

when the adolescent norms are used. As stated earlier, it often is difficult to decide which profile better reflects the adolescent's adjustment level. A good rule of thumb is that in nonclinical settings, where the MMPI is being used for screening purposes, the profile based on adult norms is likely to lead to overestimates of psychopathology. However, in clinical settings, where subjects are known to have significant psychopathology, the profile based on adult norms may more accurately reflect the level of psychopathology. Often, when MMPI scores of very disturbed adolescents are plotted on adolescent norms, the resulting profiles fall within "normal limits." Archer (1987) recommended that if adolescent norms are used clinicians should interpret scores below 70 as clinically significant. He suggested a cutoff score of T > 65 in these instances.

The next step is to identify the two-point code for each profile. Marks, Seeman, and Haller (1974) suggested that if an adolescent's code type does not appear in their book the third highest score should be used instead of the second highest score to identify a two-point code. For the adult profile, pro-cedures for defining code types described in Chapter 5 should be used. Con-sider both the adolescent-based and adult-based descriptors. Descriptors that are congruent for both profiles for the subject should be accepted with greatest confidence. Descriptors that are not consistent for the two profiles should be viewed more cautiously, and reference to data other than the MMPI profile may help in deciding between incongruent descriptors. Williams (1986) provided suggestions for learning more about adolescent clients by discussing the inter-pretations of their MMPIs with them.

Not much information is available concerning the meaning of adolescents' scores on MMPI supplementary scales. Archer (1987) reported some adolescent normative data for a number of supplementary scales. Archer, Gordon, Ander-son, and Giannetti (in press) reported some empirical correlate data for some supplementary scales for adolescent subjects. Available data suggest that the MacAndrew Alcoholism (MAC) scale can be interpreted for adolescents sim-ilarly to its interpretation for adults (Wisniewski, Glenwick, & Graham, 1985; Wolfson & Erbaugh, 1984).

Blacks

Because the standardization sample for the original MMPI did not include any black subjects, whether it is appropriate to use with black subjects has been discussed at length. Some studies have reported significant item and scale differences between black and white subjects (Greene, 1980; Gynther & Green, 1980; Pritchard and Rosenblatt, 1980; Greene, 1987). The general finding was that blacks tended to score higher than whites on scales F, 8, and 9, with a difference between blacks and whites of approximately 5 T-score points (1 or 2 raw score points). When black and white groups were of comparable age, education, and other demographic characteristics, the differences were smaller and often not significant (Dahlstrom, Lachar, & Dahlstrom, 1986).

Various interpretations of these differences were offered. Greene (1980)

concluded that the small differences between blacks and whites probably were of limited significance clinically. Gynther and Green (1980) suggested that the differences meant that normal blacks were more likely than normal whites to be incorrectly identified as abnormal. Pritchard and Rosenblatt (1980) maintained that the meaning of the differences could not be determined in most studies. It could not be assumed that the higher scores for blacks meant that the MMPI was biased against blacks. The higher scores for blacks could mean that the blacks had more psychopathology than the whites. Unfortunately, most studies did not include reliable and unbiased measures of psychopathology for black or white subjects.

Pritchard and Rosenblatt (1980) maintained that the only meaningful way of analyzing racial differences on the MMPI was to use what they called the "accuracy test." This approach involved determining if inferences made from MMPI scores were differentially accurate for different racial groups. Pritchard and Rosenblatt, as well as Greene (1987), noted the lack of well-designed studies that address the accuracy test. Butcher, Braswell, and Raney (1983) reported that MMPI differences between black and white psychiatric inpatients were meaningfully associated with actual symptomatic differences between the groups. Dahlstrom, Lachar, and Dahlstrom (1986) reported analyses suggesting that MMPI scores based on the standard test norms were not differentially related to psychopathology for black and white psychiatric patients. Additionally, Dahlstrom et al. reported that the use of special norms based exclusively on black subjects overcorrected deviations and failed to identify many black subjects who had serious emotional problems and were in need of professional intervention.

Dahlstrom et al. suggested that the more elevated MMPI scores of black subjects, especially young males, might reflect the various coping and defense mechanisms to which some minority subjects may resort in their efforts to deal with the special circumstances that they all too often encounter in America today. These investigators made some reasonable recommendations concerning the interpretation of the MMPIs of black subjects. They felt that the best procedure was to accept the pattern of MMPI scores that results from the use of the standard profile sheet and, when the profile is markedly deviant, to take special pains to explore in detail the subjects' life circumstances to understand as fully as possible the nature and degree of their problems and demands and the adequacy of their efforts in dealing with them. No data have been published concerning the MMPI-2 performance of black and white subjects. However, the investigators involved in revising the MMPI analyzed normative data separately for various ethnic groups and concluded that differences between the groups were small and did not justify separate norms for the ethnic groups included in the normative samples.

Special comment is necessary concerning the use of the revised MacAndrew Alcoholism scale (MAC-R) with black subjects. As indicated in Chapter 7, several studies have suggested caution in using the MAC with black subjects (Graham & Mayo, 1985; Walters, Greene, & Jeffrey, 1984; Walters, Greene, Jeffrey, Kruzich, & Haskin, 1983). These studies have indicated that black alcoholics tended to

obtain relatively high scores on the MAC, but classification rates for black subjects were not very good because nonalcoholic black psychiatric patients also tended to obtain rather high MAC scores. All these studies utilized military personnel or veterans, so the extent to which the findings can be generalized to other black subjects is unclear. However, until additional information is available, great caution should be exercised when the MAC-R scale is used with black subjects.

Other Ethnic Groups

There have been few empirical studies concerning the MMPI performance of ethnic subjects other than blacks. Greene (1987) identified only ten studies comparing Hispanic and white subjects on the MMPI. Although these studies found some significant differences between Hispanic and white subjects, Greene concluded that there was no pattern to the differences. The data did not support Greene's earlier contention (Greene, 1980) that Hispanics frequently score higher on the L scale and lower on scale 5. It also appeared that there were fewer differences between Hispanics and whites on the MMPI than between black and white subjects.

Greene (1987) identified only seven studies that compared the MMPI performance of American Indians and whites. Although American Indians tended to score higher than whites on some clinical scales, there was no clear pattern to these differences across the studies. Uecker, Boutilier, and Richardson (1980) reported no differences between American Indian and white alcoholics on the MacAndrew Alcoholism scale (MAC). However, these results are difficult to interpret because no data were presented for nonalcoholic American Indians and whites on the MAC.

Greene (1987) reported only three studies comparing MMPI performance of Asian-Americans and white subjects. Sue and Sue (1974) reported that male Asian-American college student counselees obtained higher scores than white counselees on most of the MMPI scales. However, other studies of Asian-Americans, which utilized normal persons and medical patients as subjects, reported fewer differences between Asian-Americans and whites. In summary, little is known about using the MMPI with Asian-American subjects, and clinicians should be cautious when the test is used with such subjects.

No data have been published concerning differences between white subjects and Hispanic, American Indian, or Asian-American subjects. However, given the continuity between the MMPI-2 and the original MMPI, it seems appropriate to be very cautious in using the MMPI-2 with members of these groups.

Medical Patients

The original MMPI was used frequently in medical settings. Although no data have been published yet concerning the use of the MMPI-2 in medical settings, it

seems likely that it will be used there even more frequently than the original instrument. Until new data are available concerning the use of the MMPI-2 in such settings, it will be necessary to rely on information concerning the use of the original MMPI.

Osborne (1979) and Henrichs (1981) presented overviews of the use of the MMPI in medical settings. Swenson, Pearson, and Osborne (1973) reported item, scale, and pattern data for 50,000 medical patients at the Mayo Clinic. Swenson, Rome, Pearson, and Brannick (1965) reported data indicating that most medical patients (89 percent) readily agreed to take the MMPI and completed and returned the test booklet. Swenson et al. (1965) also surveyed 158 physicians who had used the MMPI routinely for at least four months. For all 14 items on the questionnaire, 70 percent to 85 percent of the physicians indicated that the MMPI was useful with their patients. It will not be possible in this chapter to review even briefly the voluminous research literature concerning the relationship between MMPI data and characteristics of medical patients. Rather, an attempt will be made to indicate the general purposes for which the MMPI has been used in medical settings.

One important use of the MMPI with medical patients has been to screen for serious psychopathology that might have gone unreported or been minimized by patients. The indicators of serious psychopathology discussed elsewhere in this book (e.g., F scale level; overall profile elevation) should be considered when examining the profiles of medical patients.

Many clinicians have assumed that medical problems are going to upset patients and that this upset would be reflected in very deviant scores on the MMPI. It thus is important to develop some expectations concerning typical MMPI scores and profiles produced by medical patients. Swenson, Pearson, and Osborne (1973) reported summary MMPI data for approximately 25,000 male and 25,000 female patients at the Mayo Clinic. The mean profiles for both male and female patients fell within normal limits, the validity scales suggested a slightly defensive test-taking attitude, and T-scores on scales 1, 2, and 3 were near 60. Apparently, the medical problems of these patients were not psychologically distressing enough to lead to grossly elevated MMPI scale scores. How might the profiles of these patients appear had the tests been scored using MMPI-2 norms? The profiles probably would still be within normal limits, with T-scores on scales 1, 2, and 3 being between 55 and 60 and scores on the rest of the clinical scales being near the mean.

The MMPI-2 can be useful in alerting clinicians to the possibility of substance abuse problems among medical patients. Some patients develop physical symptoms because of chronic substance abuse; some develop substance abuse problems because of their medical problems; and some have substance abuse problems not directly related to their physical symptoms. Regardless of reasons for substance abuse problems among medical patients, early awareness of such problems facilitates treatment planning.

Research with the original MMPI did not reveal a single pattern of MMPI scales associated with substance abuse problems (e.g., Graham & Strenger, 1988). However, there is convincing evidence that scale 4 is likely to be elevated

among groups of persons who abuse substances. Scale 4 typically is not significantly elevated among medical patient groups. Thus, when a person is presenting primarily physical symptoms in a medical setting and has significant scale
4 elevation, the possibility of some abuse of substances should be considered.

Fordyce (1979) suggested that chronic pain patients can easily become ad-
dicted to narcotics, barbiturates, or muscle relaxants. He reported that such
persons often obtain elevations on scales 2 and 9. When both these scales are
elevated above T = 65, the possibility of addiction to prescription medications
should be considered.

The 24/42 two-point code type of the original MMPI has often been the most
typical pattern found among male alcoholics in treatment, and this same code
type and the 46/64 code type have been the ones most often found for female
alcoholics in treatment. Neither code type is common among medical patients
who do not abuse alcohol. Thus, when these code types are encountered in
medical patients (particularly if the scores are greater than T = 65), the
possibility of alcohol abuse should be explored carefully.

The MacAndrew Alcoholism Scale-Revised (MAC-R) was described in Chapter 7 of this book. Although the original MAC was developed by comparing item
responses of male alcoholic outpatients and male psychiatric outpatients, subsequent research indicated that the scale was very useful for identifying substance
abuse problems of various kinds for men and women in a variety of settings
(Graham & Strenger, 1988). If significant elevation is found on the MAC-R for
patients in a medical setting, careful consideration should be given to the
possibility that the person is abusing substances. As discussed in Chapter 7,
MAC-R raw scores of 28 or above strongly suggest substance abuse. Scores
between 24 and 27 are somewhat suggestive of such abuse. Scores below 24
strongly contraindicate a substance abuse problem. It should be emphasized
that research concerning the MAC has emphasized abuse of alcohol and other
nonprescription drugs. Little is known about the sensitivity of the MAC-R to the
abuse of prescribed drugs, such as those used by chronic pain patients.

The original MMPI often was used to try to determine if the physical symptoms presented by patients were organic or functional in origin. It is never
appropriate to use the MMPI-2 alone to diagnose an organic condition or to
rule it out. The most that the MMPI-2 can do is to give some information
concerning the underlying personality characteristics of the patient. This information can be used, along with other available information, to make inferences
concerning the compatibility of the personality characteristics and a functional
explanation of symptoms.

Osborne (1979) summarized studies with the original MMPI that tried to
determine if patients' symptoms were functional or organic. The symptoms
studied have included low back pain, sexual impotence, neurologic-like complaints, and others. In general, the research has indicated that patients whose
symptoms were exclusively or primarily psychological in origin tended to score
higher on scales 1, 2, and 3 than patients with similar symptoms that were
organic in origin. Particularly common among groups of patients with symp-

toms of psychological origin was the 13/31 two-point code. When this code type is found, and when scales 1 and 3 are elevated above T = 65 and are considerably higher than scale 2, the likelihood of functional origin increases. However, Osborne pointed out that the differences between the functional and organic groups have not been large enough to suggest that prediction from the test data alone would be very accurate.

Several supplementary scales have been developed specifically to try to determine if physical symptoms are of functional or organic origin. Two of the most commonly used of these scales are the Low Back Pain (Lb) scale (Hanvik, 1949, 1951) and the Caudality (Ca) scale (H. L. Williams, 1952). Because of inadequate research data to support the usefulness of these scales, they were not included in MMPI-2.

The MMPI-2 can be used to understand how persons with medical problems of clearly organic origin are affected psychologically by the physical problems. When using the MMPI-2 for this purpose, the clinician should rely on indicators of emotional disturbance that have been previously discussed in this book. For example, significant elevation on scale 2 suggests that the medical patient is experiencing dysphoria/depression, and elevated scores on scale 7 and/or Welsh's Anxiety scale would indicate that the medical patient is anxious, worried, and tense. Empirically derived correlates of various MMPI code types for patients of an internist were given by Guthrie (1949), and Henrichs (1981) provided a useful summary table describing characteristics associated with MMPI profile patterns of medical patients. Although these correlates have not yet been demonstrated for the MMPI-2, the continuity between the original and revised instruments suggests that they will apply.

The MMPI-2 also can provide important information concerning how medical patients are likely to respond psychologically to medical interventions. Several examples illustrate this potential use. Henrichs and Waters (1972) investigated the extent to which MMPIs administered preoperatively to cardiac patients could predict emotional or behavioral reactions to surgery. Based on prior literature concerning cardiac patients, five types were conceptualized and rules for classifying MMPI profiles into these types were developed. Using these rules, the investigators were able to classify 97 percent of MMPIs given to patients preoperatively. Postoperative course was recorded for all patients to determine if they had behavioral or emotional problems. The occurrence of such postoperative problems was significantly different for the different MMPI types. Only 6 percent of patients who were in the well-adjusted MMPI type preoperatively had postoperative emotional or behavioral problems. By contrast, 44 percent of persons having seriously disturbed preoperative MMPIs had postoperative behavioral or emotional problems. Henrichs and Waters pointed out that different types of preoperative interventions could be developed to address anticipated postoperative problems.

Sobel and Worden (1979) demonstrated that the MMPI was useful in predicting the psychosocial adjustment of patients who had been diagnosed as having cancer. The MMPI typically was administered following cancer surgery, and

patients studied six months afterward. Patients were classified as having high distress or low distress at follow-up on the basis of multiple measures of emotional turmoil, physical symptoms, and effectiveness of coping with the demands of their life situations. Using multiple regression analyses of MMPI scores, 75 percent of patients were correctly classified as having high distress or low distress. The authors pointed out that interventions could be developed to assist cancer patients who are considered to be at high risk for psychosocial problems.

Persons who are well adjusted emotionally before they develop serious medical problems and/or before they are treated for such problems generally seem to handle the illness-related stress better than persons who are emotionally less well adjusted. In addition, better adjusted persons seem to have better postoperative courses than do less well adjusted persons. However, not all studies have found positive relationships between MMPI results and response to medical interventions. Although the MMPI-2 seems to have a great deal of potential in predicting response to medical interventions, additional research is needed to establish more clearly the extent to which the MMPI-2 can and should be used for this purpose. It should be noted that the Negative Treatment Factors content scale may be especially useful in this regard.

Correctional Subjects

Dahlstrom, Welsh, and Dahlstrom (1975) briefly reviewed the major uses of the MMPI with correctional subjects and cited references concerning its use with these subjects. According to these investigators, the MMPI profiles of prisoners have seemed remarkably homogeneous. Numerous studies show that scale 4 usually is the most elevated scale in mean profiles of prisoners and identify the 4-2 and 4-9 code types as those most frequently occurring for prisoners.

A major use of the MMPI in correctional settings is to classify prisoners. Accurate classification permits correctional administrators to make more efficient use of limited resources and to avoid providing resources for offenders who do not require them. Early work by Panton and his associates in North Carolina (e.g., Panton, 1958) and by Fox and his associates in California (e.g., Fox, Gould, & Andre, 1965) indicated moderate success in using the MMPI to classify prisoners in meaningful ways when they entered the correctional system.

A comprehensive and useful system of classifying criminal offenders based on the MMPI was developed by Megargee and his associates (Megargee, Bohn, Meyer, & Sink, 1979). These investigators used hierarchical profile analysis to identify clusters among the MMPIs of offenders. Classification rules were then developed for placing offenders into the groups defined by the cluster analyses. Following some use of this system with other samples of offenders, the original classification rules were refined and expanded.

The resulting classification system involved ten types of offender MMPIs and

explicit rules for classifying offenders into the type to which they were most similar. Megargee (1979) reported that in a variety of correctional settings mechanical application of the rules classified about two thirds of offender profiles. Most of the remaining one third of the profiles could be classified by clinicians using published guidelines and additional data. Overall, 85 percent to 95 percent of offender profiles could be classified using the ten profile types. Although the derivational work for the Megargee system took place in a federal facility and involved primarily young, male offenders, subsequent data indicated that the classification system also worked well in other settings (e.g., state prisons, county jails) and with other kinds of offenders (e.g., women, older persons) (Megargee, 1979).

If a classification system for offenders is to be useful, the groups it identifies must differ from one another on important nontest variables. Research data have identified important nontest differences among the groups in the Megargee system. Megargee, Bohn, Meyer, & Sink (1979) found significant differences among the Megargee types on demographic characteristics, criminal behavior patterns, rated personality characteristics, measures of institutional adjustment (including frequency of disciplinary infractions, incidence of reports to sick call, interpersonal relations, and work performance), and recidivism rates. Readers interested in details concerning the classification system should consult the book by Megargee et al. (1979) for more information. Whether the same classification rules appropriate for the original MMPI can also be used for the MMPI-2 is not clear at present, though apparently research in this area is underway.

Subjects in Nonclinical Settings

The MMPI was developed in a psychiatric hospital setting, and most of the research done with it was with subjects in clinical settings. However, the use of the MMPI with nonclinical subjects increased dramatically in the years before its revision (Graham & McCord, 1985). In relation to selection of employees or students, the MMPI was used in two basic ways (Butcher, 1979, 1985b). First, the test was used to screen for psychopathology among applicants. Second, it was used to try to predict quality of job performance by matching individuals with certain personal characteristics to jobs or positions that are believed to require such characteristics.

Using the MMPI-2 to screen for psychopathology among applicants is most justified when individuals are being considered for employment in occupations involving susceptibility to occupational stress, personal risk, and personal responsibility. Such sensitive occupations include air traffic controller, airline pilot, police officer, and nuclear power plant operator. However, routine use of the MMPI-2 for personnel selection is not recommended. For many jobs the primary requirements are appropriate training and ability, and personality factors may be unimportant or irrelevant.

Research data suggest that the MMPI could be used effectively to screen for psychopathology in normal groups. Lachar (1974c) demonstrated that the MMPI could predict serious psychopathology leading Air Force cadets to drop out. Strupp and Bloxom (1975) found that men with certain MMPI code types were likely to have difficulty adjusting personally, graduating from college, finding a job, and deciding on a career.

Data also suggest that the MMPI could be used to predict effective hotline workers (Evans, 1977), competent clergymen (Jansen & Garvey, 1973), and successful businessmen (Harrell & Harrell, 1973). Its success in police applicant selection is well documented (e.g., Bernstein, 1980; Costello, Schoenfeld, & Kobos, 1982). The MMPI also has been used successfully in selecting physicians' assistants (Crovitz, Huse, & Lewis, 1973), medical assistants (Stone, Bassett, Brosseau, Demers, & Stiening, 1972), psychiatric residents (Garetz & Anderson, 1973), clinical psychology graduate students (Butcher, 1979), nurses (Kelly, 1974), fire fighters (Avery, Mussio, & Payne, 1972), probation officers (Solway, Hays, & Zieben, 1976), and nuclear power plant personnel (Dunnette, Bownas, & Bosshardt, 1981). In virtually all these studies the most useful way to use the MMPI has been to exclude persons with very elevated scores on one or more of the clinical scales. No data have been published yet concerning the use of the MMPI-2 to screen for psychopathology in applicants or to predict effective functioning in various occupations or training programs. However, given the continuity between the original MMPI and the MMPI-2 one would expect the revised instrument to be at least as effective as the original one for these purposes. The Negative Work Attitudes content scale may prove to be especially useful in this regard.

Not much information is available concerning use of the MMPI to match persons having certain personality characteristics with jobs requiring those characteristics. Using the instrument in this manner is problematic for several reasons. First, only limited information is available concerning the personality characteristics of normal persons with particular MMPI scores and profiles. Graham and McCord (1985) suggested a strategy for generating inferences about the personality characteristics of normal persons who did not have extremely elevated MMPI scores. For such persons clinicians were advised to use the descriptive information generated for clinical subjects but to eliminate those inferences dealing with serious psychopathology. For example, a normal person with a 6-8 two-point code and no T-scores above 70 might be described as suspicious and distrustful of others, deficient in social skills, and wary of deep emotional ties. However, a normal person with this kind of profile should not be seen as having confused thinking, delusions, or hallucinations. Although Graham and McCord presented some data indicating that this approach is justified, they stressed the need for additional research before the approach could be recommended for use on a routine basis.

A second problem in using the MMPI-2 to match persons having certain personality characteristics with jobs requiring those characteristics is that for most jobs the kinds of personality characteristics associated with successful

performance are not clearly understood. Future research in this area should emphasize thorough job analyses prior to attempts to use the MMPI-2 to identify persons suitable for certain jobs.

There are several other important considerations in using the MMPI-2 for personnel selection purposes. It has been suggested that requiring applicants for jobs to complete tests like the MMPI-2 is an invasion of privacy (Brayfield, 1965). Many persons feel that items dealing with sex, religious beliefs, or bowel and bladder functioning are inappropriate for job applicants because there is not likely to be any relationship between these items and job success (Butcher & Tellegen, 1966). The elimination of many objectional items from the MMPI-2 item pool was intended to address these concerns. Furthermore, it can be argued that some invasion of privacy is justified when evaluating applicants for psychologically sensitive or stress-vulnerable occupations. Applicants are less likely to object to taking the MMPI-2 if they are told how the test works and why they are being asked to take it.

Because job applicants understandably are motivated to present themselves in the best possible light, they are likely to produce defensive profiles (Butcher, 1979). If a profile is considered invalid because of the defensiveness, it should not be interpreted and the applicant should be evaluated by other means (e.g., an interview). Butcher (1985a) suggested some guidelines for interpreting defensive profiles that are not considered invalid. If there are T-scores above 65 on any of the clinical scales of the MMPI-2, the elevations probably accurately reflect important problems because they were obtained when the person was presenting a very favorable view of herself or himself. Since the person was trying to present an overly favorable view, T-scores in the 60 to 65 range on the clinical scales should also be interpreted as indicating significant problems. If all clinical scale T-scores are below 60, the profile will not provide much useful information. It is not possible to determine if such a profile indicates a person who is not functioning very well and is being defensive or a person who is functioning within normal limits.

9

An Interpretive Strategy

In 1956 Paul Meehl made a strong plea for a "good cookbook" for psychological test interpretation. Meehl's proposed cookbook was to provide detailed rules for categorizing test responses and empirically determined extratest correlates for each category of test responses. The rules could be applied automatically by a nonprofessional worker (or by a computer) and the interpretive statements selected for a particular type of protocol from a larger library of statements. Although some efforts have been made to construct such a cookbook (e.g., Gilberstadt & Duker, 1965; Marks & Seeman, 1963; Marks, Seeman, & Haller, 1974), the current status of psychological test interpretation is far from the automatic process Meehl envisioned. All tests, including the MMPI-2, provide opportunities for standardized observation of current behavior of examinees. On the basis of these test behaviors, inferences are made about other extratest behaviors. The clinician serves both as information processor and clinical judge in the assessment process. The major purpose of this chapter is to suggest one approach (but by no means the only one) to using MMPI-2 data to make meaningful inferences about examinees.

The MMPI-2 should be used solely to generate hypotheses or inferences about an examinee, for the interpretive data presented earlier will not apply completely and unfailingly to each and every person with a specified MMPI-2 protocol. In interpreting MMPI-2s, one must deal in probabilities. Some particular extratest characteristic is more likely than another to hold true for a person with a particular type of MMPI-2 protocol, but one can never be completely certain that it will. The inferences generated from an individual's MMPI-2 protocol should thus be validated against other test and nontest information available about that individual.

The MMPI-2 will be most valuable as an assessment tool when it is used in conjunction with other psychological tests, interview and observational data, and appropriate background information. Although blind interpretation of the MMPI-2 certainly is possible, and in fact is the procedure involved in computerized interpretations of the MMPI-2, such interpretations should be used only to generate hypotheses, inasmuch as more accurate person-specific inferences are likely to occur when the MMPI-2 is viewed in the context of all

200

information available about an individual. This position is consistent with research findings by investigators such as Kostlan (1954) and Sines (1959).

Two kinds of interpretive inferences can be made on the basis of MMPI-2 data. First, some characteristics of an examinee with a particular kind of MMPI-2 protocol can be used, with better than chance probability, to differentiate that examinee from other persons in a particular setting (e.g., hospital, clinic). For example, one might infer from a hospitalized patient's MMPI-2 profile that he or she is likely to abuse alcohol or other substances. Because most patients do not abuse substances, this inference clearly differentiates this particular patient from most other patients. A second kind of inference involves a characteristic common to many individuals in a particular setting. For example, the inference that a hospitalized psychiatric patient does not know how to handle stress effectively is probably true for most patients in that setting. Although the differential, patient-specific inferences tend to be more useful than the general ones, the latter are important in understanding an individual case, particularly for clinicians and others involved in the treatment process who might not understand clearly what behaviors are shared by most persons in a particular setting.

Whereas Meehl envisioned the assessment process as dealing exclusively with nontest behaviors directly and empirically tied to specific aspects of test performance, the current status of the assessment field is such that only limited relationships of this sort have been identified. Often it is both possible and necessary to make higher order inferences about examinees based on a conceptualization of their personalities. For example, currently no clear data indicate that a particular kind of MMPI-2 profile is predictive of a future suicide attempt. However, if we have inferred from an individual's MMPI-2 that he or she is extremely depressed, agitated, emotionally uncomfortable, and impulsive and shows poor judgment much of the time, the higher order inference that such a person has a higher risk of suicide than patients in general is a logical one. Although relying on such higher order inferences in interpreting the MMPI-2 is legitimate, one should have greater confidence in the inferences more directly related to MMPI-2 scores and configurations.

A GENERAL STRATEGY

In his own clinical work the author utilizes an approach to MMPI-2 interpretation that involves trying to answer the following questions about each MMPI-2 protocol:

1. What was the test-taking attitude of the examinee, and how should this attitude be taken into account in interpreting the protocol?
2. What is the general level of adjustment of the examinee?

3. What kinds of behaviors (symptoms, attitudes, defenses, etc.) can be inferred about or expected from the examinee?
4. What etiology or set of psychological dynamics underlies these behaviors?
5. What are the most appropriate diagnostic labels for the examinee?
6. What are the implications for treatment of the examinee?

Test-taking Attitude

The ideal examinee is one who approaches the task of completing the MMPI-2 in a serious and cooperative manner. This individual reads each MMPI-2 item and responds to it honestly and directly. When such an ideal situation is realized, the examiner can feel confident that the test responses are a representative sample of the examinee's behavior and can proceed with the interpretation of the protocol. However, as suggested in Chapter 3, for various reasons examinees may approach the test-taking task with an attitude that deviates from the ideal. Specification of the test-taking attitude for each examinee is important because such differential attitudes must be considered in generating inferences from the MMPI-2 protocol. In addition, such attitudes may predict similar approaches to other nontest aspects of the examinee's life situation.

Qualitative aspects of an examinee's test behavior often serve to augment inferences based on the more quantitative scores and indices. One such aspect is the amount of time required to complete the MMPI-2. As stated in Chapter 2, the typical examinee takes between 1 and 1½ hours to complete the test. Extremely long testing times may indicate indecisiveness, psychomotor retardation, confusion, or passive resistance to the testing procedures. Extremely short times suggest that either examinees were quite impulsive in responding to the test items or they did not read and consider the content of each individual item.

Examinees occasionally become very tense, agitated, or otherwise upset when taking the MMPI-2. Such behavior may be predictive of similar responses to other stressful situations. Some examinees, who are indecisive and/or obsessive in their thinking, write qualifications to their true-false responses in the margins of the answer sheet. This author is aware of one case in which the examinee attempted to eat the box form cards. Needless to say, such behavior has important diagnostic significance.

Although the qualitative features of test performance just discussed can offer important information about an examinee, the validity scales are the primary objective sources of inferences about test-taking attitude. The Cannot Say (?) score indicates the number of items omitted by the examinee. A large number of omitted items may indicate indecisiveness, ambivalence, or an attempt to avoid admitting negative things about oneself without deliberately lying. Examinees who answer all or most of the items are forgoing this simplistic way of attempting to present a positive picture of themselves.

In judging test-taking attitude from the L scale, the examinee's educational or

socioeconomic status must be considered (see Chapter 3). If the L scale is higher than expected when these factors are taken into account, one should consider the possibility that the examinee is using a rather naive and global denial of problems and shortcomings in an attempt to present himself or herself favorably.

Scores on the F scale show how an examinee's responses to a finite pool of items compare with those of the standardization samples, with higher F scores reflecting greater deviance. Scores that are considerably higher than average suggest that examinees are admitting to many clearly deviant behaviors and attitudes. There are several reasons for such admissions (see Chapter 3). Examinees might have responded randomly to the test items or with a deliberate intention of appearing very emotionally disturbed. They might be emotionally disabled persons using the MMPI-2 as a cry for help. F scale scores that are considerably below average indicate that the examinees are admitting fewer than an average number of deviant attitudes and behaviors. They may be overly defensive and trying to create unrealistically positive pictures of themselves. F scale scores in the average range indicate that the examinees have been neither hypercritical of themselves nor overly denying in responding to the test items.

Whereas F scale scores provide information about examinees' attitudes in responding to approximately the first 370 items of the test, the Backside F scale (Fb) provides similar information for items that occur later in the test booklet. High and low Fb scores can be interpreted very similarly to those of the standard F scale.

The K scale can serve as another index of defensiveness, but in interpreting this scale education and socioeconomic status must be taken into account (see Chapter 3). If scores on the K scale are significantly higher than expected given educational and socioeconomic background, one should suspect that the examinee has been rather defensive. Scores lower than expected for a person with a given educational and socioeconomic background indicate a lack of defensiveness and a highly self-critical attitude. K scale scores in the middle range suggest that the examinee has been neither overly defensive nor overly self-critical in endorsing the MMPI-2 items.

The Variable Response Inconsistency (VRIN) and True Response Inconsistency (TRIN) scales offer additional information concerning the possibility of response sets that can invalidate the protocol (see Chapter 3). Significantly elevated scores on VRIN indicate that the examinee probably responded to the items without reading and considering their content. When the TRIN scale is elevated (in either the true or false direction), the possibility of an acquiescence or nonacquiescence response set must be considered.

As discussed in Chapter 3, the configuration of the validity scales is important for understanding examinees' test-taking attitudes. In general, persons who approach the test with the intention of presenting themselves in an overly favorable way have L and K scale scores greater than the F scale score, producing a V-shape in the validity scale portion of the profile. On the other hand,

persons who are using the test to be overly self-critical and/or to exaggerate their problems produce an inverted V-shape in the validity scales (i.e., the L and K scores will be significantly lower than the F scale score).

In summary, a first step in interpreting an MMPI-2 profile is to make some judgments concerning the test-taking attitude of the examinee. If the decision is made that the test was approached in a manner that invalidates the protocol (e.g., random responding or faking bad), no additional interpretation of the profile is in order. If less extreme response sets are operating (e.g., defensiveness or exaggeration), making some tentative interpretations of the profile may be possible, but adjustments in interpretations must be made to take into account these response sets.

Adjustment Level

There are two important components to psychological adjustment level. First, how emotionally comfortable or uncomfortable are individuals? Second, how well do they carry out the responsibilities of their life situations irrespective of how conflicted they might be? For most people these two components are very much related. Persons who are psychologically comfortable tend to function well and vice versa. However, for some individuals (e.g., some neurotics) a great deal of discomfort and turmoil can be present, but adequate functioning continues. For other persons (e.g., chronic schizophrenics), quite serious impairment in coping with responsibilities can be found without an accompanying emotional discomfort. The MMPI-2 potentially can permit inferences about both these aspects of adjustment level.

The F scale seems to be the single best MMPI-2 index of degree of psychopathology. If one rules out the possibility of deviant response sets or styles that can invalidate the protocol (e.g., the angry adolescent who decides to answer true to all the deviant items), high F scale scores suggest intense emotional turmoil and/or serious impairment in functioning. For example, most acutely psychotic subjects tend to obtain high scores on the F scale. However, some neurotic individuals and persons undergoing severe situational stress also achieve high F scale scores. On the other hand, some clearly psychotic individuals, particularly those in whom the disorder has been present for quite some time, do not achieve very high F scale scores.

A second simple but meaningful index of adjustment has to do with the overall elevation of the clinical scales. In general, as more of the clinical scales are elevated (and as the degree of elevation increases), the greater is the probability that some serious psychopathology and poor levels of functioning are present. To obtain a crude, quantitative index of degree of this psychopathology, some clinicians find it useful to compute a mean T-score for eight clinical scales (excluding scales 5 and 0). Another index of psychopathology is the number of clinical scales with T-scores above 65. Higher mean scores and more scores above 65 are indicative of greater psychopathology.

The slope of the profile also yields important inferences about adjustment level. If the clinical scales are elevated and a positive slope (left side low, right side high) is present, the likelihood of severe psychopathology, and perhaps even psychosis, should be considered. A negative slope (left side high, right side low) is more indicative of a neurotic individual or one who is internally conflicted and miserable but who still is able to function fairly well.

Scores on several of the standard clinical and special scales also can serve as indices of level of adjustment. Welsh's Anxiety (A) and Barron's Ego Strength (Es) scales are measures of general maladjustment. High scorers on A and low scorers on Es tend to be rather disturbed emotionally. The A scale seems to be more sensitive to subjective emotional turmoil than inability to cope behaviorally. The Es scale indicates an individual's ability to cope with the stresses and problems of everyday life, with high scorers generally better able to cope than low scorers. Scale 2 (Depression) is a good indicator of dissatisfaction with one's life situation. As scores on scale 2 become higher, greater dissatisfaction is suggested. Scale 7 (Psychasthenia) is perhaps the single best measure of feelings of anxiety and agitation. High scale 7 scorers usually are overwhelmed by anxiety, tension, fear, and apprehension.

It may be helpful to check responses to the Koss-Butcher or Lachar-Wrobel critical items. These items deal with some blatantly psychotic behaviors and attitudes, sexual deviation, excessive use of alcohol, homicidal and/or suicidal impulses, and other manifestations of serious maladjustment. The critical item lists are reproduced in Appendix J of this book. As was discussed in Chapter 6, care should be taken not to overinterpret these individual item responses.

Characteristic Traits and Behaviors

At this point in the interpretive process, the clinician's goal is to describe the examinee's symptoms, traits, behaviors, attitudes, defenses, and so forth in enough detail to allow an overall understanding of the person. Although not every protocol permits inferences about all the points listed below, in general this author tries to make some statements or inferences about each:

1. symptoms
2. major needs (e.g., dependency, achievement, autonomy)
3. perceptions of the environment, particularly of significant other people in the examinee's life situation
4. reactions to stress (coping strategies, defenses)
5. self-concept
6. sexual identification
7. emotional control
8. interpersonal relationships
9. psychological resources

Inferences about these various aspects of behavior and personality are based primarily on analysis of individual validity and clinical scales and on two- and three-point configurations (see Chapters 3, 4, and 5). In addition, special scales, discussed in Chapters 6 and 7, often add important information about the examinee. One way for the beginner with the MMPI-2 to utilize the standard and supplementary scales is to consider each high score, low score, and configuration of scores in turn, to consult the appropriate sections in earlier chapters of this book, and to write down the appropriate hypotheses or inferences for each scale or configuration.

Initially, there may appear to be some incongruencies among the various inferences that have been generated. The clinician should first consider the possibility that the apparent incongruencies are accurately reflecting different facets of the examinee's personality and behavior. Consider, for example, a profile with T-score elevations greater than 65 on both scales 2 and 4. The scale 2 elevation suggests sensitivity to the needs and feelings of others, whereas the scale 4 elevation suggests insensitivity to these needs and feelings. It is possible that the same individual may show both characteristics at different times. In fact, research with the 24/42 code type indicates that persons with this code tend to alternate between periods of great sensitivity to others and periods of gross insensitivity to others.

Sometimes incongruencies in inferences cannot be reconciled as easily as they can in the preceding example. In these instances the clinician must decide in which inferences to have the most confidence. In general, greater confidence should be placed in inferences based on several scales or configurations than in those based on only a single scale. Inferences based on grossly elevated scales should receive greater emphasis than those based on moderate elevations. Finally, in most instances more confidence should be placed in inferences based on the standard validity and clinical scales than on the supplementary scales because more research underlies the standard scale inferences.

As mentioned earlier in this chapter, some inferences about an examinee do not result directly from scores on a scale or from configurations of scales. Rather, they are higher order inferences generated from a basic understanding of the examinee. For example, no data indicate that scores on particular MMPI-2 scales are predictive of success as a real estate salesperson. However, one might predict that an examinee whose MMPI-2 scores had led to inferences of strong achievement needs, competitiveness, and ability to create a good impression would be likely to be successful in real estate sales.

Dynamics and Etiology

In most assessment situations it is desirable to go beyond a description of an individual's behavior and to make inferences about the dynamics underlying the behavior or about the etiology of a particular problem or condition. For some MMPI-2 scales and configurations, the interpretive information presented

in previous chapters of this book includes some statements about these underlying factors. In addition, it is possible and/or necessary to make some higher order inferences about dynamics. For example, if one infers from an examinee's MMPI-2 protocol that he or she fears emotional involvement with other people because of a fear of being hurt or exploited, one might then speculate that the person has been hurt and/or exploited in earlier emotional relationships. Or if one interprets an MMPI-2 protocol as indicating strong resentment of authority, it is reasonable to infer that the resentment has its origins in parent-child relationships. The higher order inferences often are based on MMPI-2 data combined with other information about examinees and on the clinician's basic understanding of behavior, personality, and psychopathology.

Diagnostic Impression

Although the usefulness of psychiatric diagnoses per se has been questioned by many clinicians, referral sources often request information about diagnosis. In addition, assigning diagnostic labels is often necessary for purposes such as insurance claims, disability status, or competency status. Many of the interpretive sections in earlier chapters of this book present diagnostic information for the individual clinical scales and for two- and three-point code types. In addition, it can be useful to consider the slope of the profile. As stated earlier, a negative slope (left side high, right side low) suggests nonpsychotic disorders, whereas a positive slope (left side low, right side high) suggests psychotic disorders.

Goldberg (1965) derived a linear regression equation for discriminating between psychotic and neurotic profiles. To compute the Goldberg index, one simply inserts T-score values into the following formula: $L + Pa + Sc - Hy - Pt$. Goldberg found for his samples that a cutoff of 45 on his index provided the best discrimination between psychotic and neurotic profiles. However, it is recommended that a specific cutoff score be derived in each setting where the index is utilized. Further, it should be noted that the index is useful only when the clinician is relatively sure that the person being considered is either psychotic or neurotic. When the index is applied to the scores of normal persons or those with personality disorder diagnoses, most are found to be psychotic. It also should be noted that the index was based on data from the original MMPI. Data have not yet been published concerning the use of the index with MMPI-2. However, the performance of the index is expected to be similar for MMPI and MMPI-2.

In using the MMPI-2 for diagnostic purposes, the clinician must consider that the research studies concerning diagnostic inferences were based on the original MMPI and the original standardization samples. However, because of the continuity between the original MMPI and the MMPI-2, data based on the original instrument are expected to apply to the revision. It also is important to know that most of the studies of the relationship between MMPI data and

diagnoses were conducted prior to the publication of DSM-III and DSM-III-R. In presenting diagnostic inferences for particular scores and configurations of scores in this book, the earlier diagnostic labels were translated into the more contemporary ones.

Treatment Implications

A primary goal in most assessments is to make meaningful recommendations about treatment. Sometimes, when demand for treatment exceeds the resources available, the decision simply is whether or not to accept a particular person for treatment. Such a decision may involve clinical judgment about how much the person needs treatment as well as how likely he or she is to respond favorably to available treatment procedures. When differential treatment procedures are available, the assessment may be useful in deciding which procedures are most appropriate. When a particular treatment procedure already has been chosen, the assessment can provide information about problem areas to be considered in treatment and alert the therapist (or others involved in treatment) to assets and liabilities that could facilitate or hinder progress in therapy. The MMPI-2 can provide information relevant to all these aspects of treatment. Butcher (1990) has provided a detailed account of the use of the MMPI-2 in treatment planning.

Many of the inferences generated from scores on individual validity and clinical scales and from code types will have direct relevance to treatment considerations. Of special importance is the pattern of scores on the standard validity scales. A defensive validity scale pattern (L and K scales considerably more elevated than F scale) suggests that the examinee is not admitting to problems or symptoms and thus is not likely to be very receptive to therapeutic intervention. By contrast, an examinee whose F scale is considerably more elevated than the L and K scales is apparently admitting to problems, symptoms, and emotional distress. This person is likely to be motivated to enter and remain in treatment.

Several of the MMPI-2 supplementary scales can provide useful information concerning treatment. The Ego Strength (Es) scale, which was discussed in Chapter 7, was designed to predict response to psychotherapy. If one is dealing with a neurotic individual, a high Es score is likely to mean that such a person will benefit from traditional, individual psychotherapy. With other kinds of persons and/or treatment procedures the relationship between Es scores and treatment outcome is less clear, but in general, higher Es scores can be interpreted as suggesting greater psychological resources that can be used in treatment. It should be noted that persons who approach the MMPI-2 in a defensive manner tend to achieve relatively high Es scores that do not indicate a positive prognosis for treatment. Also, persons who try to exaggerate problems and symptoms tend to achieve very low Es scores, which do not necessarily indicate a negative prognosis. The Negative Treatment Indicators (TRT) scale is likely to

be helpful in predicting response to psychological treatment. Although no research concerning the relationship between scores on the TRT scale and response to treatment has yet been published, examination of the content of the scale's items suggests that higher scorers perceive themselves as unwilling or unable to change their life situations, pessimistic about the possibility of positive change, uncomfortable discussing problems with others, and likely to be rigid and noncompliant in therapy.

As was discussed in relation to characteristic traits and behaviors, many of the inferences about treatment will not come directly from scores on specific MMPI-2 scales or configurations of scales. Rather, they are higher order inferences based on other inferences that already have been made about the examinee. For example, if one has inferred from the MMPI-2 that an examinee is in considerable emotional turmoil, it can further be inferred that this person is likely to be motivated enough to change in psychotherapy. On the other hand, if one has inferred that a person is very reluctant to accept responsibility for her or his own behavior and blames others for problems and shortcomings, the prognosis for traditional psychotherapy is very poor. A person who has been described from the MMPI-2 as very suggestible is likely to respond more favorably to direct advice-giving than to insight-oriented therapy. A person described as psychopathic (based on elevations on scales 4 and 9) who enters therapy rather than going to jail is likely to terminate therapy prematurely. Obviously, there are many other examples of higher order inferences related to treatment.

SPECIFIC REFERRAL QUESTIONS

The interpretive strategy just discussed is intended to help the clinician generate as many meaningful inferences as possible about subjects' MMPI-2s. It should be recognized that very often persons are given the MMPI-2 in an attempt to try to answer some very specific questions about them or to make some very specific predictions about their behavior. Unless these specific questions or predictions are dealt with directly, it is unlikely that the MMPI-2 interpretation will be regarded as useful.

Specific issues for which the MMPI-2 may be useful include, but are not limited to, detecting suicide potential, acting out behaviors, psychotic disorders, and substance abuse problems; differentiating functional from organic somatic disorders; and predicting response to treatment. Sometimes data directly relevant to the issue of concern are available. For example, scores on the MacAndrew Alcoholism Scale-Revised (MAC-R) permit inferences about substance abuse. At other times, conclusions about issues of concern are dependent on the clinical integration of many different kinds of MMPI-2 data and second order inferences. The prediction of suicide potential is a good example of this latter situation. There are no specific scales for predicting such behavior and no actuarial formulas for this purpose. However, MMPI-2 inferences about degree

of clinical depression, energy level, impulsiveness, and similar characteristics can be integrated with history and observational data in helping clinicians to make this very difficult and important prediction.

AN ILLUSTRATIVE CASE

In order to help the reader understand the strategy discussed above, an actual case is now considered and a step-by-step analysis of the MMPI-2 protocol presented. As a practice exercise, readers can interpret the profiles (Figures 9.1–9.4) and then compare their interpretations with the one presented below.

Background Information

Greg is a 22-year-old white male. He has never been married, and he continues to live with his parents. He graduated from a vocational high school where his grades were about average. He did not participate in sports or other school activities, and he did not have any close friends. He has never had a serious relationship with a woman. Since completing school he has held a number of temporary and part-time jobs, including janitorial and restaurant kitchen work.

The MMPI-2 was administered to Greg approximately one week following his admission to a state-supported psychiatric hospital. He was cooperative, and he completed the MMPI-2 in about two hours. He had been hospitalized many times previously and had been diagnosed as paranoid schizophrenic. Hospital records also indicated the possible abuse of alcohol and marijuana. At admission Greg was quite anxious, fearful, and agitated. He reported that people were following him and trying to kill him, but he did not state any reason why they might want to do so. He admitted that he had been hearing voices telling him that he was a bad person. During his hospitalization, Greg was treated with antipsychotic medications and supportive psychotherapy, and his symptoms improved. After several weeks in the hospital, he was discharged to his family as improved, and outpatient treatment at a local mental health center was recommended.

Test-Taking Attitude

Greg completed the MMPI-2 in about an average amount of time for a psychiatric patient, indicating that he was neither excessively indecisive nor impulsive in responding to the items. He omitted no items, suggesting that he was cooperative and did not use this rather simple way of avoiding unfavorable self-statements. His raw score of 5 on the L scale was only slightly above average for someone of his educational and socioeconomic background, so we may infer

that he was not blatantly defensive and denying in his approach to the test. Greg's T-score of 89 on the F scale suggests that he was admitting to a large number of deviant attitudes and behaviors. The F scale score was not high enough to suggest random responding or a fake bad response set, nor was the VRIN raw score of 11 (T = 73) high enough to suggest random responding. Also, the absence of elevation on clinical scales other than 6 and 8 is not consistent with an invalid profile. His raw score of 17 (T = 112) on the backside F (Fb) scale suggests that he might have been responding invalidly to items that appeared later in the booklet. However, psychiatric inpatients who are responding validly to the test often endorse large numbers of items on both the F and Fb scales.

For a person of his educational and socioeconomic level, we would expect a K scale score in a range of 55 to 60. Greg's T-score of 39 on the K scale indicates that he was very self-critical in responding to the items. Such low K scale scores are rather common among recently admitted psychiatric inpatients. Greg's configuration of scores on the validity scales resembles the inverted V-shape discussed previously. Such a pattern sometimes indicates an attempt to fake bad in responding to test items, but Greg's F minus K score of seven (17–10) is below the cutoff suggestive of faking bad. Thus, the low K scale score is interpreted as indicating a very self-critical attitude in a person who is likely to feel overwhelmed by the responsibilities of everyday life.

In summary, Greg seems to have approached the MMPI-2 in an honest and open manner. He admitted to a large number of deviant attitudes and behaviors, and this admission accurately reflects his status rather than indicating an invalid approach to the test. Thus, interpretation of the clinical and supplementary scales can be undertaken.

Adjustment Level

Greg's F scale T-score of 89 indicates serious psychopathology. Because we previously ruled out profile invalidity, the interpretation of the F scale at this level is that Greg is likely manifesting blatantly psychotic symptoms and probably will have difficulty in handling even the routine responsibilities of everyday life. Greg's mean T-score on the eight clinical scales (excluding scales 5 and 0) is 57. Although this mean is not particularly high, the fact that scales 6 and 8 are elevated at 79 and 81, respectively, suggests serious psychopathology. The slope of the profile is clearly positive (left side low, right side high), also suggesting severe psychopathology and perhaps psychosis. The high score on the Anxiety (A) scale (T = 73) and the very low score on the Ego Strength (Es) scale (T = 30) both suggest serious maladjustment and inability to cope with the stresses and problems of everyday life. The absence of significant elevation on scales 2 and 7 indicates that Greg is not likely to be feeling particularly overwhelmed by anxiety, depression, and other emotional turmoil. Examination of Greg's endorsement of the Koss-Butcher and Lachar-Wrobel critical items (see the com-

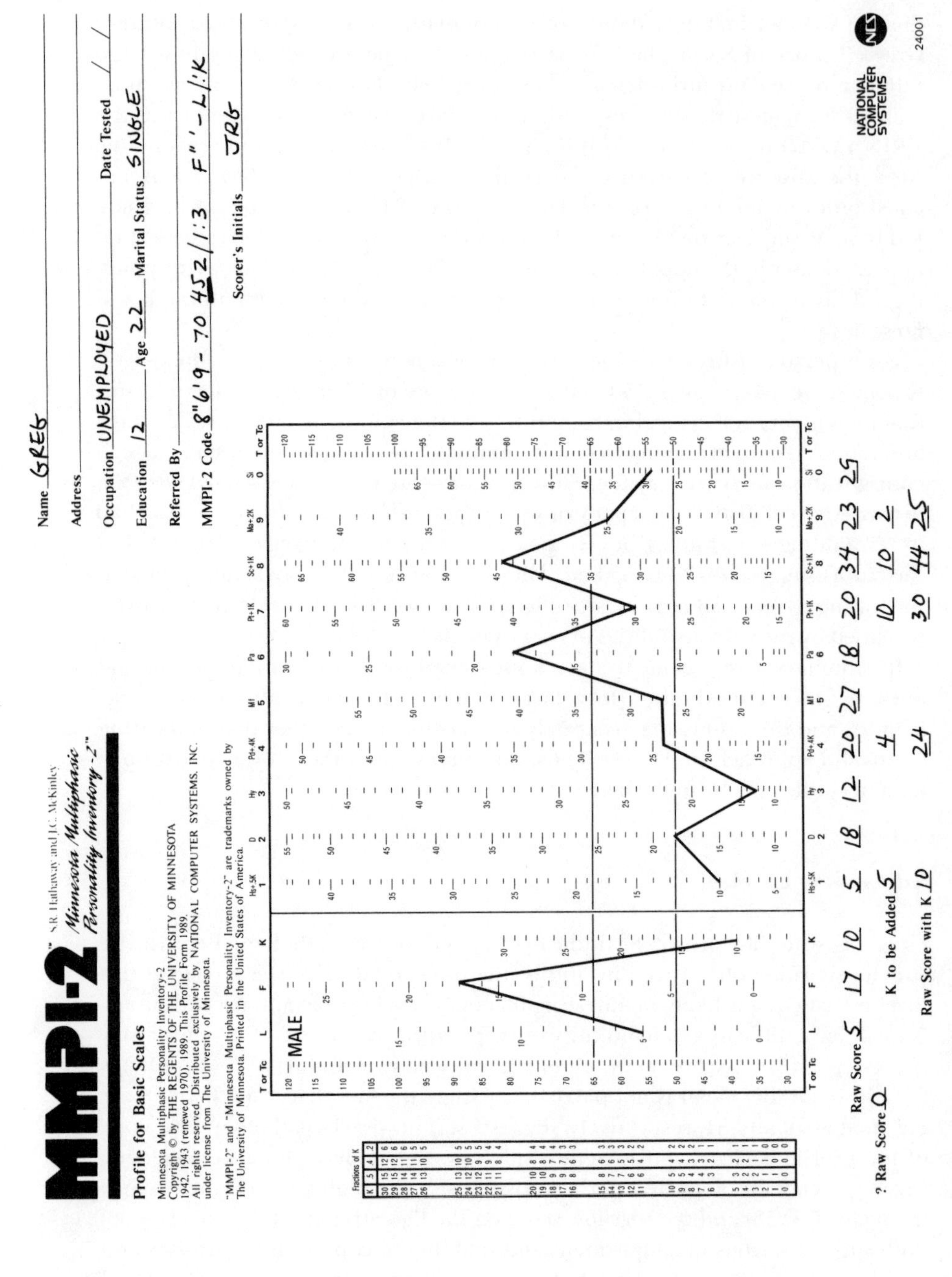

MMPI-2™

S.R. Hathaway and J.C. McKinley

Minnesota Multiphasic Personality Inventory -2™

Profile for Basic Scales

Minnesota Multiphasic Personality Inventory-2
Copyright © by THE REGENTS OF THE UNIVERSITY OF MINNESOTA
1942, 1943 (renewed 1970). 1989. This Profile Form 1989.
All rights reserved. Distributed exclusively by NATIONAL COMPUTER SYSTEMS, INC.
under license from The University of Minnesota.

"MMPI-2" and "Minnesota Multiphasic Personality Inventory-2" are trademarks owned by
The University of Minnesota. Printed in the United States of America.

Name GREG

Address

Occupation UNEMPLOYED   Date Tested / /

Education 12   Age 22   Marital Status SINGLE

Referred By

MMPI-2 Code 8'6'9 - 70 452/1:3   F"-L/:K

Scorer's Initials JRG

MALE

	Raw Score	L 5	F 17	K 10	Hs+.5K 5	D 18	Hy 12	Pd+.4K 20	Mf 27	Pa 18	Pt+1K 20	Sc+1K 34	Ma+.2K 23	Si 25
? Raw Score 0	K to be Added				5			4			10	10	2	
	Raw Score with K				10			24			30	44	25	

NATIONAL COMPUTER SYSTEMS

24001

Figure 9.1. MMPI-2 profile for basic scales for practice case (Greg).

212

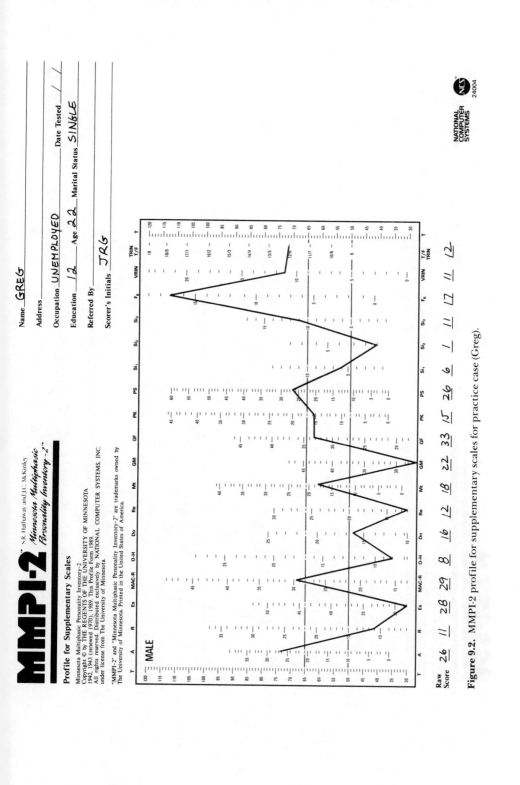

Figure 9.2. MMPI-2 profile for supplementary scales for practice case (Greg).

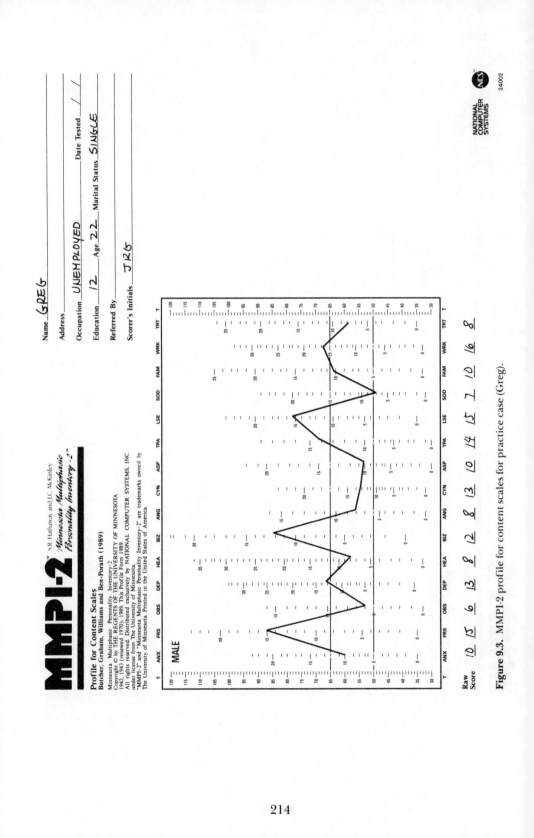

Figure 9.3. MMPI-2 profile for content scales for practice case (Greg).

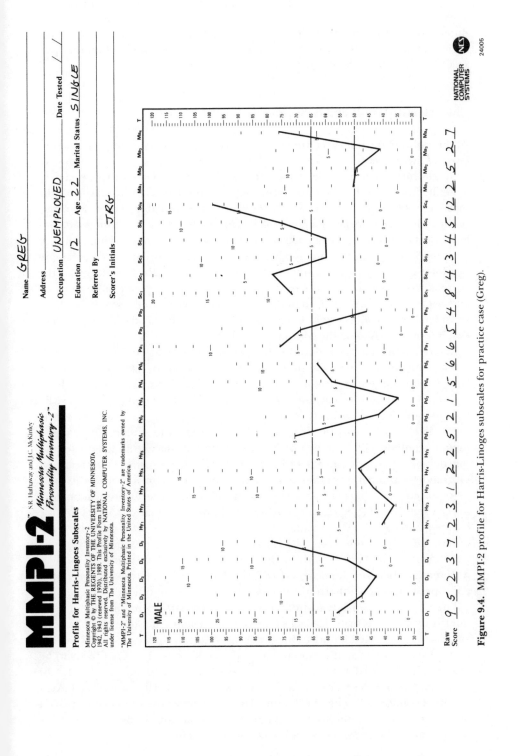

Figure 9.4. MMPI-2 profile for Harris-Lingoes subscales for practice case (Greg).

215

puterized interpretation in Chapter 10) reveals that he admitted to a wide variety of deviant attitudes and behaviors, including confused thinking, persecutory ideas, and sexual concerns.

Characteristic Traits and Behaviors

At this point in the interpretation we want to generate as many inferences about Greg as we possibly can from his MMPI-2 scores. A first step in trying to generate inferences is to determine the code types for Greg's profile and to generate inferences for them by consulting Chapter 5. It is best to start with the most complex code type for which information is available. The 8-6-9 three-point code is appropriate for his profile. Unfortunately, no published data are available for this three-point code, so no descriptive data are presented for it in Chapter 5. His two-point code is 8-6. This is a commonly occurring code type in psychiatric settings, and considerable information is available concerning the correlates of this code. Because the two scales in the code type are quite elevated and because they are much more elevated than other clinical scales, we have considerable confidence that Greg would have the same code if retested and that inferences based on the code are likely to fit him well.

Reference to Chapter 5 permits the generation of many inferences for this two-point code. The 8-6 code suggests that the most likely Axis I diagnosis for Greg is schizophrenia (paranoid type). This is particularly likely because both scales 8 and 6 are very elevated and are both considerably higher than scale 7. Consequently, Greg is likely to manifest clearly psychotic behavior. His thinking is likely to be autistic, fragmented, tangential, and circumstantial, and thought content is likely to be bizarre. Difficulties in concentrating and attending, deficits in memory, and poor judgment are likely. Delusions of persecution or grandeur and hallucinations may be present, and feelings of unreality may be reported. He is likely to be preoccupied with abstract or theoretical matters to the exclusion of specific, concrete aspects of his life situation. Affect may be blunted, and speech may be rapid and at times incoherent. Greg does not seem to have effective defenses, and he is likely to respond to stress and pressure by withdrawing into fantasy and daydreaming. Often it is difficult for him to differentiate between fantasy and reality. Medical consultation to determine appropriateness of psychotropic medication should be considered.

The 8-6 code also leads to inferences that Greg harbors intense feelings of inferiority and insecurity. He lacks self-confidence and self-esteem, and he feels guilty about perceived failures. He is likely to withdraw from everyday activities, to display emotional apathy, and to have suicidal ideation. He is not likely to be emotionally involved with other people. He is suspicious and distrustful of others and avoids deep emotional ties. He is seriously deficient in social skills and most comfortable when he is alone. He is quite resentful of demands placed on him, and other people see him as moody, irritable, unfriendly, and negativistic. In general, his life-style can be characterized as schizoid.

Several other configural aspects of the profile can be examined. The relationship among scales 1, 2, and 3 tells us something about the use of denial and repression. Because Greg's scale 2 score is higher than scores on scales 1 and 3, we would infer that he is not well defended and may be reporting a variety of symptoms and complaints. Greg's scale 5 score is about average in the profile, so it does not permit inferences about impulse control. Because his scale 4 score is considerably higher than that of scale 3, we might infer problems with impulse control. However, because his scale 4 score is still average, we would not expect overt asocial or antisocial behaviors. The relative scores on scales 7 and 8 can be helpful in making inferences about thought disorder. Because Greg's scale 8 score is considerably higher than his scale 7 score, we would infer that he is likely to have a thought disorder.

We next would examine Greg's scores on the validity scales and consult Chapter 3 for inferences based on those scores.

L (T = 56). This score is only slightly higher than what is expected from someone of Greg's educational and socioeconomic background; thus, we infer that he is not particularly defensive or denying.

F (T = 89). This score is considerably higher than we would expect; Greg admitted to many deviant behaviors and ideas including some that were clearly psychotic in nature; he endorsed items on the F scale having to do with confused thinking, persecutory ideas, and periods of activity during which he was not aware of what he was doing.

K (T = 39). This is a very low score, suggesting that Greg is self-critical and self-dissatisfied. He tends to be ineffective in dealing with problems in his daily life, and he is likely to have little insight into his own motives and behavior. He is likely to be somewhat socially retiring, and when he has interactions with others they may be blunt and harsh. He has a cynical, skeptical, caustic, and disbelieving outlook toward life. He also tends to be quite suspicious about the motivations of other people.

Next, inferences are generated based on Greg's scores on the clinical scales. Consult Chapter 4 for a summary of inferences that are appropriate for clinical scale scores at various levels.

Scale 1 (T = 42). The absence of elevation on this scale indicates that Greg is not likely to be overly concerned about health, illness, and bodily functioning. The score is in an average range, so no additional inferences are made.

Scale 2 (T = 50). This score suggests that Greg is not likely to be experiencing clinical depression. Because it is in an average range, no additional inferences are made.

Scale 3 (T = 34). This is considered a low score on this scale. It suggests that

Greg does not worry excessively about his health. In addition, it leads to inferences that he tends to be rather constricted, conventional, and conforming in everyday behavior. He is described by others as unadventurous, lacking industriousness, and having a narrow range of interests. He is cold and aloof, and he may display blunted affect. He is very limited in social interests and participation, and he tends to avoid leadership responsibilities. Others see him as unfriendly, and he is hard to get to know. He is suspicious and has difficulty trusting other people. He seems to be content with what others would judge as a rather dull, uneventful life-style.

Scale 4 (T = 52). This is an average score on this scale, so no inferences are made.

Scale 5 (T = 52). This is an average score for a person of this educational level, so no inferences are made.

Scale 6 (T = 79). This very high score suggests frankly psychotic behavior. Greg's thinking may be disturbed, and he may have delusions of persecution and/or grandeur. He may feel mistreated and picked on. He may be angry and resentful and he harbors grudges. Projection is a common defense mechanism. A diagnosis of schizophrenia or paranoid disorder may be appropriate.

Scale 7 (T = 57). This score is only slightly above average, and no inferences are made.

Scale 8 (T = 81). Scores at this level suggest the possibility of a psychotic disorder. Confusion, disorganization, and disorientation may be present, as may unusual thoughts or attitudes, delusions, hallucinations, and extremely poor judgment. Greg is likely to have a schizoid life-style. He tends to feel that he is not a part of his social environment. He feels isolated, alienated, misunderstood, and unaccepted by peers. He is likely to be withdrawn, seclusive, secretive, and inaccessible. He may avoid dealing with new people and new situations. Others describe him as shy, aloof, and uninvolved. He may experience a great deal of apprehension and generalized anxiety. He may feel very resentful, hostile, and aggressive, but he is unable to express such feelings. He typically responds to stress by withdrawing into daydreams and fantasies, and he may have difficultly separating reality from fantasy. He may be plagued by self-doubts and feelings of inferiority, incompetence, and dissatisfaction. Sexual preoccupation and sex role confusion may be present. Others may see his behavior as nonconforming, unusual, unconventional, and eccentric. He may have longstanding physical complaints. At times he may be stubborn, moody, and opinionated, and at other times he is seen as generous, peaceable, and sentimental. He may be described by others as immature, impulsive, adventurous, sharp-witted, and high-strung. His goals are abstract and vague, and he may lack the basic information required for problem solving. The prognosis for

psychotherapy is not good because of the longstanding nature of his problems and his reluctance to relate in a meaningful way to the therapist. However, he may stay in therapy longer than many patients and may eventually come to trust the therapist. Medical consultation to evaluate the appropriateness of chemo-therapy is indicated.

Scale 9 (T = 62). This is a slightly elevated score, so we would infer that Greg has somewhat above average energy and activity levels. However, because the score is within an average range, no additional inferences are made.

Scale 0 (T = 54). This score is in an average range, so no inferences are made.

Having examined the standard validity and clinical scales individually and in configuration, we then would turn to the supplementary scales for additional inferences. Examination of the Harris-Lingoes subscales often helps to clarify the meaning of elevated clinical scales.

D5—Brooding (T = 79). Although Greg's scale 2 score is about average, his elevated score on this scale 2 subscale would lead us to infer that he broods, ruminates, and cries much of the time. He lacks the energy to cope with problems and may have concluded that life is no longer worthwhile. He feels inferior, unhappy, and useless, and his feelings are easily hurt. He may feel that he is losing control of his thought processes.

Hy2—Need for Affection (T = 36). Because his scale 3 score is very low, all of the Harris-Lingoes subscale scores for this scale also are low. Only the Hy2 subscale score is low enough (T < 40) to permit inferences. This low score leads to inferences that Greg has very negative, critical, and suspicious attitudes toward other people. He sees others as dishonest, selfish, and unreasonable. He admits to negative feelings toward other people who are perceived as treating him badly.

Pd1—Familial Discord (T = 71). The relatively high score on this subscale indicates that Greg sees his family situation as unpleasant. He describes his home as lacking in love, understanding, and support and his family as critical, quarrelsome, and refusing to permit him adequate freedom and independence. He has felt like leaving his home situation.

Pd3—Social Imperturbability (T = 35). The low score on this subscale indicates that Greg experiences a great deal of discomfort and anxiety in social situations. He does not like to meet new people, and he finds it difficult to talk in interpersonal situations. He does not express personal opinions and attitudes openly.

Pa1—Persecutory Ideas (T = 76). The high score on this subscale suggests that Greg views the world as a threatening place and others as having unfairly

blamed or punished him. He feels misunderstood and thinks that he is getting a raw deal from life.

Pa2—Poignancy (T = 69). This relatively high score means that Greg sees himself as more sensitive and high-strung than other people, and he says that he feels things more intensely than others do. He feels lonely and misunderstood. At times he looks for risky or exciting activities to make him feel better.

Sc1—Social Alienation (T = 72). This relatively high score suggests that Greg feels that other people do not understand him, have it in for him, and are trying to harm him. He feels that he is getting a raw deal from life. He describes his family as not being loving or supportive and as treating him more as a child than an adult. He reports hatred and hostility toward family members, feels lonely and empty, and admits that he has never had a love relationship with anyone. He avoids social situations and interpersonal relationships whenever possible.

Sc2—Emotional Alienation (T = 78). This high score indicates that Greg may feel depressed, apathetic, and frightened, and he may feel that life is not worthwhile. He may exhibit sadistic and/or masochistic needs.

Sc5—Lack of Ego Mastery, Defective Inhibition (T = 75). This score means that Greg tends to be restless, hyperactive, and irritable. He may feel that he is not in control of his emotions and impulses and is frightened by this perceived loss of control. He may report episodes during which he did not know what he was doing and later could not remember what he had done.

Sc6—Bizarre Sensory Experiences (T = 9). This extremely high subscale score may indicate that Greg has feelings that his body is changing in strange and unusual ways. These experiences may be delusional and/or hallucinatory in nature.

Ma4—Ego Inflation (T = 76). This elevated score suggests that Greg has unrealistically positive evaluations of his own abilities and self-worth. He is resentful when others make demands on him, particularly when the persons making the demands are perceived as less capable than he is.

Reference to the Ben-Porath, Hostetler, Butcher, and Graham subscales for scale 0 can sometimes be helpful in understanding the social introversion-extraversion of subjects. Because his scale 0 score is about average, we would not expect his subscales to be very elevated.

Si3—Self/Other Alienation (T = 68). This moderately elevated subscale score suggests that Greg has low self-esteem. He lacks interest in activities, and he feels unable to effect changes in his life situation.

Other supplementary scales also should be examined to determine if additional inferences are indicated.

Anxiety (A) (T = 73). This elevated score indicates general maladjustment. Greg is likely to be submissive and overcontrolled emotionally. He lacks self-confidence. He may be experiencing enough discomfort that he is motivated to change in psychotherapy.

Ego Strength (Es) (T = 30). Very low scores on this scale often are encountered in psychiatric inpatients, and they tend to be associated with psychotic diagnoses. Greg is not well adjusted psychologically and is not well equipped to deal with problems and stresses. His problems are likely to be longstanding in nature, and the prognosis for positive change in psychotherapy is very poor.

MacAndrew Alcoholism Scale-Revised (MAC-R) (Raw Score = 29). This score is at a level suggesting strongly that Greg may abuse alcohol and/or other substances. Corroborating information should be obtained from significant others.

Overcontrolled-Hostility (O-H) (T = 35). Based on this low score we would not expect Greg to display the overcontrolled-hostility syndrome that was described in Chapter 7. It is not possible to know from this low score whether he is a chronically aggressive person or someone who is quite appropriate in the expression of his aggression.

Social Responsibility (Re) (T = 30). This low score suggests that Greg does not accept responsibility for his own behavior. He is lacking or deficient in dependability, trustworthiness, and sense of responsibility to the group. He is not likely to be interested in positions of leadership and responsibility. Because of his relatively young age, he may be denying the value system of his parents and trying to develop one of his own to substitute for theirs.

Masculine Sex Role (GM) (T < 30). This is a very low score on this scale. It could suggest the absence of stereotypically masculine interests and activities and presentation of the self as dependent, indecisive, and lacking in self-confidence.

The final supplementary scales to be examined are the content scales developed by Butcher, Graham, Williams, and Ben-Porath.

Fears (FRS) (T = 87). This very high score indicates that Greg feels fearful and uneasy much of the time. He may report multiple specific fears or phobias.

Depression (DEP) (T = 66). This mildly elevated score suggests that Greg feels depressed, pessimistic, and hopeless. He feels fatigued and lacks interest in things. He may recently have been preoccupied with thoughts of death and suicide.

Bizarre Mentation (BIZ) (T = 84). This very high score is suggestive of psychotic thought processes. Greg may be experiencing hallucinations and may report feelings of unreality. He feels that other people are saying bad thing about him, can read his mind or control his thinking or behavior, and are trying to harm him.

Type A Behavior (TPA) (T = 68). This moderately elevated score indicates that Greg may be agitated, irritable, hostile, and easily annoyed. He may be overbearing and critical in relationships and tends to hold grudges. He may feel as if there is never enough time to get things done.

Low Self Esteem (LSE) (T = 77). This score suggests that Greg has a very poor self-concept; he anticipates failure and gives up easily. He is overly sensitive to criticism and rejection, and he finds it difficult to accept compliments. He is also passive and indecisive, and he tends to have many worries and fears.

Work Interference (WRK) (T = 67). This moderately elevated score indicates that Greg is reporting a wide variety of attitudes and behaviors that are likely to contribute to poor work performance. He may be uncertain about vocational or career goals. In work situations he tends to express negative attitudes toward co-workers. He is likely to have difficulty making decisions, and he may show poor judgment in work situations.

Negative Treatment Indicators (TRT) (T = 59). This score is only slightly above average, so not much emphasis is placed on it. However, even this moderate elevation would suggest a rather poor prognosis for psychological treatment. Greg seems to believe that he has problems that will not be understood by others and feels unable to make significant changes in his life. He is not a good problem solver, often shows poor judgment, and gives up easily when problems are encountered.

A careful examination of the numerous hypotheses generated about Greg from his scores on the various scales reveals that there is remarkable overlap and agreement among the hypotheses generated from the different scores. Only a few of the hypotheses are generated from a single scale. The reader will note a few apparent inconsistencies among the hypotheses. Obviously, greater emphasis should be placed on those hypotheses that result from several or more scales, whereas hypotheses resulting from a single scale should be discarded or treated as very tentative. In dealing with the inconsistent hypotheses, greater emphasis should be placed on hypotheses based on scales with more extreme scores and on hypotheses generated from empirical data.
generated from empirical data.

It may be helpful to discuss how several of the apparent inconsistencies in inferences would be handled. Greg's low score on scale 3 (T = 34) led to an inference that he tends to be conventional and conforming. Yet his high score on scale 8 (T = 81) led to an inference that he tends to be nonconforming and

unconventional. Because there has been considerably more research on the meaning of high scores than on the meaning of low scores, we would place more emphasis on the inference based on scale 8. Greg's average score on scale 2 (T = 50) led to an inference that he is not likely to be clinically depressed. Yet his high score on Harris-Lingoes D5 subscale (T = 79) led to inferences that he is unhappy, feels useless, and may at times feel that life is no longer worthwhile. Because there has been much more empirical research on the meaning of scores on scale 2 than on the meaning of scores on the D5 subscale, we would place greater emphasis on the scale 2 inference. However, it is possible that the inferences really are not inconsistent. Greg could feel unhappy and dissatisfied without having symptoms of clinical depression, such as sleep disturbance, weight loss, and psychomotor retardation.

Symptoms. There is rather clear agreement from various aspects of the MMPI-2 protocol that Greg is likely to have psychotic symptoms. His thinking tends to be autistic, fragmented, tangential, and circumstantial. He has problems with concentration, attention, and memory, and at times he seems to be confused, disorganized, and disoriented. Feelings of unreality, hallucinations, and delusions of persecution and/or grandeur may be present. He sometimes feels that his body is changing in strange and unusual ways. He often feels out of control of his emotions, and he experiences periods during which he seems unaware of what he is doing.

Although the overall impression from the MMPI-2 profile is that Greg is not overwhelmed by depression, anxiety, and other emotional turmoil, analyses of subscales and supplementary scales reveal that he is not very satisfied with his life situation. He broods and ruminates a great deal. He is unhappy and pessimistic about things getting better for him. He may experience some thoughts about life's not being worthwhile. Because of an average score on scale 2, one would not expect to find evidence of clinical depression (e.g., sleep disturbance, weight loss, psychomotor retardation). There is some evidence that Greg is experiencing some generalized fears and anxieties that may interfere with many aspects of daily functioning, but they probably are not related directly to stressors in his life situation. He may at times feel quite agitated and restless, and he may display hyperactive behavior patterns.

The MAC-R raw score of 29 is quite high and would lead to the inference that Greg may abuse alcohol and other substances. This inference is supported by hospital records that indicated possible abuse of alcohol and marijuana.

Major Needs. The MMPI-2 does not offer much information about Greg's major needs. Perhaps the most striking inferences in this regard have to do with irritability, anger, and resentment. These feelings may result from perceptions that other people expect too much from him and are not supportive enough. He is not likely to express negative emotions very effectively. Often he withdraws into fantasy when he is upset, but sometimes he may be quite harsh and blunt in interactions with others. There is also some indication that Greg might like to

be more independent and free from family influence. He sees his family as treating him more as a child than as an adult. Finally, some of his responses suggest that he may at times exhibit sadistic and/or masochistic needs.

Perceptions of the Environment. Many different aspects of the MMPI-2 suggest that Greg views the world as a demanding and threatening place. He believes that other people are unreasonable, dishonest, and selfish. He feels mistreated, misunderstood, and picked on. He seems to feel that he is getting a raw deal from life. Greg has many negative perceptions of family members. He sees them as demanding and critical and not as loving, understanding, or supportive. He feels that his family has not permitted him to be adequately free and independent, and he has felt like running away from home. Greg does not feel a part of his social environment, and he often feels lonely, isolated, and alienated.

Reactions to Stress. From the MMPI-2 it would appear that Greg is poorly equipped to deal with stress and pressure. He feels overwhelmed by the responsibilities of everyday life. He may be preoccupied with abstract or theoretical matters to the exclusion of specific, concrete aspects of his life situation. He tends to respond to stress by withdrawing into fantasy and daydreaming, and often it is difficult for him to differentiate between fantasy and reality. When he is feeling blue or dysphoric, he may seek out risky or exciting activities as a way of trying to make himself feel better. In work situations Greg is likely to express negative opinions of co-workers, to be indecisive, and to show poor judgment.

Self-concept. At times Greg may express unrealistically positive evaluations of his abilities and self-worth. However, he basically has very low self-esteem. He is plagued by feelings of inferiority, incompetency, and self-dissatisfaction. He feels inadequately prepared to respond to the demands of daily life. He tends to anticipate failure, and he gives up easily.

Sexual Identification. In responding to the MMPI-2 items Greg admitted to preoccupation with sexual matters. There appears to be an absence of stereotypically masculine interests and activities. Sex role confusion may be present. It seems unlikely that Greg will have mature heterosexual relationships.

Emotional Control. Although Greg is likely to harbor feelings of anger and resentment toward other people who are perceived as critical, demanding, and unsupportive, he is not very comfortable with such feelings. He may at times express irritability toward others, but most of the time he is likely to be emotionally constricted and overcontrolled. At times he feels as if he will lose emotional control, and this is very frightening to him. He describes having had episodes during which he did not know what he was doing and later could not remember what he had done.

Interpersonal Relationships. Greg has a schizoid life-style. He is not likely to be

emotionally involved with others on a regular basis. He is suspicious and distrustful in relationships, and he avoids deep emotional ties. He admits to never having had a love relationship with anyone. He is deficient in social skills, and it is difficult for him to talk in interpersonal situations. He is most comfortable when he is alone. Other people describe him as shy, cold, aloof, and hard to get to know. He is also seen as unfriendly, moody, and negativistic. When he is involved with other people, he is likely to be overbearing, harsh, and blunt.

Psychological Resources. Careful examination of the inferences generated from various aspects of Greg's MMPI-2 scores reveals very few positive statements. He seems to have very limited resources for coping with the demands of his life situation. In some circumstances he may be described by others as generous, peaceable, sentimental, or sharp-witted. From the MMPI-2 it is not possible to understand under what specific circumstances these perceptions take place.

Dynamics and Etiology

As often is the case, the MMPI-2 results do not offer direct inferences concerning dynamics and etiology. We would have to rely on other data sources and/or higher order inferences to try to understand how Greg came to be as he is described so far. For example, one might hypothesize that substance abuse could result from attempts to deal with feelings of inferiority and alienation. His perceptions of the world as demanding and critical could be related to unrealistically high expectations of his parents. This hypothesis seems reasonable because Greg responded to MMPI-2 items indicating that he saw family members as critical and demanding. His lack of involvement with other people could be viewed as a defense against being rejected or exploited by others.

Diagnostic Impressions

The MMPI-2 data consistently suggested that an Axis I psychotic diagnosis would be appropriate for Greg. The positive slope of the profile is consistent with such a diagnosis. Likewise, the Goldberg index value of 125 is at a level suggestive of psychosis. The 6-8 two-point code and elevated scores on scale 6, scale 8, and the BIZ content scale all support a psychotic diagnosis. Although both schizophrenic disorder, (paranoid type) and paranoid disorder were mentioned, most indicators support the former diagnosis rather than the latter. Because of the elevated MAC-R score and indications of possible substance abuse in hospital records, Axis I substance abuse diagnoses should also be considered.

No direct inferences can be made concerning Axis II diagnoses for Greg. However, the symptoms and personality characteristics described above are consistent with a schizoid personality disorder diagnosis.

Implications for Treatment

Both direct and second order inferences can be made concerning implications for treatment. Based on previously generated inferences, it is clear that Greg has very serious psychological problems and is likely to have considerable difficulty meeting the demands of his daily life situation. Were he not already in an inpatient psychiatric facility, one would infer that he should be. The 8-6 two-point code suggests that a medical consultation is indicated to determine the appropriateness of antipsychotic medication. If corroborating information supports the hypothesis of substance abuse, a treatment program should include a substance abuse component.

The prognosis for psychological treatment is not good. Greg's problems are serious and longstanding. Although he may agree to enter treatment because he is feeling overwhelmed, he is likely to experience considerable difficulty in accepting responsibility for his own behavior. His distrust of other people will make it difficult for him to relate meaningfully to a therapist. However, he is likely to stay in treatment longer than many patients and could eventually come to trust a therapist. In therapy he will want to deal with vague and abstract issues rather than concrete and practical matters. He believes that his problems will not be understood by others, and he feels unable to make significant changes in his life. He is not a good problem solver, and he gives up easily.

Summary

The preceding analysis of this single case is lengthy in its presentation because it is meant as a teaching-learning tool for the beginning MMPI-2 user. The experienced MMPI-2 user would write a much briefer interpretation of the protocol. Specifically, the following is what the author would write about Greg in a clinic chart, to the referring source, or for his own psychotherapy notes.

> The MMPI-2 protocol produced by Greg appears to be valid. He was not overly defensive in responding to the MMPI-2 items. He admitted to a large number of deviant attitudes and behaviors, but this admission is seen as an accurate reporting of serious problems.
>
> Greg appears to be having very serious psychological problems. He is likely to have great difficulty in responding to the demands of his everyday life situation. He is likely to have psychotic symptoms, including hallucinations, delusions of persecution or grandeur, and feelings of unreality. He feels out of control of his emotions and experiences periods during which he is unaware of what he is doing. Although he does not seem to be clinically depressed, he is quite dissatisfied with his life and pessimistic about things getting better. He may at times feel that it is no longer worth being alive. There is some indication that Greg may abuse alcohol and/or other substances in an attempt to make himself feel better.
>
> Greg views the world as a threatening place and other people as critical and demanding. He sees other people as unreasonable, dishonest, and

selfish. He is suspicious and untrusting, and he avoids deep emotional involvement. He is especially angry and resentful toward family members and sees them as critical, demanding, and not permitting freedom and independence.

Greg is poorly equipped to deal with stress and pressure. He feels overwhelmed with the responsibilities of daily life. He prefers to deal with abstract issues rather than concrete and specific aspects of his life situation. He tends to respond to stress by withdrawing into fantasy and daydreaming, and at times he may find it difficult to differentiate between fantasy and reality.

Greg has a very poor self-concept. He is plagued by feelings of inferiority, incompetency, and self-dissatisfaction. He anticipates failure and gives up easily. He does not have a very strong masculine identification, and it is unlikely that he will have mature heterosexual relationships. Although Greg harbors many feelings of anger and resentment, he generally does not express such feelings openly and directly. At times he fears that he might lose emotional control.

Greg has a schizoid life-style. He is suspicious and distrustful in relationships and avoids deep emotional ties. He is deficient in social skills and prefers to be alone. When he is involved with others, he is likely to be overbearing, harsh, and blunt.

The most appropriate Axis I diagnosis for Greg is schizophrenic disorder (paranoid type). Substance abuse diagnoses also should be considered. His symptoms and personality characteristics are consistent with an Axis II diagnosis of schizoid personality disorder.

Greg needs treatment and may initially require inpatient psychiatric hospitalization. Medical referral to determine the appropriateness of antipsychotic medication is indicated. His inability to relate to other people, reluctance to accept responsibility for his own behavior, and belief that he cannot make significant changes in his life indicate a poor prognosis for psychological treatment. In addition to antipsychotic medications, if they are judged to be appropriate by medical personnel, Greg could benefit from some supportive therapy that would help him to focus on specific and concrete aspects of his current life situation.

ADDITIONAL PRACTICE PROFILES

Brief interpretations of two additional MMPI-2 profiles will now be presented. As a learning exercise, clinicians can write their own interpretations of each profile and then compare their interpretations with the ones presented below.

Jane

Figures 9.5 and 9.6 present the MMPI-2 basic scale and content scale profiles for Jane, a 35-year-old white female. She was evaluated shortly after her admission

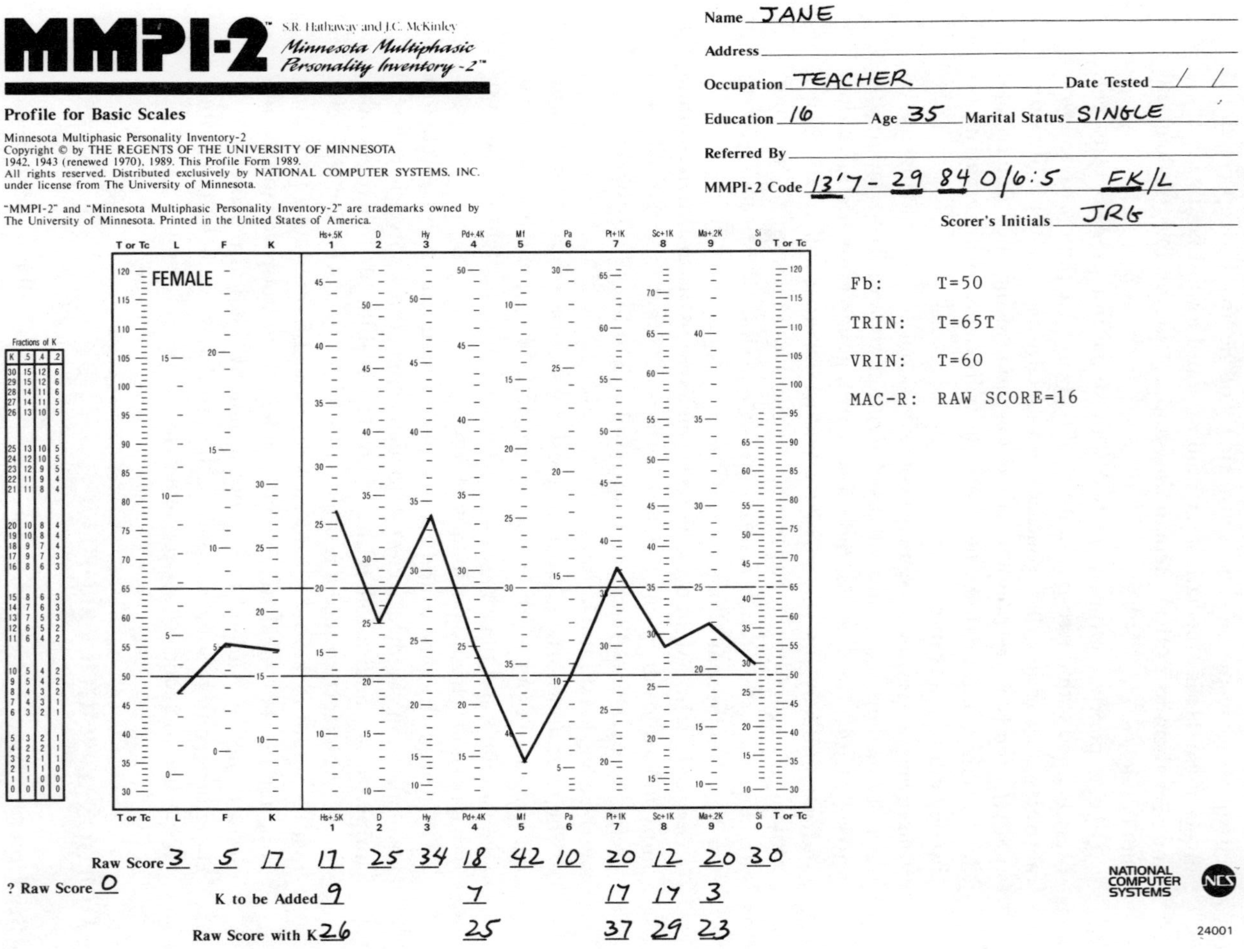

MMPI-2 S.R. Hathaway and J.C. McKinley
Minnesota Multiphasic Personality Inventory -2™

Profile for Basic Scales

Minnesota Multiphasic Personality Inventory-2
Copyright © by THE REGENTS OF THE UNIVERSITY OF MINNESOTA
1942, 1943 (renewed 1970), 1989. This Profile Form 1989.
All rights reserved. Distributed exclusively by NATIONAL COMPUTER SYSTEMS, INC.
under license from The University of Minnesota.

"MMPI-2" and "Minnesota Multiphasic Personality Inventory-2" are trademarks owned by
The University of Minnesota. Printed in the United States of America.

Name JANE

Address

Occupation TEACHER   Date Tested /

Education 16   Age 35   Marital Status SINGLE

Referred By

MMPI-2 Code 13'7 - 29 84 0/6:5   EK/L

Scorer's Initials JRG

Fb: T=50

TRIN: T=65T

VRIN: T=60

MAC-R: RAW SCORE=16

FEMALE

	T or Tc	L	F	K	Hs+.5K 1	D 2	Hy 3	Pd+.4K 4	Mf 5	Pa 6	Pt+1K 7	Sc+1K 8	Ma+.2K 9	Si 0	T or Tc
Raw Score		3	5	17	11	25	34	18	42	10	20	12	20	30	
K to be Added					9			7			17	17	3		
Raw Score with K					26			25			37	29	23		

? Raw Score 0

Figure 9.5. MMPI-2 profile for basic scales for practice case (Jane).

228

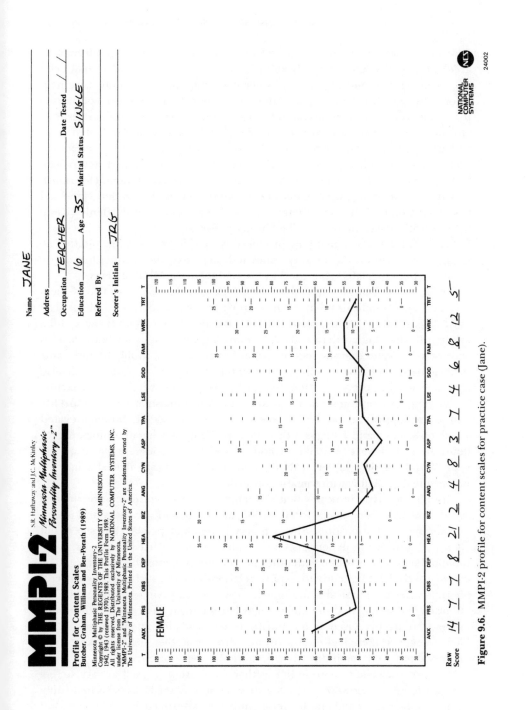

Figure 9.6. MMPI-2 profile for content scales for practice case (Jane).

229

to a chronic pain treatment unit. She had been involved in a minor automobile accident several years previously and periodically since the accident had been experiencing pain and discomfort in her neck and back. Comprehensive neurological evaluation had not indicated any physical basis for her continuing pain. Jane was the only child of middle class parents. Her father was a salesman, and her mother had not worked outside of the home. Jane graduated from college with a degree in elementary education. She had taught third and fourth grades at several different schools since her graduation. She had never been married, but she had been engaged while she was a college student. Her fiancé ended the relationship after he became involved with another student. Jane had been taking pain medication off and on since her accident, but she denied using the medications except as prescribed by her physician.

The MMPI-2 protocol that Jane produced is considered valid. She omitted no items. Her scores on the validity scales indicated that she was neither overly defensive nor especially self-critical in responding to the MMPI-2 items.

Having three clinical scales with T-scores greater than 65 (with two of them greater than 75) indicates that she has significant psychological problems. The most salient feature of the profile is the 1-3 two-point code. Both scales 1 and 3 are significantly higher than scale 2, forming a conversion valley pattern. This code type indicates that she sees herself as having medical problems and wants medical treatment. The very high score on the Health (HEA) content scale also indicates somatic preoccupation. She lacks insight into psychological factors underlying her symptoms. She tends to have a Pollyannaish attitude toward life and to use repression and denial excessively. The absence of marked elevated scores on scales 2 and 7 suggests that she is not experiencing disabling anxiety, depression, or other emotional turmoil. However, the moderate elevations on scale 7 and on the Anxiety (ANX) content scale indicate that she may be preoccupied, probably with somatic concerns.

The 1-3 code type indicates that she tends to be immature, egocentric, and selfish. She has strong needs for attention, affection, and sympathy and is very demanding in relationships. She is a very dependent person, but she is not comfortable with the dependency and experiences conflict because of it. Although she may be involved with other people, her relationships are likely to be quite superficial. She tends to exploit relationships to satisfy her own needs. She may use her physical symptoms as a way of justifying her demands for attention and support. Although Jane may harbor anger and resentment toward others who are perceived as not fulfilling her needs for attention, she is not likely to express these feelings openly and directly. Rather, they are likely to be expressed passively and indirectly or in periodic angry outbursts.

Her very low scale 5 score indicates that she presents herself as very stereotypically feminine. However, the 1-3 code suggests that she lacks skills in dealing with the opposite sex and may be deficient in heterosexual drive.

Based on the 1-3 code type, the elevated HEA content scale score, history, and presenting complaints, an Axis I diagnosis of somatoform pain disorder seems to be appropriate. Although no direct inference concerning an Axis II diagnosis

is indicated, the personality characteristics described above are consistent with a diagnosis of dependent personality disorder.

Because of her unwillingness to acknowledge psychological factors underlying her symptoms, Jane would be difficult to motivate in traditional psychotherapy. If a therapist were to stress the link between symptoms and psychological factors, she is likely to terminate therapy. It may be possible to get her to discuss problems in her life situation as long as no direct link to somatic symptoms is suggested. Because persons with the 1-3 code tend to be suggestible, Jane may be willing to try activities suggested by a therapist.

Steve

Figures 9.7 and 9.8 present the MMPI-2 basic scale and content scale profiles for Steve, a 30-year-old white male. The MMPI-2 was administered when he and his wife consulted a community mental health agency for help with marital problems. Steve and his wife had been married for six years and had two children. His wife was a high school graduate who was not employed outside the home. Steve had been employed by several different companies as a salesman since graduation from high school. Steve's wife complained that he was selfish, insensitive, and inconsiderate. She said that he used alcohol excessively and that he often stayed out late at night without telling her where he was. Although Steve felt that his wife's concerns were exaggerated, he agreed to seek professional help when she threatened to divorce him if he did not do so.

It would appear that Steve completed the MMPI-2 in a valid manner. He omitted no item, and his scores on the three validity scales did not suggest defensiveness, exaggeration, or other response sets.

The MMPI-2 profile suggests that Steve is not presenting himself as experiencing psychological distress or as being psychologically maladjusted. Only two T-scores are elevated above 65, and neither is above 70. The F scale score of approximately 65 suggests that he was admitting to some deviant attitudes and behaviors, but it was not high enough to suggest serious psychopathology. The scores on scales 2 and 7 were about average, suggesting that he is not overwhelmed by depression, anxiety, or other emotional turmoil. However, a moderate elevation on the Depression (DEP) content scale indicates that he may be dissatisfied with his current life situation.

When the 4-9 code type is significantly more elevated than in Steve's profile, a marked disregard for social standards and values and asocial or antisocial behavior are suggested. At this less elevated level, the code type suggests rebellion, nonconformity, and resentment of authority. However, the very elevated Antisocial Practices (ASP) content scale score raises some concern that he may act out in asocial or antisocial ways. Steve's history would be helpful in deciding to what extent we might expect him to act out in the future. The possibility of substance abuse raised by the 4-9 code type is reinforced by the MAC-R raw score of 29 and is consistent with his wife's allegation that he uses alcohol excessively.

Figure 9.7. MMPI-2 profile for basic scales for practice case (Steve).

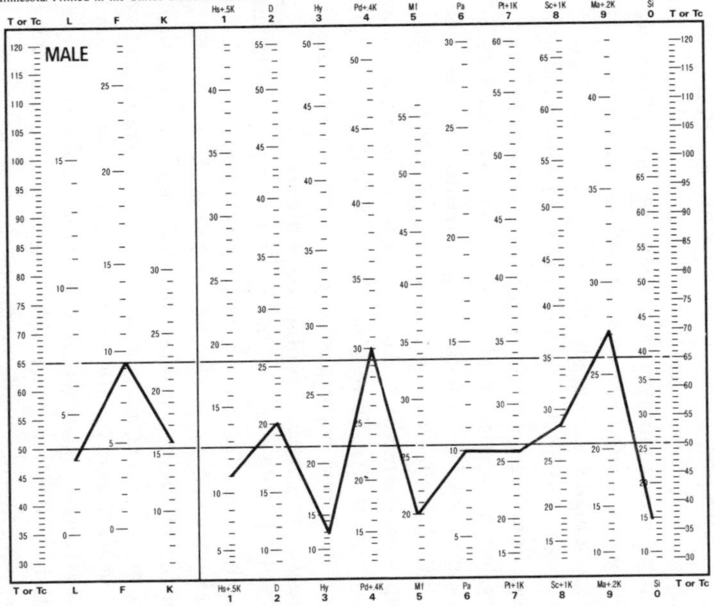

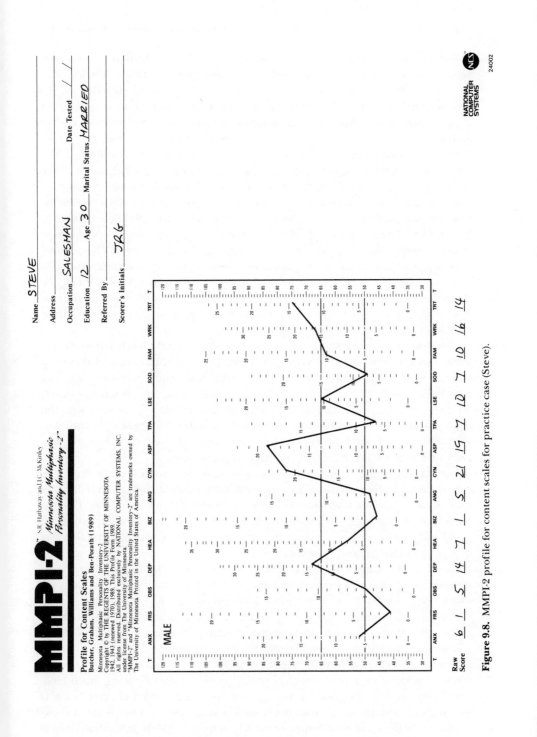

Figure 9.8. MMPI-2 profile for content scales for practice case (Steve).

233

The 4-9 code type and the very low scale 0 score (T = 37) lead us to infer that Steve is an ambitious and energetic person and that he may be restless and overactive. He is likely to seek out excitement and emotional stimulation. He can be expected to be extroverted and talkative and to create good first impressions. This configuration of scores also suggests that Steve is narcissistic and self-indulgent. He may show poor judgment, often acting without consid-ering the consequences of his actions. He is unwilling to accept responsibility for his own behavior and is quick to blame failures and difficulties on other people. He has a low tolerance for frustration and harbors intense feelings of anger and hostility that may be expressed in occasional emotional outbursts. Because of his self-centeredness, his relationships with other people are likely to be superficial. He seems incapable of deep emotional ties, and he keeps others at an emotional distance. The elevated score on the Cynicism (CYN) content scale suggests that he sees other people as dishonest, selfish, and untrustworthy. The 4-9 code type suggests that beneath an outward facade of self-confidence and security, he may be a rather immature, insecure, and dependent person. The moderately elevated score on the Low Self Esteem (LSE) content scale reinforces the inference concerning self-doubts.

Based on the very low score on scale 3 (T = 35), we might infer that Steve has limited social interests and participation, that he is not impulsive, and that he is content with a dull, uneventful life-style. Obviously, such inferences are not consistent with those based on the 4-9 code type. Because there is more research on interpretation of the 4-9 code type than on the meaning of low scores on the clinical scales, we would tend to emphasize the inferences based on the code type. One would want to explore the possibility that the low 3 score may indicate that Steve is cold, aloof, and hard to get to know.

The very low scale 5 score (T = 37) suggests that Steve is presenting himself as very stereotypically masculine. Exaggerated gender role attitudes and behaviors may be compensating for some basic doubts about his own masculinity. The low 5 score also suggests that he may be inflexible and unoriginal in his approach to problems, that he prefers action to thought, and that he is not at all comfortable dealing with feelings and emotions.

Based on the elevated MAC-R score and his wife's allegations of excessive alcohol abuse, the appropriateness of an Axis I substance abuse diagnosis should be considered. A very elevated 4-9 profile would indicate an Axis II diagnosis of antisocial personality disorder. Steve's moderately elevated 4-9 profile does not justify such a diagnosis, but many of the personality characteris-tics associated with this personality disorder may be present.

Several inferences about treatment implications are appropriate. Because he does not acknowledge psychological problems, is not experiencing much emo-tional turmoil, and does not accept responsibility for his own behavior, Steve is not likely to benefit much from traditional psychotherapy. The elevated score on the Negative Treatment Indicators (TRT) content scale suggests that Steve is likely to have negative attitudes toward mental health treatment, to feel that

others cannot understand his problems, and to believe that he is unable to make significant changes in his life. He may agree to treatment to avoid something more negative (e.g., divorce), but he is likely to terminate prematurely after the immediate crisis passes.

10

Computerized Administration, Scoring, and Interpretation

In an era of almost unbelievable advances in computer technology, it is not at all surprising that increasing efforts have been made to automate the testing process. Automation in psychological testing occurs whenever a computer performs functions previously carried out by the human examiner. Computers can be used to administer, score, and interpret tests. Although automation has been applied to a variety of psychological tests, objective personality inventories, such as the MMPI-2, lend themselves most readily to automation.

Computers have some definite advantages over human clinicians in the testing enterprise. First, they are fast. Operations that would take a person minutes, or even hours, to complete can be completed by computers in seconds. Second, computers are accurate and reliable. Assuming that the computer has been accurately programmed, the functions that it performs are perfectly reliable. Third, the computer has far greater storage capacity than the human clinician. A virtually infinite number of bits of information can be stored by the computer, to be called upon as needed in the testing process. Fourth, the flexibility provided by computer technology offers the possibility of developing tests or sets of test items tailored to the individual examinee. Programs can be written to interact with the examinee so that the answer to any specific item determines the next item to be presented, skipping irrelevant data and/or exploring some areas in more depth. Although such computer-tailored assessment procedures have been employed in ability testing and diagnostic interviewing, this potential has not been widely exploited in personality testing. (Butcher, Keller, & Bacon, 1985). However, Ben-Porath, Waller, Slutsky, & Butcher (1988) demonstrated that adaptive testing procedures could be employed with the MMPI.

AUTOMATED ADMINISTRATION OF THE MMPI-2

Instead of using the traditional test booklets and answer sheets, subjects can complete the MMPI-2 on a computer terminal or personal computer. The

typical procedure is for subjects to sit at the machine while the MMPI-2 items are individually displayed on a monitor. A response is made to each item by pressing designated keys on the machine. Each response is recorded automatically and saved in the computer memory for later processing. Programs can permit subjects to change responses after they are made and to omit items and then reconsider them at the end of the test.

Automated administration has several advantages. First, many subjects find it more interesting than the traditional procedure and are more motivated to complete the task (Carr, Ghosh, & Ancill, 1983; Evan & Miller, 1969; Greist & Klein, 1980; Lucas, Mullin, Luna, & McInroy, 1977). Second, because subjects enter response data into the computer, no professional or clerical time is used for this purpose. However, a major disadvantage is that each administration consumes an hour or more of computer time. Also, some subjects, particularly upset and confused clients or patients, may be overwhelmed by the task.

As discussed previously, the MMPI-2 is a very robust instrument. Various forms of the original MMPI (e.g., booklet, audio tape recording) yielded essentially equivalent results. However, we must be concerned about the equivalence of the computer-administered and more traditional versions of the test. Guidelines for computer-based testing developed by the American Psychological Association (1986) clearly specify that the equivalence of traditional and computer-administered procedures must be demonstrated. Biskin and Kolotkin (1977) found that subjects gave many more Cannot Say responses with computerized administration than with traditional administration. To explain this difference, it was hypothesized that whereas the conventional Cannot Say response is a rather passive one, that is, leaving the item blank on the answer sheet, computerized administration entails actively choosing the Cannot Say response alternative. In a subsequent study subjects were asked actively to enter Cannot Say responses in both traditional and computerized administration, and the differences in use of this response alternative disappeared.

Some studies have found that subjects are more willing to admit to deviant behaviors when tests are computer-administered than when a standard administration is used (Evan & Miller, 1969; Koson, Kitchen, Kochen, & Stodolosky, 1970). However, at least one study found that patients produced more pathological profiles when the MMPI was administered in the usual fashion than when it was administered via computer (Bresolin, 1984). Several studies reported no significant differences in self-report when interviews and personality scales were administered in traditional ways and by computer (Katz & Dalby, 1981; Skinner & Allen, 1983; Lukin, Dowd, Plake, & Kraft, 1985). Moreland (1985a) reviewed data concerning the equivalence of tests administered using computers and in traditional ways and concluded that differences typically are small and probably of little practical consequence. There have not yet been any data published concerning equivalence of traditional and computer administrations of MMPI-2. Based on data from the original MMPI and from other assessment procedures, it seems likely that the scores resulting from standard and computerized procedures for MMPI-2 administration will result in equivalent

scores. However, empirical studies concerning this equivalence for the MMPI-2 are needed before we may feel comfortable about the routine use of computerized administration of the instrument.

The technology for on-line administration of tests is changing rapidly. Because of copyright issues, at present persons wanting to use on-line administration of the MMPI-2 must buy from the test distributor (National Computer Systems, or NCS) software that can be used with personal computers. Persons wanting to explore this option for administration should contact NCS.

AUTOMATED SCORING OF THE MMPI-2

Programming a computer to score the MMPI-2 is not a very difficult task. The computer's memory stores information that determines which items and which responses are scored for each scale. Dozens, and even hundreds, of scales can be scored in a matter of seconds. Because test norms also can be stored in the computer's memory, raw scores on the various scales can be converted easily to T-scores, and profiles based on these T-scores can be printed. This entire process can be accomplished in a fraction of the time needed to score and plot even the basic validity and clinical scales by hand.

The use of MMPI-2 scoring information is covered by copyright standards, so permission to develop scoring programs must be obtained from the test publisher. It is anticipated that several companies, in addition to NCS, will be licensed to offer computerized scoring of the MMPI-2.

NCS has available several different procedures for computer scoring of MMPI-2. Software is available for scoring using personal computers. If the MMPI-2 has been administered on-line, the individual responses have been saved in the computer's memory and are ready for immediate scoring. If the subject uses a test booklet and answer sheet, an examiner or clerk can enter the subject's responses from an answer sheet via a computer keyboard. With a little practice, the 567 items can be entered in a very short time (5 to 10 minutes). For high-volume users special answer sheets can be processed by relatively inexpensive scanners that can be attached to personal computers. Another option is for response data to be entered on a keyboard and transmitted via teleprocessing equipment to Minneapolis where the scoring is done on a mainframe computer operated by the test distributor. The resulting scores are printed on the test user's computer printer, so they are available almost immediately. A final option is for special answer sheets to be used and mailed to Minneapolis for scoring. Ordinarily the resulting scores are sent by return mail within 24 hours of receipt. Persons who anticipate using computerized scoring should consult with the test distributor to determine the most convenient and economical method for their particular circumstances and to make sure that appropriate materials are used.

AUTOMATED INTERPRETATION OF THE MMPI-2

Automated interpretation of the MMPI-2 is not as simple and straightforward as are administration and scoring. Interpretive statements are written for various scores and patterns of scores, and these statements are stored in the computer's memory. When an MMPI-2 is administered to a specific subject and scored, the computer searches its memory to find interpretive statements that previously were judged appropriate for these particular scores and patterns of scores. These statements are then selected and printed.

It is important to distinguish between automated and actuarial interpretation (Graham & Lilly, 1984). Automation refers to the use of computers to store interpretive statements and to select and assign particular statements to particular scores and patterns of scores. The decisions about which statements are to be assigned to which scores may be based on research, actuarial tables, or clinical experience. Regardless of how the decisions are made initially, they are made automatically by the computer after the test is administered and scored.

In actuarial interpretations, the assignment of interpretive statements to scores and patterns of scores is based entirely on previously established empirical relationships between test scores and the behaviors included in the interpretive statements. Experience and intuition play no part in actuarial interpretation. This is the procedure that Meehl seemed to have in mind when he made his pleas for a good cookbook for test interpretation (Meehl, 1956).

The MMPI-2 interpretive services currently available are not actuarial in nature. They are what Wiggins (1973) called automated clinical prediction. On the basis of published research, clinical hypotheses, and clinical experience, a clinician generates interpretive statements judged to be appropriate for particular sets of MMPI-2 scores. The statements are stored in the computer and called upon as needed. It should be made perfectly clear that the accuracy (validity) of these kinds of interpretations depends on the knowledge and skill of the clinicians who generated the interpretive statements. The validity of these interpretations should not be assumed and needs to be demonstrated every bit as much as the validity of a test (Moreland, 1985c). The validity of existing interpretive programs has not been adequately established.

Numerous interpretive programs and services were offered for the original MMPI, and it is reasonable to expect that services for the MMPI-2 will also proliferate. At this time, in addition to the computerized interpretation services available from the test distributor, another service, Caldwell Reports, has made arrangements to offer computerized interpretations of the MMPI-2. Based on the services available for the original MMPI, it seems likely that the quality of the interpretive services for the MMPI-2 will vary considerably. Some programs will be written by persons with considerable knowledge of MMPI and MMPI-2 research and adequate experience with the original and revised instruments. Others will be written by persons knowing very little about the MMPI or MMPI-2. Because most interpretive services do not make available the al-

gorithms underlying their programs, it is difficult to evaluate their accuracy. Ben-Porath and Butcher (1986) suggested that potential users of computerized interpretation services should ask the following questions before deciding which service, if any, will be used:

1. To what extent has the validity of the reports been studied?
2. To what extent do the reports rely on empirical findings in generating interpretations?
3. To what extent do the reports incorporate all the currently available validated descriptive information?
4. Do the reports take demographic variables into account?
5. Are different versions of the reports available for various referral questions (e.g., employment screening versus clinical diagnosis)?
6. Do the reports include practical suggestions?
7. Are the reports periodically revised to reflect newly acquired information?

These seem to be very reasonable questions for potential users to ask of the services that they are considering. Additionally, they may want to find out who actually wrote the interpretive programs and determine their professional qualifications to do so. Services that cannot or will not provide answers to these questions should not be considered.

SAMPLE OF COMPUTERIZED INTERPRETIVE REPORT

In order to illustrate automated interpretation of the MMPI-2, the answer sheet of the subject discussed in detail in Chapter 9 (Greg) was sent to NCS for processing, and the resulting Minnesota Report is presented in its entirety at the end of this chapter. The Minnesota Report was written almost entirely by one interpretive expert, Dr. James N. Butcher at the University of Minnesota, incorporating both his knowledge of research data and his personal clinical experience. The program is built hierarchically around code type interpretations (Butcher, Keller, & Bacon, 1985; Butcher, 1989). If a profile fits an established code type, a standard report for that configural pattern is printed. Additions and modifications are based on elevations of scores on other scales. If the profile does not fit an established code type, the report is based on a scale-by-scale analysis.

The version of the Minnesota Report appropriate for the MMPI-2 relies heavily on research findings on the original MMPI and the report author's clinical experience with the original and revised versions of the MMPI (Butcher, 1989). According to the user's guide for the Minnesota Report (Butcher, 1989), several demographic and situational variables are taken into consideration in generating interpretive statements about scores. Gender, age, educational level, marital status, and type of setting in which the test was completed are all considered.

Several different options are available for persons who want to use the

computerized services provided by NCS. It is possible to obtain scoring only for the basic validity and clinical scales or for these scales plus a large number of supplementary scales and indices. In addition to the Minnesota Adult Clinical Report, which is the one illustrated in this chapter, there is a separate report for use in personnel screening situations. Readers requiring more information about these services should consult a recent NCS catalog or contact NCS.

As the reader can see in the sample report, the Minnesota Adult Clinical Report includes scores for the basic validity and clinical scales and for a large number of supplementary scales. In addition, two profile codes are reported for each case. The old Welsh code is based on K-corrected T-scores resulting from a comparison of the subject's raw scores with data from the original normative sample. The new Welsh code is based on K-corrected T-scores resulting from a comparison of the subject's raw scores with data from the 1989 normative sample. Other indices, such as the Goldberg Index and Henrichs Rules, are calculated and reported.

The narrative portion of the report contains several sections. The first section deals with the validity of the profile. If the profile is judged not to be valid, scores are reported, but no further interpretive statements are made. The second section provides a description of the most salient symptoms suggested by the test results. The third section describes how the subject likely interacts with other people. The fourth section gives statements predicting whether the symptoms and other characteristics described in other sections are likely to remain stable or change over time. The fifth section provides the most likely DSM-III-R diagnoses for the subject. The sixth and final section addresses treatment considerations. Following the narrative sections of the report, there are listings of the Koss-Butcher and Lachar-Wrobel critical items and of individual item responses to the 567 items in the MMPI-2.

It is important to note that the Minnesota Report includes a cautionary note indicating that its descriptions, inferences, and recommendations need to be verified by other sources of clinical information and that the information in the report should be most appropriately used by a trained, qualified test interpreter.

COMPARISON OF COMPUTERIZED AND CLINICIAN-GENERATED INTERPRETATIONS

A comparison of the Minnesota Report and the clinician-generated report for the same profile that was presented in Chapter 9 (Greg) reveals considerable agreement between the interpretations. Both interpretations conclude that the MMPI-2 profile is valid and interpretable, although they both indicate that Greg might have been careless in responding to items that occur later in the test. The Minnesota Report raised the possibility of random responding. The clinician-generated interpretation considers this possibility but rejects it because neither

the F scale score nor the VRIN scale score is high enough and because the overall shape of the profile is not similar to that obtained from subjects who respond randomly. The Minnesota Report also raised the possibility that Greg might have been exaggerating problems or malingering when he took the test. This possibility was considered and rejected in the clinician-generated interpretation because the F scale score is not elevated enough and because the F minus K index is only 7, well below the cutoff score suggestive of faking bad. The clinician-generated interpretation notes that the rather low K scale score suggests that Greg was very self-critical in responding to the MMPI-2 items. Because of his status as a recently admitted psychiatric inpatient, it seems likely that this self-report probably reflects accurately his severe psychopathology rather than an invalidating response set. In relation to profile validity, it is important to note that the Minnesota Report correctly raised some issues of profile invalidity that the clinician should consider. However, the computerized report was not able to consider all the variables necessary for making a decision about validity and interpretability.

The two interpretations are remarkably similar in describing Greg as being very seriously maladjusted and having symptoms of thought disorder. Both interpretations state that the most likely Axis I diagnosis is schizophrenic disorder (paranoid type) or paranoid disorder. The need to explore the possibility of substance abuse also is mentioned in both interpretations. Although fearfulness and agitation are mentioned in the clinician-generated interpretation, the computerized interpretation does not include these symptoms. Nor does it mention specifically most likely Axis II diagnoses, whereas the clinician-generated report notes that the symptoms and characteristics inferred from the MMPI-2 are consistent with a diagnosis of schizoid personality disorder.

Descriptions of Greg's personality characteristics and behaviors are remarkably similar in the two interpretations. There is clear agreement that Greg sees the world as very threatening and is suspicious of the motives of other people. He is likely to have disturbed interpersonal relationships. It is unlikely that he has formed meaningful love relationships, and heterosexual relationships are likely to be absent or troubled. His tendency to respond to stress by withdrawing into fantasy and daydreaming is mentioned in both interpretations. Negative perceptions of family are included in the clinician-generated interpretation but not in the computerized interpretation. Although one could infer from the Minnesota Report that Greg has very low self-esteem, this likelihood is addressed more directly in the clinician-generated interpretation. Likewise, the clinician-generated report more directly addresses Greg's chronic anger and irritability and his inability to express feelings in modulated ways. Although neither interpretation addresses directly the dynamics or etiology underlying Greg's psychopathology, the clinician-generated interpretation makes some higher order inferences concerning possible etiological factors.

The two interpretations include very similar statements concerning implications for treatment. They agree that Greg probably needs psychiatric hospitalization and psychotropic medications. The Minnesota Report additionally sug-

gests that a day treatment program might be helpful. Both interpretations agree that insight-oriented therapy is not indicated and that therapy should be structured and should deal with specific problems that Greg will have to face when he leaves the hospital. The interpretations both infer that he will have difficulty in trusting a therapist, and the clinician-generated interpretation states that he is likely to stay in treatment longer than most patients and eventually could learn to trust a therapist. The clinician-generated report addresses in more detail attitudes that could represent negative factors in treatment. In addition, the clinician-generated report suggests the possibility of exploring substance abuse treatment.

In summary, the overall agreement between the computerized and clinician-generated interpretations is remarkable. Although there are some specific differences in emphasis, these two interpretations are very similar. The agreement is not really unexpected. The clinician who developed the interpretive program for the Minnesota Report and the clinician who did the interpretation in Chapter 9 were basing their interpretations on basically the same research data. For this sample case the clinician-generated interpretation is more detailed than the computerized interpretation and tends to base more inferences on the content scales.

This comparison of interpretations should not be considered as general support for the validity of computerized interpretations of the MMPI-2. However, one must consider that the clinician-generated interpretation was completed before the author had access to the Minnesota Report. Further, the case used for this comparison is not a very difficult or complicated one. There is a clearly defined two-point code that has been researched extensively. There are few internal inconsistencies in the test scores. Less agreement between computerized and clinician-generated interpretations might very well occur with other, less clear-cut MMPI-2 profiles.

EVALUATION OF AUTOMATED SERVICES

Many different automated programs and services were available for the original MMPI, and evaluating the accuracy and usefulness of all these services is difficult. The author is aware of some scoring programs that used incorrect item numbers for some of the scales and inappropriate procedures for converting raw scores to T-scores. Because of recent clarifications of copyright standards, it seems likely that many fewer computerized scoring programs will be available for the MMPI-2 and that the test publisher can monitor more adequately their accuracy. However, the ultimate responsibility for assessing the accuracy of computerized services rests with the clinicians who use them (American Psychological Association, 1986).

Copyright standards do not apply to the interpretation of MMPI-2 scores. Therefore, we can expect that a large number of interpretive programs and

services for the MMPI-2 will be forthcoming. Although evaluating the adequacy of these services will be an extremely difficult task, clinicians using the services are responsible for doing so.

Some important issues are involved in the use of automated MMPI-2 interpretations. One concerns the extent to which the automated reports are integrated by adequately trained clinicians with other data available about test subjects. Although most of the services advise users that inferences in the test reports need to be verified by other data sources, in practice some clinicians use the automated reports instead of a comprehensive assessment. This is not good clinical practice.

Another concern is that computer-generated reports are seen as valid and questions rarely asked about research demonstrating their validity. In fact, Ziskin (1981) recommended the use of automated reports in forensic cases because the computer-generated profiles and reports impress judges and jurors as more scientific. Nevertheless, the validity of automated interpretations must be demonstrated empirically.

The qualifications of users of automated services are very important. Although services purport to assess the qualifications of potential users to make sure that they use the interpretive reports appropriately, many users are not qualified professionally to use them. Some psychologists who are trained and licensed to practice psychology do not know enough about the MMPI-2 to evaluate the appropriateness of the automated interpretations. The services also are available to physicians, social workers, and others who are licensed to offer mental health services. Typically, these professionals are not adequately trained to evaluate the appropriateness of the automated interpretations.

Most computer services list scores for large numbers of supplementary scales, many of which clearly are experimental in nature. Although information about the development, reliability, and validity of these scales sometimes is provided in materials supplied to users, the typical reader of computerized reports does not have readily accessible information permitting informed decisions about the relative importance of the various scores provided. It would be very helpful if reports would indicate which scales are considered experimental so that users could use appropriate caution in interpreting them.

Most services also provide numerous indices, such as the Goldberg Index and the Henrichs modification of the Meehl-Dahlstrom rules. APA guidelines indicate that when such indices are presented in computerized interpretations, information concerning hit rates and other validity data should be available to users. Such information typically has not been provided by computer services.

The automated services for the original MMPI almost all listed critical items that test subjects endorsed in the scored direction. Although critical item endorsements represent an important additional source of hypotheses concerning test subjects, many users of the services overinterpreted such endorsements. Each critical item is, in fact, a single item scale whose reliability is very questionable. Thus, extreme cautions must be exercised in interpreting the critical items.

As Butcher (1978) noted, automated interpretive systems often become fixed at a rather naive level. Although the potential exists for modifying the systems as new interpretive data become available, there has been a tendency not to change systems that have been operating smoothly and producing a profit for companies. Butcher discussed several instances where, in response to critics, only minor cosmetic changes or no changes at all were made in existing interpretive programs.

PROFESSIONAL GUIDELINES FOR COMPUTERIZED ASSESSMENT

In an effort to try to address some of the potential problems involved in the use of automated assessment services, in 1966 the American Psychological Association developed some interim standards for such services (Fowler, 1969a). The standards made it clear that organizations offering the services have primary responsibility for ensuring that the services are used by qualified persons and for demonstrating the reliability and validity of the interpretations included in the reports. More recently, the Committee on Professional Standards and the Committee on Psychological Tests and Assessment of the American Psychological Association (APA, 1986) published updated guidelines for computer-based tests and interpretations. These updated guidelines state that it is the responsibility of test developers of computer-based test services to demonstrate the equivalence of computerized and conventional versions of a test. Developers offering interpretations of test scores should describe how the interpretive statements are derived from the original scores and should make clear the extent to which interpretive statements are based on quantitative research versus clinical opinion. When statements in an interpretive report are based on expert clinical opinion, users should be given information allowing them to weight the credibility of the opinion. Developers are expected to provide whatever information is needed to permit review by qualified professionals engaged in scholarly review of their interpretive services.

The updated guidelines make it very clear that professionals are responsible for any use they make of computer-administered tests or computer-generated interpretations. Users should be aware of the method employed in generating the scores and interpretations and sufficiently familiar with the test to evaluate its applicability to the purpose for which it will be used. For each test-taker the user should judge the validity of the computerized test report based on his or her professional knowledge of the total context of testing and the test-taker's performance and characteristics.

Clearly, the developers of computerized testing services and the clinicians who use these services share responsibility for assuring that the results are valid and they are used appropriately. In the past, it has seemed that each of these parties has assumed that the other has major responsibility.

EVALUATING THE VALIDITY OF COMPUTERIZED INTERPRETATIONS

Demonstrating empirically the validity of computer-generated interpretations of MMPI-2 results is desirable. Because the MMPI-2 only recently has been published and made available for general clinical use, research has not yet been published concerning the validity of computerized interpretations of MMPI-2 scores. Several different approaches were used to try to determine the validity of automated interpretations of the original MMPI (Moreland, 1985c). Early efforts involved asking users of the automated services to provide an overall rating of the accuracy of each automated report (e.g., Fowler, 1969b; Klett, 1971; Webb, 1970; Webb, Miller, & Fowler, 1969, 1970). Other studies were a bit more sophisticated. Ratings were made of the accuracy of individual paragraphs or individual statements within each report (e.g., Lachar, 1974a; Lushene & Gilberstadt, 1972). Not surprisingly, the users rated most reports as being accurate. A major problem with these studies is that judgments about what patients really were like and impressions from the MMPI-based reports were confounded. In addition, judging to what extent reports were rated as accurate is not possible because of the inclusion of glittering generalities (Baillargeon & Danis, 1984) in the reports.

The most acceptable validity studies have been those in which external criterion information has been collected by persons with no knowledge of MMPI results or of the automated reports. The interpretive statements in the reports were compared with the external criterion information about patients (e.g., Anderson, 1969; Hedlund, Morgan, & Master, 1972). The results of such studies suggested at best moderate validity for the MMPI automated reports. However, the level of accuracy of the automated reports was not much different from that previously reported when clinicians examined MMPI profiles of subjects and generated descriptions of the subjects (e.g., Graham, 1967; Little & Shneidman, 1959; Sines, 1959).

In a well-designed study, Moreland and Onstad (1985) attempted to overcome some of the problems of earlier studies. They asked clinicians to rate the accuracy of sections of automated reports for 66 patients. To assess discriminant validity, clinicians also rated "bogus" reports that were not actually those of the patients indicated but were for other profiles of the same general code types and elevations as those of the patients. These investigators found that the genuine reports were rated as more accurate than the bogus reports overall and for five of the six sections of the reports.

Eyde, Kowal, & Fishburne (1987) studied the accuracy of statements in computerized interpretations of MMPIs provided by seven different computer services. Experienced clinical psychologists rated the accuracy of individual statements in computerized reports for six military test subjects, some of whom were patients and some of whom were subjects in a normative study. Case history materials were used as the criterion. The results indicated that the accuracy of statements varied considerably among the services. When the seven

services were ranked according to overall accuracy, the Minnesota Report was ranked as most accurate. However, it should be noted that the accuracy for even the highest ranked report was only modest. The percentages of Minnesota Report statements rated as accurate ranged from 25 percent to 58 percent for the various subjects studied. An interesting feature of the study was that data for black and white test subjects were analyzed separately. The authors concluded that differences in accuracy of computerized interpretations for black and white subjects were quite minimal. Although the Eyde et al. (1987) study represents an improvement methodologically over most earlier studies, it has several important limitations, the most important of which are the small number of subjects studied and the limited number of MMPI code types represented.

CONCLUSIONS AND RECOMMENDATIONS

The use of computers for the administration of the MMPI-2 is not likely to become a widespread practice. The computer time required for subjects to take the test on-line is so great that in most settings this form of administration is not appropriate. MMPI-2 users who intend to use computerized administration procedures are cautioned that no data exist concerning the equivalence of MMPI-2 scores for standard and computerized administration procedures. Based on data from the original MMPI, it seems likely that equivalence can be demonstrated, but equivalence should not be assumed until appropriate data are available.

The use of computerized scoring of the MMPI-2 permits the clinician to obtain scores on numerous MMPI-2 scales in a very efficient manner. As long as the accuracy of the scoring programs can be determined, their use is recommended. Because copyright standards apply to computerized scoring of the MMPI-2, it seems likely that the test publisher and test distributor will be assured adequate quality control of scoring programs.

The computerized interpretation of MMPI-2 scores is not covered by copyright standards, so anyone is free to develop computer programs for interpreting scores. As a result, one can expect the appearance of a large number of such programs in the near future. The accuracy (validity) of these interpretations must be demonstrated empirically and cannot be assumed, and it is the responsibility of the developers of the computerized interpretations to do so. Users are responsible for obtaining the information needed to make intelligent decisions concerning the use of the interpretations.

With all of the problems and concerns about computerized interpretations, what conclusions can be reached concerning their use with the MMPI-2? This author agrees with Matarazzo (1986) and Fowler and Butcher (1986) that computerized interpretations should not serve as the equivalent of or substitute for a comprehensive psychological assessment conducted by a properly trained

clinician. The automated reports are intended as professional-to-professional consultations, and the hypotheses generated should be considered in the context of other information available about the test subjects. It is the responsibility of the users of these reports to determine to what extent the interpretations apply to particular test subjects. When used in this manner by qualified professionals, the automated interpretive reports have considerable potential. When used instead of a comprehensive psychological assessment conducted by a qualified clinician, their use is irresponsible and not recommended.

Based on data for the original MMPI, it would appear that the accuracy of interpretive statements in automated reports varies considerably from service to service and from code type to code type within each service. The level of accuracy of the interpretive statements is at best modest but in many cases is no less than the accuracy of clinician-generated descriptions of clients based on the same data. Moreland (1984) suggested that clinicians be especially skeptical of automated reports when the profiles involved are rare ones. In these instances, authors of the automated systems have had to rely less on empirical data and more on clinical lore and individual experience in generating interpretive statements.

CHAPTER APPENDIX

MMPI-2^{TM}

MINNESOTA MULTIPHASIC PERSONALITY INVENTORY-2^{TM}

By Starke R. Hathaway and J. Charnley McKinley

THE MINNESOTA REPORT:^{TM}
ADULT CLINICAL SYSTEM
INTERPRETIVE REPORT

By James N. Butcher

```
        Client ID:  0014398
      Report Date:  31-JUL-89
             Age:  22
             Sex:  Male
          Setting:  Inpatient Mental Health
        Education:  12
   Marital Status:  Never Married
```

PROFILE VALIDITY

The client's responses to items in the latter portion of the MMPI-2 were
somewhat inconsistent with his response to earlier items. There is some
possibility that he responded to these later items carelessly or in a random
manner, thereby invalidating that portion of the test. Although the
standard validity and clinical scales are scored from items in the first
two-thirds of the test, caution should be taken with interpreting the MMPI-2
Content scales and Supplementary scales which depend upon responses to items
found throughout the entire item pool.

This MMPI-2 profile should be interpreted with caution. There is some
possibility that the clinical report is an exaggerated picture of the
client's present situation and problems. He is presenting an unusual number
of psychological symptoms. This extreme response set could result from poor
reading ability, confusion, disorientation, stress, or a need to seek a
great deal of attention for his problems.

His test-taking attitudes should be evaluated for the possibility that he
has produced an invalid profile. He may be showing a lack of cooperation
with the testing or he may be "malingering" by attempting to present a false
claim of mental illness. Determining the sources of his confusion, whether
conscious distortion or personality deterioration, is important since
immediate attention may be required. Clinical patients with this validity
profile are often confused, distractible, and show memory problems.
Evidence of delusions and thought disorder may be present. He may be
showing a high degree of distress and personality deterioration.

SYMPTOMATIC PATTERNS

A severe psychological disorder is reflected in this profile. The client
appears to be experiencing a florid psychotic process which includes
personality decompensation, social withdrawal, disordered affect, and
erratic, possibly assaultive, behavior. He appears to be quite confused,
withdrawn, and preoccupied with occult or abstract ideas, and may feel that
others are against him because of his beliefs. He may appear quite
apathetic, tends to spend a great deal of time in fantasy, and might suffer
from hallucinations, blunted or inappropriate affect, and hostile, irritable
behavior. He appears confused and disoriented, and may behave in
unpredictable, highly aggressive ways.

INTERPERSONAL RELATIONS

Disturbed interpersonal relationships are characteristic of individuals with
this profile type. The client feels socially inadequate and has very poor
social skills. He is rather introverted and is fearful and suspicious of
others. He may be blatantly negative in social interactions. Many
individuals with this profile type are unable to develop loving heterosexual
relationships and never trust anyone enough to marry.

```
        TM                                                            page 2
MMPI-2                 TM
THE MINNESOTA REPORT:                    ID: 0014398    REPORT DATE: 31-JUL-89
ADULT CLINICAL SYSTEM
INTERPRETIVE REPORT
```

BEHAVIORAL STABILITY

This MMPI-2 profile reflects chronic maladjustment, although he may presently be experiencing an intensification of problems. Personality decompensation and disorganization are likely. His interpersonal style is not likely to change significantly if retested at a later date.

DIAGNOSTIC CONSIDERATIONS

The most likely diagnosis for individuals with this profile type is Schizophrenia, possibly Paranoid type, or a Paranoid Disorder.

There is a strong possibility that this client has some difficulty with substance use or abuse. His personality pattern and score on the MacAndrew Alcoholism Scale - Revised suggest that possible addiction problems may warrant further evaluation.

TREATMENT CONSIDERATIONS

Individuals with this profile may be experiencing a great deal of personality deterioration, which may require hospitalization if they are considered dangerous to themselves or others. Psychotropic medication may reduce their thinking disturbance and mood disorder. Outpatient treatment may be complicated by their regressed or disorganized behavior. Day treatment programs or other such structured settings may be helpful in providing a stabilizing treatment environment.

Long-term adjustment is a problem. Frequent, brief "management" therapy contracts may be helpful in structuring their activities. Insight-oriented or uncovering therapies tend not to be helpful for individuals with this profile, and may actually exacerbate the problems. He is unlikely to be able to establish a trusting working relationship with a therapist.

NOTE: This MMPI-2 interpretation can serve as a useful source of hypotheses about clients. This report is based on objectively derived scale indexes and scale interpretations that have been developed in diverse groups of patients. The personality descriptions, inferences and recommendations contained herein need to be verified by other sources of clinical information since individual clients may not fully match the prototype. The information in this report should most appropriately be used by a trained, qualified test interpreter. The information contained in this report should be considered confidential.

```
        TM
MMPI-2                    TM
THE MINNESOTA REPORT:                      ID: 0014398      RPT DATE: 31-JUL-89
ADULT CLINICAL SYSTEM                      SEX: Male        EDUC: 12
INTERPRETIVE REPORT                        AGE: 22          MARS: Never Married
                                       SETTING: Inpatient Mental Health
```

	L	F	K	Hs	D	Hy	Pd	Mf	Pa	Pt	Sc	Ma	Si	A	R	MAC-R
Raw Score:	5	17	10	5	18	12	20	27	18	20	34	23	29	26	11	29
K Corr.				5			4			10	10	2				
T Scr.	56	89	39	42	50	34	52	52	79	57	81	62	54	73	41	67

```
                        FB (Raw): 17       Goldberg Index: 125
? Cannot Say (Raw): 0   F-K (Raw): 7       Henrichs Rule: Not Applicable

Welsh Code (new): 8"6'9-70452/1:3#    F"'-L/:K#     Percent True :   59
Welsh Code (old): 8*"69'754-02/13:    F"'-L/K?:     Percent False:   41
                                                    Profile Elev.: 57.1
```

Content Scales Profile
Butcher, Graham, Williams, and Ben-Porath (1989)

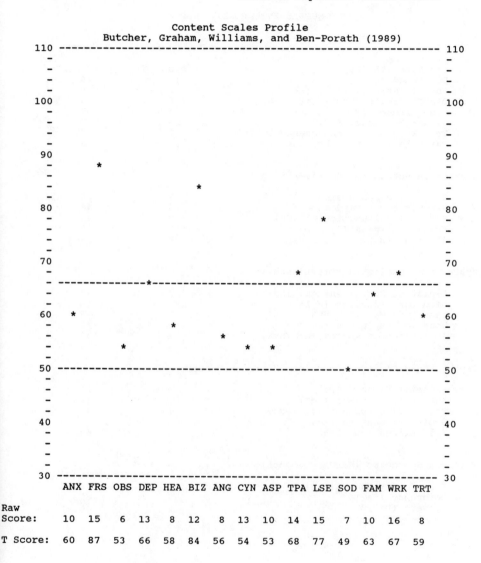

	ANX	FRS	OBS	DEP	HEA	BIZ	ANG	CYN	ASP	TPA	LSE	SOD	FAM	WRK	TRT
Raw Score:	10	15	6	13	8	12	8	13	10	14	15	7	10	16	8
T Score:	60	87	53	66	58	84	56	54	53	68	77	49	63	67	59

SUPPLEMENTARY SCORE REPORT

	Raw Score	T Score
Ego Strength (Es)	28	30
Dominance (Do)	16	48
Social Responsibility (Re)	12	30
Overcontrolled Hostility (O-H)	8	35
PTSD - Keane (PK)	15	62
PTSD - Schlenger (PS)	26	69
True Response Inconsistency (TRIN)	12	72T
Variable Response Inconsistency (VRIN)	11	73

Depression Subscales (Harris-Lingoes):

Subscale	Raw	T
Subjective Depression (D1)	9	56
Psychomotor Retardation (D2)	5	48
Physical Malfunctioning (D3)	2	43
Mental Dullness (D4)	3	53
Brooding (D5)	7	79

Hysteria Subscales (Harris-Lingoes):

Subscale	Raw	T
Denial of Social Anxiety (Hy1)	2	40
Need for Affection (Hy2)	3	36
Lassitude-Malaise (Hy3)	1	43
Somatic Complaints (Hy4)	2	48
Inhibition of Aggression (Hy5)	2	40

Psychopathic Deviate Subscales (Harris-Lingoes):

Subscale	Raw	T
Familial Discord (Pd1)	5	71
Authority Problems (Pd2)	2	42
Social Imperturbability (Pd3)	1	35
Social Alienation (Pd4)	5	57
Self-Alienation (Pd5)	6	63

Paranoia Subscales (Harris-Lingoes):

Subscale	Raw	T
Persecutory Ideas (Pa1)	6	76
Poignancy (Pa2)	5	69
Naivete (Pa3)	4	46

	Raw Score	T Score
Schizophrenia Subscales (Harris-Lingoes):		
Social Alienation (Sc1)	8	72
Emotional Alienation (Sc2)	4	78
Lack of Ego Mastery, Cognitive (Sc3)	3	60
Lack of Ego Mastery, Conative (Sc4)	4	60
Lack of Ego Mastery, Def. Inhib. (Sc5)	5	75
Bizarre Sensory Experiences (Sc6)	12	99
Hypomania Subscales (Harris-Lingoes):		
Amorality (Ma1)	2	50
Psychomotor Acceleration (Ma2)	5	49
Imperturbability (Ma3)	2	41
Ego Inflation (Ma4)	7	76

Social Introversion Subscales (Ben-Porath, Hostetler, Butcher, & Graham):

	Raw Score	T Score
Shyness / Self-Consciousness (Si1)	6	53
Social Avoidance (Si2)	1	41
Alienation--Self and Others (Si3)	11	68

Uniform T scores are used for Hs, D, Hy, Pd, Pa, Pt, Sc, Ma, and the Content
Scales; all other MMPI-2 scales use linear T scores.

255

CRITICAL ITEMS

The following critical items have been found to have possible significance in analyzing a client's problem situation. Although these items may serve as a source of hypotheses for further investigation, caution should be taken in interpreting individual items because they may have been inadvertently checked.

Acute Anxiety State (Koss-Butcher Critical Items)

   5. I am easily awakened by noise. (T)
  15. I work under a great deal of tension. (T)
 218. I have periods of such great restlessness that I cannot sit long in a
      chair. (T)
 444. I am a high-strung person. (T)
 463. Several times a week I feel as if something dreadful is about to
      happen. (T)
 469. I sometimes feel that I am about to go to pieces. (T)

Depressed Suicidal Ideation (Koss-Butcher Critical Items)

  38. I have had periods of days, weeks, or months when I couldn't take care
      of things because I couldn't "get going." (T)
 130. I certainly feel useless at times. (T)
 146. I cry easily. (T)
 215. I brood a great deal. (T)
 273. Life is a strain for me much of the time. (T)
 411. At times I think I am no good at all. (T)
 454. The future seems hopeless to me. (T)
 506. I have recently considered killing myself. (T)
 518. I have made lots of bad mistakes in my life. (T)
 524. No one knows it but I have tried to kill myself. (T)

Threatened Assault (Koss-Butcher Critical Items)

 213. I get mad easily and then get over it soon. (T)

Situational Stress Due to Alcoholism (Koss-Butcher Critical Items)

 518. I have made lots of bad mistakes in my life. (T)

Mental Confusion (Koss-Butcher Critical Items)
  24. Evil spirits possess me at times. (T)
  32. I have had very peculiar and strange experiences. (T)
 311. I often feel as if things are not real. (T)

Persecutory Ideas (Koss-Butcher Critical Items)

 124. I often wonder what hidden reason another person may have for doing
      something nice for me. (T)
 145. I feel that I have often been punished without cause. (T)
 216. Someone has been trying to rob me. (T)
 259. I am sure I am being talked about. (T)
 333. People say insulting and vulgar things about me. (T)
 361. Someone has been trying to influence my mind. (T)

Antisocial Attitude (Lachar-Wrobel Critical Items)

  84. I was suspended from school one or more times for bad behavior. (T)
 266. I have never been in trouble with the law. (F)

Family Conflict (Lachar-Wrobel Critical Items)

  21. At times I have very much wanted to leave home. (T)
  83. I have very few quarrels with members of my family. (F)

Somatic Symptoms (Lachar-Wrobel Critical Items)

  53. Parts of my body often have feelings like burning, tingling, crawling,
      or like "going to sleep." (T)
 182. I have had attacks in which I could not control my movements or speech
      but in which I knew what was going on around me. (T)
 229. I have had blank spells in which my activities were interrupted and I
      did not know what was going on around me. (T)
 247. I have numbness in one or more places on my skin. (T)
 295. I have never been paralyzed or had any unusual weakness of any of my
      muscles. (F)
 464. I feel tired a good deal of the time. (T)

Sexual Concern and Deviation (Lachar-Wrobel Critical Items)

  12. My sex life is satisfactory. (F)
  34. I have never been in trouble because of my sex behavior. (F)
 166. I am worried about sex. (T)
 268. I wish I were not bothered by thoughts about sex. (T)

257

Anxiety and Tension (Lachar-Wrobel Critical Items)
  15. I work under a great deal of tension. (T)
  218. I have periods of such great restlessness that I cannot sit long in a
       chair. (T)
  261. I have very few fears compared to my friends. (F)
  463. Several times a week I feel as if something dreadful is about to
       happen. (T)

Sleep Disturbance (Lachar-Wrobel Critical Items)

   5. I am easily awakened by noise. (T)
  30. I have nightmares every few nights. (T)
  328. Sometimes some unimportant thought will run through my mind and bother
       me for days. (T)
  471. I have often been frightened in the middle of the night. (T)

Deviant Thinking and Experience (Lachar-Wrobel Critical Items)

  32. I have had very peculiar and strange experiences. (T)
  122. At times my thoughts have raced ahead faster than I could speak
       them. (T)
  298. Peculiar odors come to me at times. (T)
  307. At times I hear so well it bothers me. (T)

Depression and Worry (Lachar-Wrobel Critical Items)

  130. I certainly feel useless at times. (T)
  273. Life is a strain for me much of the time. (T)
  339. I have sometimes felt that difficulties were piling up so high that I
       could not overcome them. (T)
  411. At times I think I am no good at all. (T)
  415. I worry quite a bit over possible misfortunes. (T)
  454. The future seems hopeless to me. (T)

Deviant Beliefs (Lachar-Wrobel Critical Items)

  216. Someone has been trying to rob me. (T)
  259. I am sure I am being talked about. (T)
  333. People say insulting and vulgar things about me. (T)
  355. At one or more times in my life I felt that someone was making me do
       things by hypnotizing me. (T)
  361. Someone has been trying to influence my mind. (T)
  466. Sometimes I am sure that other people can tell what I am thinking. (T)

Substance Abuse   (Lachar-Wrobel Critical Items)

  168. I have had periods in which I carried on activities without knowing
      later what I had been doing.   (T)

Problematic Anger   (Lachar-Wrobel Critical Items)

  213. I get mad easily and then get over it soon.   (T)

References

Alker, H.A. (1978). Minnesota Multiphasic Personality Inventory. In O.K. Buros (Ed.), *Eighth mental measurements yearbook* (pp. 931–935). Highland Park, NJ: Gryphon.

American Psychological Association. (1986). *Guidelines for computer-based tests and interpretations.* Washington, DC: APA.

Anderson, B.N. (1969). *The utility of the Minnesota Multiphasic Personality Inventory in a private psychiatric hospital setting.* Unpublished master's thesis, Ohio State University, Columbus.

Anderson, W., & Bauer, B. (1985). Clients with MMPI high D-Pd: Therapy implications. *Journal of Clinical Psychology, 41,* 181–189.

Anthony, N. (1971). Comparison of clients' standard, exaggerated, and matching MMPI profiles. *Journal of Consulting and Clinical Psychology, 36,* 100–103.

Apfeldorf, M., & Huntley, P.J. (1975). Application of MMPI alcoholism scales to older alcoholics and problem drinkers. *Journal of Studies on Alcohol, 37,* 645–653.

Archer, R.P. (1987). *Using the MMPI with adolescents.* Hillsdale, NJ: Lawrence Erlbaum Associates.

Archer, R.P., Ball, J.D., & Hunter, J.A. (1985). MMPI characteristics of borderline psychopathology in adolescent inpatients. *Journal of Personality Assessment, 49,* 47–55.

Archer, R.P., & Gordon, R.A. (1988). MMPI and Rorschach indices of schizophrenic and depressive diagnoses among adolescent inpatients. *Journal of Personality Assessment, 52,* 277–287.

Archer, R.P., Gordon, R.A., Giannetti, R., & Singles, J.M. (1988). MMPI scale clinical correlates for adolescent inpatients. *Journal of Personality Assessment, 52,* 707–721.

Archer, R.P., Gordon, R.A., Anderson, G.L., & Giannetti, R. (in press). MMPI special scale clinical correlates for adolescent inpatients. *Journal of Personality Assessment.*

Avery, R.D., Mussio, S.J., & Payne, G. (1972). Relationships between MMPI scores and job performance measures of fire fighters. *Psychological Reports, 31,* 199–202.

Baillargeon, J., & Danis, C. (1984). Barnum meets the computer: Critical test. *Journal of Personality Assessment, 48,* 415–419.

Ball, J.C. (1962). *Social deviancy and adolescent personality.* Lexington: University of Kentucky Press.

Barker, H.R., Fowler, R.D., & Peterson, L.P. (1971). Factor analytic structure of the short form MMPI in a VA hospital population. *Journal of Clinical Psychology, 27,* 228–233.

Barron, F. (1953). An ego strength scale which predicts response to psychotherapy. *Journal of Consulting Psychology, 17,* 327–333.

Barron, F. (1956). Ego-strength and the management of aggression. In G.S. Welsh and W.G. Dahlstrom (Eds.), *Basic readings on the MMPI in psychology and medicine.* (pp. 579–585). Minneapolis: University of Minnesota Press.

Barron, F., & Leary, T. (1955). Changes in psychoneurotic patients with and without psychotherapy. *Journal of Consulting Psychology, 19,* 239–245.

Baughman, E.E., & Dahlstrom, W.G. (1968). *A psychological study in the rural south.* New York: Academic Press.

Ben-Porath, Y.S., & Butcher, J.N. (1986). Computers in personality assessment: A brief past, an ebullient present, and an expanding future. *Computers in Human Behavior, 2,* 167–182.

Ben-Porath, Y.S., & Butcher, J.N. (1989). The psychometric stability of rewritten MMPI items. *Journal of Personality Assessment, 53,* 645–653.

Ben-Porath, Y.S., Hostetler, K., Butcher, J.N., & Graham, J.R. (1989). New sub-scales for the MMPI-2 social introversion (SI) scale. *Psychological Assessment: A Journal of Consulting and Clinical Psychology, 1,* 169–174.

Ben-Porath, Y.S., Waller, N.G., Slutsky, W., & Butcher, J.N. (1988, August). *Psychological assessment by computer: A comparison of two methods for adaptive administration of MMPI-2 content scales.* Paper presented at the 96th Annual Convention of the American Psychological Association, Atlanta, GA.

Bernstein, I.H. (1980). Security guards' MMPI profiles: Some normative data. *Journal of Personality Assessment, 44,* 377–380.

Biskin, B., & Kolotkin, R.L. (1977). Effects of computerized administration on scores on the Minnesota Multiphasic Personality Inventory. *Applied Psychological Measurement, 1,* 534–549.

Black, J.D. (1953). *The interpretation of MMPI profiles of college women.* Unpublished doctoral dissertation, University of Minnesota, Minneapolis.

Block, J. (1965). *The challenge of response sets: Unconfounding meaning, acquiescence, and social desirability in the MMPI.* New York: Appleton-Century-Crofts.

Block, J., & Bailey, D.Q. (1955). Q-sort item analyses of a number of MMPI scales. *Officer Education Research Laboratory, Technical Memorandum.* (OERL-TM-55-7).

Boerger, A.R., Graham, J.R., & Lilly, R.S. (1974). Behavioral correlates of single-scale MMPI code types. *Journal of Consulting and Clinical Psychology, 42,* 398–402.

Brayfield, A.H. (Ed.). (1965). Testing and public policy. *American Psychologist, 20,* 857–1005.

Bresolin, M.J., Jr. (1984). *A comparative study of computer administration of the Minnesota Multiphasic Personality Inventory in an inpatient psychiatric setting.* Unpublished doctoral dissertation, Loyola University, Chicago, IL.

Buechley, R., & Ball, H. (1952). A new test of "validity" for the group MMPI. *Journal of Consulting Psychology, 16,* 299–301.

Burkhart, B.R., Christian, W.L., & Gynther, M.D. (1978). Item subtlety and faking on the MMPI: A paradoxical relationship. *Journal of Personality Assessment, 42,* 76–80.

Burkhart, B.R., Gynther, M.D., & Fromuth, M.E. (1980). The relative validity of subtle versus obvious items on the MMPI Depression scale. *Journal of Clinical Psychology, 36,* 748–751.

Butcher, J.N. (1972). *Objective personality assessment: Changing perspectives.* New York: Academic Press.

Butcher, J.N. (1978). Computerized scoring and interpreting services. In O.K. Buros (Ed.), *Eighth mental measurments yearbook* (pp. 942–945). Highland Park, NJ: Gryphon.

Butcher, J.N. (1979). Use of the MMPI in personnel selection. In J.N. Butcher (Ed.), *New developments in the use of the MMPI* (pp. 165–201). Minneapolis: University of Minnesota Press.

Butcher, J.N. (1985a). Interpreting defensive profiles. In J.N. Butcher & J.R. Graham (Eds.), *Clinical applications of the MMPI* (No.3). Minneapolis: Department of Conferences, University of Minnesota.

Butcher, J.N. (1985b). Personality assessment in industry: Theoretical issues and illustrations. In H.J. Bernardin (Ed.), *Personality assessment in organizations* (pp. 277–310). New York: Praeger.

Butcher, J.N. (1989). *Minnesota Multiphasic Personality Inventory-2, user's guide, the Minnesota Report: Adult clinical system.* Minneapolis: National Computer Systems.

Butcher, J.N. (1990). *Assessing patients in psychotherapy: Use of the MMPI-2 for treatment planning.* New York: Oxford University Press.

Butcher, J.N., Braswell, L., & Raney, D. (1983). A cross-cultural comparison of American Indian, black, and white inpatients on the MMPI and presenting symptoms. *Journal of Consulting and Clinical Psychology, 51,* 587–594.

Butcher, J.N., Dahlstrom, W.G., Graham, J.R., Tellegen, A., & Kaemmer, B. (1989). *Minnesota Multiphasic Personality Inventory (MMPI-2). Manual for administration and scoring.* Minneapolis: University of Minnesota Press.

Butcher, J.N., Graham, J.R., Williams, C.L., & Ben-Porath, Y.S. (1990). *Development and use of the MMPI-2 content scales.* Minneapolis: University of Minnesota Press.

Butcher, J.N., Keller, L.S., & Bacon, S.F. (1985). Current developments and future directions in computerized personality assessment. *Journal of Consulting and Clincal Psychology, 53,* 803–815.

Butcher, J.N., Kendall, P.C., & Hoffman, N. (1980). MMPI short forms: CAUTION. *Journal of Consulting Psychology, 48,* 275–278.

Butcher, J.N., & Tellegen, A. (1966). Objections to MMPI items. *Journal of Consulting and Clinical Psychology, 30,* 527–534.

Caldwell, A.B. (1969). *MMPI critical items.* Unpublished manuscript. (Available from Caldwell Report, 1545 Sawtelle Bl., No. 14, Los Angeles, CA 90025).

Calvin, J. (1974). *Two dimensions or fifty: Factor analytic studies with the MMPI.* Unpublished materials, Kent State University, Kent, OH.

Calvin, J. (1975). *A replicated study of the concurrent validity of the Harris subscales for the MMPI.* Unpublished doctoral dissertation, Kent State University, Kent, OH.

Cannon, D.S., Bell, W.E., Andrews, R.H., & Finkelstein, A.S. (1987). Correspondence between MMPI PTSD measures and clinical diagnosis. *Journal of Personality Assessment, 51,* 517–521.

Carr, A.C., Ghosh, A., & Ancill, R.J. (1983). Can a computer take a psychiatric history? *Psychological Medicine, 13,* 151–158.

Carson, R.C. (1969). Interpretive manual to the MMPI. In J.N. Butcher (Ed.), *Research developments and clinical applications* (pp. 279–296). New York: McGraw-Hill.

Chang, A.F., Caldwell, A.B., & Moss, T. (1973). Stability of personality traits in alcoholics during and after treatment as measured by the MMPI: A one-year follow-up study. *Proceedings of the 81st Annual Convention of the American Psychological Association, 8,* 387–388.

Chase, T.V., Chaffin, S., & Morrison, S.D. (1975). False positive adolescent MMPI profiles. *Adolescence, 40,* 507–519.

Chu, C. (1966). *Object cluster analysis of the MMPI.* Unpublished doctoral dissertation, University of California, Berkeley.

Clayton, M.R., & Graham, J.R. (1979). Predictive validity of Barron's Es scale: The role of symptom acknowledgment. *Journal of Consulting and Clinical Psychology, 47,* 424–425.

Colligan, R.C., Osborne, D., & Offord, K.P. (1980). Linear transformation and the interpretation of MMPI T-scores. *Journal of Clinical Psychology, 36,* 162–165.

Comrey, A.L. (1957a). A factor analysis of items on the MMPI depression scale. *Educational and Psychological Measurement, 17,* 578–585.

Comrey, A.L. (1957b). A factor analysis of items on the MMPI hypochondriasis scale. *Educational and Psychological Measurement, 17,* 566–577.

Comrey, A.L. (1957c). A factor analysis of items on the MMPI hysteria scale. *Educational and Psychological Measurement, 17,* 586–592.

Comrey, A.L. (1958a). A factor analysis of items on the F scale of the MMPI. *Educational and Psychological Measurement, 18,* 621–632.

Comrey, A.L. (1958b). A factor analysis of items on the MMPI hypomania scale. *Educational and Psychological Measurement, 18,* 313–323.

Comrey, A.L. (1958c). A factor analysis of items on the MMPI paranoia scale. *Educational and Psychological Measurement, 18,* 99–107.

Comrey, A.L., (1958d). A factor analysis of items on the MMPI psychasthenia scale. *Educational and Psychological Measurement, 18,* 293–300.

Comrey, A.L. (1958e). A factor analysis of items on the MMPI psychopathic deviate scale. *Educational and Psychological Measurement, 18,* 91–98.

Comrey, A.L., & Marggraff, W. (1958). A factor analysis of items on the MMPI schizophrenia scale. *Educational and Psychological Measurement, 18,* 301–311.

Costello, R.M., Schoenfeld, L.S., & Kobos, J. (1982). Police applicant screening: An analogue study. *Journal of Clinical Psychology, 38*, 216–221.

Cottle, W.C. (1950). Card versus booklet forms of the MMPI. *Journal of Applied Psychology, 34*, 255–259.

Crovitz, E., Huse, M.N., & Lewis, D.E. (1973). Selection of physicians' assistants. *Journal of Medical Education, 48*, 551–555.

Dahlstrom, W.G. (1972). Whither the MMPI? In J.N. Butcher (Ed.), *Objective personality assessment: Changing perspectives* (pp. 85–115). New York: Academic Press.

Dahlstrom, W.G. (1980). Altered versions of the MMPI. In W.G. Dahlstrom & L. Dahlstrom (Eds.), *Basic readings on the MMPI: A new selection on personality measurement.* (pp. 386–393). Minneapolis: University of Minnesota Press.

Dahlstrom, W.G., & Dahlstrom, L. (Eds.). (1980). *Basic readings on the MMPI: A new selection on personality measurement.* Minneapolis: University of Minnesota Press.

Dahlstrom, W.G., Lachar, D., & Dahlstrom, L.E. (1986). *MMPI patterns of American minorities.* Minneapolis: University of Minnesota Press.

Dahlstrom, W.G., & Welsh, G.S. (1960). *An MMPI handbook: A guide to use in clinical practice and research.* Minneapolis: University of Minnesota Press.

Dahlstrom, W.G., Welsh, G.S., & Dahlstrom, L.E. (1972). *An MMPI handbook: Vol. I. Clinical interpretation.* Minneapolis: University of Minnesota Press.

Dahlstrom, W.G., Welsh, G.S., & Dahlstrom, L.E. (1975). *An MMPI handbook: Vol. II. Research applications.* Minneapolis: University of Minnesota Press.

Davis, K.R., & Sines, J.O. (1971). An antisocial behavior pattern associated with a specific MMPI profile. *Journal of Consulting and Clinical Psychology, 36*, 229–234.

Deiker, T.E. (1974). A cross-validation of MMPI scales of aggression on male criminal criterion groups. *Journal of Consulting and Clinical Psychology, 42*, 196–202.

Dikmen, S., Hermann, B.P., Wilensky, A.J., & Rainwater, G. (1983). Validity of the Minnesota Multiphasic Personality Inventory (MMPI) to psychopathology in patients with epilepsy. *Journal of Nervous and Mental Disease, 171*, 114–122.

Distler, L.S., May, P.R., & Tuma, A.H. (1964). Anxiety and ego strength as predictors of response to treatment in schizophrenic patients. *Journal of Consulting Psychology, 28*, 170–177.

Dodrill, C.B. (1986). Psychosocial consequences of epilepsy. In S. Filskov & T. Boll (Eds.), *Handbook of clinical neuropsychology, Vol. II* (pp. 338–363). New York: Wiley.

Drake, L.E. (1946). A social I.E. scale for the MMPI. *Journal of Applied Psychology, 30*, 51–54.

Drake, L.E., & Oetting, E.R. (1959). *An MMPI codebook for counselors.* Minneapolis: University of Minnesota Press.

Dubinsky, S., Gamble, D.J., & Rogers, M.L. (1985). A literature review of subtle-obvious items on the MMPI. *Journal of Personality Assessment, 49*, 62–68.

Duckworth, J., & Anderson, W. (1986). *MMPI interpretation manual for counselors and clinicians.* Muncie, IN: Accelerated Development, Inc.

Duckworth, J.C., & Duckworth, E. (1975). *MMPI interpretation manual for counselors and clinicians.* Muncie, IN: Accelerated Development, Inc.

Duff, F.L. (1965). Item subtlety in the personality inventory scales. *Journal of Consulting Psychology, 29*, 565–570.

Dunnette, M.D., Bownas, D.A., & Bosshardt, M.J. (1981). *Electric power plant study: Prediction of inappropriate, unreliable or aberant job behavior in nuclear power plant settings.* Minneapolis, MN: Personnel Decisions Research Institute.

Edwards, A.L. (1957). *The social desirability variable in personality assessment and research.* New York: Dryden.

Edwards, A.L. (1964). Social desirability and performance on the MMPI. *Psychometrika, 29*, 295–308.

Ehrenworth, N.V. (1984). A comparison of the utility of interpretive approaches with adolescent MMPI profiles. Unpublished doctoral dissertation, Virginia Consortium for Professional Psychology, Norfolk.

Ehrenworth, N.V., & Archer, R.P. (1985). A comparison of clinical accuracy ratings of inter-pretive approaches for adolescent MMPI responses. *Journal of Personality Assessment, 49*, 413–421.

Eichman, W.J. (1961). Replicated factors on the MMPI with female NP patients. *Journal of Consulting Psychology, 25*, 55–60.

Eichman, W.J. (1962). Factored scales for the MMPI: A clinical and statistical manual. *Journal of Clinical Psychology, 18*, 363–395.

Ends, E.J., & Page, C.W. (1957). Functional relationships among measures of anxiety, ego strength, and adjustment. *Journal of Clinical Psychology, 13*, 148–150.

Eschenback, A.E., & Dupree, L. (1959). The influence of stress on MMPI scale scores. *Journal of Clinical Psychology, 15*, 42–45.

Evan, W.M., & Miller, J.R. (1969). Differential effects on response bias of computer vs. conven-tional administration of a social science questionnaire. *Behavior Science, 14*, 216–227.

Evans, D.R. (1977). Use of the MMPI to predict effective hotline workers. *Journal of Clinical Psychology, 33*, 1113–1114.

Eyde, L., Kowal, D., & Fishburne, J. (1987, August). Clinical implications of validity research on computer-based interpretation of the MMPI. Paper presented at the 95th Annual Meet-ing of the American Psychological Association, New York.

Fisher, G. (1970). Discriminating violence eminating from over-controlled vs. under-controlled aggressivity. *British Journal of Social and Clinical Psychology, 9*, 54–59.

Fordyce, W.E. (1979). Use of the MMPI in the assessment of chronic pain (*Clinical Notes on the MMPI No. 3*). Minneapolis, MN: National Computer Systems.

Fowler, R.D. (1969a). Automated interpretation of personality test data. In J.N. Butcher (Ed.), *MMPI: Research developments and clinical applications* (pp. 105–126). New York: McGraw-Hill.

Fowler, R.D. (1969b). The current status of computer interpretation of psychological tests. *American Journal of Psychiatry, 125*, 21–27.

Fowler, R.D. (1975). *A method for the evaluation of the abuse prone patient*. Paper presented at the meeting of the American Academy of Family Physicians, Chicago, IL.

Fowler, R.D., & Butcher, J.N. (1986). Critique of Matarazzo's views on computerized testing: All sigma and no meaning. *American Psychologist, 41*, 94–96.

Fowler, R.D., & Coyle, F.A. (1968). Overlap as a problem in atlas classification of MMPI profiles. *Journal of Clinical Psychology, 24*, 435.

Fowler, R.D., Teel, S.K., & Coyle, F.A. (1967). The measurement of alcoholic response to treatment by Barron's ego strength scale. *Journal of Psychology, 67*, 65–68.

Fox, J., Gould, E., & Andre, J. (1965). *Crime classification and personality patterns*. Unpublished manuscript.

Fredericksen, S.J. (1976, March). *A comparison of selected personality and history variables in highly violent, mildly violent, and nonviolent female offenders*. Paper presented at the 11th Annual MMPI Symposium, Minneapolis, MN.

Garb, H.N. (1984). The incremental validity of information used in personality assessment. *Clinical Psychology Review, 4*, 641–655.

Garetz, F.K., & Anderson, R.W. (1973). Patterns of professional activities of psychiatrists: A follow-up of 100 psychiatric residents. *American Journal of Psychiatry, 130*, 981–984.

Gayton, W.F., Burchstead, G.N., & Matthews, G.R. (1986). An investigation of the utility of an MMPI posttraumatic stress disorder subscale. *Journal of Clinical Psychology, 42*, 916–917.

Getter, H., & Sundland, D.M. (1962). The Barron ego strength scale and psychotherapy out-come. *Journal of Consulting Psychology, 26*, 195.

Gilberstadt, H., & Duker, J. (1965). *A handbook for clinical and actuarial MMPI interpretation*. Philadelphia: Saunders.

Gocka, E. (1965). *American Lake norms for 200 MMPI scales*. Unpublished materials, Veterans Administration Hospital, American Lake, WA.

Gocka, E., & Holloway, H. (1963). *Normative and predictive data on the Harris and Lingoes subscales*

for a neuropsychiatric population (Report No. 7). American Lake, WA: Veterans Administration Hospital.

Goldberg, L.R. (1965). Diagnosticians vs. diagnostic signs: The diagnosis of psychosis vs. neurosis for the MMPI. *Psychological Monographs, 79* (9, Whole No. 602).

Goldberg, L.R. (1968). Simple models or simple processes. *American Psychologist, 23,* 483–496.

Good, P.K., & Brantner, J.P. (1961). *The physician's guide to the MMPI.* Minneapolis: University of Minnesota Press.

Gottesman, I.I. (1959). More construct validation of the ego-strength scale. *Journal of Consulting Psychology, 23,* 342–346.

Gottesman, I.I., & Prescott, C.A. (1989). Abuses of the MacAndrew MMPI alcoholism scale: A critical review. *Clinical Psychology Review, 9,* 223–242.

Gough, H.G. (1950). The F minus K dissimulation index for the MMPI. *Journal of Consulting Psychology, 14,* 408–413.

Gough, H.G. (1954). Some common misconceptions about neuroticism. *Journal of Consulting Psychology, 18,* 287–292.

Gough, H.G., McClosky, H., & Meehl, P.E. (1951). A personality scale for dominance. *Journal of Abnormal and Social Psychology, 46,* 360–366.

Gough, H.G., McClosky, H., & Meehl, P.E. (1952). A personality scale for social responsibility. *Journal of Abnormal and Social Psychology, 47,* 73–80.

Gough, H.G., McKee, M.G., & Yandell, R.J. (1955). Adjective check list analyses of a number of selected psychometric and assessment variables. *Officer Education Research Laboratory. Technical Memorandom* (OERL-TM-5S-10)

Graham, J.R. (1967). A Q-sort study of the accuracy of clinical descriptions based on the MMPI. *Journal of Psychiatric Research, 5,* 297–305.

Graham, J.R. (1977a). *Stability of MMPI configurations in a college setting.* Unpublished manuscript, Kent State University, Kent, OH.

Graham, J.R. (1977b). *The MMPI: A practical guide.* New York: Oxford.

Graham, J.R. (1978). A review of some important MMPI special scales. In P. McReynolds (Ed.), *Advances in psychological assessment, Vol. IV* (pp. 311–331). San Francisco: Jossey-Bass.

Graham, J.R. (1987). *The MMPI: A practical guide (2d ed.).* New York: Oxford.

Graham, J.R. (1988, August). *Establishing validity of the revised form of the MMPI.* Symposium presentation at the 96th Annual Convention of the American Psychological Association, Atlanta, GA.

Graham, J.R., & Lilly, R.S. (1984). *Psychological testing.* Englewood Cliffs, NJ: Prentice Hall.

Graham, J.R., & Lilly, R.S. (1986, March). *Linear T-scores versus normalized T-scores: An empirical study.* Paper presented at the 21st Annual Symposium on Recent Developments in the use of the MMPI, Clearwater Beach, FL.

Graham, J.R., & Mayo, M.A. (1985, March). *A comparison of MMPI strategies for identifying black and white male alcoholics.* Paper presented at the 20th Annual Symposium on Recent Developments in the use of the MMPI, Honolulu, HI.

Graham, J.R., & McCord, G. (1985). Interpretation of moderately elevated MMPI scores for normal subjects. *Journal of Personality Assessment, 49,* 477–484.

Graham, J.R., Schroeder, H.E., & Lilly, R.S. (1971). Factor analysis of items on the Social Introversion and Masculinity-Femininity scales of the MMPI. *Journal of Clinical Psychology, 27,* 367–370.

Graham, J.R., Smith, R.L., & Schwartz, G.F. (1986). Stability of MMPI configurations for psychiatric inpatients. *Journal of Consulting and Clinical Psychology, 54,* 375–380.

Graham, J.R., & Strenger, V.E. (1988). MMPI characteristics of alcoholics: A review. *Journal of Consulting and Clinical Psychology, 56,* 197–205.

Grayson, H.M. (1951). *A psychological admissions testing program and manual.* Los Angeles: Veterans Administration Center, Neuropsychiatric Hospital.

Greene, R.L. (1978). An empirically derived MMPI carelessness scale. *Journal of Clinical Psychology, 34,* 407–410.

Greene, R.L. (1980). *The MMPI: An interpretive manual.* New York: Grune & Stratton.

Greene, R.L. (1987). Ethnicity and MMPI performance: A review. *Journal of Consulting and Clinical Psychology, 55*, 497–512.

Greist, J.H., & Klein, M.H. (1980). Computer programs for patients, clinicians, and researchers in psychiatry. In J.B. Sidowski, J.H. Johnson, & T.A. Williams (Eds.), *Technology in mental health care delivery systems* (pp. 161–182). Norwood, NJ: Ablex.

Guthrie, G.M. (1949). *A study of the personality characteristics associated with the disorders encountered by an internist.* Doctoral dissertation, University of Minnesota, Minneapolis.

Guthrie, G.M. (1952). Common characteristics associated with frequent MMPI profile types. *Journal of Clinical Psychology, 8*, 141–145.

Gynther, M.D., Altman, H., & Sletten, I.W. (1973). Replicated correlates of MMPI two-point types: The Missouri Actuarial System. *Journal of Clinical Psychology* (Suppl. 39).

Gynther, M.D., Altman, H., & Warbin, W. (1973). Interpretation of uninterpretable Minnnesota Multiphasic Personality Inventory profiles. *Journal of Consulting and Clinical Psychology, 40*, 78–83.

Gynther, M.D., & Brillant, P.J. (1968). The diagnostic utility of Welsh's A-R categories. *Journal of Projective Techniques and Personality Assessment, 32*, 572–574.

Gynther, M.D., Burkhart, B.R., & Hovanitz, C. (1979). Do face-valid items have more predictive validity than subtle items? The case of the MMPI Pd scale. *Journal of Consulting and Clinical Psychology, 47*, 295–300.

Gynther, M.D., & Green, S.B. (1980). Accuracy may make a difference, but does a difference make for accuracy? A response to Pritchard and Rosenblatt. *Journal of Consulting and Clinical Psychology, 48*, 268–272.

Hanvik, L.J. (1949). *Some psychological dimensions of low back pain.* Doctoral dissertation, University of Minnesota, Minneapolis.

Hanvik, L. J. (1951). MMPI profiles in patients with low back pain. *Journal of Consulting Psychology, 15*, 250–253.

Harrell, T.W., & Harrell, M.S. (1973). The personality of MBAs who reach general management early. *Personnel Psychology, 26*, 127–134.

Harris, R., & Christiansen, C. (1946). Prediction of response to brief psychotherapy. *Journal of Psychology, 21*, 269–284.

Harris, R., & Lingoes, J. (1955). *Subscales for the Minnesota Multiphasic Personality Inventory.* Mimeographed materials, The Langley Porter Clinic.

Harris, R., & Lingoes, J. (1968). *Subscales for the Minnesota Multiphasic Personality Inventory.* Mimeographed materials, The Langley Porter Clinic.

Hathaway, S.R. (1947). A coding system for MMPI profiles. *Journal of Consulting Psychology, 11*, 334–337.

Hathaway, S.R. (1956). Scales 5 (Masculinity-Femininity), 6 (Paranoia), and 8 (Schizophrenia). In G.S. Welsh & W.G. Dahlstrom (Eds.), *Basic readings on the MMPI in psychology and medicine* (pp. 104–111). Minneapolis: University of Minnesota Press.

Hathaway, S.R. (1965). Personality inventories. In B.B. Wolman (Ed.), *Handbook of clinical psychology* (pp. 451–476). New York: McGraw-Hill.

Hathaway, S.R., & Briggs, P.F. (1957). Some normative data on new MMPI scales. *Journal of Clinical Psychology, 13*, 364-368.

Hathaway, S.R., & McKinley, J.C. (1940). A multiphasic personality schedule (Minnesota): I. Construction of the schedule. *Journal of Psychology, 10*, 249–254.

Hathaway, S.R., & McKinley, J.C. (1942). A multiphasic personality schedule (Minnesota): III. The measurement of symptomatic depression. *Journal of Psychology, 14*, 73–84.

Hathaway, S.R., & McKinley, J.C. (1983). *The Minnesota Multiphasic Personality Inventory manual.* New York: Psychological Corporation.

Hathaway, S.R., & Meehl, P.E. (1952). *Adjective check list correlates of MMPI scores.* Unpublished materials, University of Minnesota.

Hathaway, S.R., & Monachesi, E.D. (1963). *Adolescent personality and behavior: MMPI patterns of normal, delinquent, dropout, and other outcomes.* Minneapolis: University of Minnesota Press.

Hawkinson, J.R. (1961). A study of the construct validity of Barron's Ego Strength scale with a

state mental hospital population. Unpublished doctoral dissertation, University of Minnesota, Minneapolis.

Hedlund, J.L. (1977). MMPI clinical scale correlates. *Journal of Consulting and Clinical Psychology, 45,* 739–750.

Hedlund, J.L., Morgan, D.W., & Master, F.D. (1972). The Mayo Clinic automated MMPI program: Cross-validation with psychiatric patients in an army hospital. *Journal of Clinical Psychology, 28,* 505–510.

Henrichs, T.F. (1964). Objective configural rules for discriminating MMPI profiles in a psychiatric population. *Journal of Clinical Psychology, 20,* 157–159.

Henrichs, T.F. (1981). Using the MMPI in medical consultation (*Clinical Notes on the MMPI, No. 6*). Minneapolis, MN: National Computer Systems.

Henrichs, T.F., & Waters, W.F. (1972). Psychological adjustment and responses to open-heart surgery: Some methodological considerations. *British Journal of Psychiatry, 120,* 491–496.

Himelstein, P. (1964). Further evidence of the Ego Strength scale as a measure of psychological health. *Journal of Consulting Psychology, 28,* 90–91.

Hoffman, H., Loper, R.G., & Kammeier, M.L. (1974). Identifying future alcoholics with the MMPI alcoholism scales. *Quarterly Journal of Studies on Alcohol, 35,* 490–498.

Holmes, D.S. (1967). Male-female differences in MMPI Ego Strength: An artifact. *Journal of Consulting Psychology, 31,* 408–410.

Hovey, H.B. (1953). MMPI profiles and personality characteristics. *Journal of Consulting Psychology, 17,* 142–146.

Hovey, H.B., & Lewis, E.G. (1967). *Semiautomatic interpretation of the MMPI.* Brandon, VT: Clinical Psychology Publishing Company.

Hsu, L.M. (1984). MMPI T-scores: Linear verus normalized. *Journal of Consulting and Clinical Psychology, 52,* 821–823.

Huber, N.A., & Danahy, S. (1975). Use of the MMPI in predicting completion and evaluating changes in long-term alcoholism treatment program. *Journal of Studies on Alcohol, 36,* 1230–1237.

Huff, F.W. (1965). Use of actuarial description of abnormal personality in a mental hospital. *Psychological Reports, 17,* 224.

Hyer, L., Fallon, J.H., Jr., Harrison, W.R., & Boudewyns, P.A. (1987). MMPI overreporting by Vietnam combat veterans. *Journal of Clinical Psychology, 43,* 79–83.

Jansen, D.G., & Garvey, F.J. (1973). High-, average-, and low-rated clergymen in a state hospital clinical program. *Journal of Clinical Psychology, 29,* 89–92.

Johnson, J.R., Null, C., Butcher, J.N., & Johnson, K.N. (1984). Replicated item level factor analysis of the full MMPI. *Journal of Personality and Social Psychology, 47,* 105–114.

Katz, L., & Dalby, J.T. (1981). Computer and manual administration of the Eysenck Personality Inventory. *Journal of Clinical Psychology, 37,* 586–588.

Keane, T.M., Malloy, P.F., & Fairbank, J.A. (1984). Empirical development of an MMPI subscale for the assessment of combat-related posttraumatic stress disorder. *Journal of Consulting and Clinical Psychology, 52,* 888–891.

Keller, J.W., & Piotrowski, C. (1989, March). *Psychological testing patterns in outpatient mental health facilities: A national study.* Paper presented at the meeting of the Southeastern Psychological Association, Washington, DC.

Kelly, W.L. (1974). Psychological prediction of leadership in nursing. *Nursing Research, 23,* 38–42.

King, G.D. (1978). Minnesota Multiphasic Personality Inventory. In O.K. Buros (Ed.), *Eighth mental measurments yearbook* (pp. 935–938). Highland Park, NJ: Gryphon.

Kleinmuntz, B. (1960). An extension of the construct validity of the Ego Strength scale. *Journal of Consulting Psychology, 24,* 463–464.

Kleinmuntz, B. (1961). The college maladjustment scale (Mt): Norms and predictive validity. *Educational and Psychological Measurement, 21,* 1029–1033.

Kleinmuntz, B. (1963). MMPI decision rules for the identification of college maladjustment: A digital computer approach. *Psychological Monographs, 77,* (14, Whole No. 577).

Klett, W. (1971). The utility of computer interpreted MMPIs at St. Cloud VA Hospital. *Newsletter of Research in Psychology, 13*, 45–47.

Knapp, R.R. (1960). A reevaluation of the validity of MMPI scales of dominance and responsibility. *Educational and Psychological Measurement, 20*, 381–386.

Koson, D., Kitchen, C., Kochen, M., & Stodolosky, D. (1970). Psychological testing by computer: Effect on response bias. *Educational and Psychological Measurement, 30*, 803–810.

Koss, M.P. (1979). MMPI item content: Recurring issues. In J.N. Buther (Ed.), *New developments in the use of the MMPI* (pp. 3–38). Minneapolis: University of Minnesota Press.

Koss, M.P. (1980). Assessing psychological emergencies with the MMPI. In J. Butcher, G. Dahlstrom, M. Gynther, & W. Schofield (Eds.), *(Clinical notes on the MMPI,* No. 4). Minneapolis, MN: National Computer Systems.

Koss, M.P., Butcher, J.N., & Hoffman, N. (1976). The MMPI critical items: How well do they work? *Journal of Consulting and Clinical Psychology, 44*, 921–928.

Kostlan, A. (1954). A method for the empirical study of psychodiagnosis. *Journal of Consulting Psychology, 18*, 83–88.

Kranitz, L. (1972). Alcoholics, heroin addicts and non-addicts: Comparisons on the MacAndrew Alcoholism scale on the MMPI. *Quarterly Journal of Studies on Alcohol, 33*, 807–809.

Lachar, D. (1974a). Accuracy and generalization of an automated MMPI interpretation system. *Journal of Consulting and Clinical Psychology, 42*, 267–273.

Lachar, D. (1974b). *The MMPI: Clinical assessment and automated interpretation.* Los Angeles: Western Psychological Services.

Lachar, D. (1974c). Prediction of early U.S. Air Force cadet adaptation with the MMPI. *Journal of Counseling Psychology, 21*, 404–408.

Lachar, D., Klinge, V., & Grisell, J.L. (1976). Relative accuracy of automated MMPI narratives generated from adult norm and adolescent norm profiles. *Journal of Consulting and Clinical Psychology, 44*, 20–24.

Lachar, D., & Wrobel, T.A. (1979). Validation of clinicians' hunches: Construction of a new MMPI critical item set. *Journal of Consulting and Clinical Psychology, 47*, 277–284.

Lane, P.J. (1976). *Annotated bibliography of the Megargee et al.'s Overcontrolled-Hostility (O-H) scale and the overcontrolled personality literature.* Unpublished materials, Florida State University, Tallahassee.

Lanyon, R.I. (1968). *A handbook of MMPI group profiles.* Minneapolis: University of Minnesota Press.

Lewandowski, D., & Graham, J.R. (1972). Empirical correlates of frequently occurring two-point code types: A replicated study. *Journal of Consulting and Clinical Psychology, 39*, 467–472.

Lewinsohn, P.M. (1965). Dimensions of MMPI change. *Journal of Clinical Psychology, 21*, 37–43.

Lingoes, J. (1960). MMPI factors of the Harris and Wiener subscales. *Journal of Consulting Psychology, 24*, 74–83.

Little, K.B., & Shneidman, E.S. (1959). Congruencies among interpretations of psychological test and anamnestic data. *Psychological Monographs, 73*, (6, Whole No. 476).

Lubin, B., Larsen, R.M., & Matarazzo, J.D. (1984). Patterns of psychological test usage in the United States: 1935–1982. *American Psychologist, 39*, 451–454.

Lucas, R.W., Mullin, P.J., Luna, C.B., & McInroy, D.C. (1977). Psychiatrists and a computer as interrogators of patients with alcohol-related illnesses: A comparison. *British Journal of Psychiatry, 131*, 160–167.

Lukin, M.E., Dowd, E.T., Plake, B.S., & Kraft, R.G. (1985). Comparing computerized versus traditional psychological assessment. *Computers in Human Behavior, 1*, 49–58.

Lushene, R.E. (1967). *Factor structure of the MMPI item pool.* Unpublished master's thesis, Florida State University, Tallahassee.

Lushene, R.E., & Gilberstadt, H. (1972, March). *Validation of VA MMPI computer-generated reports.* Paper presented at the Veterans Administration Cooperative Studies Conference, St. Louis, MO.

MacAndrew, C. (1965). The differentiation of male alcoholic out-patients from nonalcoholic

psychiatric patients by means of the MMPI. *Quarterly Journal of Studies on Alcohol, 26*, 238–246.

MacDonald, G.L. (1952). A study of the shortened group and individual forms of the MMPI. *Journal of Clinical Psychology, 8*, 309–311.

Marks, P.A., & Seeman, W. (1963). *Actuarial description of abnormal personality.* Baltimore, MD: Williams & Wilkins.

Marks, P.A., Seeman, W., & Haller, D.L. (1974). *The actuarial use of the MMPI with adolescents and adults.* Baltimore,MD: Williams & Wilkins.

Matarazzo, J.D. (1986). Computerized clinical psychological test interpretations: Unvalidated plus all mean and no sigma. *American Psychologist, 41*, 14–24.

McKinley, J.C., & Hathaway, S.R. (1940). A multiphasic personality schedule (Minnesota): II. A differential study of hypochondriasis. *Journal of Psychology, 10*, 255–268.

McKinley, J.C., & Hathaway, S.R. (1944). The MMPI: V. Hysteria, hypomania, and psychopathic deviate. *Journal of Applied Psychology, 28*, 153–174.

McKinley, J.C., Hathaway, S.R., & Meehl, P.E. (1948). The MMPI: VI. The K scale. *Journal of Consulting Psychology, 12*, 20–31.

Meehl, P.E. (1951). *Research results for counselors.* St. Paul, MN: State Department of Education.

Meehl, P.E. (1956). Wanted—a good cookbook. *American Psychologist, 11*, 263–272.

Meehl, P.E., & Dahlstrom, W.G. (1960). Objective configural rules for discriminating psychotic from neurotic MMPI profiles. *Journal of Consulting Psychology, 24*, 375–387.

Meehl, P.E., & Hathaway, S.R. (1946). The K factor as a suppressor variable in the MMPI. *Journal of Applied Psychology, 30*, 525–564.

Megargee, E.I. (1979). Development and validation of an MMPI-based system for classifying criminal offenders. In J.N. Butcher (Ed.), *New developments in the use of the MMPI* (pp. 303–324). Minneapolis: University of Minnesota Press.

Megargee, E.I., Bohn, M.J., Meyer, J.E., Jr., & Sink, F. (1979). *Classifying criminal offenders: A new system based on the MMPI.* Beverly Hills, CA: Sage.

Megargee, E.I., Cook, P.E., & Mendelsohn, G.A. (1967). The development and validation of an MMPI scale of assaultiveness in overcontrolled individuals. *Journal of Abnormal Psychology, 72*, 519–528.

Meikle, S., & Gerritse, R. (1970). MMPI cookbook pattern frequencies in a psychiatric unit. *Journal of Clinical Psychology, 26*, 82–84.

Messick, S., & Jackson, D.N. (1961). Acquiescence and the factorial interpretation of the MMPI. *Psychological Bulletin, 58*, 299–304.

Moore, D.D., Handal, P.J. (1980). Adolescents' MMPI performance, cynicism, estrangement, and personal adjustment. *Psychology, 36*, 932–936.

Moreland, K.L. (1984). Intelligent use of automated psychological reports. *Critical Items, 1*, 4–5. (Distributed by National Computer Systems, Minneapolis, MN).

Moreland, K.L. (1985a). Computer-assisted psychological assessment in 1986: A practical guide. *Computers in Human Behavior, 1*, 221–233.

Moreland, K.L. (1985b). *Test-retest reliability of 80 MMPI scales.* Unpublished materials. (Available from National Computer Systems, Minneapolis, MN).

Moreland, K.L. (1985c). Validation of computer-based test interpretations: Problems and prospects. *Journal of Consulting and Clinical Psychology, 53*, 816–825.

Moreland, K.L. (1987). Computerized psychological assessment: What's available? In J.N. Butcher (Ed.), *Computerized psychological assessment* (pp. 26–49). New York: Basic Books.

Moreland, K.L., & Onstad, J.A. (1985, March). *Validity of the Minnesota Clinical Report, I: Mental health outpatients.* Paper presented at the 20th Annual Symposium on Recent Developments in the Use of the MMPI, Honolulu, HI.

Nelson, L.D., & Marks, P.A. (1985). Empirical correlates of infrequently occurring MMPI code types. *Journal of Clinical Psychology, 41*, 477–482.

Newmark, C.S., Gentry, L., & Whitt, J.K. (1983). Utility of MMPI indices of schizophrenia with adolescents. *Journal of Clinical Psychology, 39*, 170–172.

Olmstead, D.W., & Monachesi, E.D. (1956). A validity check on MMPI scales of responsibility and dominance. *Journal of Abnormal and Social Psychology, 53*, 140–141.

Osborne, D. (1979). Use of the MMPI with medical patients. In J.N. Butcher (Ed.), *New developments in the use of the MMPI* (pp. 141–163). Minneapolis: University of Minnesota Press.

Panton, J.H. (1958). MMPI profile configurations among crime classification groups. *Journal of Clinical Psychology, 14*, 305–308.

Panton, J.H. (1959). The response of prison inmates to MMPI subscales. *Journal of Social Therapy, 5*, 233–237.

Parker, C.A. (1961). The predictive use of the MMPI in a college counseling center. *Journal of Counseling Psychology, 8*, 154–158.

Pepper, L.J., & Strong, P.N. (1958). *Judgmental subscales for the Mf scale of the MMPI.* Unpublished materials, Hawaii Department of Health, Honolulu, HI.

Persons, R.W., & Marks, P.A. (1971). The violent 4–3 MMPI personality type. *Journal of Consulting and Clinical Psychology, 36*, 189–196.

Peterson, C.D. (1989). *Masculinity and femininity as independent dimensions on the MMPI.* Unpublished doctoral dissertation, University of North Carolina, Chapel Hill.

Peterson, D.R. (1954). Predicting hospitalization of psychiatric outpatients. *Journal of Abnormal and Social Psychology, 49*, 260–265.

Piotrowski, C., & Lubin, B. (in press). Assessment practices of division 38 practitioners. *Health Psychology.*

Pritchard, D.A., & Rosenblatt, A. (1980). Racial bias in the MMPI: A methodological review. *Journal of Consulting and Clinical Psychology, 48*, 263–267.

Quay, H. (1955). The performance of hospitalized psychiatric patients on the ego-strength scale of the MMPI. *Journal of Clinical Psychology, 11*, 403–405.

Query, W.T., Megran, J., & McDonald, G. (1986). Applying posttraumatic stress disorder MMPI subscale to World War II POW veterans. *Journal of Clinical Psychology, 42*, 315–317.

Rhodes, R.J. (1969). The MacAndrew Alcoholism scale: A replication. *Journal of Clinical Psychology, 25*, 189–191.

Rich, C.C., & Davis, H.G. (1969). Concurrent validity of MMPI alcoholism scales. *Journal of Clinical Psychology, 25*, 425–426.

Rohan, W.P. (1972). MMPI changes in hospitalized alcoholics: A second study. *Quarterly Journal of Studies on Alcohol, 33*, 65–76.

Rohan, W.P., Tatro, R.L., & Rotman, S.R. (1969). MMPI changes in alcoholics during hospitalization. *Quarterly Journal of Studies on Alcohol, 30*, 389–400.

Rosen, A. (1963). Diagnostic differentiation as a construct validity indication for the MMPI ego-strength scale. *Journal of General Psychology, 69*, 65–68.

Rosenberg, N. (1972). MMPI alcoholism scales. *Journal of Clinical Psychology, 28*, 515–522.

Rutter, M., Graham, P., Chadwick, O.F.D., & Yule, W. (1976). Adolescent turmoil: Fact or fiction? *Journal of Child Psychology, 17*, 35–56.

Schlenger, W.E., & Kulka, R.A. (1987). *Performance of the Keane-Fairbank MMPI scale and other self-report measures in identifying post-traumatic stress disorder.* Paper presented at the 95th annual meeting of the American Psychological Association, New York.

Schlenger, W.E., Kulka, R.A., Fairbank, J.A., Hough, R.L., Jordan, B.K., Marmar, C.R., & Weiss, D.S. (1989). *The prevalence of post-traumatic stress disorder in the Vietnam generation: Findings from the National Vietnam Veterans Readjustment study.* Report from Research Triangle Institute, Research Triangle Park, NC.

Schretlen, D.J. (1988). The use of psychological tests to identify malingered symptoms of mental disorder. *Clinical Psychology Review, 8*, 451–476.

Schubert, H.J.P. (1973). *A wide-range MMPI manual.* Unpublished materials.

Schwartz, G.F. (1977). *An investigation of the stability of single scale and two-point MMPI code types for psychiatric patients.* Unpublished doctoral dissertation, Kent State University, Kent, OH.

Schwartz, M.F., & Graham, J.R. (1979). Construct validity of the MacAndrew Alcoholism scale. *Journal of Consulting and Clinical Psychology, 47,* 1090–1095.

Serkownek, K. (1975). *Subscales for scales 5 and 0 of the Minnesota Multiphasic Personality Inventory.* Unpublished materials.

Sherriffs, A.C., & Boomer, D.S. (1954). Who is penalized by the penalty for guessing? *Journal of Educational Psychology, 45,* 81–90.

Simmett, E.R. (1962). The relationship between the Ego Strength scale and rated in-hospital improvement. *Journal of Clinical Psychology, 18,* 46–47.

Sines, L.K. (1959). The relative contribution of four kinds of data to accuracy in personality assessment. *Journal of Consulting Psychology, 23,* 483–492.

Skinner, H.A., & Allen, B.A. (1983). Does the computer make a difference? Computerized vs. face to face vs. self-report assessment of alcohol, drug, and tobacco use. *Journal of Consulting and Clinical Psychology, 51,* 267–275.

Snyter, C.M., & Graham, J.R. (1984). The utility of subtle and obvious MMPI subscales. *Journal of Clinical Psychology, 40,* 981–985.

Sobel, H.J., & Worden, W. (1979). The MMPI as a predictor of psychosocial adaptation to cancer. *Journal of Consulting and Clinical Psychology, 47,* 716–724.

Solway, K.S., Hays, J.R., & Zieben, M. (1976). Personality characteristics of juvenile probation officers. *Journal of Community Psychology, 4,* 152–156.

Spiegel, D.E. (1969). SPI and MMPI predictors of psychopathology. *Journal of Projective Techniques and Personality Assessment, 33,* 265–273.

Stein, K.B. (1968). The TSC scales: The outcome of a cluster analysis of the 550 MMPI items. In P. McReynolds (Ed.), *Advances in psychological assessment, Vol. I* (pp. 80–104). Palo Alto, CA: Science and Behavior Books.

Stone, L.A., Bassett, G.R., Brousseau, J.D., Demers, J., & Stiening, J.A. (1972). Psychological test scores for a group of MEDEX trainees. *Psychological Reports, 31,* 827–831.

Strenger, V.E. (1989). Content homogeneous subscales for scale 7 of the MMPI. Unpublished masters thesis, Kent State University, Kent, OH.

Strupp, H.H., & Bloxom, A.L. (1975). An approach to defining a patient population in psychotherapy research. *Journal of Counseling Psychology, 22,* 231–237.

Sue, S., & Sue, D.W. (1974). MMPI comparisons between Asian-American and non-Asian students utilizing a student health psychiatric clinic. *Journal of Counseling Psychology, 21,* 423–427.

Sullivan, D.L., Miller, C., & Smelser, W. (1958). Factors in the length of stay and progress in psychotherapy. *Journal of Consulting Psychology, 22,* 1–9.

Swenson, W.M., Pearson, J.S., & Osborne, D. (1973). *An MMPI source book: Basic item, scale, and pattern data for 50,000 medical patients.* Minneapolis: University of Minnesota Press.

Swenson, W.M., Rome, H.P., Pearson, J.S., & Brannick, T.L. (1965). A totally automated psychological test: Experience in a medical center. *Journal of the American Medical Association, 191,* 925–950.

Taft, R. (1957). The validity of the Barron Ego Strength scale and the Welsh Anxiety index. *Journal of Consulting Psychology, 21,* 247–249.

Tamkin, A.S. (1957). An evaluation of the construct validity of Barron's Ego-Strength scale. *Journal of Consulting Psychology, 13,* 156–158.

Tamkin, A.S., & Klett, C.J. (1957). Barron's Ego Strength scale: A replication of an evaluation of its construct validity. *Journal of Consulting Psychology, 21,* 412.

Taulbee, E.S., & Sisson, B.D. (1957). Configural analysis of MMPI profiles of psychiatric groups. *Journal of Consulting Psychology, 21,* 413–417.

Terman, L.M., & Miles, C.C. (1936). *Sex and personality: Studies in masculinity and femininity.* New York: McGraw-Hill.

Tryon, R.C. (1966). Unrestricted cluster and factor analysis, with application to the MMPI and Holzinger-Harman problems. *Multivariate Behavioral Research, 1,* 229–244.

Tryon, R.C., & Bailey, D. (Eds.). (1965). *Users' manual of the BC TRY system of cluster and factor analysis* (Taped version). Berkeley: University of California Computer Center.

Uecker, A.E. (1970). Differentiating male alcoholics from other psychiatric inpatients: Validity of the MacAndrew scale. *Quarterly Journal of Studies on Alcohol, 31*, 379–383.

Uecker, A.E., Boutilier, L.R., & Richardson, E.H. (1980). "Indianism" and MMPI scores of men alcoholics. *Journal of Studies on Alcohol, 41*, 357–362.

Vanderploeg, R.D., Sison, G.F.P., & Hickling, E.J. (1987). A reevaluation of the use of the MMPI in the assessment of combat-related posttraumatic stress disorder. *Journal of Personality Assessment, 51*, 140–150.

Walters, G.D., Greene, R.L., & Jeffrey, T.B. (1984). Discriminating between alcoholic and nonalcoholic blacks and whites on the MMPI. *Journal of Personality Assessment, 48*, 486–488.

Walters, G.D., Greene, R.L., Jeffrey, T.B., Kruzich, D.J., & Haskin, J.J. (1983). Racial variations on the MacAndrew Alcoholism scale of the MMPI. *Journal of Consulting and Clinical Psychology, 51*, 947–948.

Webb, J.T. (1970). Validity and utility of computer-produced reports with Veterans Administration psychiatric populations. *Proceedings of the 78th Annual Convention of the American Psycholigical Association, 5*, 541–542.

Webb, J.T., Miller, M.L., & Fowler, R.D. (1969). Validation of a computerized MMPI interpretation system. *Proceedings of the 77th Annual Convention of the American Psychological Association, 4*, 523–524.

Webb, J.T., Miller, M.L., & Fowler, R.D. (1970). Extending professional time: A computerized MMPI interpretation service. *Journal of Clinical Psychology, 26*, 210–214.

Welsh, G.S. (1948). An extension of Hathaway's MMPI profile coding system. *Journal of Consulting Psychology, 12*, 343–344.

Welsh, G.S. (1956). Factor dimensions A and R. In G.S. Welsh & W.G. Dahlstrom (Eds.), *Basic readings on the MMPI in psychology and medicine* (pp. 264–281). Minneapolis: University of Minnesota Press.

Welsh, G.S. (1965). MMPI profiles and factors A and R. *Journal of Clinical Psychology, 21*, 43–47.

Wiener, D.N. (1947). Differences between the individual and group forms of the MMPI. *Journal of Consulting Psychology, 11*, 104–106.

Wiener, D.N. (1948). Subtle and obvious keys for the MMPI. *Journal of Consulting Psychology, 12*, 164–170.

Wiggins, J.S. (1969). Content dimensions in the MMPI. In J.N. Butcher (Ed.), *MMPI: Research developments and clinical applications* (pp. 127–180). New York: McGraw-Hill.

Wiggins, J.S. (1973). *Personality and prediction: Principles of personality assessment.* Reading, MA: Addison-Wesley.

Wilderman, J.E. (1984). *An investigation of the clinical utility of the College Maladjustment scale.* Unpublished master's thesis, Kent State University, Kent, OH.

Williams, A.F., McCourt, W.F., & Schneider, L. (1971). Personality self-descriptions of alcoholics and heavy drinkers. *Quarterly Journal of Studies on Alcohol, 32*, 310–317.

Williams, C.L. (1986). MMPI profiles from adolescents: Interpretive strategies and treatment considerations. *Journal of Child and Adolescent Psychotherapy, 3*, 179–193.

Williams, C.L., & Butcher, J.N. (in press, a). I. An MMPI study of adolescents: Empirical validity of the standard scales. *Psychological Assessment: A Journal of Consulting and Clinical Psychology.*

Williams, C.L., & Butcher, J.N. (in press, b). II. An MMPI study of adolescents: Verification and limitations of codetype classifications. *Psychological Assessment: A Journal of Consulting and Clinical Psychology.*

Williams, H.L. (1952). The development of a caudality scale for the MMPI. *Journal of Clinical Psychology, 8*, 293–297.

Wimbish, L.G. (1984). *The importance of appropriate norms for the computerized interpretation of adolescent MMPI profiles.* Unpublished doctoral dissertation, Ohio State University, Columbus.

Wirt, R.D. (1955). Further validation of the Ego-Strength scale. *Journal of Consulting Psychology, 19*, 444.

Wirt, R.D. (1956). Actuarial prediction. *Journal of Consulting Psychology, 20,* 123–124.

Wisniewski, N.M., Glenwick, D.S., & Graham, J.R. (1985). MacAndrew scale and socio-demographic correlates of adolescent alcohol and drug use. *Addictive Behaviors, 10,* 55–67.

Wolfson, K.P., & Erbaugh, S.E. (1984). Adolescent responses to the MacAndrew Alcoholism scale. *Journal of Consulting and Clinical Psychology, 52,* 625–630.

Ziskin, J. (1981). Use of the MMPI in forensic settings (*Clinical Notes on the MMPI, No. 9*). Minneapolis, MN: National Computer Systems.

Appendices

Appendix A. Composition of Standard Validity and Clinical Scales

L Scale
True: NONE
False: 16, 29, 41, 51, 77, 93, 102, 107, 123, 139, 153, 183, 203, 232, 260

F Scale
True: 18, 24, 30, 36, 42, 48, 54, 60, 66, 72, 84, 96, 114, 138, 144, 150, 156, 162, 168, 180, 198, 216, 228, 234, 240, 246, 252, 258, 264, 270, 282, 288, 294, 300, 306, 312, 324, 336, 349, 355, 361
False: 6, 12, 78, 90, 102, 108, 120, 126, 132, 174, 186, 192, 204, 210, 222, 276, 318, 330, 343

K Scale
True: 83
False: 29, 37, 58, 76, 110, 116, 122, 127, 130, 136, 148, 157, 158, 167, 171, 196, 213, 243, 267, 284, 290, 330, 338, 339, 341, 346, 348, 356, 365

Scale 1—Hypochondriasis (Hs)
True: 18, 28, 39, 53, 59, 97, 101, 111, 149, 175, 247
False: 2, 3, 8, 10, 20, 45, 47, 57, 91, 117, 141, 143, 152, 164, 173, 176, 179, 208, 224, 249, 255

Scale 2—Depression (D)
True: 5, 15, 18, 31, 38, 39, 46, 56, 73, 92, 117, 127, 130, 146, 147, 170, 175, 181, 215, 233
False: 2, 9, 10, 20, 29, 33, 37, 43, 45, 49, 55, 68, 75, 76, 95, 109, 118, 134, 140, 141, 142, 143, 148, 165, 178, 188, 189, 212, 221, 223, 226, 238, 245, 248, 260, 267, 330

Scale 3—Hysteria (Hy)
True: 11, 18, 31, 39, 40, 44, 65, 101, 166, 172, 175, 218, 230
False: 2, 3, 7, 8, 9, 10, 14, 26, 29, 45, 47, 58, 76, 81, 91, 95, 98, 110, 115, 116, 124, 125, 129, 135, 141, 148, 151, 152, 157, 159, 161, 164, 167, 173, 176, 179, 185, 193, 208, 213, 224, 241, 243, 249, 253, 263, 265

Scale 4—Psychopathic Deviate (Pd)
True: 17, 21, 22, 31, 32, 35, 42, 52, 54, 56, 71, 82, 89, 94, 99, 105, 113, 195, 202, 219, 225, 259, 264, 288
False: 9, 12, 34, 70, 79, 83, 95, 122, 125, 129, 143, 157, 158, 160, 167, 171, 185, 209, 214, 217, 226, 243, 261, 263, 266, 267

Scale 5—Masculinity-Femininity (Mf)—Male
True: 4, 25, 62, 64, 67, 74, 80, 112, 119, 122, 128, 137, 166, 177, 187, 191, 196, 205, 209, 219, 236, 251, 256, 268, 271
False: 1, 19, 26, 27, 63, 68, 69, 76, 86, 103, 104, 107, 120, 121, 132, 133, 163, 184, 193, 194, 197, 199, 201, 207, 231, 235, 237, 239, 254, 257, 272

Scale 5—Masculinity-Femininity (Mf)—Female
True: 4, 25, 62, 64, 67, 74, 80, 112, 119, 121, 122, 128, 137, 177, 187, 191, 196, 205, 219, 236, 251, 256, 271
False: 1, 19, 26, 27, 63, 68, 69, 76, 86, 103, 104, 107, 120, 132, 133, 163, 166, 184, 193, 194, 197, 199, 201, 207, 209, 231, 235, 237, 239, 254, 257, 268, 272

Scale 6—Paranoia (Pa)
True: 16, 17, 22, 23, 24, 42, 99, 113, 138, 144, 145, 146, 162, 234, 259, 271, 277, 285, 305, 307, 333, 334, 336, 355, 361
False: 81, 95, 98, 100, 104, 110, 244,

Source: *Minnesota Multiphasic Personality Inventory-2 (MMPI-2): Manual for administration and scoring.* S. R. Hathaway & J. C. McKinley with J. N. Butcher, W. G. Dahlstrom, J. R. Graham, A. Tellegen, & B. Kaemmer. Minneapolis: The University of Minnesota Press. Reproduced by permission.

255, 266, 283, 284, 286, 297, 314, 315

Scale 7—Psychasthenia (Pt)

True: 11, 16, 23, 31, 38, 56, 65, 73, 82, 89, 94, 130, 147, 170, 175, 196, 218, 242, 273, 275, 277, 285, 289, 301, 302, 304, 308, 309, 310, 313, 316, 317, 320, 325, 326, 327, 328, 329, 331

False: 3, 9, 33, 109, 140, 165, 174, 293, 321

Scale 8—Schizophrenia (Sc)

True: 16, 17, 21, 22, 23, 31, 32, 35, 38, 42, 44, 46, 48, 65, 85, 92, 138, 145, 147, 166, 168, 170, 180, 182, 190, 218, 221, 229, 233, 234, 242, 247, 252, 256, 268, 273, 274, 277, 279, 281, 287, 291, 292, 296, 298, 299, 303, 307, 311, 316, 319, 320, 322, 323, 325, 329, 332, 333, 355

False: 6, 9, 12, 34, 90, 91, 106, 165, 177, 179, 192, 210, 255, 276, 278, 280, 290, 295, 343

Scale 9—Hypomania (Ma)

True: 13, 15, 21, 23, 50, 55, 61, 85, 87, 98, 113, 122, 131, 145, 155, 168, 169, 182, 190, 200, 205, 206, 211, 212, 218, 220, 227, 229, 238, 242, 244, 248, 250, 253, 269

False: 88, 93, 100, 106, 107, 136, 154, 158, 167, 243, 263

Scale 0—Social Introversion (Si)

True: 31, 56, 70, 100, 104, 110, 127, 135, 158, 161, 167, 185, 215, 243, 251, 265, 275, 284, 289, 296, 302, 308, 326, 337, 338, 347, 348, 351, 352, 357, 364, 367, 368, 369

False: 25, 32, 49, 79, 86, 106, 112, 131, 181, 189, 207, 209, 231, 237, 255, 262, 267, 280, 321, 328, 335, 340, 342, 344, 345, 350, 353, 354, 358, 359, 360, 362, 363, 366, 370

Appendix B. T-Score Conversions for Standard Validity and Clinical Scales

T-SCORE CONVERSIONS WITH K-CORRECTIONS*

Males

Raw score	L	F	K	Hs+.5K	D	Hy	Pd+.4K	Mf	Pa	Pt+1K	Sc+1K	Ma+.2K	Si
73													
72													
71													
70													100
69													99
68													98
67											120		97
66											118		96
65											117		94
64											115		93
63											113		92
62											111		91
61											110		
60										120	108		90
59										119	106		89
58										117	105		87
57										115	103		86
56								109		113	101		85
55					120			107		111	99		84
54					119			105		109	98		83
53					117			103		106	96		82
52					115			101		104	94		80
51					114		120	99		102	93		79
50					112	120	117	97		100	91		78
49					110	119	115	95		98	89		77
48					108	116	112	93		96	87		76
47					106	114	110	91		94	86		75
46					104	111	107	89		91	84		73
45					102	109	105	87		89	82	120	72
44				120	100	106	102	85		87	81	117	71
43				119	98	104	100	83		85	79	114	70
42				116	97	101	97	81		83	77		69
41				114	95	99	95	79		81	75		68

Females

Raw score	Hs+.5K	D	Hy	Pd+.4K	Mf	Pa	Pt+1K	Sc+1K	Ma+.2K	Si
73								120		
72								119		
71								118		
70								116		
69								115		95
68								113		94
67							120	112		93
66							119	111		91
65							117	109		90
64							115	108		89
63							114	106		88
62							112	105		87
61							110	103		86
60							108	102		85
59							106	100		84
58							105	99		83
57							103	97		82
56							101	96		81
55							99	94		79
54							97	93		78
53		120					95	91		77
52		118	120				94	90		76
51		116	118				92	88		75
50		114	115	120			90	87		74
49		112	113	118			88	85		73
48		109	111	115			86	84		72
47		107	108	113			84	82		71
46	120	105	106	110			83	81		70
45	118	103	104	107			81	79		69
44	116	101	101	105	30		79	78	120	67
43	113	99	99	102	33		77	76	118	66
42	111	96	96	100	35		75	75	115	65
41	109	94	94	97	38			73	112	64

278

40	63	109	72	73		40	94	92	92	107			66	110	74	79		78	92	96	93	112				
39	62	106	70	72		43	92	89	90	105			65	107	72	77		76	90	94	91	110				
38	61	103	69	70		45	89	87	88	103			64	104	70	74		74	87	91	89	108				
37	60	100	67	68		47	87	84	86	101			63	101	69	72		72	84	89	87	105				
36	59	97	66	66		50	84	82	83	99			62	98	67	70		70	82	86	85	103				
35	58	94	65	64		52	81	80	81	97			61	94	65	68		68	79	84	83	101				
34	57	91	63	62		55	79	77	79	95			59	91	63	66		66	77	81	81	99				
33	55	88	62	61		57	76	75	77	92			58	88	62	64		64	74	79	80	97				
32	54	85	60	59		60	73	73	75	90			57	85	60	62		62	72	76	78	94				
31	53	82	59	57		62	71	70	72	88			56	81	58	59		60	69	74	76	92				
30	52	79	57	55	120	65	68	68	70	86	83		55	78	56	57		58	67	71	74	90	81			
29	51	76	55	53	118	67	66	65	68	84	81		54	75	55	55		56	64	69	72	88	79			
28	50	74	53	51	114	69	63	63	66	82	78		52	72	53	53		54	62	66	70	86	77	120		
27	49	71	52	49	111	72	60	61	64	80	76		51	69	51	51		52	59	64	68	84	75	119		
26	48	68	50	47	107	74	58	58	62	78	74		50	65	49	49		50	57	61	66	81	72	116		
25	47	65	48	44	103	77	55	56	59	76	72		49	62	47	47	120	48	54	59	64	79	70	113		
24	46	62	46	42	100	79	53	54	57	74	70	120	48	59	45	44	119	46	52	57	62	77	68	110		
23	45	59	44	40	96	82	51	51	55	71	67	116	47	56	43	43	116	44	50	54	60	75	66	107		
22	43	56	42	39	92	84	49	49	53	69	65	113	45	53	42	41	113	42	48	52	59	73	64	104		
21	42	53	41	37	89	87	47	47	51	67	63	109	44	51	40	39	108	40	46	50	57	70	62	101		
20	41	51	39	35	85	89	45	45	49	65	61	106	43	49	39	37	105	38	44	47	54	68	60	98		
19	40	49	37	34	81	92	43	43	47	63	59	103	42	47	37	36	101	36	42	45	52	66	58	95		
18	39	47	36	32	78	94	41	41	46	61	56	99	41	45	36	34	97	34	40	43	50	64	56	92		
17	38	45	34	31	74	96	39	39	44	59	54	96	40	43	35	33	94	32	39	42	47	62	54	89		
16	37	43	33	30	70	99	37	38	42	57	52	92	38	41	33	32	90	30	37	40	45	59	51	85		100
15	36	41	32		67	101	36	36	40	54	50	89	37	39	32	31	86		35	38	42	57	49	82	105	96
14	35	39	31		63	104	34	35	38	51	48	85	36	38	31	30	83		34	37	40	54	47	79	100	91
13	34	37	30		59	106	32	34	36	49	46	82	35	36	30		79		33	35	38	51	45	76	95	87
12	33	35			56	109	30	32	34	46	43	79	34	35			75		31	34	36	48	43	73	90	83
11	32	33			52	111		31	32	43	41	75	33	33			72		30	33	34	45	41	70	86	78
10	30	31				114		30	30	40	39	72	31	31			68			32	32	42	39	67	81	74
9		30				116				38	37	68	30	30			64			31	30	39	37	64	76	70
8						118				35	35	65					61			30		37	35	61	71	65
7						120				33	32	61					57					35	33	58	66	61
6										30	30	58					53					33	30	55	62	56
5												55					49					32		51	57	52
4												51					46					31		48	52	47
3												47					42					31		45	47	43
2												44					39					30		42	43	38
1												41					37							39	38	35
0												38					34							36	33	

*Uniform T-scores are presented for scales Hs, D, Hy, Pd, Pa, Pt, Sc, and Ma. Linear T-scores are presented for scores L, F, K, Mf, and Si.

Appendix B (continued)
T-SCORE CONVERSIONS WITHOUT K-CORRECTIONS*

Males

Raw score	L	F	K	Hs + .5K	D	Hy	Pd + .4K	Mf	Pa	Pt + 1K	Sc + 1K	Ma + .2K	Si
72													
71													
70						120					120		100
69						119					119		99
68						116					117		98
67						114					116		97
66						111					115		96
65						109					114		94
64						106					113		93
63						104					111		92
62						101							91
61						99							
60					120						110		90
59					119						109		89
58					117						108		87
57					115						107		86
56					114			109			105		85
55								107			104		84
54								105			103		83
53								103			102		82
52								101			100		80
51								99			99		79
50					112			97			98		78
49					110			95			97		77
48					108		120	93		104	96		76
47					106		117	91		103	94		75
46					104		115	89		101	93		73
45					102		113	87		100	92		72
44					100		111	85		98	91		71
43					98		109	83		97	90		70
42					97		106	81		95	88	120	69
41					95		104	79		94	87	118	68

Females

Raw score	Hs + .5K	D	Hy	Pd + .4K	Mf	Pa	Pt + 1K	Sc + 1K	Ma + .2K	Si
72								120		
71								118		
70								117		
69								116		95
68								115		94
67								114		93
66								113		91
65								112		90
64								111		89
63								109		88
62								108		87
61								107		86
60								106		85
59								105		84
58								104		83
57								103		82
56								102		81
55								100		79
54		120						99		78
53		118	120					98		77
52		116	118					97		76
51								96		75
50		114	115					95		74
49		112	113				98	94		73
48		109	111	120			97	93		72
47		107	108	118			95	92		71
46		105	106	116			94	90		70
45		103	104	113			93	89		69
44		101	101	111	30		91	88		67
43		99	99	109	33		90	87	120	66
42		96	96	106	35		89	86	119	65
41		94	94		38			85	116	64

MMPI-2 uniform and linear T-score conversion table (male). Raw scores appear in the bold columns at both the left and right margins (40 down to 0). Values are the corresponding T-scores for each scale.

Raw	L	F	K	Hs	D	Hy	Pd	Mf	Pa	Pt	Sc	Ma	Si	Raw
40		115			92	96	102	40	120	114	84	87	63	40
39		112			91	94	100	43	118	111	83	86	62	39
38		109			89	91	97	45	114	108	81	84	61	38
37		106			87	89	95	47	111	105	80	83	60	37
36		103			84	86	93	50	107	102	79	82	59	36
35		100			82	84	91	52	103	100	78	80	58	35
34		97			80	81	89	55	100	97	77	79	57	34
33		94			77	79	86	57	96	94	76	78	55	33
32		91		100	75	76	84	60	92	91	75	76	54	32
31		88		98	72	74	82	62	89	89	74	75	53	31
30		85	83	97	70	71	80	65	85	86	72	73	52	30
29		82	81	95	68	69	77	67	81	83	71	72	51	29
28		79	78	93	65	66	75	69	78	80	70	71	50	28
27		76	76	91	63	64	73	72	74	77	69	69	49	27
26		73	74	89	61	61	72	74	70	75	68	68	48	26
25		70	72	87	59	59	70	77	67	73	67	67	47	25
24		67	70	85	56	57	69	79	63	69	66	65	46	24
23		64	67	83	54	54	67	82	59	66	65	64	45	23
22		61	65	82	51	52	66	84	56	64	63	62	43	22
21		58	63	80	49	50	64	87	52	61	62	61	42	21
20		56	61	78	47	47	63	89	49	58	61	60	41	20
19		53	59	76	45	45	61	92	45	55	59	58	40	19
18		51	56	74	43	43	60	94	42	53	58	57	39	18
17		49	54	72	41	42	58	96	39	51	57	56	38	17
16		47	52	70	39	40	57	99	37	49	56	55	37	16
15	100	45	50	69	38	38	55	101	34	47	55	53	36	15
14	96	43	48	67	35	37	53	104	32	45	53	52	35	14
13	91	42	46	65	34	35	52	106	31	43	52	51	34	13
12	87	40	43	63	32	33	51	109	30	41	51	50	33	12
11	83	38	41	61	30	30	50	111		40	50	48	32	11
10	78	37	39	59			48	114		38	48	47	30	10
9	74	35	37	57			47	116		36		46		9
8	70	33	35	56			46	118		34		44		8
7	65	31	32	54			44	120		32		43		7
6	61	30	30	52			43			30		41		6
5	56			49			41					39		5
4	52			47								37		4
3	48			44								35		3
2	43			41								33		2
1	39			37								31		1
0	35			33								30		0

*Uniform T-scores are presented for scales Hs, D, Hy, Pd, Pt, Pa, Sc, and Ma. Linear T-scores are presented for scales L, F, K, Mf, and Si.

Source: Minnesota Multiphasic Personality Inventory-2 (MMPI-2): Manual for administration and scoring. S. R. Hathaway & J. C. McKinley with J. N. Butcher, W. G. Dahlstrom, J. R. Graham, A. Tellegen, & B. Kaemmer. Minneapolis: The University of Minnesota Press. Reproduced by permission.

Appendix C. T-Score Conversions for Adolescents

T-SCORE CONVERSIONS WITHOUT K-CORRECTIONS FOR ADOLESCENT MALES AGE 14 AND BELOW

Raw score	L	F	K	1	2	3	4	5	6	7	8	9	0	Raw score
0	32	36	23	34	9	10	10	0	23	30	32	15	11	0
1	37	38	25	37	12	13	12	3	25	32	33	17	12	1
2	42	40	27	40	15	16	14	5	27	33	35	19	14	2
3	46	42	29	43	17	18	16	8	30	34	36	21	15	3
4	51	44	31	46	19	20	18	10	33	36	37	23	16	4
5	56	46	33	49	21	22	21	12	35	37	38	25	18	5
6	61	48	35	52	23	25	23	15	38	38	39	27	19	6
7	66	50	37	55	26	27	25	17	41	40	40	29	20	7
8	71	52	39	58	28	29	28	20	44	41	41	31	22	8
9	76	54	41	61	30	31	30	22	46	43	42	33	23	9
10	80	56	43	64	32	33	32	24	49	44	43	35	24	10
11	85	58	45	67	35	36	35	27	52	45	44	37	26	11
12	90	60	48	70	37	38	37	29	55	47	45	39	27	12
13	95	62	50	73	39	40	39	31	57	48	46	41	28	13
14	100	64	52	76	41	42	42	34	60	49	47	43	30	14
15	105	66	54	79	43	44	44	36	63	51	48	45	31	15
16		68	56	82	46	47	46	38	65	52	50	47	33	16
17		70	58	84	48	49	49	41	68	54	51	49	34	17
18		71	60	87	50	51	51	43	71	55	52	50	35	18
19		73	62	90	52	53	53	46	74	56	53	52	37	19
20		75	64	93	55	56	56	48	76	58	54	54	38	20
21		77	66	96	57	58	58	50	79	59	55	56	39	21
22		79	68	99	59	60	60	53	82	60	56	58	41	22
23		81	70	102	61	62	62	55	84	62	57	60	42	23
24		83	72	105	63	64	65	57	87	63	58	62	43	24
25		85	74	108	66	67	67	60	90	65	59	64	45	25
26		87	76	111	68	69	69	62	93	66	60	66	46	26
27		89	79	114	70	71	72	65	95	67	61	68	47	27
28		91	81	117	72	73	74	67	98	69	62	70	49	28
29		93	83	120	75	75	76	69	101	70	63	72	50	29
30		95	85	123	77	78	79	72	104	71	65	74	51	30
31		97		126	79	80	81	74	106	73	66	76	53	31
32		99		129	81	82	83	76	109	74	67	78	54	32
33		101		132	83	84	86	79	112	75	68	80	56	33
34		103			86	87	88	81	114	77	69	82	57	34
35		105			88	89	90	83	117	78	70	84	58	35

Raw score	T-scores													Raw score
	L	F	K	1	2	3	4	5	6	7	8	9	0	
36		107			90	91	93	86	120	80	71	86	60	36
37		109			92	93	95	88	123	81	72	88	61	37
38		111			95	95	97	91	125	82	73	90	62	38
39		113			97	98	100	93	128	84	74	92	64	39
40		115			99	100	102	95	131	85	75	94	65	40
41		117			101	102	104	98		86	76	96	66	41
42		119			103	104	106	100		88	77	98	68	42
43		121			106	107	109	102		89	78	100	69	43
44		123			108	109	111	105		91	80	101	70	44
45		125			110	111	113	107		92	81	103	72	45
46		127			112	113	116	109		93	82	105	73	46
47		129			115	115	118	112		95	83		75	47
48		131			117	118	120	114		96	84		76	48
49		133			119	120	123	117			85		77	49
50		135			121	122	125	119			86		79	50
51		137			123	124		121			87		80	51
52		139			126	126		124			88		81	52
53		141			128	129		126			89		83	53
54		143			130	131		128			90		84	54
55		145			132	133		131			91		85	55
56		147			135	135		133			92		87	56
57		149			137	138		135			93		88	57
58		151			139	140		138			95		89	58
59		153			141	142		140			96		91	59
60		155			143	144		143			97		92	60
61		157									98		93	61
62		159									99		95	62
63		161									100		96	63
64		163									101		98	64
65											102		99	65
66											103		100	66
67											104		102	67
68											105		103	68
69											106		104	69
70											107		106	70
71											108			71
72											110			72
73											111			73
74											112			74
75											113			75
76											114			76
77											115			77
78											116			78

Note: The MMPI-2 should not be used for subjects younger than 18 years. The original MMPI should be used for such subjects. These norms are for the original MMPI.

T-SCORE CONVERSIONS WITHOUT K-CORRECTIONS FOR ADOLESCENT MALES AGE 15

Raw score	L	F	K	1	2	3	4	5	6	7	8	9	0	Raw score
0	32	37	22	36	9	12	10	6	27	29	33	15	10	0
1	37	38	24	39	11	15	13	8	29	31	34	17	12	1
2	42	40	26	41	13	17	15	10	31	32	35	19	13	2
3	46	41	28	44	15	20	17	12	33	34	36	21	15	3
4	50	43	30	46	18	22	19	14	35	35	37	22	16	4
5	55	45	32	48	20	24	22	16	37	37	38	24	17	5
6	59	46	34	51	22	26	24	18	40	38	39	26	19	6
7	63	48	37	53	24	28	26	20	42	39	40	28	20	7
8	67	50	39	55	27	30	28	22	44	41	41	30	21	8
9	72	52	41	58	29	32	30	24	46	42	42	32	23	9
10	76	53	43	60	31	34	32	26	48	44	43	34	24	10
11	80	55	45	62	33	36	34	28	50	45	44	36	25	11
12	85	57	47	65	36	38	37	31	52	46	45	38	27	12
13	89	58	49	67	38	40	39	33	54	48	46	40	28	13
14	93	60	51	69	40	42	41	35	56	49	47	42	30	14
15	98	62	53	72	43	44	43	37	58	51	48	43	31	15
16		63	55	74	45	46	45	39	60	52	49	45	32	16
17		65	58	76	47	48	47	41	63	54	50	47	34	17
18		67	60	79	49	50	49	43	65	55	51	49	35	18
19		68	62	81	52	52	52	45	67	56	52	51	36	19
20		70	64	84	54	54	54	47	69	58	53	53	38	20
21		72	66	86	56	57	56	49	71	59	54	55	39	21
22		73	68	88	58	59	58	51	73	61	55	57	40	22
23		75	70	91	61	61	60	53	75	62	56	59	42	23
24		77	72	93	63	63	62	56	77	64	57	61	43	24
25		78	74	95	65	65	64	58	79	65	58	63	44	25
26		80	76	98	67	67	66	60	81	66	59	65	46	26
27		82	78	100	70	69	69	62	83	68	60	66	47	27
28		83	81	102	72	71	71	64	86	69	61	68	48	28
29		85	83	105	74	73	73	66	88	71	62	70	50	29
30		87	85	107	77	75	75	68	90	72	63	72	51	30
31		88		109	79	77	77	70	92	73	64	74	52	31
32		90		112	81	79	79	72	94	75	65	76	54	32
33		92		114	83	81	81	74	96	76	66	78	55	33
34		93			86	83	84	76	98	78	67	80	56	34
35		95			88	85	86	79	100	79	68	82	58	35
36		97			90	87	88	81	102	81	69	84	59	36
37		98			92	89	90	83	104	82	70	86	60	37
38		100			95	91	92	85	106	83	71	87	62	38
39		102			97	94	94	87	109	85	72	89	63	39

Raw score							T-scores							Raw score
	L	F	K	1	2	3	4	5	6	7	8	9	0	
40		103			99	96	96	89	111	86	73	91	64	40
41		105			101	98	99	91		88	74	93	66	41
42		107			104	100	101	93		89	75	95	67	42
43		108			106	102	103	95		90	76	97	69	43
44		110			108	104	105	97		92	77	99	70	44
45		112			111	106	107	99		93	78	101	71	45
46		114			113	108	109	101		95	79	103	73	46
47		115			115	110	111	104		96	80		74	47
48		117			117	112	114	106		98	81		75	48
49		119			120	114	116	108			82		77	49
50		120			122	116	118	110			83		78	50
51		122			124	118		112			84		79	51
52		124			126	120		114			85		81	52
53		125			129	122		116			86		82	53
54		127			131	124		118			87		83	54
55		129			133	126		120			88		85	55
56		130			135	128		122			89		86	56
57		132			138	131		124			90		87	57
58		134			140	133		127			91		89	58
59		135			142	135		129			92		90	59
60		137			145	137		131			93		91	60
61		139									94		93	61
62		140									95		94	62
63		142									96		95	63
64		144									97		97	64
65											98		98	65
66											99		99	66
67											100		101	67
68											101		102	68
69											102		103	69
70											103		105	70
71											104			71
72											105			72
73											106			73
74											107			74
75											108			75
76											109			76
77											110			77
78											111			78

Note: The MMPI-2 should not be used for subjects younger than 18 years. The original MMPI should be used for such subjects. These norms are for the original MMPI.

T-SCORE CONVERSIONS WITHOUT K-CORRECTIONS FOR ADOLESCENT MALES AGE 16

Raw score	L	F	K	1	2	3	4	5	6	7	8	9	0	Raw score
0	31	35	20	33	8	10	10	0	34	28	30	11	8	0
1	35	37	22	36	11	12	12	3	35	30	32	13	10	1
2	40	39	24	39	13	15	15	5	36	31	33	15	11	2
3	44	40	27	42	15	17	17	8	37	33	35	17	12	3
4	49	42	29	45	18	19	19	10	39	34	36	19	14	4
5	53	44	31	47	20	21	21	12	40	36	37	21	15	5
6	58	46	33	50	22	23	23	15	42	37	38	23	17	6
7	62	47	36	53	24	26	25	17	43	39	39	25	18	7
8	67	49	38	56	27	28	28	20	45	40	40	28	20	8
9	71	51	40	59	29	30	30	22	46	42	41	30	21	9
10	76	53	42	62	31	32	32	24	48	43	42	32	22	10
11	80	54	45	64	33	34	34	27	49	45	43	34	24	11
12	85	56	47	67	36	37	36	29	51	46	44	36	25	12
13	89	58	49	70	38	39	38	31	52	48	45	38	27	13
14	94	60	51	73	40	41	41	34	54	49	46	40	28	14
15	99	61	54	76	42	43	43	36	55	51	48	43	29	15
16		63	56	78	45	45	45	39	57	52	49	45	31	16
17		65	58	81	47	47	47	41	58	54	50	47	32	17
18		66	60	84	49	50	49	43	60	55	51	49	34	18
19		68	63	87	51	52	51	46	61	56	52	51	35	19
20		70	65	90	54	54	53	48	63	58	53	53	37	20
21		72	67	93	56	56	56	50	64	59	54	55	38	21
22		73	70	95	58	58	58	53	66	61	55	58	39	22
23		75	72	98	60	61	60	55	67	62	56	60	41	23
24		77	74	101	63	63	62	57	68	64	57	62	42	24
25		79	76	104	65	65	64	60	70	65	58	64	44	25
26		80	79	107	67	67	66	62	71	67	59	66	45	26
27		82	81	109	69	69	69	65	73	68	61	68	46	27
28		84	83	112	71	71	71	67	74	70	62	70	48	28
29		86	85	115	74	74	73	69	76	71	63	73	49	29
30		87	88	118	76	76	75	72	77	73	64	75	51	30
31		89		121	78	78	77	74	79	74	65	77	52	31
32		91		124	80	80	79	76	80	76	66	79	54	32
33		92		126	83	82	82	79	82	77	67	81	55	33
34		94			85	85	84	81	83	79	68	83	56	34
35		96			87	87	86	84	85	80	69	85	58	35
36		98			89	89	88	86	86	82	70	88	59	36
37		99			92	91	90	88	88	83	71	90	61	37
38		101			94	93	92	91	89	85	72	92	62	38
39		103			96	96	95	93	91	86	74	94	63	39

Raw score	L	F	K	1	2	3	4	5	6	7	8	9	0	Raw score
										T-scores				
40		105			98	98	97	95	92	87	75	96	65	40
41		106			101	100	99	98		89	76	98	66	41
42		108			103	102	101	100		90	77	100	68	42
43		110			105	104	103	103		92	78	103	69	43
44		112			107	106	105	105		93	79	105	71	44
45		113			110	109	107	107		95	80	107	72	45
46		115			112	111	110	110		96	81	109	73	46
47		117			114	113	112	112		98	82		75	47
48		118			116	115	114	114		99	83		76	48
49		120			119	117	116	117			84		78	49
50		122			121	120	118	119			85		79	50
51		124			123	122		121			86		81	51
52		125			125	124		124			88		82	52
53		127			128	126		126			89		83	53
54		129			130	128		129			90		85	54
55		131			132	130		131			91		86	55
56		132			134	133		133			92		88	56
57		134			137	135		136			93		89	57
58		136			139	137		138			94		90	58
59		138			141	139		140			95		92	59
60		139			143	141		143			96		93	60
61		141									97		95	61
62		143									98		96	62
63		144									99		98	63
64		146									101		99	64
65											102		100	65
66											103		102	66
67											104		103	67
68											105		105	68
69											106		106	69
70											107		107	70
71											108			71
72											109			72
73											110			73
74											111			74
75											112			75
76											114			76
77											115			77
78											116			78

Note: The MMPI-2 should not be used for subjects younger than 18 years. The original MMPI should be used for such subjects. These norms are for the original MMPI.

T-SCORE CONVERSIONS WITHOUT K-CORRECTIONS FOR ADOLESCENT MALES AGES 17 AND 18

Raw score	T-scores												Raw score
	L	F	K	1	2	3	4	5	6	7	8	9	0	
0	30	32	20	35	16	13	6	5	19	27	31	12	6	0
1	34	34	23	38	17	15	9	7	22	28	32	14	8	1
2	38	36	25	40	19	17	11	9	25	30	33	16	9	2
3	43	39	27	43	21	19	13	11	28	32	34	18	11	3
4	47	41	29	45	23	21	16	13	31	33	35	20	12	4
5	51	43	31	48	24	23	18	16	34	35	36	22	14	5
6	55	45	34	50	26	25	20	18	37	36	37	24	15	6
7	59	47	36	53	28	27	23	20	40	38	38	26	17	7
8	63	50	38	55	30	29	25	22	43	39	39	28	18	8
9	68	52	40	58	32	30	27	24	46	41	40	31	20	9
10	72	54	42	60	34	32	29	26	49	42	41	33	21	10
11	76	56	45	63	35	34	32	29	52	44	43	35	23	11
12	80	58	47	65	37	36	34	31	55	45	44	37	24	12
13	84	60	49	68	39	38	36	33	58	47	45	39	26	13
14	88	63	51	70	41	40	39	35	61	48	46	41	27	14
15	93	65	53	73	43	42	41	37	64	50	47	43	29	15
16		67	56	75	44	44	43	40	67	52	48	45	30	16
17		69	58	78	46	46	46	42	70	53	49	48	32	17
18		71	60	80	48	48	48	44	72	55	50	50	33	18
19		73	62	83	50	49	50	46	75	56	51	52	35	19
20		76	64	85	52	51	52	48	78	58	52	54	36	20
21		78	67	88	54	53	55	50	81	59	53	56	38	21
22		80	69	90	55	57	57	53	84	61	55	58	39	22
23		82	71	93	57	59	59	55	87	62	56	60	41	23
24		84	73	95	59	61	62	57	90	64	57	62	42	24
25		87	75	98	61	63	64	59	93	65	58	65	44	25
26		89	78	100	63	65	66	61	96	67	59	67	45	26
27		91	80	103	64	67	69	63	99	69	60	69	47	27
28		93	82	105	66	68	71	66	102	70	61	71	49	28
29		95	84	108	68	70	73	68	105	72	62	73	50	29
30		97	86	110	70	72	75	70	108	73	63	75	52	30
31		100		113	72	74	78	72	111	75	64	77	53	31
32		102		115	73	76	80	74	114	76	66	79	55	32
33		104		118	75	78	82	77	117	78	67	82	56	33
34		106			77	80	85	79	120	79	68	84	58	34
35		108			79	82	87	81	123	81	69	86	59	35
36		110			81	84	89	83	126	82	70	88	61	36
37		113			83	86	91	85	128	84	71	90	62	37
38		115			84	87	94	87	131	86	72	92	64	38
39		117			86	89	96	90	134	87	73	94	65	39

Raw score								T-scores							Raw score
	L	F	K	1	2	3	4	5	6	7	8	9	0	
40		119			88	91	98	92	137	89	74	96	67	40
41		121			90	93	101	94		90	75	99	68	41
42		124			92	95	103	96		92	77	101	70	42
43		126			93	97	105	98		93	78	103	71	43
44		128			95	99	108	100		95	79	105	73	44
45		130			97	101	110	103		96	80	107	74	45
46		132			99	103	112	105		98	81	109	76	46
47		134			101	105	114	107		99	82		77	47
48		137			102	107	117	109		101	83		79	48
49		139			104	108	119	111			84		80	49
50		141			106	110	121	114			85		82	50
51		143			108	112		116			86		83	51
52		145			110	114		118			88		85	52
53		147			112	116		120			89		86	53
54		150			113	118		122			90		88	54
55		152			115	120		124			91		89	55
56		154			117	122		127			92		91	56
57		156			119	124		129			93		92	57
58		158			121	126		131			94		94	58
59		161			122	127		133			95		95	59
60		163			124			135			96		97	60
61		165									97		98	61
62		167									99		100	62
63		169									100		101	63
64		171									101		103	64
65											102		104	65
66											103		106	66
67											104		107	67
68											105		109	68
69											106		110	69
70											107		112	70
71											108			71
72											109			72
73											111			73
74											112			74
75											113			75
76											114			76
77											115			77
78											116			78

Note: The MMPI-2 should not be used for subjects younger than 18 years. The original MMPI should be used for such subjects. These norms are for the original MMPI.

T-SCORE CONVERSIONS WITHOUT K-CORRECTIONS FOR ADOLESCENT FEMALES AGE 14 AND BELOW

Raw score	L	F	K	1	2	3	4	5	6	7	8	9	0	Raw score
0	31	36	19	36	11	7	14	126	28	29	32	16	13	0
1	36	39	22	39	13	9	16	124	30	30	34	18	15	1
2	41	41	24	41	15	11	19	122	32	32	35	20	16	2
3	46	44	27	44	17	13	21	120	34	33	36	22	18	3
4	50	46	29	46	20	15	23	118	36	34	37	24	19	4
5	55	49	31	49	22	18	25	115	38	36	38	26	20	5
6	59	51	33	51	24	20	27	113	40	37	40	28	21	6
7	64	54	35	54	26	22	29	111	43	39	41	30	23	7
8	69	56	38	56	28	24	31	109	45	40	42	32	24	8
9	73	59	40	59	30	27	34	107	47	42	43	35	25	9
10	78	61	42	61	32	29	36	104	49	43	45	37	26	10
11	83	64	44	64	34	31	38	102	51	44	46	39	28	11
12	87	66	47	66	36	33	40	100	54	46	47	41	29	12
13	92	69	49	69	38	35	42	99	56	47	48	43	30	13
14	97	71	51	71	41	38	44	97	58	49	49	45	32	14
15	101	74	53	74	43	40	46	95	60	50	51	47	33	15
16		76	56	76	45	42	49	92	62	52	52	49	34	16
17		79	58	79	47	44	51	90	65	53	53	51	35	17
18		81	60	81	49	46	53	88	67	54	54	54	37	18
19		84	62	84	51	49	55	86	69	56	56	56	38	19
20		86	65	86	53	51	57	84	71	57	57	58	39	20
21		89	67	89	55	53	59	81	73	59	58	60	40	21
22		91	69	91	57	55	61	79	75	60	59	62	42	22
23		94	71	94	59	58	64	77	78	62	60	64	43	23
24		96	73	96	62	60	66	75	80	63	62	66	44	24
25		99	76	99	64	62	68	73	82	64	63	68	45	25
26		101	78	101	66	64	70	70	84	66	64	70	47	26
27		104	80	104	68	66	72	68	86	67	65	72	48	27
28		106	82	106	70	69	74	66	89	69	67	75	49	28
29		109	85	109	72	71	76	64	91	70	68	77	51	29
30		111	87	111	74	73	79	62	93	72	69	79	52	30
31		114		113	76	75	81	59	95	73	70	81	53	31
32		116		116	78	78	83	57	97	74	71	83	54	32
33		119		118	80	80	85	55	99	76	73	85	56	33
34		121			83	82	87	53	102	77	74	87	57	34
35		124			85	84	89	51	104	79	75	89	58	35
36		126			87	86	92	48	106	80	76	91	59	36
37		129			89	89	94	46	108	82	77	94	61	37
38		131			91	91	96	44	110	83	79	96	62	38
39		134			93	93	98	42	113	84	80	98	63	39

Raw score	T-scores												Raw score
	L	F	K	1	2	3	4	5	6	7	8	9	0	
40		136			95	95	100	40	115	86	81	100	64	40
41		139			97	98	102	37		87	82	102	66	41
42		141			99	100	104	35		89	84	104	67	42
43		144			102	102	107	33		90	85	106	68	43
44		146			104	104	109	31		92	86	108	69	44
45		149			106	106	111	29		93	87	110	71	45
46		151			108	109	113	26		94	88	113	72	46
47		154			110	111	115	24		96	90		73	47
48		156			112	113	117	22		97	91		75	48
49		159			114	115	119	20			92		76	49
50		161			116	118	122	18			93		77	50
51		164			118	120		15			95		78	51
52		166			120	122		13			96		80	52
53		169			123	124		11			97		81	53
54		172			125	126		9			98		82	54
55		174			127	129		7			99		83	55
56		177			129	131		4			101		85	56
57		179			131	133		2			102		86	57
58		182			133	135					103		87	58
59		184			135	138		− 2			104		88	59
60		187			137	140		− 4			106		90	60
61		189									107		91	61
62		192									108		92	62
63		194									109		94	63
64		197									110		95	64
65											112		96	65
66											113		97	66
67											114		99	67
68											115		100	68
69											117		101	69
70											118		102	70
71											119			71
72											120			72
73											121			73
74											123			74
75											124			75
76											125			76
77											126			77
78											128			78

Note: The MMPI-2 should not be used for subjects younger than 18 years. The original MMPI should be used for such subjects. These norms are for the original MMPI.

T-SCORE CONVERSIONS WITHOUT K-CORRECTIONS FOR ADOLESCENT FEMALES AGE 15

Raw score	L	F	K	1	2	3	4	5	6	7	8	9	0	Raw score
0	31	36	21	37	9	9	13	120	26	29	32	19	13	0
1	36	38	23	39	11	11	15	118	29	31	34	20	14	1
2	40	41	25	41	13	13	17	115	31	32	35	22	15	2
3	45	43	27	43	15	15	19	113	33	33	36	24	17	3
4	49	45	29	46	17	17	21	111	36	35	37	26	18	4
5	53	47	32	48	19	19	23	109	38	36	39	28	19	5
6	58	50	34	50	21	21	25	107	40	37	40	29	21	6
7	62	52	36	52	24	23	27	105	42	39	41	31	22	7
8	66	54	38	55	26	25	30	103	44	40	42	33	23	8
9	70	57	40	57	28	27	32	101	47	41	43	35	24	9
10	75	59	42	59	30	29	34	100	49	43	44	37	26	10
11	79	61	45	61	32	31	36	98	51	44	45	39	27	11
12	83	63	47	64	34	33	38	96	53	45	46	41	28	12
13	88	66	49	66	37	35	40	94	55	47	47	42	30	13
14	92	68	51	68	39	37	42	92	58	48	48	44	31	14
15	96	70	53	70	41	39	44	90	60	49	49	46	32	15
16		73	56	72	43	42	46	88	62	51	50	48	33	16
17		75	58	75	45	44	48	86	64	52	51	50	35	17
18		77	60	77	47	46	51	84	66	53	53	52	36	18
19		79	62	79	49	48	53	82	68	55	54	54	37	19
20		82	64	81	52	50	55	79	71	56	55	56	39	20
21		84	67	84	54	52	57	77	73	58	56	57	40	21
22		86	69	86	56	54	59	75	75	59	57	59	41	22
23		89	71	88	58	56	61	73	77	60	58	61	42	23
24		91	73	90	60	58	63	71	79	62	59	63	44	24
25		93	75	93	62	60	65	69	82	63	60	65	45	25
26		95	77	95	65	62	67	67	84	64	61	67	46	26
27		98	80	97	67	64	69	65	86	66	62	69	48	27
28		100	82	99	69	66	71	63	88	67	63	70	49	28
29		102	84	102	71	68	74	61	90	68	64	72	50	29
30		104	86	104	73	70	76	59	93	70	65	74	52	30
31		107		106	75	72	78	57	95	71	66	76	53	31
32		109		108	78	74	80	55	97	72	68	78	54	32
33		111		110	80	76	82	53	99	74	69	80	55	33
34		114			82	79	84	51	101	75	70	82	57	34
35		116			84	81	86	49	103	76	71	83	58	35
36		118			86	83	88	47	106	78	72	85	59	36
37		120			88	85	90	45	108	79	73	87	61	37
38		123			90	87	92	42	110	80	74	89	62	38
39		125			93	89	95	40	112	82	75	91	63	39

Raw score	L	F	K	1	2	3	4	5	6	7	8	9	0	Raw score
40		127			95	91	97	38	114	83	76	93	64	**40**
41		130			97	93	99	36		85	77	95	66	**41**
42		132			99	95	101	34		86	78	96	67	**42**
43		134			101	97	103	32		87	79	98	68	**43**
44		136			103	99	105	30		89	80	100	70	**44**
45		139			106	101	107	28		90	82	102	71	**45**
46		141			108	103	109	26		91	83	104	72	**46**
47		143			110	105	111	24		93	84		73	**47**
48		146			112	107	113	22		94	85		75	**48**
49		148			114	109	115	20			86		76	**49**
50		150			116	111	118	18			87		77	**50**
51		152			119	113		16			88		79	**51**
52		155			121	115		14			89		80	**52**
53		157			123	118		12			90		81	**53**
54		159			125	120		10			91		82	**54**
55		162			127	122		8			92		84	**55**
56		164			129	124		6			93		85	**56**
57		166			131	126		3			94		86	**57**
58		168			134	128		1			95		88	**58**
59		171			136	130		−1			97		89	**59**
60		173			138	132		−3			98		90	**60**
61		175									99		92	**61**
62		178									100		93	**62**
63		180									101		94	**63**
64		182									102		95	**64**
65											103		97	**65**
66											104		98	**66**
67											105		99	**67**
68											106		101	**68**
69											107		102	**69**
70											108		103	**70**
71											109			**71**
72											110			**72**
73											112			**73**
74											113			**74**
75											114			**75**
76											115			**76**
77											116			**77**
78											117			**78**

Note: The MMPI-2 should not be used for subject younger than 18 years. The original MMPI should be used for such subjects. These norms are for the original MMPI.

T-SCORE CONVERSIONS WITHOUT K-CORRECTIONS FOR ADOLESCENT FEMALES AGE 16

Raw score	L	F	K	1	2	3	4	5	6	7	8	9	0	Raw score
0	29	35	22	35	8	10	11	127	21	27	32	12	10	0
1	34	37	24	37	10	12	14	125	24	29	33	14	12	1
2	38	39	26	40	12	14	16	122	27	30	34	17	13	2
3	42	41	28	42	14	16	18	120	29	32	35	19	15	3
4	47	44	30	44	16	18	20	118	32	33	36	21	16	4
5	51	46	33	47	18	20	23	116	35	34	38	23	17	5
6	56	48	35	49	20	22	25	113	37	36	39	26	18	6
7	60	50	37	51	22	24	27	111	40	37	40	28	20	7
8	64	53	39	54	24	26	29	109	42	38	41	30	21	8
9	69	55	41	56	26	28	31	106	45	40	42	32	22	9
10	73	57	44	58	28	30	33	104	48	41	43	35	23	10
11	78	59	46	61	30	32	36	102	50	42	44	37	24	11
12	82	62	48	63	32	34	38	100	53	44	45	39	26	12
13	86	64	50	65	34	36	40	98	55	45	46	41	27	13
14	91	66	52	67	36	38	42	96	58	46	47	44	28	14
15	95	68	55	70	38	40	44	94	61	48	48	46	29	15
16		71	57	72	40	42	47	91	63	49	49	48	31	16
17		73	59	74	43	44	49	89	66	50	50	50	32	17
18		75	61	77	45	46	51	87	68	52	51	53	33	18
19		77	63	79	47	48	53	84	71	53	52	55	34	19
20		80	66	81	49	50	55	82	74	54	53	57	36	20
21		82	68	84	51	52	57	80	76	56	54	59	37	21
22		84	70	86	53	54	60	77	79	57	55	62	38	22
23		86	72	88	55	56	62	75	81	58	56	64	39	23
24		89	74	91	57	57	64	73	84	60	58	66	41	24
25		91	77	93	59	59	66	70	87	61	59	68	42	25
26		93	79	95	61	61	68	68	89	62	60	71	43	26
27		95	81	98	63	63	71	66	92	64	61	73	44	27
28		98	83	100	65	65	73	64	94	65	62	75	46	28
29		100	85	102	67	67	75	61	97	66	63	77	47	29
30		102	88	105	69	69	77	59	99	67	64	80	48	30
31		104		107	71	71	79	57	102	69	65	82	49	31
32		107		109	73	73	82	54	105	70	66	84	51	32
33		109		112	75	75	84	52	107	71	67	86	52	33
34		111			77	77	86	50	110	73	68	89	53	34
35		113			79	79	88	47	112	74	69	91	54	35
36		116			81	81	90	45	115	75	70	93	55	36
37		118			83	83	92	43	118	77	71	95	57	37
38		120			85	85	95	40	120	78	72	98	58	38
39		122			87	87	97	38	123	79	73	100	59	39

Raw score	L	F	K	1	2	3	4	5	6	7	8	9	0	Raw score
							T-scores							
40		125			89	89	99	36	125	81	74	102	60	40
41		127			92	91	101	34		82	75	104	62	41
42		129			94	93	103	31		83	77	106	63	42
43		131			96	95	106	29		85	78	109	64	43
44		134			98	97	108	27		86	79	111	65	44
45		136			100	99	110	24		87	80	113	67	45
46		138			102	101	112	22		89	81	115	68	46
47		140			104	103	114	20		90	82		69	47
48		143			106	105	116	17		91	83		70	48
49		145			108	107	119	15			84		72	49
50		147			110	109	121	13			85		73	50
51		149			112	111		10			86		74	51
52		152			114	113		8			87		75	52
53		154			116	115		6			88		77	53
54		156			118	117		4			89		78	54
55		158			120	119		1			90		79	55
56		161			122	121		−1			91		80	56
57		163			124	123		−3			92		82	57
58		165			126	124		−6			93		83	58
59		167			128	126		−8			94		84	59
60		170			130	128		−10			95		85	60
61		172									97		86	61
62		174									99		88	62
63		176									100		89	63
64		178									101		90	64
65											102		91	65
66											103		93	66
67											104		94	67
68											105		95	68
69											106		96	69
70											107		98	70
71											108			71
72											109			72
73											110			73
74											111			74
75											112			75
76											113			76
77											114			77
78														78

Note: The MMPI-2 should not be used for subjects younger than 18 years. The original MMPI should be used for such subjects. These norms are for the original MMPI.

T-SCORE CONVERSIONS WITHOUT K-CORRECTIONS FOR ADOLESCENT FEMALES AGES 17 AND 18

Raw score	L	F	K	1	2	3	4	5	6	7	8	9	0	Raw score
0	28	32	18	31	5	7	7	125	21	25	29	15	7	0
1	33	35	21	34	7	9	10	122	24	27	31	17	9	1
2	37	37	23	36	9	11	12	120	27	28	32	19	10	2
3	41	40	26	38	11	13	14	117	30	30	33	22	11	3
4	45	42	28	41	13	15	17	115	33	31	35	24	13	4
5	49	45	31	43	15	17	19	113	35	33	36	26	14	5
6	54	47	33	45	17	19	21	111	38	34	37	28	15	6
7	58	49	36	48	20	21	24	108	41	36	38	30	17	7
8	62	52	38	50	22	23	26	106	44	37	39	32	18	8
9	66	54	41	52	24	25	28	104	47	39	40	34	19	9
10	70	57	44	55	26	27	31	102	50	40	41	37	21	10
11	74	59	46	57	28	29	33	100	53	42	43	39	22	11
12	79	62	49	59	30	31	35	98	56	43	44	41	23	12
13	83	64	51	61	32	33	37	96	59	44	45	43	25	13
14	87	67	54	64	35	35	40	94	61	46	46	45	26	14
15	91	69	56	66	37	37	42	92	64	47	47	47	27	15
16		72	59	68	39	39	44	89	67	49	48	50	29	16
17		74	61	71	41	41	47	87	70	50	49	52	30	17
18		77	64	73	43	43	49	85	73	52	50	54	31	18
19		79	66	75	45	45	51	83	76	53	52	56	33	19
20		81	69	77	47	47	54	80	79	55	53	58	34	20
21		84	71	80	50	49	56	78	82	56	54	60	35	21
22		86	74	82	52	51	58	76	84	58	55	63	37	22
23		89	76	84	54	53	61	74	87	59	56	65	38	23
24		91	79	87	56	55	63	71	90	60	57	67	39	24
25		94	81	89	58	57	65	69	93	62	58	69	41	25
26		96	84	91	60	59	67	67	96	63	60	71	42	26
27		99	86	93	62	61	70	65	99	65	61	73	43	27
28		101	89	96	65	63	72	62	102	66	62	76	45	28
29		104	91	98	67	65	74	60	105	68	63	78	46	29
30		106	94	100	69	67	77	58	108	69	64	80	47	30
31		109		103	71	69	79	56	110	71	65	82	49	31
32		111		105	73	71	81	53	113	72	66	84	50	32
33		113		107	75	73	84	51	116	74	68	86	51	33
34		116			78	75	86	49	119	75	69	89	53	34
35		118			80	77	88	47	122	77	70	91	54	35
36		121			82	79	91	44	125	78	71	93	55	36
37		123			84	81	93	42	128	79	72	95	57	37
38		126			86	83	95	40	131	81	73	97	58	38
39		128			88	85	98	38	134	82	74	99	59	39
40		131			90	87	100	36	136	84	76	101	61	40
41		133			93	89	102	33		85	77	104	62	41

Raw score	L	F	K	1	2	3	4	5	6	7	8	9	0	Raw score
							T-scores							
42		136			95	91	104	31		87	78	106	63	42
43		138			97	93	107	29		88	79	108	65	43
44		141			99	95	109	27		90	80	110	66	44
45		143			101	97	111	24		91	81	112	67	45
46		145			103	99	114	22		93	82	114	69	46
47		148			105	101	116	20		94	84		70	47
48		150			108	103	118	18		95	85		71	48
49		153			110	105	121	15			86		73	49
50		155			112	107	123	13			87		74	50
51		158			114	109		11			88		75	51
52		160			116	111		9			89		77	52
53		163			118	113		6			90		78	53
54		165			120	115		4			92		79	54
55		168			123	117		2			93		81	55
56		170			125	119					94		82	56
57		173			127	121		−3			95		83	57
58		175			129	123		−5			96		85	58
59		177			131	125		−7			97		86	59
60		180			133	127		−9			98		87	60
61		182									100		89	61
62		185									101		90	62
63		187									102		91	63
64		190									103		93	64
65											104		94	65
66											105		95	66
67											106		97	67
68											108		98	68
69											109		99	69
70											110		101	70
71											111			71
72											112			72
73											113			73
74											114			74
75											116			75
76											117			76
77											118			77
78											119			78

Note: The MMPI-2 should not be used for subjects younger than 18 years. The original MMPI should be used for such subjects. These norms are for the original MMPI.

Source: Minnesota Multiphasic Personality Inventory-2 (MMPI-2): Manual for administration and scoring. (1989). S. R. Hathaway & J. C. McKinley with J. N. Butcher, W. G. Dahlstrom, J. R. Graham, A. Tellegen, & B. Kaemmer. Minneapolis: The University of Minnesota Press. Reproduced by permission.

Appendix D. Composition of Harris–Lingoes Subscales

SCALE 2—DEPRESSION

D1—Subjective Depression
True: 31, 38, 39, 46, 56, 73, 92, 127, 130, 146, 147, 170, 175, 215, 233
False: 2, 9, 43, 49, 75, 95, 109, 118, 140, 148, 178, 188, 189, 223, 260, 267, 330

D2—Psychomotor Retardation
True: 38, 46, 170, 233
False: 9, 29, 37, 49, 55, 76, 134, 188, 189, 212

D3—Physical Malfunctioning
True: 18, 117, 175, 181
False: 2, 20, 45, 141, 142, 143, 148

D4—Mental Dullness
True: 15, 31, 38, 73, 92, 147, 170, 233
False: 9, 10, 43, 75, 109, 165, 188

D5—Brooding
True: 38, 56, 92, 127, 130, 146, 170, 215
False: 75, 95

SCALE 3—HYSTERIA

Hy1—Denial of Social Anxiety
True: None
False: 129, 161, 167, 185, 243, 265

Hy2—Need for Affection
True: 230
False: 26, 58, 76, 81, 98, 110, 124, 151, 213, 241, 263

Hy3—Lassitude-malaise
True: 31, 39, 65, 175, 218
False: 2, 3, 9, 10, 45, 95, 125, 141, 148, 152

Hy4—Somatic Complaints
True: 11, 18, 40, 44, 101, 172
False: 8, 47, 91, 159, 164, 173, 176, 179, 208, 224, 249

Hy5—Inhibition of Aggression
True: None
False: 7, 14, 29, 115, 116, 135, 157

SCALE 4—PSYCHOPATHIC DEVIATE

Pd1—Familial Discord
True: 21, 54, 195, 202, 288
False: 83, 125, 214, 217

Pd2—Authority Problems
True: 35, 105
False: 34, 70, 129, 160, 263, 266

Pd3—Social Imperturbability
True: None
False: 70, 129, 158, 167, 185, 243

Pd4—Social Alienation
True: 17, 22, 42, 56, 82, 99, 113, 219, 225, 259
False: 12, 129, 157

Pd5—Self-alienation
True: 31, 32, 52, 56, 71, 82, 89, 94, 113, 264
False: 9, 95

SCALE 6—PARANOIA

Pa1—Persecutory Ideas
True: 17, 22, 42, 99, 113, 138, 144, 145, 162, 234, 259, 305, 333, 336, 355, 361
False: 314

Pa2—Poignancy
True: 22, 146, 271, 277, 285, 307, 334
False: 100, 244

Pa3—Naiveté
True: 16
False: 81, 98, 104, 110, 283, 284, 286, 315

SCALE 8—SCHIZOPHRENIA

Sc1—Social Alienation
True: 17, 21, 22, 42, 46, 138, 145, 190, 221, 256, 277, 281, 291, 292, 320, 333
False: 90, 276, 278, 280, 343

Sc2—Emotional Alienation
True: 65, 92, 234, 273, 303, 323, 329, 332

Source: Minnesota Multiphasic Personality Inventory-2 (MMPI-2): Manual for administration and scoring. S. R. Hathaway & J. C. McKinley with J. N. Butcher, W. G. Dahlstrom, J. R. Graham, A. Tellegen, & B. Kaemmer. Minneapolis: The University of Minnesota Press. Reproduced by permission.

False: 9, 210, 290

Sc3—Lack of Ego Mastery, Cognitive

True: 31, 32, 147, 170, 180, 299, 311, 316, 325

False: 165

Sc4—Lack of Ego Mastery, Conative

True: 31, 38, 48, 65, 92, 233, 234, 273, 299, 303, 325

False: 9, 210, 290

Sc5—Lack of Ego Mastery, Defective Inhibition

True: 23, 85, 168, 182, 218, 242, 274, 320, 322, 329, 355

False: None

Sc6—Bizarre Sensory Experiences

True: 23, 32, 44, 168, 182, 229, 247, 252, 296, 298, 307, 311, 319, 355

False: 91, 106, 177, 179, 255, 295

SCALE 9—HYPOMANIA

Ma1—Amorality

True: 131, 227, 248, 250, 269

False: 263

Ma2—Psychomotor Acceleration

True: 15, 85, 87, 122, 169, 206, 218, 242, 244

False: 100, 106

Ma3—Imperturbability

True: 155, 200, 220

False: 93, 136, 158, 167, 243

Ma4—Ego Inflation

True: 13, 50, 55, 61, 98, 145, 190, 211, 212

False: None

Appendix E. Linear T-Score Conversions for Harris–Lingoes Subscales

	Males																													
Raw score	D1	D2	D3	D4	D5	Hy1	Hy2	Hy3	Hy4	Hy5	Pd1	Pd2	Pd3	Pd4	Pd5	Pa1	Pa2	Pa3	Sc1	Sc2	Sc3	Sc4	Sc5	Sc6	Ma1	Ma2	Ma3	Ma4	Raw score
32	116																												**32**
31	114																												**31**
30	111																												**30**
29	108																												**29**
28	106																												**28**
27	103																												**27**
26	100																												**26**
25	98																												**25**
24	95																												**24**
23	93																												**23**
22	90																												**22**
21	87																												**21**
20	85															120													**20**
19	82															117													**19**
18	79									120						113								120					**18**
17	77															109													**17**

Males

Raw score	D1	D2	D3	D4	D5	Hy1	Hy2	Hy3	Hy4	Hy5	Pd1	Pd2	Pd3	Pd4	Pd5	Pa1	Pa2	Pa3	Sc1	Sc2	Sc3	Sc4	Sc5	Sc6	Ma1	Ma2	Ma3	Ma4	Raw score
16	74								115										105					119					16
15	71			110				106	111										101					114					15
14	69	98		105				102	106							120			97			114		109					14
13	66	92		101				97	101					99		118			92			109		104					13
12	64	87		96			71	93	96					94	91	112			88			103		99					12
11	61	81	116	91			67	88	91					88	87	106			84			98	117	95		78			11
10	58	76	108	86	96		63	84	86					83	82	100			80		103	92	110	90		73			10
9	56	70	100	82	91		59	79	82	98				78	77	94	96	70	76	120	96	87	103	85		68		89	9
8	53	65	91	77	85		55	75	77	91	81			73	72	88	89	65	72	117	90	82	96	80		63	77	82	8
7	50	59	83	72	79		51	70	72	84	74			67	67	82	82	60	68	107	84	76	89	75		58	71	76	7
6	48	54	75	67	74	61	47	66	67	78	68	64		62	63	76	76	56	64	98	78	71	82	70	81	53	65	69	6
5	45	48	67	62	68	56	43	61	62	71	61	58		57	58	70	69	51	59	88	72	65	75	65	74	49	59	63	5
4	42	43	59	58	62	51	40	57	57	65	55	52		51	53	64	62	46	55	78	66	60	68	60	66	44	53	56	4
3	40	37	51	53	57	45	36	52	52	58	48	46		46	48	58	55	41	51	69	60	55	61	55	58	39	47	50	3
2	37	32	43	48	51	40	32	48	48	51	42	40		41	43	52	48	36	47	59	54	49	54	51	50	34	41	43	2
1	35	30	35	43	45	34	30	43	43	45	35	35		36	38	46	41	32	43	50	48	44	47	46	42	30	35	37	1
0	32		30	38	40	30		38	38	38	30	30		30	34	40	34	30	39	40	42	39	40	41	35		30	30	0

301

Appendix E (*continued*)

Females

Raw score	D1	D2	D3	D4	D5	Hy1	Hy2	Hy3	Hy4	Hy5	Pd1	Pd2	Pd3	Pd4	Pd5	Pa1	Pa2	Pa3	Sc1	Sc2	Sc3	Sc4	Sc5	Sc6	Ma1	Ma2	Ma3	Ma4	Raw score
32	108																												**32**
31	105																												**31**
30	103																												**30**
29	101																												**29**
28	98																												**28**
27	96																												**27**
26	94																												**26**
25	91																												**25**
24	89																												**24**
23	86																												**23**
22	84																												**22**
21	82																			119										**21**
20	79																			115										**20**
19	77																			111										**19**
18	75																			108						120				**18**
17	72						105													104						118				**17**

302

Females

Raw score	D1	D2	D3	D4	D5	Hy1	Hy2	Hy3	Hy4	Hy5	Pd1	Pd2	Pd3	Pd4	Pd5	Pa1	Pa2	Pa3	Sc1	Sc2	Sc3	Sc4	Sc5	Sc6	Ma1	Ma2	Ma3	Ma4	Raw score
16	70								101										100					113					16
15	67			106				99	97										96					109					15
14	65	95		102				95	93										92			111		104					14
13	63	90		97				91	89					97					88			106		100					13
12	60	84		93			71	87	85					92	92				84			100		95					12
11	58	79	107	88			67	83	81					86	87	105			81			95	110	91		80			11
10	56	73	100	84	89		63	79	77							99			77		104	90	104	86		75			10
9	53	68	93	79	83		59	75	73		92					91	69	93	73	120	98	85	97	81		70		86	9
8	51	62	85	75	78		55	71	69		86					84	65	87	69	113	92	80	91	77		65	82	80	8
7	48	57	78	70	73		50	67	65	80	80					78	60	81	65	104	86	75	85	72		60	75	74	7
6	46	51	70	66	68		46	63	61	74	74					72	55	75	61	95	80	70	78	68		55	69	68	6
5	44	46	63	61	63		42	59	57	68	68					65	50	69	57	86	74	64	72	63		50	62	62	5
4	41	41	56	57	58		38	55	53	62	62					59	45	63	53	76	67	59	65	59		45	56	56	4
3	39	35	48	52	53		34	51	49	56	56					53	41	57	50	67	61	54	54	54		40	50	49	3
2	37	30	41	48	47		30	47	45	50	50					46	36	53	46	58	55	49	49	50		35	43	43	2
1	34		34	43	42	43		43	44	40	44					40	31	49	42	49	49	44	44	45		30	37	37	1
0	32		30	38	37	39		39	41	38	40					34		43	38	40	43	39	39	41			30	31	0

Source: *Minnesota Multiphasic Personality Inventory-2 (MMPI-2): Manual for administration and scoring.* S. R. Hathaway & J. C. McKinley with J. N. Butcher, W. G. Dahlstrom, J. R. Graham, A. Tellegen, & B. Kaemmer. Minneapolis: The University of Minnesota Press. Reproduced by permission.

Appendix F. Composition of Si Subscales

Si1 (Shyness/Self-Consciousness)
  True: 158, 161, 167, 185, 243, 265, 275, 289
  False: 49, 262, 280, 321, 342, 360
Si2 (Social Avoidance)
  True: 337, 367
  False: 86, 340, 353, 359, 363, 370
Si3 (Self/Other Alienation)
  True: 31, 56, 104, 110, 135, 284, 302, 308, 326, 328, 338, 347, 348, 358, 364, 368, 369
  False: None

Source: Minnesota Multiphasic Personality Inventory-2 (MMPI-2): Manual for administration and scoring. (1989). S. R. Hathaway & J. C. McKinley with J. N. Butcher, W. G. Dahlstrom, J. R. Graham, A. Tellegen, & B. Kaemmer. Minneapolis: The University of Minnesota Press. Reproduced by permission.

Appendix G. Linear T-Score Conversions for Si Subscales

Raw score	Males			Females		
	Si1	Si2	Si3	Si1	Si2	Si3
1	39	41	38	38	42	38
2	42	45	41	41	47	41
3	45	49	44	44	51	44
4	48	54	47	46	56	47
5	51	58	50	49	60	49
6	53	62	53	52	65	52
7	56	67	56	55	69	55
8	59	71	59	57	74	58
9	62		62	60		60
10	65		65	63		63
11	68		68	65		66
12	71		71	68		69
13	74		74	71		72
14	77		77	73		74
15			80			77
16			83			80
17			86			83

Source: Minnesota Multiphasic Personality Inventory-2 (MMPI-2): Manual for administration and scoring. S. R. Hathaway & J. C. McKinley with J. N. Butcher, W. G. Dahlstrom, J. R. Graham, A. Tellegen, & B. Kaemmer. Minneapolis: The University of Minnesota Press. Reproduced by permission.

Appendix H. Composition of Content Scales

ANX—Anxiety
True: 15, 30, 31, 39, 170, 196, 273, 290, 299, 301, 305, 339, 408, 415, 463, 469, 509, 556
False: 140, 208, 223, 405, 496

FRS—Fears
True: 154, 317, 322, 329, 334, 392, 395, 397, 435, 438, 441, 447, 458, 468, 471, 555
False: 115, 163, 186, 385, 401, 453, 462

OBS—Obsessiveness
True: 55, 87, 135, 196, 309, 313, 327, 328, 394, 442, 482, 491, 497, 509, 547, 553
False: None

DEP—Depression
True: 38, 52, 56, 65, 71, 82, 92, 130, 146, 215, 234, 246, 277, 303, 306, 331, 377, 399, 400, 411, 454, 506, 512, 516, 520, 539, 546, 554
False: 3, 9, 75, 95, 388

HEA—Health Concerns
True: 11, 18, 28, 36, 40, 44, 53, 59, 97, 101, 111, 149, 175, 247
False: 20, 33, 45, 47, 57, 91, 117, 118, 141, 142, 159, 164, 176, 179, 181, 194, 204, 224, 249, 255, 295, 404

BIZ—Bizarre Mentation
True: 24, 32, 60, 96, 138, 162, 198, 228, 259, 298, 311, 316, 319, 333, 336, 355, 361, 466, 490, 508, 543, 551
False: 427

ANG—Anger
True: 29, 37, 116, 134, 302, 389, 410, 414, 430, 461, 486, 513, 540, 542, 548

False: 564

CYN—Cynicism
True: 50, 58, 76, 81, 104, 110, 124, 225, 241, 254, 283, 284, 286, 315, 346, 352, 358, 374, 399, 403, 445, 470, 538
False: None

ASP—Antisocial Practices
True: 26, 35, 66, 81, 84, 104, 105, 110, 123, 227, 240, 248, 250, 254, 269, 283, 284, 374, 412, 418, 419
False: 266

TPA—Type A
True: 27, 136, 151, 212, 302, 358, 414, 419, 420, 423, 430, 437, 507, 510, 523, 531, 535, 541, 545
False: None

LSE—Low Self-esteem
True: 70, 73, 130, 235, 326, 369, 376, 380, 411, 421, 450, 457, 475, 476, 483, 485, 503, 504, 519, 526, 562
False: 61, 78, 109

SOD—Social Discomfort
True: 46, 158, 167, 185, 265, 275, 281, 337, 349, 367, 479, 480, 515
False: 49, 86, 262, 280, 321, 340, 353, 359, 360, 363, 370

FAM—Family Problems
True: 21, 54, 145, 190, 195, 205, 256, 292, 300, 323, 378, 379, 382, 413, 449, 478, 543, 550, 563, 567
False: 83, 125, 217, 383, 455

WRK—Work Interference
True: 15, 17, 31, 54, 73, 98, 135, 233, 243, 299, 302, 339, 364, 368,

Source: Minnesota Multiphasic Personality Inventory-2 (MMPI-2): Manual for administration and scoring. S. R. Hathaway and J. C. McKinley with J. N. Butcher, W. G. Dahlstrom, J. R. Graham, A. Tellegen, & B. Kaemmer. Minneapolis: The University of Minnesota Press. Reproduced by permission.

394, 409, 428, 445, 464, 491,   True: 22, 92, 274, 306, 364, 368, 373,
505, 509, 517, 525, 545, 554,   375, 376, 377, 391, 399, 482,
559, 566   488, 491, 495, 497, 499, 500,
False: 10, 108, 318, 521, 561   504, 528, 539, 554
TRT—Negative Treatment Indicators   False: 493, 494, 501

Appendix I. Uniform T-Score Conversions for Content Scales

								Males							
Raw score	ANX	FRS	OBS	DEP	HEA	BIZ	ANG	CYN	ASP	TPA	LSE	SOD	FAM	WRK	TRT
36					112										
35					110										
34					108										
33				100	106									98	
32				99	105									96	
31				97	103									94	
30				95	101									92	
29				94	99									90	
28				92	97									89	
27				90	95									87	
26				88	93									85	104
25				87	91								105	83	101
24				85	89						101	89	102	81	99
23	92	113		83	87	120		83			98	86	99	79	96
22	90	110		82	85	119		80	94		96	84	97	78	94
21	87	107		80	83	115		77	90		93	81	94	76	91
20	85	103		78	81	112		74	87		91	78	91	74	89
19	82	100		77	80	108		71	83	89	88	76	88	72	86
18	80	97		75	78	105		68	79	85	85	73	85	70	84
17	77	93		73	76	101		65	76	81	83	71	82	68	81
16	75	90	87	71	74	98	86	62	72	77	80	68	80	67	79
15	72	87	84	70	72	94	82	59	69	72	77	65	77	65	76
14	70	84	80	68	70	91	78	56	65	68	75	63	74	63	74
13	67	80	77	66	68	88	74	54	62	64	72	60	71	61	71
12	65	77	73	65	66	84	70	52	58	60	70	58	68	59	69
11	62	74	70	63	64	81	67	51	55	56	67	55	66	57	66
10	60	70	66	61	62	77	63	49	53	53	64	54	63	56	64
9	57	67	63	59	60	74	59	48	51	50	62	52	60	54	61
8	55	64	59	58	58	70	56	47	49	48	59	50	57	52	59
7	53	60	56	56	56	67	53	46	47	46	57	49	55	50	56
6	52	57	53	55	53	63	50	44	46	44	55	47	52	48	54
5	50	54	50	53	51	60	48	43	44	43	53	45	50	46	52
4	47	51	47	51	48	57	46	41	42	41	51	43	47	44	49
3	45	48	44	48	44	54	43	40	40	38	48	41	44	41	47
2	42	45	41	45	41	51	40	38	37	36	45	39	41	39	43
1	39	41	37	41	37	46	36	35	34	32	41	35	37	36	39
0	35	35	33	36	33	39	32	32	30	30	35	32	33	33	35

Females

ANX	FRS	OBS	DEP	HEA	BIZ	ANG	CYN	ASP	TPA	LSE	SOD	FAM	WRK	TRT	Raw score
				107											**36**
				105											**35**
				103											**34**
			97	101									99		**33**
			95	100									97		**32**
			93	98									95		**31**
			92	96									92		**30**
			90	94									90		**29**
			88	92									88		**28**
			87	90									86		**27**
			85	89									84	102	**26**
			83	87								99	82	100	**25**
			82	85						97	87	96	80	97	**24**
89	101		80	83	113		83			94	84	94	78	95	**23**
86	98		78	81	110		80	98		92	82	91	76	92	**22**
84	94		77	79	108		77	94		89	80	89	73	89	**21**
81	91		75	77	105		75	91		86	77	86	71	87	**20**
79	88		73	76	102		72	88	94	84	75	83	69	84	**19**
76	85		72	74	99		69	85	90	81	72	81	67	82	**18**
74	81		70	72	96		67	82	86	78	70	78	65	79	**17**
71	78	87	68	70	93	88	64	79	81	76	68	75	63	77	**16**
69	75	83	67	68	90	84	61	75	77	73	65	73	61	74	**15**
66	72	79	65	66	87	80	58	72	73	70	63	70	59	72	**14**
64	68	75	63	64	84	76	56	69	69	68	60	68	57	69	**13**
61	65	71	62	63	81	72	54	66	64	65	58	65	55	67	**12**
59	62	67	60	61	79	68	53	63	60	62	56	62	54	64	**11**
56	59	63	58	59	76	64	51	59	56	60	54	60	52	61	**10**
55	56	59	57	57	73	60	50	56	53	57	52	57	51	59	**9**
53	53	56	55	55	70	56	48	54	50	55	51	55	50	57	**8**
51	51	53	54	53	67	53	47	52	48	54	49	52	48	55	**7**
49	48	50	52	51	64	50	46	49	45	52	48	50	46	53	**6**
47	46	48	50	49	61	47	44	47	43	51	46	47	45	51	**5**
45	43	46	48	46	58	45	42	45	41	49	44	45	43	49	**4**
43	41	44	45	43	56	42	40	42	38	47	41	42	40	43	**3**
40	38	41	42	40	52	39	38	39	36	44	39	39	37	43	**2**
37	35	37	39	36	47	36	35	36	33	40	35	36	34	39	**1**
34	31	32	34	32	39	31	32	33	30	35	32	32	31	35	**0**

Source: Minnesota Multiphasic Personality Inventory-2 (MMPI-2): Manual for administration and scoring. S. R. Hathaway & J. C. McKinley with J. N. Butcher, W. G. Dahlstrom, J. R. Graham, A. Tellegen, & B. Kaemmer. Minneapolis: The University of Minnesota Press. Reproduced by permission.

Appendix J. Critical Item Lists

KOSS-BUTCHER CRITICAL ITEMS

Acute Anxiety State

2. I have a good appetite. (F)
3. I wake up fresh and rested most mornings. (F)
5. I am easily awakened by noise. (T)
10. I am about as able to work as I ever was. (F)
15. I work under a great deal of tension. (T)
28. I am bothered by an upset stomach several times a week. (T)
39. My sleep is fitful and disturbed. (T)
59. I am troubled by discomfort in the pit of my stomach every few days or oftener. (T)
140. Most nights I go to sleep without thoughts or ideas bothering me. (F)
172. I frequently notice my hand shakes when I try to do something. (T)
208. I hardly ever notice my heart pounding and I am seldom short of breath. (F)
218. I have periods of such great restlessness that I cannot sit long in a chair. (T)
223. I believe I am no more nervous than most others. (F)
301. I feel anxiety about something or someone almost all the time. (T)
444. I am a high-strung person. (T)
463. Several times a week I feel as if something dreadful is about to happen. (T)
469. I sometimes feel that I am about to go to pieces. (T)

Depressed Suicidal Ideation

9. My daily life is full of things that keep me interested. (F)
38. I have had periods of days, weeks, or months when I couldn't take care of things because I couldn't "get going". (T)
65. Most of the time I feel blue. (T)
71. These days I find it hard not to give up hope of amounting to something. (T)
75. I usually feel that life is worthwhile. (F)
92. I don't seem to care what happens to me. (T)
95. I am happy most of the time. (F)
130. I certainly feel useless at times. (T)
146. I cry easily. (T)
215. I brood a great deal. (T)
233. I have difficulty in starting to do things. (T)
273. Life is a strain for me much of the time. (T)
303. Most of the time I wish I were dead. (T)
306. No one cares much what happens to you. (T)
388. I very seldom have spells of the blues. (F)
411. At times I think I am no good at all. (T)
454. The future seems hopeless to me. (T)
485. I often feel that I'm not as good as other people. (T)
506. I have recently considered killing myself. (T)
518. I have made lots of bad mistakes in my life. (T)
520. Lately I have thought a lot about killing myself. (T)
524. No one knows it but I have tried to kill myself. (T)

Threatened Assault

37. At times I feel like smashing things. (T)
85. At times I have a strong urge to do

310

something harmful or shocking. (T)

134. At times I feel like picking a fist fight with someone. (T)

213. I get mad easily and then get over it soon. (T)

389. I am often said to be hotheaded. (T)

Situational Stress Due to Alcoholism

125. I believe that my home life is as pleasant as that of most people I know. (F)

264. I have used alcohol excessively. (T)

487. I have enjoyed using marijuana. (T)

489. I have a drug or alcohol problem. (T)

502. I have some habits that are really harmful. (T)

511. Once a week or more I get high or drunk. (T)

518. I have made lots of bad mistakes in my life. (T)

Mental Confusion

24. Evil spirits possess me at times. (T)

31. I find it hard to keep my mind on a task or job. (T)

32. I have had very peculiar and strange experiences. (T)

72. My soul sometimes leaves my body. (T)

96. I see things or animals or people around me that others do not see. (T)

180. There is something wrong with my mind. (T)

198. I often hear voices without knowing where they come from. (T)

299. I cannot keep my mind on one thing. (T)

311. I often feel as if things are not real. (T)

316. I have strange and peculiar thoughts. (T)

325. I have more trouble concentrating than others seem to have. (T)

Persecutory Ideas

17. I am sure I get a raw deal from life. (T)

42. If people had not had it in for me, I would have been much more successful. (T)

99. Someone has it in for me. (T)

124. I often wonder what hidden reason another person may have for doing something nice for me. (T)

138. I believe I am being plotted against. (T)

144. I believe I am being followed. (T)

145. I feel that I have often been punished without cause. (T)

162. Someone has been trying to poison me. (T)

216. Someone has been trying to rob me. (T)

228. There are persons who are trying to steal my thoughts and ideas. (T)

241. It is safer to trust nobody. (T)

251. I have often felt that strangers were looking at me critically. (T)

259. I am sure I am being talked about. (T)

314. I have no enemies who really wish to harm me. (F)

333. People say insulting and vulgar things about me. (T)

361. Someone has been trying to influence my mind. (T)

LACHAR-WROBEL CRITICAL ITEMS

Anxiety and Tension

15. I work under a great deal of tension. (T)

17. I am sure I get a raw deal from life. (T)

172. I frequently notice my hand shakes when I try to do something. (T)

218. I have periods of such great restlessness that I cannot sit long in a chair. (T)

Appendix J (*continued*)

223. I believe I am no more nervous than most others. (F)
261. I have very few fears compared to my friends. (F)
299. I cannot keep my mind on one thing. (T)
301. I feel anxiety about something or someone almost all the time. (T)
320. I have been afraid of things or people that I knew could not hurt me. (T)
405. I am usually calm and not easily upset. (F)
463. Several times a week I feel as if something dreadful is about to happen. (T)

Depression and Worry

2. I have a good appetite. (F)
3. I wake up fresh and rested most mornings. (F)
10. I am about as able to work as I ever was. (F)
65. Most of the time I feel blue. (T)
73. I am certainly lacking in self-confidence. (T)
75. I usually feel that life is worthwhile. (F)
130. I certainly feel useless at times. (T)
150. Sometimes I feel as if I must injure either myself or someone else. (T)
165. My memory seems to be all right. (F)
180. There is something wrong with my mind. (T)
273. Life is a strain for me much of the time. (T)
303. Most of the time I wish I were dead. (T)
339. I have sometimes felt that difficulties were piling up so high that I could not overcome them. (T)
411. At times I think I am no good at all. (T)

415. I worry quite a bit over possible misfortunes. (T)
454. The future seems hopeless to me. (T)

Sleep Disturbance

5. I am easily awakened by noise. (T)
30. I have nightmares every few nights. (T)
39. My sleep is fitful and disturbed. (T)
140. Most nights I go to sleep without thoughts or ideas bothering me. (F)
328. Sometimes some unimportant thought will run through my mind and bother me for days. (T)
471. I have often been frightened in the middle of the night. (T)

Deviant Beliefs

42. If people had not had it in for me I would have been much more successful. (T)
99. Someone has it in for me. (T)
106. My speech is the same as always (not faster or slower, no slurring or hoarseness). (F)
138. I believe I am being plotted against. (T)
144. I believe I am being followed. (T)
162. Someone has been trying to poison me. (T)
216. Someone has been trying to rob me. (T)
228. There are persons who are trying to steal my thoughts and ideas. (T)
259. I am sure I am being talked about. (T)
314. I have no enemies who really wish to harm me. (F)
333. People say insulting and vulgar things about me. (T)
336. Someone has control over my mind. (T)

355. At one or more times in my life I felt that someone was making me do things by hypnotizing me. (T)
361. Someone has been trying to influence my mind. (T)
466. Sometimes I am sure that other people can tell what I am thinking. (T)

Deviant Thinking and Experiences

32. I have had very peculiar and strange experiences. (T)
60. When I am with people, I am bothered by hearing very strange things. (T)
96. I see things or animals or people around me that others do not see. (T)
122. At times my thoughts have raced ahead faster than I could speak them. (T)
198. I often hear voices without knowing where they come from. (T)
298. Peculiar odors come to me at times. (T)
307. At times I hear so well it bothers me. (T)
316. I have strange and peculiar thoughts. (T)
319. I hear strange things when I am alone. (T)
427. I have never seen a vision. (F)

Substance Abuse

168. I have had periods in which I carried on activities without knowing later what I had been doing. (T)
264. I have used alcohol excessively. (T)
429. Except by doctor's orders I never take drugs or sleeping pills. (F)

Antisocial Attitude

27. When people do me a wrong, I feel I should pay them back if I can, just for the principle of the thing. (T)
35. Sometimes when I was young I stole things. (T)

84. I was suspended from school one or more times for bad behavior. (T)
105. In school I was sometimes sent to the principal for bad behavior. (T)
227. I don't blame people for trying to grab everything they can get in this world. (T)
240. At times it has been impossible for me to keep from stealing or shoplifting something. (T)
254. Most people make friends because friends are likely to be useful to them. (T)
266. I have never been in trouble with the law. (F)
324. I can easily make other people afraid of me, and sometimes do for the fun of it. (T)

Family Conflict

21. At times I have very much wanted to leave home. (T)
83. I have very few quarrels with members of my family. (F)
125. I believe that my home life is as pleasant as that of most people I know. (F)
288. My parents and family find more fault with me than they should. (T)

Problematic Anger

85. At times I have a strong urge to do something harmful or shocking. (T)
134. At times I feel like picking a fist fight with someone. (T)
213. I get mad easily and then get over it soon. (T)
389. I am often said to be hotheaded. (T)

Sexual Concern and Deviation

12. My sex life is satisfactory. (F)
34. I have never been in trouble because of my sex behavior. (F)
62. I have often wished I were a girl. (or if you are a girl) I have never been sorry that I am a girl. (T/F)

Appendix J (*continued*)

121. I have never indulged in any unusual sex practices. (F)
166. I am worried about sex. (T)
268. I wish I were not bothered by thoughts about sex. (T)

Somatic Symptoms

18. I am troubled by attacks of nausea and vomiting. (T)
28. I am bothered by an upset stomach several times a week. (T)
33. I seldom worry about my health. (F)
40. Much of the time my head seems to hurt all over. (T)
44. Once a week or oftener I suddenly feel hot all over, for no real reason. (T)
47. I am almost never bothered by pains over my heart or in my chest. (F)
53. Parts of my body often have feelings like burning, tingling, crawling, or like "going to sleep". (T)
57. I hardly ever feel pain in the back of my neck. (F)
59. I am troubled by discomfort in the pit of my stomach every few days or oftener. (T)
101. Often I feel as if there is a tight band around my head. (T)

111. I have a great deal of stomach trouble. (T)
142. I have never had a fit or convulsion. (F)
159. I have never had a fainting spell. (F)
164. I seldom or never have dizzy spells. (F)
175. I feel weak all over much of the time. (T)
176. I have very few headaches. (F)
182. I have had attacks in which I could not control my movements or speech but in which I knew what was going on around me. (T)
224. I have few or no pains. (F)
229. I have had blank spells in which my activities were interrupted and I did not know what was going on around me. (T)
247. I have numbness in one or more places on my skin. (T)
255. I do not often notice my ears ringing or buzzing. (F)
295. I have never been paralyzed or had any unusual weakness of any of my muscles. (F)
464. I feel tired a good deal of the time. (T)

Source: *Minnesota Multiphasic Personality Inventory-2 (MMPI-2): Manual for administration and scoring*. S. R. Hathaway & J. C. McKinley with J. N. Butcher, W. G. Dahlstrom, A. Tellegen, & B. Kaemmer. Minneapolis: The University of Minnesota Press. Reproduced by permission.

Appendix K. Composition of Supplementary Scales

A Scale—Anxiety

True: 31, 38, 56, 65, 82, 127, 135, 215, 233, 243, 251, 273, 277, 289, 301, 309, 310, 311, 325, 328, 338, 339, 341, 347, 390, 391, 394, 400, 408, 411, 415, 421, 428, 442, 448, 451, 464, 469

False: 388

R Scale—Repression

True: None

False: 1, 7, 10, 14, 37, 45, 69, 112, 118, 120, 128, 134, 142, 168, 178, 189, 197, 199, 248, 255, 256, 297, 330, 346, 350, 353, 354, 359, 363, 365, 422, 423, 430, 432, 449, 456, 465

Es Scale—Ego Strength

True: 2, 33, 45, 98, 141, 159, 169, 177, 179, 189, 199, 209, 213, 230, 245, 323, 385, 406, 413, 425

False: 23, 31, 32, 36, 39, 53, 60, 70, 82, 87, 119, 128, 175, 196, 215, 221, 225, 229, 236, 246, 307, 310, 316, 328, 391, 394, 441, 447, 458, 464, 469, 471

MAC-R—MacAndrew Alcoholism Scale–Revised

True: 7, 24, 36, 49, 52, 69, 72, 82, 84, 103, 105, 113, 115, 128, 168, 172, 202, 214, 224, 229, 238, 257, 280, 342, 344, 407, 412, 414, 422, 434, 439, 445, 456, 473, 502, 506, 549

False: 73, 107, 117, 137, 160, 166, 251, 266, 287, 299, 325, 387

Fb Scale—Backside F

True: 281, 291, 303, 311, 317, 319, 322, 323, 329, 332, 333, 334, 387, 395, 407, 431, 450, 454, 463, 468, 476, 478, 484, 489, 506, 516, 517, 520, 524, 525, 526, 528, 530, 539, 540, 544, 555

False: 383, 404, 501

TRIN—True Response Inconsistency

3T–39T	99T–314T	125F–195F
12T–166T	125T–195T	140F–196F
40T–176T	209T–351T	152F–464F
48T–184T	359T–367T	165F–565F
63T–127T	377T–534T	262F–275F
65T– 95T	556T–560T	265F–360F
73T–239T	9F– 56F	359F–367F
83T–288T	65F– 95F	

VRIN—Variable Response Inconsistency

3T–39T	125T–195T	349F–515F
6T– 90F	125F–195F	349F–515T
6F– 90T	135F–482T	350F–521T
9F– 56F	136T–507F	353T–370F
28T–59F	136F–507T	353F–370T
31T–299F	152F–464F	364T–554T
32F–316T	161T–185F	369F–421T
40T–176T	161F–185T	372T–405F
46T–265F	165F–565F	372F–405T
48T–184T	166T–268F	380T–562F
49T–280F	166F–268T	395T–435F
73T–377F	167T–243F	395F–435T
81T–284F	167F–243T	396T–403F
81F–284T	196T–415T	396F–403T
83T–288T	199T–467F	411T–485F
84T–105F	199F–467T	411F–485T
86T–359F	226T–267F	472T–533F
95F–388T	259T–333T	472F–533T
99F–138T	262F–275F	491T–509F
103T–344F	290T–556F	506T–520F
110T–374F	290F–556T	506F–520T
110F–374T	339F–394T	513T–542F
116T–430F		

O-H Scale—Overcontrolled Hostility

True: 67, 79, 207, 286, 305, 398, 471

False: 1, 15, 29, 69, 77, 89, 98, 116, 117, 129, 153, 169, 171, 293, 344, 390, 400, 420, 433, 440, 460

Do Scale—Dominance

True: 55, 207, 232, 245, 386, 416

Source: Minnesota Multiphasic Personality Inventory-2 (MMPI-2): Manual for administration and scoring. S. R. Hathaway & J. C. McKinley with J. N. Butcher, W. G. Dahlstrom, J. R. Graham, A. Tellegen, & B. Kaemmer. Minneapolis: The University of Minnesota Press. Reproduced by permission.

Appendix K (*continued*)

False: 31, 52, 70, 73, 82, 172, 201, 202,
         220, 227, 243, 244, 275, 309, 325,
         399, 412, 470, 473

Re Scale—Social Responsibility

True: 100, 160, 199, 266, 440, 467

False: 7, 27, 29, 32, 84, 103, 105, 145, 164,
         169, 201, 202, 235, 275, 358, 412,
         417, 418, 430, 431, 432, 456, 468,
         470

Mt Scale—College Maladjustment

True: 15, 16, 28, 31, 38, 71, 73, 81, 82, 110,
         130, 215, 218, 233, 269, 273, 299,
         302, 325, 331, 339, 357, 408, 411,
         449, 464, 469, 472

False: 2, 3, 9, 10, 20, 43, 95, 131, 140, 148,
         152, 223, 405

GM Scale—Masculine Gender Role

True: 8, 20, 143, 152, 159, 163, 176, 199,
         214, 237, 321, 331, 350, 385, 388,
         401, 440, 462, 467, 474

False: 4, 23, 44, 64, 70, 73, 74, 80, 100, 137,
         146, 187, 289, 351, 364, 392, 395,
         435, 438, 441, 469, 471, 498, 509,
         519, 532, 536

GF Scale—Feminine Gender Role

True: 62, 67, 119, 121, 128, 263, 266, 353,

         384, 426, 449, 456, 473, 552

False: 1, 27, 63, 68, 79, 84, 105, 123, 133,
         155, 197, 201, 203, 220, 231, 238,
         239, 250, 257, 264, 272, 287, 406,
         417, 465, 477, 487, 510, 511, 537,
         548, 550

PK Scale—Post-traumatic Stress Disorder

True: 16, 17, 22, 23, 30, 31, 32, 37, 39, 48,
         52, 56, 59, 65, 82, 85, 92, 94, 101,
         135, 150, 168, 170, 196, 221, 274,
         277, 302, 303, 305, 316, 319, 327,
         328, 339, 347, 349, 367

False: 2, 3, 9, 49, 75, 95, 125, 140

PS Scale—Post-traumatic Stress Disorder

True: 17, 21, 22, 31, 32, 37, 38, 44, 48, 56,
         59, 65, 85, 94, 116, 135, 145, 150,
         168, 170, 180, 218, 221, 273, 274,
         277, 299, 301, 304, 305, 311, 316,
         319, 325, 328, 377, 386, 400, 463,
         464, 469, 471, 475, 479, 515, 516,
         565

False: 3, 9, 45, 75, 95, 141, 165, 208, 223,
         280, 372, 405, 564

Appendix L. Linear T-Score Conversions for Supplementary Scales

Columns 2–16 = **Males**; columns 17–31 = **Females**.

Raw score	A	R	Es	MAC-R	Fb	TRIN	VRIN	O-H	Do	Re	Mt	GM	GF	PK	PS	A	R	Es	MAC-R	Fb	TRIN	VRIN	O-H	Do	Re	Mt	GM	GF	PK	PS	Raw score
60															112															104	60
59															111															103	59
58															110															102	58
57															108															100	57
56															107															99	56
55															106															98	55
54															104															97	54
53															103															96	53
52		83													102			86												95	52
51		81													101			84												94	51
50			78												99			82												93	50
49			76	113											98			80												92	49
48			74	111											97			78												90	48
47			72	109								71			96			76								80				89	47
46			69	106								69	90	113	94			74	120							78	74	107		88	46
45			67	104								66	88	112	93			72	119							76	71	106		87	45
44			65	102								64	85	110	92			70	116							75	69	104		86	44
43			63	99								62	83	108	91			68	114							73	66	103		85	43
42			60	97								60	81	107	89			66	111							71	63	101		84	42
41			58	95							96	58	79	105	88			64	108						91	70	61	100		83	41
40			56	92							95	56	77	103	87	85		61	105						90	68	58	98		81	40
39	91		54	90							93	53	75	102	86	83		59	103						88	67	56	96		80	39
38	89		51	88							91	51	73	100	84	82		57	100						87	65	53	95		79	38
37	88	98	49	85							90	49	71	98	83	81		55	97						85	63	50	93		78	37
36	87	96	47	83							88	47	68	97	82	80	104	53	94						84	62	48	92		77	36
35	85	94	45	81							87	45	66	95	81	79	102	51	92						82	60	45	90		76	35
34	84	92	42	78							85	42	64	93	80	78	99	49	89						81	58	43	89		75	34
33	82	89	40	76							84	40	62	92	78	77	96	47	86						80	57	40	87		74	33
32	81	87	38	74							82	38	60	90	77	76	94	45	84						78	55	37	86		73	32
31	80	85	36	72							81	36	58	88	76	75	88	43	81						77	54	35	84		71	31

317

Appendix L (continued)

Males

Raw score	A	R	Es	MAC-R	Fb	TRIN	VRIN	O-H	Do	Re	Mt	GM	GF	PK	PS
30	78	83	34	69						76	79	34	56	87	74
29	77	81	31	67						73	77	31	54	85	73
28	75	78	30	65				103		70	76	30	51	83	72
27	74	76		62				99		68	74		49	82	71
26	73	74		60				96		65	73		47	80	69
25	71	72		58				93	78	63	71		45	78	68
24	70	69		55			120	89	75	60	70		43	77	67
23	68	67		53			118	86	72	57	68		41	75	66
22	67	65		51			115	82	68	55	67		39	73	64
21	65	63		48			111	79	65	52	65		37	72	63
20	64	61		46			107	76	61	50	64		34	70	62
19	63	58		44	120	120T	103	72	58	47	62		32	68	61
18	61	56		41	116	114T	99	69	55	45	60		30	67	59
17	60	54		39	112	107T	96	65	51	42	59			65	58
16	58	52		37	108	100T	92	62	48	39	57			63	57

Females

Raw score	A	R	Es	MAC-R	Fb	TRIN	VRIN	O-H	Do	Re	Mt	GM	GF	PK	PS
30	73	86	41	78						77	75	52	32	83	70
29	72	83	39	75						74	74	50	30	81	69
28	71	81	37	73				103		71	72	49		80	68
27	69	78	35	70				99		68	71	47		78	67
26	68	75	33	67				96		65	70	45		77	66
25	67	73	31	64				92	80	62	68	44		75	65
24	66	70	30	62				88	77	59	67	42		74	64
23	64	67		59			120	85	73	56	65	41		72	62
22	63	65		56			118	81	70	53	64	39		71	61
21	62	62		53			114	77	66	50	62	37		69	60
20	61	60		51	120		110	74	63	47	61	36		68	59
19	59	57		48	116	120T	106	70	59	44	60	34		66	58
18	58	54		45	112	118T	102	66	56	41	58	32		64	57
17	57	52		42	108	111T	98	63	53	38	57	31		63	56
16	56	49		40	105	103T	94	59	49	35	55			61	55

Males

Raw score	A	R	Es	MAC-R	Fb	TRIN	VRIN	O-H	Do	Re	Mt	GM	GF	PK	PS
15	57	50		34	104	93T	88	59	45	37	56			62	56
14	56	47		32	100	86T	84	55	41	34	54			60	54
13	54	45		30	96	79T	80	52	38	32	53			58	53
12	53	43			92	72T	76	48	34	30	51			57	52
11	51	41			87	65T	73	45	31		50			55	51
10	50	39			83	57T	69	41	30		48			53	49
9	49	36			79	50	65	38			46			52	48
8	47	34			75	57F	61	35			45			50	47
7	46	32			71	64F	57	31			43			48	46
6	44	30			67	71F	54	30			42			47	44
5	43				63	78F	50				40			45	43
4	42				59	85F	46				39			43	42
3	40				55	92F	42				37			42	41
2	39				51	99F	38				36			40	39
1	37				46	107F	34				34			38	38
0	36				42	114F	31				32			37	37

Females

A	R	Es	MAC-R	Fb	TRIN	VRIN	O-H	Do	Re	Mt	GM	GF	PK	PS	Raw score
54	46		37	101	95T	90	55	46	32	54			60	54	15
53	44		34	97	88T	86	52	42	30	52			58	52	14
52	41		31	93	80T	82	48	39		51			57	51	13
50	39		30	89	73T	78	44	35		50			55	50	12
49	36			85	65T	74	41	32		48			54	49	11
48	33			81	58T	70	37	30		47			52	48	10
47	31			77	50	66	33			45			51	47	9
45	30			74	58F	62	30			44			49	46	8
44				70	65F	58				42			48	45	7
43				66	73F	54				41			46	43	6
42				62	80F	50				40			45	42	5
40				58	88F	46				38			43	41	4
39				54	95F	42				37			42	40	3
38				50	103F	38				35			40	39	2
37				46	111F	34				34			39	38	1
35				42	118F	30				32			37	37	0

Source: *Minnesota Multiphasic Personality Inventory-2 (MMPI-2): Manual for administration and scoring.* S. R. Hathaway & J. C. McKinley with J. N. Butcher, W. G. Dahlstrom, J. R. Graham, A. Tellegen, & B. Kaemmer. Minneapolis: The University of Minnesota Press. Reproduced by permission.

Appendix M. Intercorrelations Among MMPI-2 Scales

Scale	L	F	K	Hs	D	Hy	Pd	Mf	Pa	Pt	Sc	Ma	Si
L		-04	37	-05	09	15	-19	-18	-04	-31	-28	-19	-08
F	-09		-36	46	36	07	52	13	29	55	69	32	35
K	28	-40		-33	-10	44	-21	-02	-01	-68	-60	-35	-43
Hs	-06	41	-45		53	41	33	04	23	53	56	15	34
D	00	34	-29	56		35	34	18	26	47	39	-21	51
Hy	10	10	24	53	35		25	22	32	-05	01	-09	-20
Pd	-19	56	-28	36	37	26		23	41	46	55	36	11
Mf	-11	-11	-03	01	12	10	01		29	22	24	07	10
Pa	-07	36	-15	24	31	22	41	13		34	39	15	05
Pt	-28	55	-71	59	61	09	51	09	43		84	33	54
Sc	-25	71	-62	60	48	15	64	-02	47	84		46	44
Ma	-17	38	-36	25	-07	01	42	-06	21	37	51		-22
Si	-03	32	-51	36	59	-13	14	09	15	58	44	-17	

Note: Correlations for males are above diagonal. Correlations for females are below diagonal.

Source: Minnesota Multiphasic Personality Inventory-2 (MMPI-2): Manual for administration and scoring. S. R. Hathaway & J. C. McKinley with J. N. Butcher, W. G. Dahlstrom, J. R. Graham, A. Tellegen, & B. Kaemmer. Minneapolis: The University of Minnesota Press. Reproduced by permission.

Appendix N. Percentile Equivalents for Uniform T-Scores

Uniform T-score	Percentile Equivalent
30	<1
35	4
40	15
45	34
50	55
55	73
60	85
65	92
70	96
75	98
80	99

Source: Unpublished data from MMPI Restandardization Project, Auke Tellegen, Department of Psychology, The University of Minnesota, Minneapolis, MN 55455.

Author Index

323

Subject Index